Dreamweaver® 8

FOR

DUMMIES®

Dreamweaver® 8 FOR DUMMIES®

Janine Warner

WILEY

Wiley Publishing, Inc.

Dreamweaver® 8 For Dummies®

Published by
Wiley Publishing, Inc.
111 River Street
Hoboken, NJ 07030-5774

www.wiley.com

WILEY

About the Author

Janine Warner is a bestselling author, journalist, and Internet consultant.

Since 1995, she's written and coauthored 10 books about the Internet, including *Creating Family Web Sites For Dummies*, *Dreamweaver For Dummies* (now in its sixth edition) and *Teach Yourself Dreamweaver Visually*.

Janine has been featured on technology news specials for ABC, NBC, and ZDTV and has been interviewed on numerous radio programs in the United States and abroad. Her articles and columns have been published in a variety of publications, including *The Miami Herald* newspaper, *Shape Magazine*, and the Pulitzer-Prize-winning *Point Reyes Light*.

Janine is a popular speaker at conferences and events throughout the US, and her fluency in Spanish has brought her many invitations to speak in Latin America and Spain. She also serves as a judge for the Arroba de Oro, a series of Internet award contests held throughout Latin America. Through her participation as a speaker at the award's events, she helped to create an Internet literacy program for high school students in Central America.

Janine has also been a part-time faculty member at the University of Southern California Annenberg School for Communication and at the University of Miami where she taught online journalism. She now serves as the Multimedia Program Manager for the Western Knight Center, a joint project of USC and UC Berkeley, funded by the Knight Foundation.

From 1998 to 2000, Janine worked fulltime for *The Miami Herald*, first as its Online Managing Editor and later as Director of New Media, managing a team of designers, programmers, and journalists who produced the online editions of *The Miami Herald* and *El Nuevo Herald*, as well as Miami.com. She also served as Director of Latin American Operations for CNET Networks, an international technology media company.

An award-winning former reporter, she earned a degree in Journalism and Spanish from the University of Massachusetts, Amherst, and worked for several years in Northern California as a reporter and editor before becoming interested in the Internet in the mid 90s.

To learn more, visit www.JCWarner.com.

Dedication

To all those who dare to dream about the possibilities of the Web: May this book make your work easier so you can make those dreams come true.

Author's Acknowledgments

Let me start by thanking my husband, David LaFontaine, whose patience and support have kept me fed, loved, and entertained, even while working long hours to make seemingly impossible deadlines.

Thanks to my wonderful contributor, Susannah Gardner, for gracing these pages with examples of her own beautiful Web design work (see it on the Web at www.hopstudios.com) and for revising Chapters 8 and 9. I recommend both of her latest books, *Buzz Marketing with Blogs For Dummies* and *BitTorrent For Dummies*.

Thanks to Frank Vera, a skilled programmer who deserves credit for revising the three most complex chapters in this book, Chapters 13, 14, and 15, on dynamic database features in Dreamweaver.

Thanks also to Sheila Castelli, who designed many of the Web sites featured in the examples. You can find her work online at www.digitalcottage.com.

Thanks to the entire editorial team: Travis Smith for his superb tech editing; Becky Huehls and Rebecca Senninger for catching the details and improving the prose; and Bob Woerner for shepherding this book through the development and publishing process.

Over the years, I've thanked many people in my books — family, friends, teachers, and mentors — but I have been graced by so many wonderful people now that no publisher will give me enough pages to thank them all. So let me conclude by thanking everyone I've ever known, just so I can go to sleep tonight and know I haven't forgotten anyone.

Publisher's Acknowledgments

We're proud of this book; please send us your comments through our online registration form located at www.dummies.com/register/.

Some of the people who helped bring this book to market include the following:

Acquisitions, Editorial, and Media Development

Project Editor: Rebecca Huehls

Acquisitions Editor: Bob Woerner

Copy Editor: Rebecca Senninger

Technical Editor: Travis Smith

Editorial Manager: Leah Cameron

Editorial Assistant: Amanda Foxworth

Cartoons: Rich Tennant
(www.the5thwave.com)

Composition Services

Project Coordinator: Adrienne Martinez

Layout and Graphics: Carl Byers, Andrea Dahl, Lauren Goddard, Stephanie D. Jumper, Barbara Moore, Barry Offringa

Proofreaders: Laura Albert, Leeann Harney, Robert Springer

Indexer: Joan Griffitts

Special Help: Mary Lagu

Publishing and Editorial for Technology Dummies

Richard Swadley, Vice President and Executive Group Publisher

Andy Cummings, Vice President and Publisher

Mary Bednarek, Executive Acquisitions Director

Mary C. Corder, Editorial Director

Publishing for Consumer Dummies

Diane Graves Steele, Vice President and Publisher

Joyce Pepple, Acquisitions Director

Composition Services

Gerry Fahey, Vice President of Production Services

Debbie Stailey, Director of Composition Services

Contents at a Glance

Table of Contents

Introduction

I've been writing about Macromedia Dreamweaver since the first version came out in the mid 1990s, and I'm pleased to say that this latest (and long-awaited) version 8 makes this program better than ever. If you've never used Dreamweaver before, don't worry; this book shows you everything you need to know about the old features, as well as the new ones. If you have used earlier versions of Dreamweaver, it's definitely time to upgrade and make sure you have all the tools available to create a fabulous Web site.

If you're like most of the Web designers I know, you don't have time to wade through a thick book before you start working on your Web site. That's why I wrote *Dreamweaver 8 For Dummies* in a way that makes it easy for you to find the answers you need quickly. You don't have to read this book cover to cover. If you're in a hurry, just go right to the information you need most and get back to work. If you're new to Web design, or you want to really get to know the intricacies of Dreamweaver, skim through the chapters to get an overview and then go back and read what's most relevant to your project in greater detail. Whether you are building a simple site for the first time or working to redesign a complex site for the umpteenth time, you find everything you need in these pages.

Why Choose Dreamweaver?

With each new version of Dreamweaver, this award-winning program becomes more efficient and powerful. Yet somehow, Macromedia continues to make Dreamweaver intuitive and easy to use, even as its programmers work long hours to keep up with the latest innovations in Web design and release a new version of this program nearly every year since its creation.

The high-end features and ease of use of Dreamweaver make it an ideal choice for professional Web designers, as well as for those new to working on the Internet. And the new features in version 8 make Dreamweaver better than ever!

I've been reviewing Web design programs since the first ones hit the market in 1994, and I can assure you that Dreamweaver is the best one I've ever worked with. But don't take my word for it — Dreamweaver has already won a slew of awards over the years, including Best of Show at Internet World, the prestigious five-mouse rating from *MacWorld*, and Best Web Authoring Tool in the Readers Choice Awards by *PC Magazine*.

Among all the Dreamweaver features, these are some of the best:

- ✔ Dreamweaver has clean HTML code and sophisticated support for the latest HTML options (such as Dynamic HTML).

- ✔ Cascading Style Sheets, better known as *CSS*, have become popular among professional Web designers. It's no wonder; this powerful part of the HTML code can save considerable time and give you greater design control than ever before. As you'd expect, Dreamweaver 8 offers more sophisticated support for CSS and better rendering within the design environment.

- ✔ Dreamweaver 8 even makes adding high-end features for creating database-driven Web sites easier. These features used to be sold separately in Dreamweaver UltraDev, but since Dreamweaver MX 2004, they've been integrated into this one powerful program. Now, in version 8, these features have been further refined and enhanced to work better than ever.

- ✔ As in previous versions, you find a state-of-the-art integrated text editor that makes switching back and forth between Dreamweaver and a text editor easier (if you prefer to look at the code, behind your pages you find some great enhancements to the text editor in this version).

If you've never written HTML before, don't be intimidated by these fancy features. The Dreamweaver graphical design environment uses carefully designed palettes and windows to make it easy for you to create high-end Web sites that include such features as animations, interactive forms, and e-commerce systems, even if you don't know HTML.

Foolish Assumptions

Although Dreamweaver is designed for *professional* developers, I don't assume you're a pro — at least not yet. In keeping with the philosophy behind the *For Dummies* series, this book is an easy-to-use guide designed for readers with a wide range of experience. Being interested in Web design and wanting to create a Web site is key, but that desire is all that I expect from you.

If you're an experienced Web designer, *Dreamweaver 8 For Dummies* is an ideal reference for you because it gets you working quickly with this program, starting with basic Web page design features and progressing to the more advanced options for DHTML and database-driven sites. If you're new to Web design, this book walks you through all you need to know to create a Web site.

About This Book

I designed *Dreamweaver 8 For Dummies* to help you find the answers you need when you need them. You don't have to read this book cover to cover and memorize it (and I don't really recommend this as beach reading). Consider this a quick study guide and a reference when you need it. Each section of the book stands alone, giving you easy answers to particular questions and step-by-step instructions for specific tasks.

Want to find out how to change the background color on a page, create a nested table, build HTML frames, or get into the really cool stuff such as style sheets and layers? Then jump right in and go directly to the section that most interests you. Oh, and don't worry about keeping all those new HTML tags in your head. You don't have to memorize anything. The next time you need to do one of these tasks, just go back and review that section. And don't worry about getting sand on this book if you do take it to the beach — I promise it won't complain!

Conventions Used in This Book

Keeping things consistent makes them easier to understand. In this book, those consistent elements are *conventions*. Notice how the word *conventions* is in italics? That's a convention I use frequently. I put new terms in italics and then define them so that you know what they mean.

When I type URLs (Web addresses) or e-mail addresses within regular paragraph text, they look like this: `www.jcwarner.com`. Sometimes, however, I set URLs off on their own lines, like this:

```
www.jcwarner.com
```

That's so you can easily spot them on a page if you want to type them into your browser to visit a site. I also assume that your Web browser doesn't require the introductory `http://` for Web addresses. If you use an older browser, remember to type this before the address (also make sure you include that part of the address when you're creating links in Dreamweaver).

Even though Dreamweaver makes knowing HTML code unnecessary, you may want to wade into HTML waters occasionally. I include HTML code in this book when I think it can help you better understand how HTML works. When

I do provide examples, such as this code which links a URL to a Web page, I set off HTML in the same monospaced type as URLs:

```
<A HREF="http://www.jcwarner.com">Janine's Web Site</A>
```

When I introduce you to a new set of features, such as options in a dialog box, I set these items apart with bullets so that you can see that they're all related. When I want you to follow instructions, I use numbered steps to walk you through the process.

How This Book Is Organized

To ease you through the learning curve associated with any new program, I organized *Dreamweaver 8 For Dummies* to be a complete reference. The following sections provide a breakdown of the parts of the book and what you can find in each one. Each chapter walks you through the features of Dreamweaver step by step, providing tips and helping you understand the vocabulary of Web design.

Part 1: Fulfilling Your Dreams

This part introduces you to Dreamweaver and covers getting started with the basics. In Chapter 1, I give you a handy reference to toolbars and menu options. I also describe the new features in version 8. You may prefer to skim this chapter as it's designed to give you an overview of the program, and you don't have to memorize the contents of each menu and toolbar. In Chapter 2, I start you on the road to creating your first Web site, including setting up your site, importing an existing site, creating new Web pages, applying basic formatting to text, and even placing images and setting links on your pages. To make this chapter more interesting and help you see how all these features come together, I walk you through creating a real Web page in this chapter as I show you how each features works.

Part II: Looking Like a Million (Even on a Budget)

Planning the design of your Web site is perhaps the most important part of Web site development — you'll save plenty of reorganizing time later. In Chapter 3, I start you out on the right foot with tips on Web site management, the principles of good design, and strategies that can save you countless hours. I also introduce you to the Dreamweaver site-management features, which can help you keep track of all the elements in your site and make sure you don't have any broken links. In Chapter 4, I introduce you to some of my favorite Dreamweaver features, including sophisticated template capabilities, that enable you to create more consistent designs and even lock sections of a page to protect them. I also love Dreamweaver's Library items, which can be used to place and update commonly used elements on your pages, such as navigation bars or copyright tags. If you work with a team of designers, you may be especially interested in the check in and check out features covered in this chapter for version control and integrated e-mail for communicating with other team members. Chapter 4 also covers tracing images, the Quick Tag Editor, Design Notes, and the History palette.

Chapter 5 introduces you to the basics of creating, converting, and optimizing graphics for the Web and shows you how to add graphic elements to your pages. You can find tools and strategies for creating the best images for your Web site, as well as tips for finding free images online and buying graphics that are specially designed for the Web.

Part III: Advancing Your Site

In Part III, I show you how to use Dreamweaver with some of the more advanced HTML features. In Chapter 6, you discover how to use HTML tables to create page layouts that work in the most common Web browsers. A highlight of this chapter is Layout mode, which makes creating complex Web designs easier than ever. In Chapter 7, you find all you need to know about designing a site with HTML frames. (This chapter helps you decide when you should and shouldn't use frames and gives you plenty of step-by-step instructions for creating HTML frames in Dreamweaver.)

Chapter 8 provides an overview of how Cascading Style Sheets work and how they can save you time. CSS has become a popular way to create designs and manage formatting on Web pages, and these features have been nicely improved in Dreamweaver 8. In this chapter, you find descriptions of the style definition options available in Dreamweaver as well as instructions for creating and applying styles.

Part IV: Making It Cool

The most important thing in Web design is looking cool, and this section of the book is designed to make sure you're part of the "cool club." In Chapter 9, I take you further into CSS and include Dynamic HTML features, such as layers and behaviors, which allow precise design control and new levels of interactivity. Chapter 10 introduces Fireworks, the Macromedia image program for the Web, and shows you how to take advantage of Dreamweaver's integration with Fireworks to more easily edit images.

In Chapter 11, you find out how easily you can add multimedia to your Web pages, including how to link a variety of file types — from Flash to Java to RealAudio — to your Web pages. Then in Chapter 12, I cover HTML forms and how to use Dreamweaver to add interactive elements, such as surveys, search engines, online discussion areas, and e-commerce systems to your pages.

Part V: Working with Dynamic Content

Part V features three chapters that cover the most advanced features in Dreamweaver 8. Chapter 13 is designed to help you understand how database-driven Web sites work and why they have become so important on the Web. In Chapter 14, you discover how to add dynamic content to your pages, define data sources, and display record sets. And in Chapter 15, you pull it all together and find out how to build master pages, create pages to search databases, and test your work with a live connection.

Part VI: The Part of Tens

In The Part of Tens, you get three quick references to help you get the most out of Dreamweaver and avoid some of the common design mistakes on the Web. In Chapter 16, you find descriptions and images of ten Web sites created with Dreamweaver to give you an idea of what's possible. In Chapter 17, you find ten great Web design ideas; and in Chapter 18, you get ten tips to save you time and make your sites work better.

Icons Used in This Book

When I want to point you toward something you can download for your use, I use this icon.

This icon points you toward valuable resources on the World Wide Web.

This icon reminds you of an important concept or procedure that you'll want to store away in your memory banks for future use.

This icon signals technical stuff that you may find informative and interesting but isn't essential for using Dreamweaver. Feel free to skip over this stuff.

This icon indicates a tip or technique that can save you time and money — and a headache — later.

This icon warns you of any potential pitfalls — and gives you the all-important information on how to avoid them.

Where to Go from Here

If you want to get familiar with what's new in Dreamweaver 8 and get an overview of the program, turn to Chapter 1. If you're ready to dive in and build your first Web site with Dreamweaver right away, jump ahead to Chapter 2. If you want to find out about a specific trick or technique, consult the Table of Contents or the Index and jump right to the section you need; you won't miss a beat as you work to make those impossible Web design deadlines. And most of all have fun!

Part I
Fulfilling Your Dreams

The 5th Wave   By Rich Tennant

©RICHTENNANT

"I have to say I'm really impressed with the interactivity on this car wash Web site."

In this part . . .

In Part I, you discover that you're not dreaming and all the wonderful advances in this powerful Web design program are real and at your fingertips. The new features of Dreamweaver 8 make Web design easier, more intuitive, and more powerful than ever. And don't worry, if you're new to Dreamweaver or need a little refresher, this part includes an introduction to this award-winning Web design program. Chapter 1 provides an overview, with highlights on what's new in version 8, as well as descriptions of the toolbars, menus, and panels that make up Dreamweaver's interface. In Chapter 2, you dive right into setting up your Web site, creating your first Web page, and adding text, images, and links.

Chapter 1

Introducing Your New Best Friend

In This Chapter

▶ Introducing the new features of Dreamweaver 8

▶ Examining your Web site objectives

▶ Finding your way around in Dreamweaver

*W*elcome to the wonderful world of Dreamweaver 8. If you're an experienced Web designer, you're going to love the power and sophistication of this Web editor. If you're new to building Web sites, you'll appreciate its simplicity and intuitive interface. Either way, this chapter starts you on your way to making the most of Dreamweaver by introducing you to the menus and panels that make this program so useful.

Dreamweaver can help you with every aspect of Web development, from designing simple pages, to fixing links, to publishing your pages on the World Wide Web. Dreamweaver can handle the simplest HTML, as well as some of the most complex and advanced features possible on the Web, including Cascading Style Sheets and Dynamic HTML (see Chapters 8 and 9 for more information on these features). Dreamweaver also integrates a powerful HTML text editor into its easy-to-use graphical design environment so you can work in the HTML code if you prefer.

If you already work in another Web design program or you're updating a site that was created in another program, don't worry — you can use Dreamweaver to modify existing Web pages and continue to develop your Web site without losing all the time you've already invested. For example, if you've been working in a program such as Microsoft FrontPage or Adobe GoLive, you can change to Dreamweaver to edit and develop your site further. All Web design programs create HTML pages, and those pages can be opened in any other Web design program. At the end of this chapter, in the "Working on Web Pages Created in Another Web Design Program" section, you find a few warnings about the challenges you may encounter because the code can vary slightly from program to program, but once you clean up those differences, you should be fine.

In this chapter, you find an introduction to the new features in Dreamweaver 8, get a tour of the desktop, and gain an overview of what makes Dreamweaver such a powerful Web design program.

So What's New in Dreamweaver 8?

Now the good stuff. All those requests you make to Macromedia, all that wishful thinking . . . believe it or not, they heard you and many of the little — and not so little — things we all have been wanting in this program are finally here, as well as a few extras you might expect!

The following list provides you a quick overview of some of the new features you find in version 8:

- ✔ When you first launch Dreamweaver 8, you'll notice a few changes to the Workspace. Although it has no dramatic changes, the programmers at Macromedia have added some clever new features, including a magnifying glass feature complete with a little icon in the status bar just below the work area. Much like the magnifiers common in image-editing programs, this new feature enables you to zoom in to view page elements in greater detail or zoom out to see the full layout of a larger page.

- ✔ You'll find some of the most extensive changes in the way Dreamweaver handles CSS — important upgrades as Cascading Style Sheets become increasingly popular among professional designers. Among other things, you'll find improved CSS rendering, better support for positioning, and a more unified CSS panel that includes the Rule Tracker, Property Grid, and a new Composite view.

- ✔ You can find one of my favorite new feature sets on the Edit menu. Paste Special enables you to paste formatted text (and even tables) from other programs, such as Microsoft Word or Excel, with options about what formatting is kept. You can choose to paste text with structural formatting, such as tables and paragraph marks; with or without basic formatting, such as bold and italics; and you can even opt to clean up the often problematic paragraph formatting from Word as you paste in the text. If you specify your choices in Dreamweaver's Preferences, anytime you use the paste feature your text is inserted based on your favorite options.

- ✔ Going beyond the predesigned templates included in previous versions, Dreamweaver now includes Starter Pages, which not only include topic-based designs. They actually include text. Of course, you can edit the text; but if you're creating a calendar of events or a product catalog, for example, the general text already in place on these pages gives you a head start.

- ✔ If you prefer working in Code view, where you can see all the HTML tags, you'll find a few enhancements to that interface, including a new toolbar that provides quick access to common commands and the capability to selectively expand and collapse code so you can focus on the area you are working on.

✔ I always recommend that you design your pages for the broadest audience, and that definitely includes designing for the disabled, such as the blind who use special browsers that read Web pages aloud. Macromedia has always been good about including accessibility features, and I'm pleased to see those features support the Priority 2 Web Content Accessibility Guidelines.

Introducing the Many Components of Dreamweaver

Dreamweaver can seem a bit overwhelming at first. It has so many features, and they are spread out in so many panels, toolbars, and dialog boxes that you can easily get lost. If you prefer to learn by poking around, have at it (and feel free to skip ahead to the next chapter where you start building your first Web page). If you want a tour before you get started, the next few sections introduce you to the interface and provide an overview of the basics of Dreamweaver. You also discover where to find common features and functions, which the rest of the book covers in more detail.

The Workspace

When you launch Dreamweaver, the Start Screen appears in the main area of the program (and it reappears anytime you don't have a file open). From the Start Screen, you can choose to create a new page from one of the many Dreamweaver pre-made templates, or you can create a new blank page by selecting HTML from the Create New options in the middle column. When you select HTML, Dreamweaver creates a new blank HTML page in the main *Workspace,* as shown in Figure 1-1. You can type text directly into any page in the Workspace and apply basic formatting with the many formatting options described later in this chapter.

You build HTML pages, templates, style sheets, and so on in the Workspace, which consists of a main window that shows the page you're working on surrounded by a number of panels and menus that provide tools you can use to design and develop your pages (shown in Figure 1-1). The Dreamweaver Workspace consists of the following basic components: the menu bar (at the very top), the Insert bar (just below it), the Document window (the main area of the screen, just below the Insert bar), the Properties inspector (at the bottom of the screen), and the Vertical Docking panels (to the right of the Document window) that expand and collapse as needed. More detailed descriptions of each of these follows.

Menu

Insert bar | Document toolbar   Document window   Vertical Docking panels

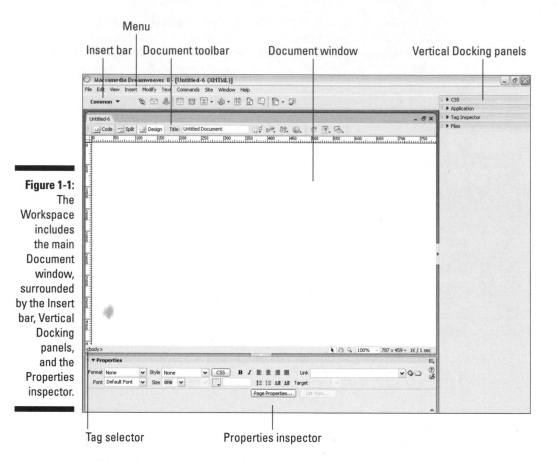

Figure 1-1:
The
Workspace
includes
the main
Document
window,
surrounded
by the Insert
bar, Vertical
Docking
panels,
and the
Properties
inspector.

Tag selector   Properties inspector

The Document window

The big, open area in the main area of the Workspace is the Document window, which is where you work on new and existing pages. If you use the Designer interface in Design view, you see your page as it would display in a Web browser. If you want to see the HTML code behind your page, click the Code button at the top of the work area. Choose the Split button to see the HTML code and Design view simultaneously (which you can see in Figure 1-2).

Pages viewed on the World Wide Web may not always look exactly the way they do in the Document window in Dreamweaver because not all browsers support the same HTML features or display them identically. For best results, always test your work in a variety of Web browsers, and design your pages to work best in the browsers that your audience are most likely to use. Fortunately, Dreamweaver includes features that help you target your page designs to specific browsers, such as the Check Target Browsers feature covered in Chapter 3.)

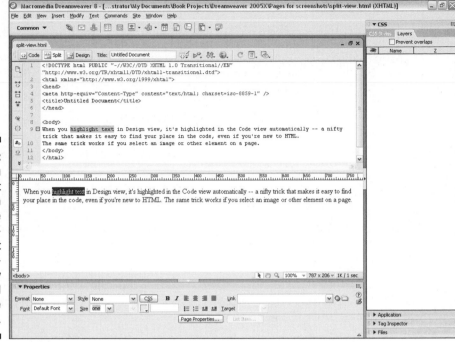

Figure 1-2:
When you select text in Design view, the corresponding text is automatically highlighted in Code view.

Customizing the interface

The docking panels, palettes, and bars in Dreamweaver provide easy access to most of the program's features. The default settings put the Properties inspector at the bottom of the page, the Insert bar at the top, and the panels on the right, but you can move these elements around the screen by selecting them and use drag and drop to move them to another part of the screen. You can also close any or all the panels on the right by clicking the tiny Options icon in the top right of each panel and selecting Close Panel from the drop-down list (it looks like three bullet points with lines next to them and a little arrow underneath, and it's really, really small). You can close them all at once by choosing Window⇨Hide Panels (or by clicking the arrow in the middle of the row of panels), and you can access any or all the panels through the various options on the Window menu. If you want to open a particular panel — the CSS Styles panel, for example — choose Window⇨CSS Styles and it expands to become visible on your screen. The Properties inspector, Insert bar, and panels are integral parts of this program, and you find a lot more information about them throughout the book. Check out the Cheat Sheet at the front of this book for a handy reference to the Properties inspector options. In Chapter 2, you discover how to use some of the most common features, such as the icon for inserting an image on the Insert bar at the top of the screen.

The Insert bar

The Insert bar, located at the top of the screen, comes with eight *subcategories*, each with a different set of icons representing common features. Click the small arrow to the right of the name to access the drop-down list to switch from displaying the buttons on one subcategory to showing the buttons for another. The options are

- **Common bar:** Displays icons for many of the most common features, including links, tables, and images.

- **Layout bar:** Displays layer and table options essential for creating complex layouts.

- **Forms bar:** Surprise! This one features all the most common form elements, such as radio buttons and boxes.

- **Text bar:** Displays common text-formatting features, including paragraphs, breaks, and lists.

- **HTML bar:** Offers a mishmash of raw HTML, such as rules, tables, frames and, scripts.

- **Application:** Use these options when building dynamic Web pages powered by database material.

- **Flash elements:** A single icon allows you to place a Flash file on your Web page.

- **Favorites:** Right-click (Windows) or Control+click (Mac) to customize your most-used HTML elements.

At the very end of the drop-down list, you find the Show as Tabs option, which enables you to display the names of the Insert bars as tabs across the top of the screen, as shown in Figure 1-3.

The Favorites Insert bar is blank by default, and you can customize it to hold your own collection of options. Simply right-click (Windows) or Control+click (Mac) in the bar and you can easily customize this bar.

Throughout the book, I refer to these Insert bars by their full names, such as the Forms Insert bar or the Layout Insert bar. You find more information on each of these in their relevant chapters. For example, Chapter 12 covers the Forms Insert bar in detail; and Chapters 13, 14, and 15 cover the Application Insert bar.

Figure 1-3 shows the Insert bar with the Common options visible and each name displayed in a tab across the top of the screen.

Figure 1-3:
The
Common
Insert bar
provides
access for
forms,
tables,
images,
and more.

The Properties inspector

The Properties inspector is docked at the bottom of the page in Dreamweaver. If you prefer it at the top of the screen, you can drag it up there, and it locks into place; but I rather like that it's handy, yet out of the way, at the bottom of the screen.

The Properties inspector displays the properties of a selected element on the page. A *property* is a characteristic of HTML — such as the alignment of an image or the size of a cell in a table — that you can assign to an element on your Web page. If you know HTML, you recognize these as HTML *attributes*.

When you select any element on a page (such as an image), the inspector changes to display the relevant properties for that element, such as the height and width of an image. You can alter these properties by changing the fields in the Properties inspector. You can also set links and create image maps using the options in the Properties inspector.

Figure 1-4 shows the image options displayed in the Properties inspector, including height and width, alignment, and the *URL* (Uniform Resource Locator or, more simply, Web address) to which the image links.

At the bottom-right corner of the Properties inspector, you see a small arrow. Click this arrow (or double-click in any open inspector space) to reveal additional attributes that let you control more advanced features, such as the image map options when a graphic is selected.

Figure 1-4:
The Properties inspector displays the attributes of any selected element, such as an image shown here.

Figure 1-5 shows the Properties inspector when you select a table. Notice that the fields in the inspector reflect the attributes of an HTML table, such as the number of columns and rows. (See Chapter 6 to find out more about HTML tables.)

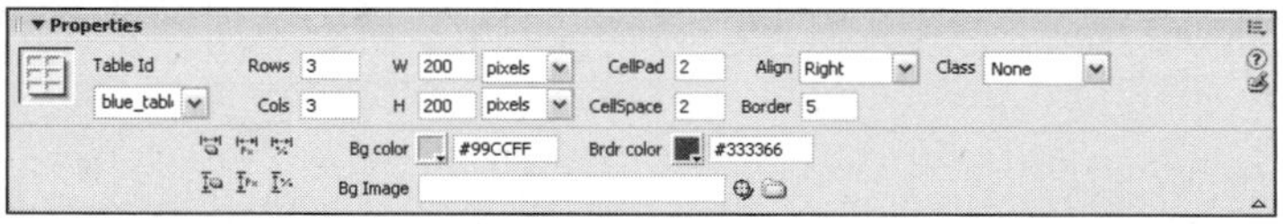

Figure 1-5:
Attributes of a selected HTML table or cell.

The Docking panels

The Docking panels, shown in Figure 1-6, are located to the right of the work area (although you can easily move them anywhere on the screen). The Docking panels display a variety of important features in Dreamweaver, including all the files and folders in a site (in the Files panel), Cascading Style Sheets (in the CSS panel) and more. You can open and close panels by clicking the small arrow to the left of the panel's name. To display more panels, select the panel name from the Window menu. To hide all the visible panels at once, click the tab with the small arrow in the middle, left of the row of panels.

Figure 1-6: The Docking panels provide easy access to CSS, tags, and all the files in a Web site, such as the list shown here in Kathryn LeMieux's cartoon site.

The following list offers a description of some of the elements that you access through the Docking panels (the others are described in greater detail in their respective sections of the book).

✔ **Files panel:** Shown in Figure 1-6, the Files panel lists all the folders and files in a Web site and helps you manage the structure and organization of the site. You can move files in and out of folders and even create new folders in this panel, and Dreamweaver automatically adjusts any related links. The Files panel is also where you access FTP *(file transfer protocol)* capabilities to upload or download files from a server. You can use the Connect button at the top of this panel to dial quickly into your server and use the Get Files and Put Files arrows to transfer pages. (See Chapter 2 for more about the Files panel and built-in FTP features.)

✔ **Assets panel:** The Assets panel, shown in Figure 1-7, automatically lists all the images, colors, external links, multimedia files, scripts, templates, and Library items in a Web site. You can add a stored item, such as a graphic, to a Web page simply by dragging the element into the work area. You find more on templates and Library items in Chapter 4.

These features work only if you define your site using the Site Definition dialog box (by choosing Site➪Manage Sites) and then identifying the main folder of your Web site. If you find that the Library or other options aren't available, follow the steps in Chapter 2 to define your site (a setup process you should go through for all your sites).

✔ **CSS panel:** The Cascading Style Sheets panel includes Layers and CSS Styles panels. CSS styles are similar to style sheets used in word processing and desktop publishing programs, such as Microsoft Word and QuarkXPress. You define a style and name it, and the style is then included in the CSS Styles panel (see Figure 1-8). The Layers panel provides access to layers options, which enable you to precisely position elements on a page. (For more information about CSS and layers, see Chapters 8 and 9.)

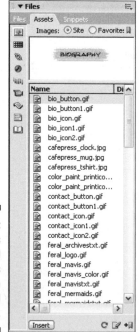

Figure 1-7:
The Assets panel presents like items in a central place.

✔ **Tag panel:** The Tag panel provides access to attributes and behaviors. In Dreamweaver, *behaviors* are scripts (usually written in JavaScript) that you can apply to objects to add interactivity to your Web page. Essentially, a behavior is made up of a specified event that, when triggered, causes an action. For example, an *event* may be a visitor clicking an image, and the resulting action may be that a sound file plays.

Figure 1-9 shows the Tag panel's Attributes tab, which displays all the attributes of a selected element. You can change attributes in the Attributes tab as well as in the Properties inspector. (Chapter 9 provides more information on creating and applying behaviors.)

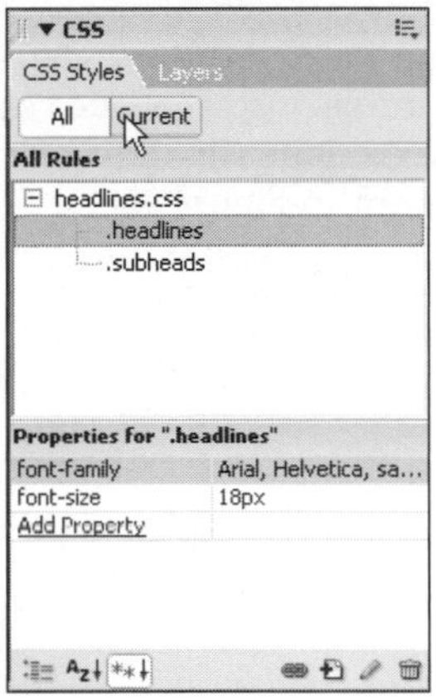

Figure 1-8:
The CSS panel makes it easy to manage styles and layers.

Figure 1-9:
The Attributes panel displays all the attributes of a selected element.

✔ **History panel:** The History panel, shown in Figure 1-10, keeps track of every action you take in Dreamweaver. You can use the History panel to undo multiple steps at once, to replay steps you performed, and to automate tasks. Dreamweaver automatically records the last 50 steps, but you can increase or decrease that number by choosing Edit⇨Preferences⇨General (Windows) or Dreamweaver⇨Preferences⇨General (Mac), and changing the maximum number of history steps.

✔ **Application panel:** This panel includes the Database, Bindings, Server Behaviors, and Components panels. These features are used only if you work with a database-driven site (the most technically complex of the features covered in this book). You find more on database options in Chapters 13, 14, and 15.

✔ **Frames panel:** If you create a site design that uses *frames*, a set of HTML tags that enable you to divide a screen into sections made up of separate pages, you use the Frames panel to manage the different pages on the screen, such as the three frames shown in Figure 1-11.

Figure 1-10: The History panel keeps track of all your actions in Dream-weaver.

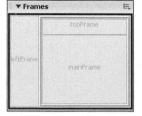

Figure 1-11: The Frames panel helps manage the different pages that make up a frameset.

The menu bar

At the top of the screen, the Dreamweaver menu bar provides easy access to all the features that you find in the Insert bar, Properties inspector, and panels, as well as a few others that are available only from the menu. The following sections provide a general description of each of the menu options.

The File menu

You find many familiar options, such as New, Open, and Save, on the File menu, shown in Figure 1-12. You also find a Revert option, which is similar to the Revert feature in Adobe Photoshop. This sophisticated undo feature enables you to return your page quickly to its last-saved version if you don't like the changes you made.

The File menu also includes access to Design Notes, a unique feature that associates private notes with HTML and other files. Take a look at Chapter 4 for more information about Design Notes and other Dreamweaver features that make collaboration easier.

You can also find features useful for checking your work in Web browsers on the File menu. Most Web design programs include some way of previewing your work in a browser. Dreamweaver takes this feature two steps further by enabling you to check your work in a number of browsers and even test the compatibility of your pages in different versions of different browsers.

Figure 1-12 shows the Check Page options, which includes Check Accessibility, Check Links, and Check Target Browsers — all great tools for testing your work. The Check Target Browsers option enables you to specify a browser and version, such as Safari 2.0, Netscape 6, or Internet Explorer 6.0. When you do a browser check, Dreamweaver generates a report listing any HTML features you use that the chosen browser doesn't support.

The Check Links feature verifies all the links in a site and produces a report with all broken and unresolved links. The Check Accessibility feature checks to make sure the page displays properly in browsers for the blind and other systems for the disabled.

The Edit menu

The Edit menu contains many features that you may find familiar, such as Cut, Copy, and Paste. One feature that may be new to you is the Edit with External Editor option, which enables you to open an element in another program, such as an image editor, and make changes without ever closing Dreamweaver.

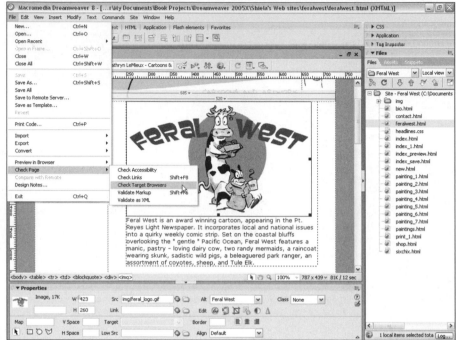

Figure 1-12:
The Check Target Browsers feature produces a list of HTML tags that older browsers do not support.

You also find the Preferences settings on the Edit menu (Windows) or on the Dreamweaver (Mac). Before you start working with a new program, go through all the Preferences options to ensure that the program is set up the best way for you.

The View menu

The View menu provides access to some helpful design features, such as grids and rulers, as well as the new zoom features. The Visual Aides option on the View menu gives you the option of turning on or off the borders of your HTML tables, frames, and layers, as well as controlling visibility of image maps and other invisible elements. This option is useful because you often want to set the border attribute of these HTML tags to zero so that they're not visible when the page displays in a browser. However, while you work on the design of your page in Dreamweaver, seeing where elements, such as tables and layers, start and stop is very useful. Checking the frame options on the View menu lets you see the borders in Dreamweaver even if you don't want them visible to your site's visitors.

The Insert menu

As shown in Figure 1-13, the Insert menu offers access to a number of features unique to Web design. From this menu, you can insert elements such as a horizontal rule, a Java applet, a form, or a plug-in file.

Figure 1-13:
The Insert menu makes adding a variety of elements to your pages, including multimedia files, easy.

Dreamweaver offers extra support for inserting Flash and Shockwave Director files, both of which are products from Macromedia. (You can find out more about using multimedia files in Chapter 11.)

The Modify menu

The Modify menu is another place where you can view and change object properties, such as the table attributes shown in Figure 1-14. The properties (usually called *attributes* in HTML) let you define elements on a page by setting alignment, height, width, and other specifications.

Page Properties

To alter properties for an entire page, such as text and link colors, use the Page Properties dialog box shown in Figure 1-15. Available from the Modify menu or by clicking the Page Properties button at the bottom of the Properties inspector, the Page Properties panel also enables you to specify the background color or to use an image as a page background.

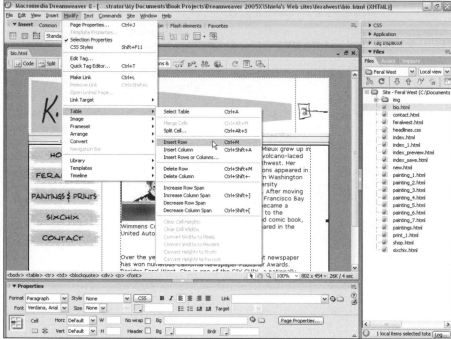

Figure 1-14:
The Modify menu makes changing object properties, such as the table attributes shown here, easy.

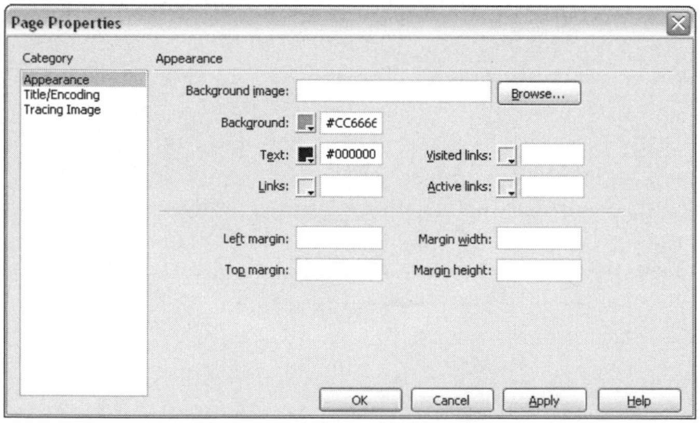

Figure 1-15:
The Page Properties dialog box provides access to background and text color attributes.

The Text menu

You can easily format text with the Text menu by using simple options, such as bold and italic, as well as more complex features, such as font styles and custom style sheets. Text formatting options have evolved dramatically on the Web. Just a few years ago, you didn't even have the option of specifying a particular font style or controlling leading and spacing. Today you have more control than ever over the look of your Web pages, although these options aren't yet universally supported. The Text menu also features options that enable you to quickly create headers and subheads, check spelling, and create lists.

The Commands menu

The Commands menu, shown in Figure 1-16, provides access to a host of options in Dreamweaver. These options include the Start and Play Recording features, which let you quickly save a series of steps and then repeat them. To use this feature, choose Commands⇨Start Recording, perform whatever actions you want to record — for example, copying and pasting some text — and then choose Stop Recording. To perform any action again, choose Commands⇨Play Recorded Command. You can download an action by choosing Commands⇨Get More Commands, which automatically launches a browser and takes you to the Macromedia Web site. You can download new commands from the Web site that add functionality to Dreamweaver.

The Clean Up XHTML and Clean up Word HTML options on the Commands menu help you correct incorrect or redundant HTML code, and the Clean Up Word HTML feature is designed especially to correct the common problems caused by the Save As HTML feature in Microsoft Word.

The Add/Remove Netscape Resize Fix option on this menu inserts or removes a JavaScript script designed to help correct an old Netscape bug by automatically reloading the page when users resize their browser windows.

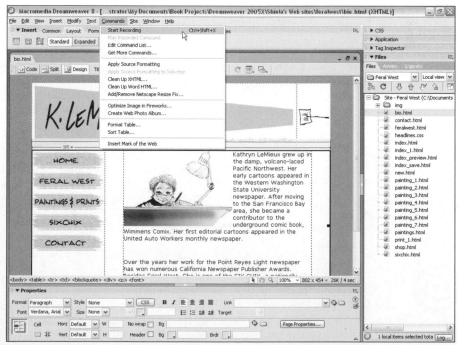

Figure 1-16:
The Commands menu offers easy access to some of Dreamweaver's most advanced features.

The Create Web Photo Album option launches Macromedia Fireworks and uses it to automate the creation of a photo album with a series of images. If you choose Optimize Image in Fireworks, a selected image automatically opens in the optimization area in Fireworks. (Both these commands require that you have Fireworks installed.)

The Site menu

The Site menu provides access to the options you need to set up your site, a process required before many of the other Dreamweaver features work properly. (Chapter 2 covers this process.) The Site menu also gives you easy access to the Check In and Check Out features, which are options that can help you keep a team of designers from overwriting each other's work. (Chapter 4 talks about this feature.)

The Window menu

The Window menu lets you control the display of panels and dialog boxes, such as Insert, Properties, and Behaviors. To make these panels visible, select the panel name so that a check mark appears next to the feature you want to display; to hide them, select again to remove the check mark. Other panels and dialog boxes, such as CSS Styles and HTML Code Inspector, are also listed on the Window menu for easy access.

The Help menu

The Help menu provides easy access to help options that can assist you in figuring out many features of Dreamweaver. You also find access to the Dreamweaver template and example files on the Help menu.

Templates and examples provide visual samples of common HTML designs, such as tables and frames, and provide design ideas and great shortcuts for creating complex layouts.

The status bar

The status bar appears at the bottom left of any open Dreamweaver document. On the right end of the status bar, you can see tool icons that control the on-screen display of your document. On the left end, you find a row of HTML codes that indicate how elements on your page are tagged. If you place your cursor in bold text that is centered, for example, the status bar might display `<BODY><CENTER><B>`. This feature makes double-checking the kind of formatting applied to any element on your page easy.

You can also use the status bar to quickly make a selection on your page. For example, if you click the name of a tag in the status bar, the section of your page where that tag is applied is highlighted. This makes selecting a certain section of a page, such as a page, easier.

Working on Web Pages Created in Another Web Design Program

In theory, all Web design programs should be compatible because HTML files are, at their heart, just ordinary text files. You can open an HTML file in any text editor, including Macintosh TextEdit and Windows Notepad. However, HTML has evolved dramatically over the years and different Web programs follow different standards, which can cause serious conflicts when a page created in one program opens in another.

One of the reasons Dreamweaver is so popular is because it creates very clean code and is considered more accurate and more respectful of HTML standards than other programs. Dreamweaver is also better at creating pages that work in different browsers and on different platforms, but importing files created in another Web program can be challenging, even in Dreamweaver.

To help with the transition, Dreamweaver includes some special features, such as the Clean Up Word HTML option, designed to fix some of the common problems with Microsoft Word's HTML code.

 Before you start working on a site that was developed in another program, you need to import the site into Dreamweaver. I recommend you make a backup of the site first so you have a copy of all the original pages (strange things can happen when you open a site created in another program). You find step-by-step instructions for importing an existing Web site in Chapter 2.

The following sections describe the most popular HTML editors and what you need to know if you're moving files from one of these programs to Dreamweaver.

Microsoft FrontPage

Microsoft FrontPage is one of the most popular HTML editors on the market, in large part because it's a part of the immensely popular Microsoft Office. FrontPage offers some powerful features as well as an attractive bundle of programs for Web developers, including Image Composer, a graphics program designed for creating images for the Web. FrontPage also includes Web components that you can use to add interactive features, such as a simple search engine or a discussion area, to your Web site. Web components work only if their corresponding programs reside on the Web server that you use, but many commercial service providers now offer FrontPage Web components.

If you are migrating a site from FrontPage to Dreamweaver, first make note of any FrontPage Web components that you use, such as search engines or forms. Dreamweaver doesn't offer these same built-in features, and you won't be able to continue editing them in Dreamweaver the way you did in FrontPage. Although you don't need to alter the code for these components, thanks to the Dreamweaver respect for unique code, you can't edit FrontPage's built-in components in Dreamweaver.

If you use CSS or layers in FrontPage, you need to pay special attention to those features as you convert your site to Dreamweaver. Microsoft FrontPage isn't as good as Dreamweaver at creating high-end features that work in both Netscape Navigator and Microsoft Internet Explorer, so you probably want to improve your code if you expect viewers to use any browser other than Internet Explorer. Because CSS and layers are more complex than HTML to code, you probably don't want to edit this code manually — converting from other editors to Dreamweaver can get pretty tricky. Tables can also get messy when you switch from one program to another. In some cases, you may find that the simplest solution is to delete the elements that you created in FrontPage and re-create them in Dreamweaver. (For more on CSS and layers, check out Chapters 8 and 9.)

Microsoft Word

Although Microsoft Word is a word processor and is not considered an HTML editor per se, it does have HTML output capabilities. As a result, you will likely encounter pages that have been created and saved in Microsoft Word at some point. The problems you find in HTML code generated from Word are similar to the problems generated from FrontPage: They both tend to create unusual and sometimes redundant code that deviates from HTML standards. Because Word-generated HTML is so common, Dreamweaver includes a special Clean Up Word HTML command. To use this feature, choose Commands⇨ Clean Up Word HTML and then specify the code you want altered in the Clean Up Word HTML dialog box. When you use this feature, Dreamweaver removes excess code, which can help your pages load faster and work better in different browsers.

After you use Dreamweaver to clean up Word HTML, you should not expect to edit the file in Word again. The code may be cleaner, but depending on the formatting options you've used, Word may no longer be able to read it.

Adobe GoLive

Adobe GoLive offers some great features for easy page design and a lot of similarities to Dreamweaver, so you should have little if any trouble migrating a site from GoLive to Dreamweaver.

If you have included any JavaScript actions in your pages using GoLive, you may not be able to edit them in Dreamweaver, but the actions should still work when the page displays in a browser. Likewise, CSS and other Dynamic HTML features created in GoLive do not always work well in Dreamweaver unless you know how to edit the code manually. If your page contains any actions or DTHML features, you may find re-creating the page in Dreamweaver your best option.

Not long before the writing of this book, Adobe purchased Macromedia and although, to date, no announcement has been made about changes to GoLive, I imagine that both GoLive and Dreamweaver are likely to see changes in the future that will either make them more compatible or make one of them obsolete. I'm betting on Dreamweaver, not only because I'm the author of this book, but because it has the largest market share; but it's hard to predict what will happen to GoLive, which is also a strong Web design program.

Other HTML editors

In the early days of the Web, lots of different visual HTML editors were being used. Today only a few major ones are left. The few that I discuss here seem to capture most of the market. Still, you may find yourself inheriting sites built in really old editors such as Claris HomePage, or Symantec VisualPage. Each of these programs present fewer problems than either Frontpage or GoLive because they aren't capable of creating the complex, high-end features that are hardest to migrate from one program to another.

For the most part, you can open any HTML page with Dreamweaver and continue developing it with little concern. If you run into problems, remember that you always have the option of re-creating the page from scratch in Dreamweaver — a sure way to get rid of any unwanted code. You may also want to use the Dreamweaver Clean Up XHTML feature to identify potentially problematic code. To use this feature, choose Commands⇨Clean Up XHTML and then select the elements you want to alter in the Clean Up HTML dialog box.

No matter what program your site is originally created in, as you consider how best to convert your work into Dreamweaver, pay special attention to unusual code output, nonstandard rules about HTML tags and syntax, and sophisticated features such as CSS, Dynamic HTML, and sophisticated programming, such as ASP, Java, or CGI scripts. These Web page elements are most likely to cause problems when you import them into Dreamweaver.

Chapter 2

Setting Up a Web Site with Dreamweaver

*I*f you're ready to dive in and start building your Web site, you've come to the right place. In this chapter, you find what you to need to start building a Web site whether you are working on an existing Web site or creating a new one. First you discover an important preliminary step — site setup, which enables Dreamweaver to keep track of the images, links, and other elements in your site. Then, you get into the fun stuff, creating your first page and adding images and text.

Before you start creating or editing individual pages, setting up your site using the site-management features in Dreamweaver is really important. Whether you're creating a new site or working on an existing site, follow the steps in the next section to get Dreamweaver ready to manage the site for you. The site-management features enable Dreamweaver to keep track of the elements in your site, automatically create links, update your server, and even manage a team of developers. With the enhancements in this latest version, all these features are even more powerful and easy to use.

You can use Dreamweaver without doing this initial site setup, but many of the features — such as automated link checking and the capability to store commonly used elements in the Library — won't work.

Setting Up a New or Existing Site

The site-management features in Dreamweaver are designed to ensure that everything works properly in your Web site by making certain that links connect and files and folders are placed correctly on your hard drive. If you don't do site setup, you risk breaking links between pages. The site setup process also gets you ready to use Dreamweaver's file transferring tools, including FTP capabilities (*File Transfer Protocol*). These tools facilitate the transfer of your pages to and from your local computer to your Web server. Dreamweaver also includes special features that help track and manage updates to your server anytime you make changes to your site.

As you go through the site setup process, you start by telling Dreamweaver which folder on your hard drive is the one that you use to store all the files and folders for your Web site. You need to keep all the files and folders for your site in one main folder because when you finish building your site and upload it to your Web server, the individual pages, images, and other elements must remain in the same relative location on the Web server as they are on your hard drive, and that's most easily accomplished by storing them all in one main folder.

If this setup seems a little confusing to you, don't worry; it's a quick easy process and as long as you keep all the files of your Web site in one main folder, you'll be fine. Just trust me; don't skip this first step.

When you use site setup for a new Web site, Dreamweaver by default creates a new folder on your hard drive to ensure that you save all the pages and other elements of your site in one place. If you prefer, you can change the location of that folder or create a new one yourself.

If you're working on an existing site, you follow the same steps for site setup, but instead of creating a new folder, you direct Dreamweaver to the folder that contains the existing site.

If you're an experienced Web designer and just want to make quick changes to a site or use the FTP features to access files on a server without doing the site setup steps, Dreamweaver does enable you to use these features without completing site setup. To access FTP features and set them up quickly, choose Site➪Manage Sites and then choose New➪FTP & RDS Server from the Manage Sites dialog box. This shortcut enables you to work directly on your server using FTP & RDS Server; but Dreamweaver does not manage link checking, and none of the other site-management features work.

FTP (*File Transfer Protocol*) is used for copying files to and from computers connected across a network, such as the Internet. FTP is the protocol you use to send your Web pages to your Web server when you're ready to publish your site on the Web.

Defining a site

The following steps walk you through the process of using the Site Definition dialog box to define your site. Whether you create a new site or work on an existing Web site, this first step is important to your Web design work because you identify your site structure, which enables Dreamweaver to set links and effectively handle many of the site-management features explained in later chapters.

If you want to work on an existing site that is on a remote Web server, follow the steps in the sidebar, "Downloading an existing Web site," later in this chapter.

To define a site using the Site Definition dialog box, follow these steps.

1. **Choose Site⇨Manage Sites.**

   The Manage Sites dialog box appears, as shown in Figure 2-1.

Figure 2-1:
The Manage Sites dialog box keeps a list of all the sites you set up in Dreamweaver and provides access to editing and setup options.

Manage Sites	
David LaFontaine	New...
Digital Family.com	
Feral West	Edit...
Graden site	
Hard News Inc.	Duplicate
JCWarner.com	
karate site	Remove
Marilyn Pittman	
Operacion Red	Export...
Our House	
Our Warner Family	Import...
Spheres Women's Circle	
Ted Perkins site	
Done	Help

2. **Click the New button and then select Site.**

   The Site Definition dialog box appears, as shown in Figure 2-2.

3. **Click the Advanced tab.**

   The Advanced window appears. If you prefer, you can use the Basic wizard that steps you through the setup process, but I find it easier to understand what's happening when I can view all the options at once on the Advanced tab.

4. **Make sure that the Local Info category is selected in the Category box.**

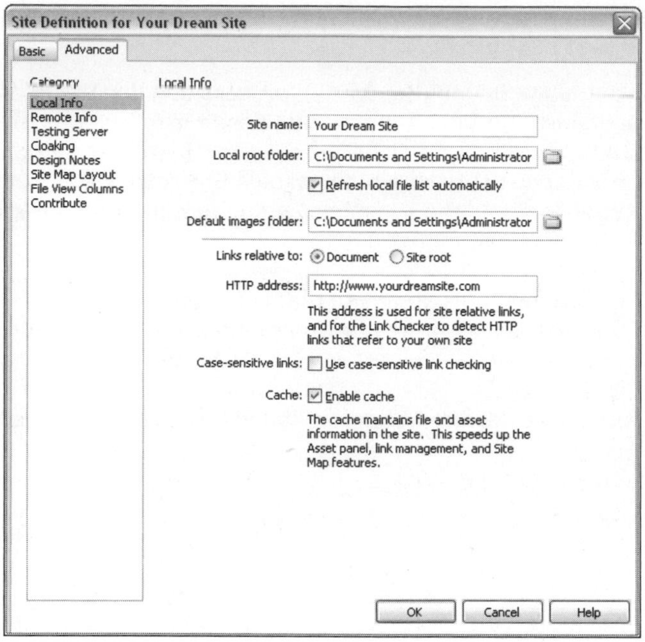

Figure 2-2:
The Site Definition dialog box enables you to set up a new or existing Web site in Dream-weaver.

5. **In the Site Name text box, type a name for your site.**

   You can call your site whatever you like; this name is only used for you to keep track of your sites. Many people work on more than one site in Dreamweaver so the program includes a way to name and keep track of them. After you name it here, the name appears as an option on the drop-down list in the Files panel. You use this list to select the site you want to work on when you open Dreamweaver. In the example shown in Figure 2-2, I named the new site I created "Your Dream Site."

6. **Click the Browse button (it resembles a file folder) next to the Local Root Folder text box to locate the folder on your hard drive that contains your Web site.**

   If you're working on a new site, create a new folder and designate that as the location of your site in Dreamweaver. If you're working an existing site, select the folder that contains the files for that site.

7. **If Refresh Local File List Automatically isn't already selected, click to place a check mark in the box next to this option if you want Dreamweaver to automatically update the list of all the new pages you add to your site.**

   This feature helps Dreamweaver work more efficiently by speeding the process of tracking and identifying files in your site.

8. **Specify the Default Images folder by entering the location or using the Browse button to locate it.**

   You do not have to identify an images folder, but it's another way Dreamweaver helps keep track of things for you. If you store images in more than one folder, you can leave this box blank. If you're setting up a new site, you can create a new folder inside your site folder and identify that as your images folder, even if it is empty. (You find more information about images in Chapter 5.)

9. **Type the URL of your Web site in the HTTP Address text box.**

   The HTTP Address is the URL, or Web address, that your site will have when published on a Web server. If you do not yet know the Web address for your site or you do not plan to publish it on a Web server, you can leave this box blank. Include the http:// at the beginning, and a / at the end.

10. **Check the Use Case-Sensitive Link Checking box.**

    Unless you know for sure that you don't have to worry about the case of your filenames, have Dreamweaver help you enforce the case sensitivity of your site's links. (See Chapter 3 for more on file naming.)

11. **Check the Enable Cache option.**

    Dreamweaver creates a local cache of your site to quickly reference the location of files in your site. The local cache speeds up many of the site-management features of the program and takes only a few seconds to create.

12. **Click OK to close the Site Definition dialog box.**

    If you haven't checked the Enable Cache option, a message box appears asking whether you want to create a cache for the site. Figure 2-2 shows what the Site Definition dialog box looks like when all the areas in the Local Info section are filled in.

Setting up Web server access for FTP

To make your life simpler, Dreamweaver incorporates FTP capability so that you can easily upload your pages to a Web server. This feature also enables Dreamweaver to help you keep track of changes you make to files on your hard drive and to ensure that they match the files on your Web server.

You enter information about the Web server where your site will be published on the Remote Info page of the Site Definition dialog box. You access this page by selecting Remote Info in the Category box on the left side of the Site Definition dialog box. The Remote Info page opens on the right side of the box, as shown in Figure 2-3.

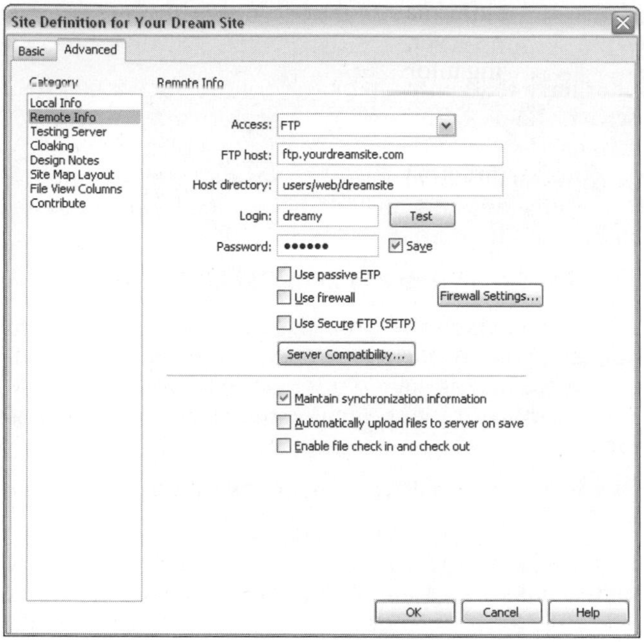

Site Definition for Your Dream Site

Basic | Advanced

Category

Local Info
Remote Info
Testing Server
Cloaking
Design Notes
Site Map Layout
File View Columns
Contribute

Remote Info

Access: FTP

FTP host: ftp.yourdreamsite.com

Host directory: users/web/dreamsite

Login: dreamy   [Test]

Password: ••••••   ☑ Save

☐ Use passive FTP
☐ Use firewall   [Firewall Settings...]
☐ Use Secure FTP (SFTP)

[Server Compatibility...]

☑ Maintain synchronization information
☐ Automatically upload files to server on save
☐ Enable file check in and check out

[OK]   [Cancel]   [Help]

Figure 2-3:
The Site
Definition
dialog box
specifies
the access
information
for a remote
Web server.

You can find several options in the Remote Info section on the Access drop-down list. In the following section, you find instructions on how to set up FTP access, which is the second choice on the drop-down list. If you aren't going to publish your site on a server, choose None from the drop-down list and go on to the next section. If you're going to send your site to a server located on your local network, choose Local/Network; then use the Browse button to specify that server's location on your network. The other options — WebDAV, RDS, and Microsoft Visual SourceSafe — are advanced options that you don't need to worry about if you're working on a site you'll host on a commercial service provider. (You can find more about working with these advanced options in Chapters 13, 14, and 15.)

The most common way to publish a Web site after you develop it is to use FTP to send the site to a remote server, such as those offered by commercial Internet service providers. If that is how you're going to publish your site, follow the upcoming steps, and you'll be all set when you're ready to publish your Web site.

If you don't have your server information, or you're anxious to start building your site on your own hard drive first, you can skip this part of the setup process and come back to it when you're ready to publish your site.

You need the following information to set up the FTP option in Dreamweaver. If you're using a remote server, such as an Internet service provider, ask your provider for the following information:

- ✔ FTP host name
- ✔ Path for the Web directory
- ✔ FTP login
- ✔ FTP password

Choose FTP from the Access drop-down list in the Remote Info page of the Site Definition dialog box (refer to Figure 2-3), and follow these steps:

1. **In the FTP Host text box, type the hostname of your Web server.**

   It should look something like `ftp.host.com` or `shell.host.com` or `ftp.domain.com`, depending on your server. (In my example, I used `ftp.yourdreamsite.com`.)

2. **In the Host Directory text box, type the directory on the remote site in which documents visible to the public are stored (also known as the *site root*).**

   It should look something like `public/html/` or `www/public/docs/`. Again, this depends on your server.

3. **In the Login and Password text boxes, type the login name and password required to gain access to your Web server. If you check the Save box, Dreamweaver stores the information and automatically supplies it to the server when you connect to the remote site.**

   This is your unique login and password information that provides you access to your server.

   Click the Test button to make sure that you've entered everything correctly. If there are no problems, Dreamweaver responds with a box saying `Dreamweaver connected to your Web server successfully`.

4. **Put a check mark in the Use Passive FTP or Use Firewall options only if your service provider or site administrator instructs you to do so.**

   If you aren't on a network but you do use a commercial service provider, you should not need to check either option.

5. **Click OK to save your Web Server Info settings and close the Site Definition dialog box.**

   If you want to continue reviewing the settings in other categories, choose Testing Server, Design Notes, Site Map Layout, File View Columns, or Contribute from the Category box on the left side of the screen. (You can find more information on these categories in Chapter 4.)

Downloading an existing Web site

If you want to work on an existing Web site and you don't already have a copy of it on your local computer's hard drive, you can use Dreamweaver to download any or all the files in the site so that you can edit the existing pages, add new pages, or use any of Dreamweaver's other features to check links and manage the site's further development. The first step is to get a copy of the site onto your computer by downloading it from the server.

To download an existing Web site, follow these steps:

1. **Create a new folder on your computer to store the existing site.**

2. **Specify this folder as the local root folder for the site with the Dreamweaver site setup features.**

   Check out the section "Defining a site," earlier in this chapter, if you're not sure how to do this.

3. **Set up the Remote Info dialog box.**

   I explain how to do this in the "Setting up Web server access for FTP" section, earlier in this chapter.

4. **Connect to the remote site by clicking the Connects to Remote Host button, which looks like the ends of two cables, in the Files panel.**

5. **Click the Get Files button, which looks like a down arrow, to download the entire site to your local drive.**

   Sometimes your Web host has files on the remote server that you don't need to download. If you want to download only specific files or folders from the site, select those files or folders in the Remote Site pane of the Files panel, and click the Get Files button. Dreamweaver automatically duplicates some or all the remote site's structure, meaning the folders in the site but not all the files within them, and places the downloaded files in the correct part of the site hierarchy. Re-creating the folder structure on your local computer is important because Dreamweaver needs to know the location of the files as they relate to other parts of the site in order to set links properly. The safest option is to download the entire site; but if you are working on a really large Web project, downloading a part and duplicating the structure enables you to work on a section of the site without downloading all of it.

   If you are working on only one page or section of a site, you should generally choose to include *dependent files*, meaning any files linked from those pages, to ensure that links set properly when you make changes.

6. **After you download the site or specific files or folders, you can edit them as you do any other file in Dreamweaver.**

Creating New Pages

Every Web site begins with a single page. Visitors are first greeted by the front page — or *home page* — of your site, and that's usually a good place to start building. Dreamweaver makes building a home page easy: When the program opens, you see a Start Screen with shortcuts to many handy features for creating new pages.

If you want to create a simple, blank Web page, choose HTML from the Create New list in the middle row (see Figure 2-4). If you are creating a dynamic site, you may choose ColdFusion, PHP, or one of the ASP options. (If you don't even know what those options mean, you probably won't need to use them, but you can find some information about these advanced options in Chapters 13, 14, and 15.)

Get in the habit of saving new Web pages into your main Web site folder as soon as you create them, even though they are still blank. As you create links or add images to your pages, Dreamweaver needs to be able to identify the location of your page, and it can't do that until you save the page.

Figure 2-4:
The Start
Screen
provides
a list of
shortcuts to
create new
files or open
existing
pages in
Dream-
weaver.

If the Start Screen is not visible because you have an existing page already open or you've opted not to show it, follow these steps to create a new page:

1. **Choose File⇨New.**

2. **Select Basic Page from the Category list.**

3. **Select HTML from the Basic Page list.**

4. **Choose File⇨Save to save your page.**

   You find many other options in the Dreamweaver New Document window, including a wide range of predesigned templates. For now, don't worry about all those. In this chapter, you start off by creating a simple blank page. You find instructions for working with templates in Chapter 4.

Make sure you add a page title to each of your pages. You can add a page title by changing the text in the Title box on the Document toolbar. By default, Dreamweaver inserts the words `Untitled Page` into the Title box, but you can put any text you want in this box. The page title doesn't appear in the body of your Web page, but it's important because this text appears at the top of the browser window, usually just to the right of the name of the browser. This text also appears in a user's list of Favorites or Bookmarks when that user bookmarks your site.

Naming Web Pages

When you save Web pages, images, and other files in your site, you need to be careful what you name them and you need to include an extension at the end to identify the file type (such as `.html` for HTML files or `.gif` for GIF images). Dreamweaver automatically adds the extension to the end of HTML files, but you can change preferences to use either `.html` or `.htm`. In theory, these extensions are interchangeable, but some servers read only `.html` so that's the safer bet.

Filenames in Web sites get incorporated into links and links are easier to manage when they don't include spaces or special characters. For example you shouldn't name a Web page with an apostrophe, such as `cat's page.html`. If you want to separate words, use the underscore (_) or the hyphen (-). For example, `cat-page.html` is a fine filename. Numbers are fine and capital letters don't really matter, as long as the filename and the link match, which Dreamweaver takes care of for you when you create links (just be careful if you ever create a link in the HTML code).

One of the most confusing and important filename rules in Web design is that the main page (or the *front page*) of your Web site must be called `index.html`. That's because most servers are set up to serve the `index.html` page first. (Although some servers also serve other filenames, such as `home.html`, or `default.asp` on dynamic sites, most prioritize and serve `index.html` before

---

Creating multiple pages to set links

Creating a new page to start a Web site may seem obvious, but consider this: You may want to create a bunch of new pages before you get too far in your development, and you may even want to start organizing the new pages in sub-directories before you have anything on them. Doing so enables you to organize the structure of your site before you start setting links. After all, you can't link to a page that doesn't exist. If you plan to have five links on your front page to other pages in your site, go ahead and create those other pages, even if you don't put anything on them yet.

For example, say you're creating a site for your department at a big company. You're likely to want a few main pages, such as a page about your staff, another about what you do, and a third with general information and resources. At this initial stage, you could create four pages — one for the front page of the site and three others for each of the subsections. With these initial pages in place, you benefit from having an early plan for organizing the site, and you can start setting links among the main pages right away. See Chapter 3 for more tips about Web site planning and organization.

---

all others.) If you want to ensure that your visitors see the right page when their browsers arrive at your Web site, make sure the front page of your site is named `index.html`. After that, you can name your files anything you like, as long as they don't include special characters or spaces.

Designing your first page

Many people are pleasantly surprised by how easily you can create a basic Web page in Dreamweaver.

If you're ready to plunge right in, create a page and click to insert your cursor at the top of the blank page (see the earlier section "Creating New Pages" if you need to start from the beginning). Type some text on the page, anything you like; you just need something to get started. If you're having trouble being creative today, try typing `My husband David is so cool`. (Okay, so I'm guilty of trying to win cheap points with my husband; but trust me, this is a great trick if you want your spouse, partner, or other significant person in your life to be interested when you show off your first Web page. Simply enter your special person's name in place of mine and you're on your way to creating a site he or she is sure to appreciate.)

Although you may be tempted to use the basic formatting options I cover in this chapter, if you're doing a lot of formatting on a site, you can save considerable time using Cascading Style Sheets instead. With CSS you can define styles for things such as headlines, and apply multiple formatting options all at once. You can also change styles and alter the formatting everywhere it's applied. Chapter 8 covers CSS in detail.

Inserting text from another program

If you have text in another program, such as Microsoft Word or Excel, you can copy and paste that text into your Dreamweaver page and even keep the formatting. The Edit menu has two paste options: Paste and Paste Special. If you use the simple Paste option, the content you paste loses any formatting and appears on your page as plain text. If you choose Paste Special, you have several options that enable you to maintain some or all the formatting applied to the text in the program you copied it from. Just click to select the radio button that corresponds to the formatting you want to preserve, and Dreamweaver automatically applies that formatting to the text as it is inserted into your page.

Creating a headline

Most Web pages have some kind of headline at the top of the page. To make your headline bold, centered, and a large font size, follow these steps:

1. **Highlight the text you want to format.**

2. **In the Properties inspector at the bottom of the page, select the B icon to make the selected text bold.**

   The heading becomes bold.

3. **In the Properties inspector at the bottom of the page, select the center icon.**

   The text automatically centers.

4. **In the Properties inspector, use the Size drop-down list and select 36.**

   The text changes to font size 36, and you have a headline at the top of your page that looks something like the headline shown in Figure 2-5.

In general, I find the Properties inspector the easiest way to apply basic formatting, but some people prefer using the drop-down lists from the Text menu bar. Both achieve the same results with the exception that Dreamweaver features font sizes in the Properties inspector (listed as sizes 9 through 36 and xx-small through xx-large) but offers only the capability to increase or decrease font size from the Text menu.

You can collapse the panels on the right side of the work area by clicking the small tab on the side of the panel set. In the following figures, I collapsed the panels in the figures in the rest of this chapter to create more room in the Workspace.

Figure 2-5:
The
Properties
inspector
provides
easy access
to common
formatting
features,
such as
bold, center,
and font
sizes.

Indenting text

Type a little more text after your headline text. (I added a few nice things about meeting and marrying my husband — call me sentimental if you must.) A single sentence is all you need, but you can add as much as text as you like. To indent that text, follow these steps:

1. **Highlight the text you want to indent.**

2. **Choose Text⇨Indent.**

   The text automatically indents. Alternatively, you can use the Text Indent and Text Outdent icons in the Properties inspector.

 If you want to continue adding text and you don't want to indent it, choose Text⇨Outdent to transition back to plain text mode without the indent. You can also use the small Indent and Outdent icons located at the bottom of the Properties inspector, just to the left of the Target field.

If you just want to indent a short paragraph or two, the Indent option is ideal. If, however, you want to create the effect of a narrower column of text on a page, you may find that putting your text in an HTML table is a better option because you can better control the width of the column. You can find information about creating HTML tables in Chapter 6. You can also achieve similar results using layers, which Chapter 9 covers.

Changing fonts and text sizes

You can change font and text sizes for the entire page or for selections of text. You find instructions on making global changes in the following section "Changing Page Properties." To change the font face and font size for a selected section of text, follow these steps:

1. **Highlight the text you want to change.**

2. **In the Properties inspector at the bottom of the work area, select a collection of fonts from the Font drop-down list.**

   The selected text changes to the font you selected.

   You can also choose the Edit Font list option and use any font, but beware that the font you apply displays on your visitor's computer only if that font is on the hard drive. (See sidebar, "Why so many fonts?" for more about how this works.)

3. **In the Properties inspector at the bottom of the work area, specify the size you want your text from the Size drop-down list.**

   Font sizes in HTML are different from the font sizes you may be used to using in a word processing or image program. Your size options are more limited, and you have the added choices of small, x-small, and so on. The numbered font sizes work much like those you may be used to, but the options specified by words like *small*, *medium*, or *large* display according to the settings of a user's browser. In general, using the numbered sizes gives you more predictable results.

You find many more text formatting options in the Properties inspector, Text menu, and Text Insert bar. Go ahead, experiment a little; you can always undo your formatting choices or change them again if you don't like the way they look.

Adding images

Now for the fun part. Adding an image to your Web page may seem almost magical at first because it is so simple with Dreamweaver. The challenge with Web graphics is not adding them to your pages, but creating good-looking images that load quickly in your viewer's browser. You need another program, such as Photoshop or Fireworks, to create, convert, and edit images. Dreamweaver just lets you place the images on your page.

For more information on finding and creating images, as well as keeping file sizes small, see Chapter 5. For now, I assume that you have a GIF or JPEG image file ready, and that you want to insert your image into your page. The

---

Why so many fonts?

Although you can specify any font you want for text on your Web pages, you don't have complete control over how that font appears on your visitor's computer. That's because the font can only display if your visitor has the font on his or her hard drive. To help ensure your text appears as you intend, Dreamweaver offers collections of similar fonts, such as Arial, Helvetica, sans-serif, or Georgia, Times New Roman, Times, serif.

Here's how it works. When you apply a collection of fonts like these, the browser displays the formatted text in the first font available on that list. For example, if you choose the font collection that starts with Georgia and your visitors don't have Georgia, the text displays in Times New Roman; if they don't have that font, it displays in Times; and if they don't even have Times, then the browser looks for another serif font. (In case you're not familiar with font terms,

serif is used to describe fonts such as Times that have those little curly things on the edges of letters; *sans serif* means no curly things, which is what you get with a font such as Arial.)

You can create your own font collections by selecting the Edit Font List option. The collection of fonts included in Dreamweaver represents some of the most common fonts and thus the ones most likely to appear on any user's computer.

The only way to ensure that text appears in the font you want is to create the text as a graphic in a program such as Photoshop or Fireworks and then insert the graphic with the text into your page. That's not a bad option for special text, such as banners or logos; but it's usually not a good option for all your text because graphics take longer to download than text and harder to update later.

---

two most common image formats you can use on your Web page are GIF and JPEG (which is often shortened to JPG). You can use any image on your Web site, as long as it's in GIF or JPEG format.

If you don't have an image handy and want one to practice the following exercise with, you can download a free JPEG from my Web site at `www.Digital Family.com/free` (you find instructions for downloading images in Chapter 5).

Most browsers also support BMP, but most designers never use it because BMP files don't optimize as well. PNG is also an accepted image format on the Web, but Web designers rarely use it because Internet Explorer for Windows has not supported PNG fully. Unless you have a compelling reason to use one of these formats, you'll do well to stick with JPEG and GIF.

You need to do two important things before inserting an image on a Web page: Save the page and ensure the image is in the proper folder. Saving your page in your Web site's folder on your hard drive is important because Dreamweaver can't properly set the link to your image until it identifies the relative locations of the page and the image.

For this same reason, you need to make sure that the image file is in your main Web site folder (the folder you identified in the site setup process at the beginning of this chapter). Many designers create a folder called *images* so they can keep all their image files in one place. If you are working on a very large site, you may want an images folder within each of the main folders of the site. An important thing to remember is that if you move the page or image to another folder after you place the image on your page, you risk breaking the link between the page and the image, and an ugly broken image icon appears when you view your page in a browser.

If you move files or folders in the Dreamweaver Files panel, it keeps the links up to date, but if you move them outside of Dreamweaver, the links break. If for some reason you do end up breaking an image link, simply click the broken image icon that appears in its place, and use the Browse button in the Properties inspector to find the image and replace it on your page.

Okay, assuming you've saved your page and the image you want to link is saved within your main Web site folder, you're ready to follow these steps to place an image on your Web page:

1. **Click the Image icon located on the Common Insert bar at the top of the work area and choose Image from the drop-down list. (*Hint:* The icon looks like a small tree.)**

   The Image dialog box opens.

2. **Click the Select button.**

   The Select Image Source dialog box opens, displaying files and folders on your hard drive.

3. **Navigate to the folder that has the image you want to insert.**

4. **Double-click to select the image you want.**

   The image automatically appears on your Web page.

   If you haven't already saved your page, a warning box appears to tell you that Dreamweaver cannot properly set the link to the image until you save the page. You see this message because Dreamweaver needs to know the location of the HTML page relative to the image to create the link. If you see this box, you have two options. You can click Cancel, save your page by choosing File⇨Save, and then repeat the preceding steps. Or, you can go ahead and choose the image, and after you save your file, Dreamweaver tries to automatically update the image link.

   If you've already saved your page, another common problem is that the image is not located within your main Web site folder. Dreamweaver offers you the option of creating a copy of the image in your main site folder. Click the Yes button if you want Dreamweaver to copy the image to your root folder (this helps ensure the image transfers to your server correctly when you upload your site to your server).

5. **Click the image on your Web page to display the image options in the Properties inspector at the bottom of the page.**

   Use the Properties inspector to specify image attributes, such as alignment, horizontal, and vertical spacing, and alternative text. (The image properties are visible in the Properties inspector in Figure 2-6.)

   With an image selected, the Properties inspector enables you to specify many attributes for an image. Table 2-1 describes those attributes. If you don't see all the attributes listed in the table on your screen, click the triangle in the bottom-right corner of the Properties inspector to reveal all the image options.

Although you can resize an image in Dreamweaver by clicking and dragging on the edge of the image or by changing the Height and Width values in the Properties inspector, I don't recommend you change an image size this way. Changing the height and width in the Properties inspector won't actually change the size of the image, just the way it displays on the page. That's a problem for two reasons. First, using this option to make an image look bigger often leads to the image looking distorted; second, using this option to make an image look smaller requires your visitor to download a larger file than necessary.

Figure 2-6:
When an image is selected, the Properties inspector provides easy access to common image attributes, such as alignment and spacing.

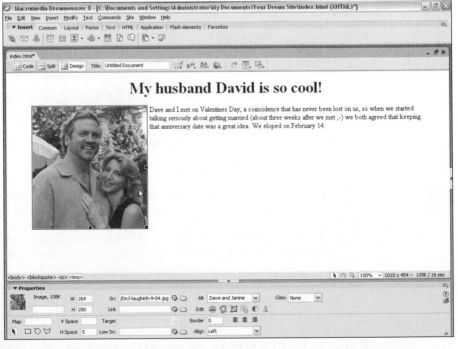

You're almost always better off using Dreamweaver's new auto resizing and cropping functions or using an image editor to change the physical size of an image. Because this is such a common thing to do, Dreamweaver includes a few shortcuts that incorporate Fireworks image-editing capabilities and enable you to edit an image in tandem with Dreamweaver. To edit an image in Fireworks from within Dreamweaver, click to select the image and then click the Fireworks icon (the yellow circle labeled FW in the Properties inspector) to open the image in Fireworks. Edit the image in Fireworks and when you save it, your changes are reflected in Dreamweaver.

See Chapter 5 for more on working with images in Dreamweaver, such as the built-in cropping tool and image map features. You can find instructions for working with Fireworks in Chapter 10.

Table 2-1	Image Attributes in the Properties Inspector	
Abbreviation	*Attribute*	*Function*
Image	N/A	Specifies the file size.
Image Name	Name	Identifies image uniquely on the page — an important detail if you use behaviors or other scripts that are triggered by the image.
Map	Map Name	Assign a name to an image map. All image maps require a name.
Hotspot tools	Image Map Coordinates	Use the Rectangle, Oval, and Polygon icons to create image map hotspots for links. (See Chapter 5 to find out how to create an image map.)
W	Width	Dreamweaver automatically specifies the width of the image based on the actual size of the image dimensions.
H	Height	Dreamweaver automatically specifies the height of the image based on the actual size of the image dimensions.

Abbreviation	Attribute	Function
Src	Source	Required. The *source* is the file-name and path from the current document to the desired image. Dreamweaver automatically sets this when you insert the image.
Link	Hyperlink	This field shows the address or path if the image links to another page. (For more about linking, see "Setting Links" later in this chapter.)
Alt	Alternate Text	The words you enter display if the image doesn't appear on your viewer's screen because images are turned off in the user's browser. Alt text is especially important for search engines and browsers used by the blind to read Web pages.
Edit	Icons for Fireworks, Optimize, Crop, Resample, Brightness and Contrast, and Sharpen	Click the Fireworks icons to launch Fireworks. Use any of the other icons to make other minor alter-ations to an image within Dreamweaver.
V Space	Vertical Space	Measured in pixels, this setting inserts blank space above and below the image.
H Space	Horizontal Space	Measured in pixels, this setting inserts blank space to the left and right of the image.
Target	Link Target	Use this option when the image appears in a page where you want to control the target, such as when a page is part of an HTML frameset or when you want a link to open a new window. The Target specifies the frame into which the linked page opens. I cover creating frames and how to set links in frames in Chapter 7.

(continued)

Table 2-1 *(continued)*

Abbreviation	Attribute	Function
Low Src	Low Source	This option enables you to link two images to the same place on a page. The Low Source image loads first and, after the rest of the page loads, is replaced by the primary image. You may find this option especially useful when you have a large image size because you can set a smaller image (such as a stretched black-and-white version) as the Low Source, which displays while the main image downloads. The combination of two images in this way creates the illusion of a simple animation.
Border	Image Border	Measured in pixels, this attribute enables you to put a border around an image. I nearly always set the image border to 0 (zero). Dreamweaver makes that the default setting when linking an image because, otherwise, the viewer sees a colored border around a linked image.
Align	Alignment	This option enables you to align the image. Text automatically wraps around images aligned to the right or left. The other options, including Baseline, Top, and Middle, control how text or other elements align next to the image. The alignment icons control the entire paragraph containing the image, and align the text left, right, or center.

Setting relative versus absolute links

If the page you want to link to is within your Web site, you want to create a *relative, or* internal link, that includes the path that describes how to get from the current page to the linked page. A relative link doesn't need to include the domain name of the server. Here's an example of what the code would look like if I created a relative link to the books page on my own Web site:

```
<A HREF="books/index.html">Janine's
        Books</A>
```

If you link to a page on a different Web site, you want to create an *absolute, or* external, link. An absolute link does include the full Internet address of the other site. Here's an example of what the code would look like behind an absolute link if you created a link from your site to the books page on my site:

```
<A
        HREF="http://www.jcwarner.com/b
        ooks/index.html">Janine's
        Books</A>
```

If all that HREF code stuff looks like Greek to you, don't worry. The following section shows you how Dreamweaver allows you to set links without even knowing what the code means.

Setting Links

Dreamweaver is truly a dream when setting links. The most important thing to keep in mind is that a link is essentially an address (URL) that tells a viewer's browser what page to go to when the viewer clicks the text or image containing the link.

Linking pages within your Web site

Linking from one page to another page in your Web site — known as a *relative* or *internal link* — is easy. The most important thing to remember is to save your pages in the folders that you want to keep them in before you start setting links. Make sure that all your files are in the root folder, as described in the section "Defining a site," earlier in this chapter. Here's how you create an internal link:

1. **In Dreamweaver, open the page on which you want to create a link.**

2. **Select the text or image that you want to serve as the link (meaning the text or image that opens the new page when a user clicks it).**

   Click and drag to highlight text or click once to select an image.

3. **Click the Browse button to the right of the Link text box in the Properties inspector.**

   The Select File dialog box opens.

4. **Click the filename to select the page that you want your image or text to link to, and then click the OK button (Windows) or Choose button (Mac).**

   The link is automatically set and the dialog box closes. If you haven't already saved your page, a message box opens, explaining that you can create a relative link only after you save the page. Always save the page you're working on before you set links. Note that to test your links, you have to view your page in a browser, covered in the "Previewing Your Page in a Browser," section later in this chapter.

If the page is part of a frameset, use the Target field in the Properties inspector to specify which frame the linked page opens into. (You find out more about setting links in frames in Chapter 7.)

Setting links to named anchors within a page

If you like to create really long pages, using anchor links to break up navigation within the page is a good idea. A *named anchor link,* often called a *jump link,* enables you to set a link to a specific part of a Web page. You can use a named anchor to link from an image or text string on one page to another place on the same page, or to link from one page to a specific part of a different page. To create a named anchor link, you first insert a named anchor in the place that you want to link to, and then use that anchor to direct the browser to that specific part of the page when a viewer follows the link.

Suppose that you want to set a link from the word *Convertible* at the top of a page to a section lower on the page that starts with the headline *Convertible Sports Cars.* You first insert a named anchor at the *Convertible Sports Cars* headline. Then you link the word *Convertible* from the top of the page to that anchor.

To insert a named anchor and set a link to it, follow these steps:

1. **Open the page on which you want to insert the named anchor.**

2. **Place your cursor next to the word or image that you want to link to on the page.**

   You don't need to select the word or image; you just need a reference point that displays when the link is selected. For this example, I placed the cursor to the left of the headline *Convertible Sports Cars.*

3. **Choose Insert⇨Named Anchor.**

   The Insert Named Anchor dialog box appears.

4. **Enter a name for the anchor.**

   You can name anchors anything you want (as long as you don't use spaces or special characters). Just make sure that you use a different name for each anchor on the same page. Then be sure that you remember what you called the anchor, because you have to type the anchor name to set the link. (Unlike other Web design programs, Dreamweaver doesn't automatically enter the anchor name.) In this example, I chose *convertible* as the anchor name because it's easy for me to remember.

5. **Click OK.**

   The dialog box closes, and a small anchor icon appears on the page where you inserted the anchor name. You can move an anchor name by clicking the anchor icon and dragging it to another location on the page.

   If you're curious about what this named anchor looks like in HTML, here's the code that appears before the headline in my example:

   ```
   <A NAME="convertible"></A>
   ```

6. **To set a link to the named anchor location, select the text or image that you want to link from.**

   You can link to a named anchor from anywhere else on the same page or from another page. In my example, I linked from the word *Convertible* that appears at the top of the page to the anchor I made next to the headline.

7. **In the Properties inspector, type the pound sign (#) followed by the anchor name.**

   You can also select the text and drag a line from the Point to File icon (next to the Link text box) to the anchor icon. The anchor name automatically appears in the Link box, saving you from typing the name again.

   In my example, I typed **#convertible** in the Link text box. The HTML code for this line looks like this:

   ```
   <A HREF="#convertible">Convertible</A>
   ```

   If you want to link to an anchor named *convertible* on another page with the filename `coolcars.html`, you type **coolcars.html#convertible** in the Link text box.

When you create a text link, Dreamweaver includes a handy little drop-down list beside the Link box, listing the most recent links you've created. To set a link to the same page or Web site, just select it from the drop-down list. Unfortunately, if you're creating a link from an image, that handy drop-down list is not available and you have to set the link by entering the URL manually or using the Browser button to locate the page you want to link to.

Linking to pages outside your Web site

Linking to a page on another Web site — called an *external link* — is even easier than linking to an internal link. All you need is the URL of the page to which you want to link, and you're most of the way there.

To create an external link, follow these steps:

1. **In Dreamweaver, open the page from which you want to link.**

2. **Select the text or image that you want to act as a link.**

3. **In the Link text box in the Properties inspector, type the URL of the page you want your text or image to link to.**

   The link is automatically set. (In the example in Figure 2-7, I created a link to my site about family-oriented Web sites at www.digitalfamily.com.)

Although in most browsers, you don't have to type the http:// at the beginning of a Web site address to get to a site, you must always use the full URL, including the http://, when you create an external link in HTML. Otherwise, the browser can't find the correct external site address and the visitor probably end ups on an error page.

Figure 2-7:
Link text or an image to another Web site.

![Properties inspector showing Link field with http://www.digitalfamily.com]

Setting a link to an e-mail address

Another common link option goes to an e-mail address. Visitors can send you messages easily with e-mail links. I always recommend that you invite visitors to contact you because they can point out mistakes in your site and give you valuable feedback about how you can further develop your site.

Setting a link to an e-mail address is just as easy as setting a link to another Web page. Before you start, you need to know the e-mail address to which you want to link. The only other thing you need to know is that e-mail links must begin with the code `mailto:` (no `//`). Here's an example of the full line of code behind an e-mail link:

```
<A HREF="mailto:janine@jcwarner.com">Send a message to
           Janine</A>
```

When visitors to your Web site click an e-mail link, their browsers automatically launch their associated e-mail programs and create a blank e-mail message to the specified e-mail address. This is a cool trick, but it can be disconcerting to your users if they don't expect it to happen. That's why I always try to notify users when I use e-mail links by labeling them so that link clearly goes to an e-mail address and not to another Web page.

To create an e-mail link in Dreamweaver, follow these steps:

1. **In Dreamweaver, open the page on which you want to create an e-mail link and insert your cursor where you want the link.**

2. **If you want to link a text block, highlight the text that you want to act as the link.**

3. **Click the Email Link icon on the Common Insert bar at the top of the screen. (It looks like a small envelope).**

    The Email Link dialog box opens. If you selected text before choosing the Email Link icon, that text is automatically entered into the Text box in the Email Link dialog box.

4. **Enter or edit the text you want to represent the link on the page in the Text box, and then enter the e-mail address (without mailto:) in the Email box.**

    The e-mail link is automatically set, and any text you added or edited appears on the page.

If you want to create a mailto link using a graphic, you can use the Properties inspector. Click to select the image you want to link, and then type **mailto:** followed by the e-mail address in the Link text area. Make sure you don't add any spaces between `mailto:` and the address. It should look like this: `mailto:name@domain.com`.

Changing Page Properties

You can change many individual elements on a page in the Properties inspector, but if you want to make changes that affect the entire page, such as altering link or text colors, you need the Page Properties dialog box. Notice in

Figure 2-8 that the Page Properties dialog box also has a Category list and that each of these sections reveals different page options. Some of these options are covered in other parts of the book, such as the Tracing Image feature (Chapter 4), and the Background Image feature (Chapter 5). For now, to keep things simple, this section focuses only on changing the background and text colors available from the Appearance category, shown in Figure 2-8, and the options in the Links category shown in Figure 2-9.

You can make global changes in the Page Properties dialog box, but you can override those options using the individual formatting options within Dreamweaver, which take precedence. For example, you could make all your text purple in the Page Properties dialog box and then change the color of some of your text to red using the Text Color swatch box in the Properties dialog box.

To change the background and text colors on a page, follow these steps:

1. **Choose Modify➪Page Properties.**

   The Appearance category of the Page Properties dialog box appears, as shown in Figure 2-8.

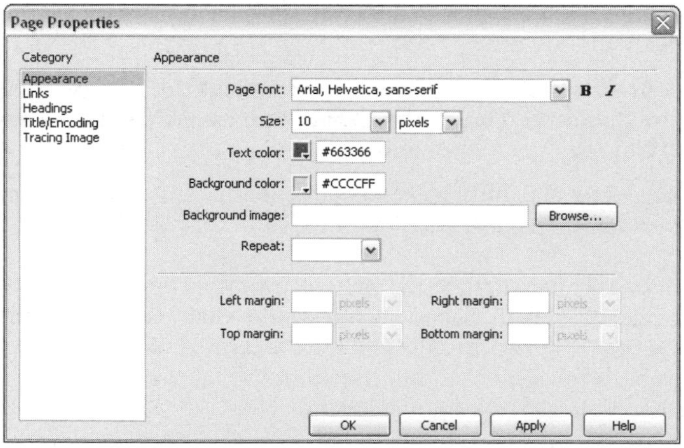

Figure 2-8:
The Appearance category in the Page Properties dialog box enables you to change text colors, font face, font size, background, and margins.

Page Properties

Category: Appearance, Links, Headings, Title/Encoding, Tracing Image

Appearance

Page font: Arial, Helvetica, sans-serif   **B** *I*

Size: 10   pixels

Text color: #663366

Background color: #CCCCFF

Background image: Browse...

Repeat:

Left margin: pixels   Right margin: pixels

Top margin: pixels   Bottom margin: pixels

OK   Cancel   Apply   Help

2. **Specify the fonts you want for the text on your page from the Page Font drop-down list.**

   If you don't specify a font, your text appears in the font specified in your user's browser, which is usually Times.

3. **Click the B or I to the right of the Page Font drop-down list if you want all the text on your page to appear bold or italic.**

   If you select one of these options, all your text appears bold or italic unless you specify other formatting options using the individual text formatting options in Dreamweaver.

4. **Specify the font size you want for the text on your page with the Size drop-down list.**

   Again, you can override these settings by changing the text size using the individual formatting options in Dreamweaver.

5. **Click the Text Color swatch box to reveal the color palette. Choose any color you like.**

   The color you select fills the color swatch box, but will not change the text color on your page until you click the Apply or OK button.

6. **Click the Background Color swatch box to reveal the color palette. Choose any color you like.**

   The color you selected fills the color swatch box. The color does not fill the background until you click the Apply or OK button.

7. **Click the Browse button next to Background Image box if you want to insert a graphic or photograph into the background of your page.**

   When you insert a background image it automatically repeats or tiles across and down the page unless you choose the no-repeat option from the Repeat drop-down list.

8. **Use the margin options at the bottom of the dialog box to change the left, right, top, or bottom margins of your page.**

9. **Click the Apply button to see how the colors look on your page. Click OK to finish and close the Page Properties dialog box.**

When you change the background, text, or link colors make sure the colors look good together and that your text is still readable. As a general rule, a light background color works best with a dark text color and vice versa.

To change the link color and underline options, follow these steps:

1. **Choose Modify⇨Page Properties.**

   The Page Properties dialog box appears.

2. **Select the Links option from the Category list.**

   The Links page opens, as shown in Figure 2-9.

Figure 2-9:
The Links
category in
the Page
Properties
dialog box
enables you
to change
link colors
and specify
if links
should be
underlined.

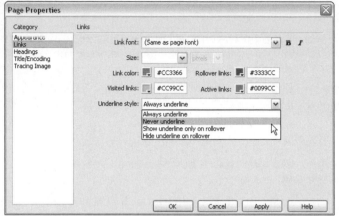

3. **Specify the fonts you want for the links on your page from the Link Font drop-down list.**

   If you don't specify a font, your links appear in the font specified for the general text of your document, or if that's not set, the font specified in your user's browser, which is usually Times.

4. **Click the B or I to the right of the Links Font drop-down list if you want all the links on your page to appear bold or italic.**

   If you select one of these options, all your links appear bold or italic unless you specify other formatting options using the individual formatting options in Dreamweaver.

5. **Specify the font size you want for the links on your page from the Size drop-down list.**

   Again, you can override these settings by changing the text size using the individual formatting options in Dreamweaver.

6. **Click the Link Color swatch box to reveal the color palette. Choose any color you like.**

   The color you selected is applied to links on your page. Notice that there are four link color options:

   Link: Specify the color a link appears if a user hasn't visited its destination page.

   Visited Links: This color is used for links pointing to pages that a visitor has already visited.

   Rollover Links: A link changes to this color when a user rolls a cursor over the link (also known as *hovering*).

   Active Link: A link changes to this color briefly while a user is clicking it.

7. **Specify if you want your links underlined from the Underline drop-down list.**

   By default, all links on a Web page appear underlined in a browser, but many designers find that distracting and opt to turn off underlining by selecting Never Underline. You can also choose Show Underline Only on Rollover to make the underline appear when users moves their cursors over the link, or Hide Underline on Rollover to make the underline disappear when users moves their cursors over a link.

8. **Click the Apply button to see how the colors look on your page. Click OK to finish and close the Page Properties dialog box.**

Adding Meta Tags for Search Engines

If you've heard of Meta tags, you probably associate them with search engines, and you'd be right. Meta tags are used for a variety of things, but the most common is to provide special text that doesn't appear on your page, but does get read by crawlers, bots, and other programs that scour the Web cataloging and ranking Web pages for sites such as Yahoo!, Google, and AltaVista.

Search engines read two common Meta tags — keyword tags and description tags. The first enables site designers to include a list of keywords they would like to be matched to in a search engine. Unfortunately, Meta keywords have been so abused and used to mislead visitors that most search engines no longer give them any weight when ranking pages. At least one search engine, Inktomi, is still using Meta keywords at the time of this writing, and you certainly won't hurt your ranking by using them, but they don't offer the benefits they once did.

The Meta description tag, however, is still widely used and is definitely worth your time. This tag is designed to let you include a written description of your Web site and is often used by search engines as the brief description that appears in search results pages. If you don't include your own text in a Meta description tag, most search engines use the first several words that appear on your front page; but depending on your design, the first few words may not be the best description of your site — they're just as likely to be your site's top navigation. Indeed, if you've ever wondered why the descriptions of some Web sites seem so random or disjointed in search engines, that's why.

To make sure your site looks good in search engine results, follow these steps to use the Meta description tag:

1. **Open the page on which you want to add your Meta description.**

   You can use Meta descriptions on any or all the pages on your Web site (some search engines link directly to internal pages on your site if they match a search), but the most important thing is to add a description to the main page of your site.

2. **Switch to the HTML Insert bar by selecting HTML from the Insert Bar drop-down list, as shown in Figure 2-10.**

   If you have set the Insert bar to display as tabs, click the HTML tab to open it.

3. **Click the small arrow next to the Head icon and choose Description.**

   The Description dialog box opens.

4. **Enter the text you want for your page description in the Description field in the Description dialog box.**

   Don't use any HTML in this box.

5. **Click OK.**

   The description text you entered is inserted into the HTML code.

If you want to add keywords, repeat Steps 1 through 5, selecting the Keywords option from the Head icon drop-down list in Step 3.

Figure 2-10: Many search engines use the description text of your Web page.

Previewing Your Page in a Browser

Although Dreamweaver displays Web pages much like a Web browser, not all of the interactive features you can add to a Web page function from Dreamweaver's work area. For example, links won't work in Dreamweaver. To test your links and verify that your page is displaying the way you intended, you need to preview your work in a Web browser.

 The simplest way to preview your work is to save the page you are working on and then click the Preview/Debug in Browser icon located at the top right of the Workspace (it looks like a small globe).

When you install Dreamweaver, it automatically finds a browser on your computer and sets it up so that when you click this button, you launch the browser. If you want to test your work in more than one browser, you can add more options to the list by choosing Edit➪Preferences and then choosing Preview in Browser from the Category list (on a Mac, you choose Dreamweaver➪ Preferences). Use the plus sign at the top of the screen to add any browsers on your hard drive to the Browser list.

Putting Your Web Site Online

In the section "Setting Up a New or Existing Site," earlier in this chapter, I show you how to set up a site and enter the address, login name, and password for your server. In this section, I show you how to put pages on your server and retrieve them by using the built-in FTP capabilities of Dreamweaver.

To transfer files between your hard drive and a remote server, follow these steps:

1. **Make sure you defined your site, as described in the "Setting Up a New or Existing Site" section in the beginning of this chapter and make sure that that the site you set up is open and displayed in the Files panel. You can open an existing site by choosing Window➪Files and then selecting the site.**

   If you do this properly, the files and folders of your site become visible on the Files tab of the Files panel on the right side of the work area. (See Figure 2-11.)

Figure 2-11:
The Files tab
of the Files
panel
features a
row of
buttons
across the
top that
control FTP
functions.

2. **Click the Connects to Remote Host button in the top left of the Files panel (it looks like a small, blue electrical plug).**

   If you're not already connected to the Internet, the Connects to Remote Host button starts your dialup connection. If you have trouble connecting this way, try establishing your Internet connection as you usually do to check e-mail or surf the Web; then return to Dreamweaver and click the Connects to Remote Host button after establishing your Internet connection. When your computer is online, Dreamweaver should have no trouble establishing an FTP connection with your host server automatically.

   If you still have trouble establishing a connection to your Web server, refer to the section, "Setting up Web server access for FTP," earlier in this chapter and make sure that you specified the server information correctly. If you still have trouble, contact your service provider or site administrator to ensure you have all the correct information for connecting to your server. Getting all this information set up correctly the first time can be tricky, and each service provider is different. The good news is that, once you get this right, Dreamweaver saves your settings so it connects automatically the next time.

   After you establish the connection, the directories on your server appear in the Files panel. You can move between views in this panel by choosing from the drop-down list at the top right (refer to Figure 2-11). The main options are Local View, which displays files on your local hard drive, and Remote View, which displays files on the server.

3. **To *upload* a file (transfer a file from your hard drive to your Web server), select the file from the Local View panel (which shows the files on your hard drive) and click the Put Files icon (the up arrow) in the Files panel.**

   The files automatically copy to your server when you transfer them. You can select multiple files or folders to be transferred simultaneously.

   After you upload files to you server, test your work by using a Web browser to view them online. Sometimes things that look and work fine on your computer (such as links) won't work on the server.

4. **To *download* files or folders (transfer files or folders from your Web server to your hard drive), select the files or folders from the Remote View panel, (which shows the files on your server) and click the Get Files button (the down arrow) in the Files panel.**

   The files automatically copy to your hard drive when you transfer them. Beware that when you copy files to or from your server, the file you're transferring overwrites the files that are already at the destination. Dreamweaver notifies you about the overwriting if it notices you're replacing a new file with an old one, but it isn't always able to correctly assess the proper time differences. When the transfer is complete, you can open the files on your hard drive.

You can see both the remote and local views simultaneously by clicking the Expand/Collapse button on the far right side of the top of the Files panel. To collapse this Site dialog box, click the same Expand/Collapse button a second time.

The arrows with the check mark and the little lock at the top of the Files panel are for the Check In/Check Out feature, which enables you to keep track of who is working on a site and prevent more than one person making changes to the same page. Chapter 4 explains this feature.

If you're not happy with the FTP capabilities in Dreamweaver, you can use a dedicated FTP program, such as Fetch for the Macintosh or WS_FTP for Windows. You can download these shareware programs from www.shareware. com or www.download.com.

Synchronizing Local and Remote Sites

One of the most valuable features in Dreamweaver's FTP options is the capability to automatically synchronize the files on your hard drive with the files on your server. This is cool because it helps you keep track of which pages you've edited and ensure that they have been updated on the server. This may not matter much to you the first time you upload your site, or if you only have a few pages in your site, but if you have a large site and you make frequent updates, this feature is a wonderful way to make sure all the changes that you make get to your server. Dreamweaver also confirms which files are updated after you complete the synchronization.

Follow these steps to synchronize your Web site:

1. **Select the name of the site you want to work on in the Files panel drop-down list.**

   If you haven't already defined your site, you first need to follow the step-by-step instructions in the "Defining a site" section earlier in this chapter.

2. **Click the Connects to Remote Host button to log on to your remote site.**

3. **Click the Expand/Collapse button at the top on the far-right side of the Files panel.**

   The Site dialog box displays both the remote and local views of the site, as shown in Figure 2-12. (To collapse this dialog box, click the same Expand/Collapse button a second time.)

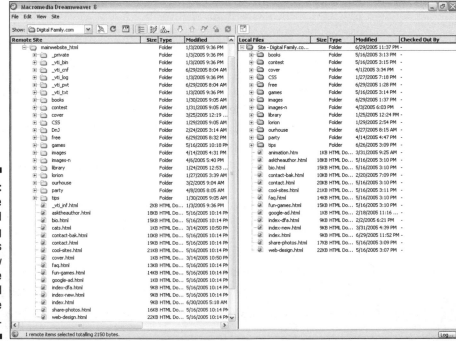

Figure 2-12:
The expanded Site dialog box lets you view both remote and local files at the same time.

4. **From the menu bar, choose Site⇨Synchronize Sitewide.**

   The Synchronize Files dialog box appears, as shown in Figure 2-13.

Figure 2-13:
The Syn-
chronize
Files dialog
box enables
you to
replace or
delete files.

5. **Choose whether to synchronize the Entire Site or Selected Files Only from the Synchronize drop-down list.**

6. **From the Direction drop-down list, choose which option you want to use to copy the files:**

   • **Put Newer Files to Remote:** This option copies the most recently modified files from your local site to the remote site. Click the Delete Remote Files Not On Local Drive box if you want those files removed from your Web site.

   • **Get Newer Files from Remote:** This option copies the most recently modified files from your remote site to the local site. Click the Delete Local Files Not On Remote Server box if you want to remove those files from your local copy.

   • **Get and Put Newer Files:** This option updates both the local and remote sites with the most recent versions of all the files.

7. **Make sure the Delete Remote files Not On Local Drive box is unchecked.**

   Be careful of this feature. As a general rule, I recommend you leave it unchecked because you may have folders and files on the server, such as log files, that do not exist on your hard drive, and you don't want to delete them inadvertently.

8. **Click the Preview button.**

   The Site FTP dialog box displays the files that are about to be changed.

   Now you have the option to verify the files you want to delete, put, and get. If you don't want Dreamweaver to alter a file, deselect it from the Site FTP dialog box now or forever live with the consequences.

9. **Click OK.**

   All approved changes are automatically made, and Dreamweaver updates the Site FTP dialog box with the status.

10. **When the synchronization finishes, you can choose to save or not save the verification information to a local file.**

    I recommend you choose to save the verification information as it can be handy if you want to review your changes after synchronization is complete.

Be very careful of the Delete Remote Files Not on Local Drive option, especially if you have special administrative pages, such as stats files, which are often added to your server space by your service provider to track traffic on your site.

Cloaking Options

The Dreamweaver Cloaking option enables you to exclude folders or files from all site operations, meaning they won't be uploaded to the live site when you're synchronizing or batching files back and forth. This feature is handy if you have sections of a site that you want to save but don't want visible to your viewers. For example, if you have a special holiday folder that you don't want visible during the rest of the year, you can use the Cloaking feature to save it locally, with the assurance that no one can accidentally publish the files with Dreamweaver until you uncloak them and publish them in December.

To use the Cloaking feature, follow these steps:

1. **On the Cloaking page of the Site Definition dialog box, select the Enable Cloaking box as shown in Figure 2-14.**

2. **If you want to cloak files of a certain type, select the Cloak Files Ending With box and enter the extension(s) in the text field.**

   For example, if you want to cloak all your original Photoshop files so they don't upload and take up space on your server, enter the extension .psd. If you want to cloak more than one file type, separate each file extension with a space. Do not use a comma or other delimiter.

3. **Click OK to close the Site Definition dialog box and then click the Done button in the Define Sites dialog box to close it.**

   Files matching the extensions specified, if any, are now cloaked. If you want to manually cloak specific folders, continue to Step 4.

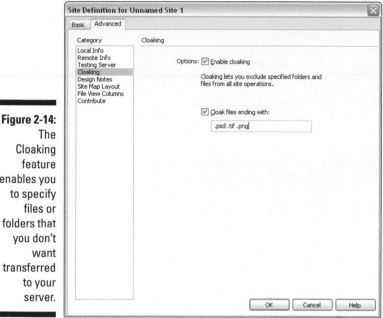

Figure 2-14:
The
Cloaking
feature
enables you
to specify
files or
folders that
you don't
want
transferred
to your
server.

4. **On the Files tab of the Files panel, select the folders you want to cloak.**

   You can't cloak individual files, for reasons known only to the Dreamweaver programmers.

5. **Right-click (Windows) or Control+click (Mac) and select Cloaking⇨ Cloak from the shortcut menu.**

To uncloak files or folders, repeat Steps 4 and 5 and select Uncloak from the shortcut menu. You can also use these steps to uncloak all the files in your current site, disable cloaking in the site, and change the cloaking settings.

If you disable cloaking for all files, any manual cloaking choices you've made are lost, even if you enable cloaking again later.

Part II
Looking Like a Million (Even on a Budget)

The 5th Wave   By Rich Tennant

"Just how accurately should my Web site reflect my place of business?"

In this part . . .

No matter how great the content on your Web site is, it seems viewers always pay most attention to the design and the images. This part starts by explaining how to design a well-planned site, an important part of creating a well-designed site. Then, you find out how to add graphics, create image maps, and bring your pages to life with images. And you discover how to save time and ensure consistency with Dreamweaver's templates and Library items.

Chapter 3

Planning and Maintaining a Web Site

*O*ne of the most common mistakes new Web designers make is plunging into developing a site without thinking through all their goals, priorities, budget, and design options. The instinct is to simply start creating pages, throw them all into one big directory, and then string stuff together with links. Then, when designers finally test the site out on an audience, they're often surprised when users say the site is hard to navigate and they can't find what they want.

Do yourself a favor and save yourself some grief by planning ahead. By having a plan, you also stand a much better chance of creating an attractive Web site that's easy to maintain and update. In this chapter, you discover many of the common planning issues of Web design. You also find out how Dreamweaver is designed to help manage a team of developers with features such as Design Notes and integrated e-mail. You also discover Dreamweaver's file management features, which make it easy to move files and folders around within the structure of your Web site without breaking links. If you do find yourself in the unfortunate predicament of trying to fix broken links, Dreamweaver makes that task easier, too. And, if you like knowing all the details, you may appreciate Dreamweaver's many report features, which automatically analyze and evaluate many aspects of your Web site.

Visualizing Your Site

Before you get too far into building Web pages, take some time to plan your site and think about its structure and organization. Begin thinking about the following questions:

- ✔ What do you want to accomplish with your Web site? (What are your goals and objectives?)
- ✔ Who is your target audience?
- ✔ Who will be working on your site? How many developers do you have to manage?
- ✔ How will you create or collect the text and images you need for your site?
- ✔ How will you organize the files in your site?
- ✔ Will you include multimedia files, such as Flash or RealAudio?
- ✔ Will you want interactive features, such as a feedback form or chat room?
- ✔ What other software will you need for specialized features (for example, Macromedia Flash for animations)?
- ✔ What kind of navigation system will you have for your site (that is, how can you make navigating through your Web site easy for visitors)?
- ✔ How will you accommodate growth and further development of the site?

With at least a basic plan for your site, you're in a better position to take advantage of the site-management features discussed in this chapter. Taking the time to get clear on your goals and objectives is time well spent and can save you lots of grief later. Set the tone for successful Web development from the beginning and make sure you spend your precious time, money, and energy on the elements and features that best serve your audience and help you reach your goals.

Preparing for Development

One of the first things I like to do when I'm working on a new site with a group or company is hold a brainstorming session with a few people who understand the goals for the Web site. The purpose of this session is to come up with proposed sections and features for the site. A good brainstorming session is a nonjudgmental free-for-all — a chance for everyone involved to make all the suggestions that they can think of, whether realistic or not.

Not discrediting ideas at the brainstorming stage is important. Often an unrealistic idea leads to a great idea that no one may have thought of otherwise. And if you stifle one person's creative ideas too quickly, that person may feel less inclined to voice other ideas in the future.

After the brainstorming session, you have a long list of possible features to develop into your site. Your challenge is to edit that list down to the best and most realistic ideas and then plan your course of development to ensure that these ideas all work well together when you're done.

Developing a New Site

In a nutshell, building a Web site involves creating individual pages and linking them to other pages. You need to have a home page (often called the *front page*) that links to pages representing different sections of the site. Those pages, in turn, can link to subsections that can then lead to additional subsections. A big part of Web site planning is determining how to divide your site into sections and deciding how pages link to one another. Dreamweaver makes creating pages and setting links easy, but how you organize the pages is up to you.

If you're new to this, you may think you don't need to worry much about how your Web site will grow and develop. Think again. All good Web sites grow, and the bigger they get, the harder they are to manage. Planning the path of growth for your Web site before you begin can make a tremendous difference later. Neglecting to think about growth is probably one of the most common mistakes among new designers. This becomes even more serious when more than one person is working on the same site. Without a clearly established site organization and some common conventions for tasks such as naming files, confusion reigns.

Managing your site's structure

Managing the structure of a Web site has two sides: the side that users see, which depends on how you set up links, and the behind-the-scenes side, which depends on how you organize files and folders.

What the user sees

The side that the user sees is all about navigation. When users arrive at your home page, where do you direct them from there? How do they move from one page to another in your site? A good Web site is designed so that users navigate easily and intuitively and can make a beeline to the information most relevant to them. As you plan, make sure that users can

- Access key information easily from more than one place in the site.
- Move back and forth between pages and sections.
- Return to main pages and subsections in one step.

Setting links is easy in Dreamweaver; the challenge is to make sure that they're easy for visitors to follow.

What you see

The second side to managing your Web site structure happens behind the scenes (where your users can't see the information, but you want some kind of organizational system to remember what's what). Before you get too far into building your site with Dreamweaver, spend some time thinking about the management issues involved in keeping track of all the files you create for your site. *Files* are all the images, HTML pages, animations, sound files, and anything else you put in your Web site. Once your Web site grows past a handful of pages, organizing them in separate folders or directories is best.

Many Web developers get 20 or 30 pages into a growing Web site and then realize that having all their files in one folder is confusing. To make matters worse, if you start moving things into new folders, you have to change all the links. Not realizing this, some people start organizing files outside of Dreamweaver, only to discover that they have broken links. Fortunately, Dreamweaver includes site-management tools that automatically adjust links when you move pages or create new folders from within the Files panel. Still, starting out with a good plan is better than having to clean up the structure later.

Before you build those first few pages, think about where you're likely to add content in the future (you always will!). For example, you may start with one page that lists all your staff; but after they see how cool it is, staff members may want to develop their own pages. In that case, you may want a separate folder dedicated to staff pages. Similarly, if you provide information for a sales team or create an online catalog, you may want a separate folder for each product.

As you add new sections, such as the staff or product pages I mention here, it's a good practice to create new subfolders to store their respective files. Creating subfolders also makes managing a site that's built by multiple people easier. If each subsection has a separate folder, then each developer can better manage his or her own files.

Naming your site's files

As you create files and folders, you have to name them; and the more consistent you are about those names, the easier it is for you and anyone else working on your site to keep track of what's in them as the site grows.

For example, say your Web site is a newsletter that includes articles about the happenings in your town. Simple names like `fire.html` and `truck.html` may make sense to you this week because you're familiar with the top stories. But six months from now, if you look for that article on the six-car-pileup that happened on Main Street, you may not remember that you called it `truck.html`. Adding dates to the end of filenames can help you identify the files that you may need months — or even years — down the road. Remember that you can't use spaces, but you can use the underscore. A good filename may be `fire2006_08_12.html` or `truck2006_08_19.html`; using dates helps you remember that you added these articles in August of 2006.

Another option is to create a folder for each new update and name it with a date. For example, a folder named stories2006_08 can contain all the stories from the August 2006 issue. Then you can put `truck.html` and any other stories from that issue in the stories2006_08 folder, and you can find them by date as well as by filename.

As you develop a filenaming system, talk to other people who may work on the site and make sure you create a system that makes sense to everyone and is easy to explain if a new person joins the team. Don't be afraid to give files a slightly longer, more descriptive name. Whatever you do, don't name files randomly and throw them all in one directory. You should also consider documenting your naming system. Printing a list of all the filenames in your site can also provide a handy reference if you're looking for a particular file.

Make sure your files work on your Web server. Dreamweaver lets you call your files any name that works on your operating system, even something like `don't forget this is the photo the boss likes.htm`, but your Web server may use a different operating system that's more restrictive. Many servers on the Web are run on UNIX machines that are case-sensitive — so stick to lowercase for filenames and extensions. Also, keep your URLs simple and easy to type by avoiding using spaces, apostrophes, or other special characters, except for the underscore (_) or hyphen (-). If you use filenames that your Web server can't read, then your site won't work until you rename all those files.

Under construction? No hard hats here!

All good Web sites are under construction — always. It's the nature of the Web. But build your site in such a way that you can add pages when they're ready instead of putting up placeholders. Don't greet your viewers with a guy in a yellow hat who seems to say, "You clicked this link for no good reason. Come back another day, and maybe we'll have something for you to see." Instead of creating "Under Construction" placeholders, create directory structures that make adding new pages later easy. You can let readers know that new things are coming by putting notices on pages that already have content — a message like "Come here next Thursday for a link to something even cooler" is a great idea. But never make users click a link and wait for a page to load, only to find that nothing but a guy with a hard hat is waiting for them.

A few examples of good filenames are `mugshot_jim.jpg`, `logo_128_x_240.gif`, or `deckchair.html`. Bad filenames would include spaces and special characters. These filenames would not work well on a Web site: `Jim'sMugShot.jpg`, `Logo.gif`, or `deck chair.HTML`. Although coming up with names that work and that everyone else on your site development team will remember can take a little more time, it's worth the effort in the long run. Now where did I save that file about organizing images. . . .

Finding files by their addresses

If you're not sure where you saved a file or what you called it, but you can get to it with your browser, you can determine the filename and location by looking at the URL in the browser's address bar. Each folder in a Web site is included in the address to a page within that folder. Folder names are separated by the forward slash /, and each filename can be distinguished because it includes an extension. For example, the address to the page displayed in the figure tells me that the file is named `dwfd.html` and that it is located in a folder called books.

Similarly, you can identify the name and location of any image you are viewing on a Web page. If you're using Internet Explorer, place your cursor over the image and right-click (Windows) and then choose Properties from the drop-down list. The Properties dialog box includes the specific URL of the image, which has the name and folder (path). In this example, the image is named tips.gif and it's stored in the images folder. If you're using the Safari browser on a Mac, it works a little differently. Control+click an image and choose Open Image in New Window from the drop-down list. In the new window, the image URL appears in the location bar.

Organizing images

Many HTML teachers and consultants suggest that you place all your images in a single folder at the top level of the directory structure and name it images. You may also find that other HTML authoring tools place all your images in one folder by default. Dreamweaver doesn't require an images folder, but it does encourage you to identify a main images folder when you set up your site (for more on site setup, see Chapter 2).

The advantage of keeping all your images in one folder is that you only have one place to look for them. However, if all your images are in one place, you'll likely end up with a long list of image files, making it harder to keep track of which image is which. When you want to change an image later, sorting through this list can be arduous work.

A good alternative is to store your images in multiple images folders and keep them within subfolders with related HTML files. For example, keep all your staff photos for your staff pages in an images folder within a staff subfolder. If you have images that link throughout the site — a logo, for example — you may want to keep those images in an images folder at the top level of your directory structure. This way, the images are easy to find from any folder in the site.

Dreamweaver makes no distinction between a folder called images and a folder called hot-stuff, or any other name for that matter. You can name your folders whatever you like, even goofy_pictures, just make sure you remember what you called them so you can find them again later.

Handling links

As you develop your site, the links only become more complicated to manage and easier to break. Fortunately, Dreamweaver includes a variety of tools that help you keep links in good working order.

Changing and moving files without breaking links

You can use the Files panel to rename and rearrange files and folders, as well as create new folders, all with drag-and-drop ease. You need to define your site for this to work (see Chapter 2).

To rename or rearrange files, follow these steps:

1. **Select the site name from the drop-down list at the top of the Files panel and choose the site you want to work on from the list.**

   When you select a site, the folders and files of that site display in the Files panel on the right side of the Dreamweaver work area.

2. **Use the plus (+) and minus (–) signs to open and close folders in the Files panel.**

3. **In the Files panel, select the file or folder that you want to change (move and/or rename):**

   To move the selected file: Drag that file or folder anywhere in the panel. For example, you can move a file into a folder, and Dreamweaver automatically changes all the related links.

   This panel works just like the Explorer window on a PC or the Finder on a Mac, except that Dreamweaver tracks and fixes links when you move files through the Files panel. By contrast, if you move or rename site files or folders in the Finder or Explorer, you break the links in existing Web pages. In Dreamweaver, when you move a linked file into a new folder, the Update Files dialog box appears with a list of links that need to be updated, as shown in Figure 3-1. To adjust the links, choose Update. If you choose Don't Update, any links to or from that file are left as they are, and likely won't work any more.

   To rename a selected file: Click the selected file, and after the cursor appears at the end of the filename, type your new filename or edit the existing name. When you finish, press Enter (Return on a Mac). Again you're prompted to update any links affected by the filename change. Choose Update to adjust the links.

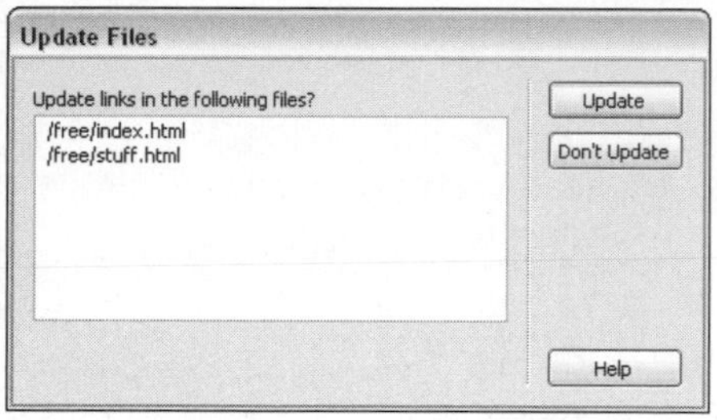

Figure 3-1:
The Update
Files dialog
box shows
you which
links
change.

Update Files

Update links in the following files?

/free/index.html
/free/stuff.html

Update

Don't Update

Help

Making global changes to links

If you want to globally change a link to point at a new URL or to some other page on your site, you can use the Change Link Sitewide option to enter the new URL and change every reference automatically. You can use this option to change any kind of link, including mailto, ftp, and script links. For example, if the e-mail address that you list at the bottom of every page on your site changes, you can use this feature to fix it automatically — a real timesaver. You can also use this feature when you want a string of text to link to a different file than it currently does. For example, you can change every instance of the words *Enter this month's contest* to link to /contest/january.htm instead of /contest/december.htm throughout your Web site.

To change all links from one page on your site to another using the Change Link Sitewide feature, follow these steps:

1. **Make sure the site you want to work on is displayed in the Files panel. (See Chapter 2 for more on this).**

2. **From the menu, choose Site⇨Change Link Sitewide.**

    The Change Link Sitewide dialog box appears (see Figure 3-2).

3. **Enter the old address and the new address you want to change it to, or click the Browse buttons to identify files where you want to change the links.**

4. **Click OK.**

    Dreamweaver updates any documents that include the specified links.

These changes occur only on the local version of your site on your hard drive and are reflected on your live site until you upload them to your server. To automatically reconcile these changes, use the Dreamweaver Synchronize Files option described in Chapter 2.

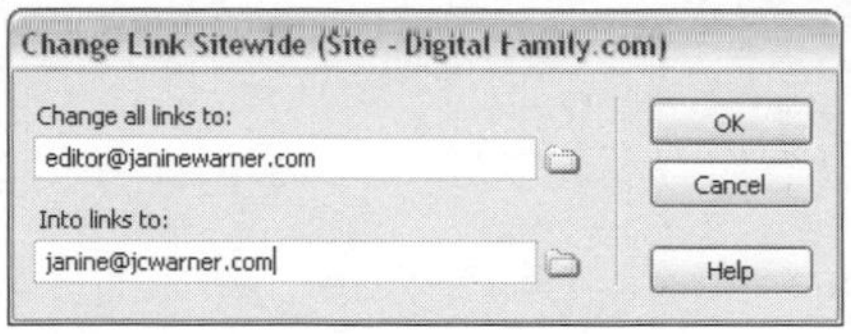

Figure 3-2:
You can
enter any
URL or
e-mail
address to
make quick
global
changes.

Change Link Sitewide (Site - Digital Family.com)

Change all links to:

editor@janinewarner.com

Into links to:

janine@jcwarner.com

OK

Cancel

Help

Finding and Fixing Broken Links

If you're trying to rein in a chaotic Web site, or if you just want to check a site for broken links, you'll be pleased to discover the Check Links feature. You can use Check Links to verify the links in a single file or an entire Web site, and you can use it to automatically fix all the referring links at once.

Here's an example of what Check Links can do. Assume that someone on your team (because you would never do such a thing yourself) changed the name of a file from `new.htm` to `old.htm` without using the Dreamweaver automatic link update features to fix the corresponding links. Maybe this person changed the name using another program or simply renamed it in the Finder on the Mac or in Explorer in Windows. Changing the filename was easy, but what this person may not have realized is that if he or she didn't change the links to the file when the file was renamed, the links are now broken.

If only one page links to the file that your clueless teammate changed, fixing the broken link isn't such a big deal. As long as you remember what file the page links from, you can simply open that page and use the Properties inspector to reset the link the same way you created the link in the first place. (You can find out all the basics of link creation in Chapter 2.)

But many times, a single page in a Web site is linked to many other pages. When that's the case, fixing all the link references can be time-consuming, and forgetting some of them is all too easy. That's why the Check Links feature is so helpful. First, it serves as a diagnostic tool that identifies broken links throughout the site (so you don't have to second-guess where someone may have changed a filename or moved a file). Then it serves as a global fix-it tool. You can use the Check Links dialog box to identify the page a broken link should go to, and Dreamweaver automatically fixes all links referring to that page. The following section walks you through this very cool process.

If you are working on a dynamic, database-driven site or if your site was altered with programming that was done outside of Dreamweaver, the Check

Links feature may not work properly. This feature works best for sites with static HTML pages.

Checking for broken links

To check a site for broken links, follow these steps:

1. **Select the site name from the drop-down list at the top of the Files panel and choose the site you want to work on from the list.**

   Link checking works only for sites listed in the Dreamweaver Site dialog box. For more information about the Site dialog box and how to set up a new site or import an existing one, see Chapter 2.

2. **From the menu, choose Site⇨Check Links Sitewide.**

   The Link Checker tab opens in the Results panel at the bottom of the page, just under the Properties inspector, as shown in Figure 3-3. The tab displays a list of internal and external links. The tab also lists any pages, images, or other items not linked from any other page in the site (Dreamweaver calls these *orphans*). Unused images can waste space on your server so this list is handy if you want to clean up old images or other elements you no longer use on the site.

Most service providers limit the amount of space on your server and charge extra if you exceed that limit. Deleting unused files helps you save valuable server space, especially if they are image or multimedia files. But remember, just because you delete them from your hard drive doesn't mean they are deleted off the server. Make sure you remove them from the Remote Site window in the Files panel as well as the Local Site panel. (For more on using FTP and synchronization to update or delete files on your server, see Chapter 2.)

If you find broken links, the next section, "Fixing broken links," shows you how Dreamweaver automatically updates multiple link references to make fixing them fast and easy.

Fixing broken links

Broken links are one of the most problematic errors a Web designer can make. After you identify a broken link in your site, you should fix it immediately. Nothing turns off visitors faster than clicking a link and getting a File Not Found error page (also known as a *404 error* because that's the official Web error code associated with the message viewers usually see if they click a broken link). Fortunately, Dreamweaver makes fixing broken links simple by providing quick access to files with broken links and automating the process of fixing multiple links to the same file.

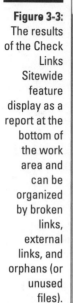

Figure 3-3:
The results
of the Check
Links
Sitewide
feature
display as a
report at the
bottom of
the work
area and
can be
organized
by broken
links,
external
links, and
orphans (or
unused
files).

After using the Link Checker feature described in the preceding section to identify broken links, follow these steps to use the Results panel to fix them:

1. **With the Results panel open at the bottom of the page, double-click a filename that Dreamweaver identified as a broken link.**

   The page and its corresponding Properties inspector opens. The Results panel remains visible.

2. **Select the broken link or image on the open page.**

   In Figure 3-4, a broken image was selected and is being fixed by using the Properties inspector to find the correct image name.

3. **In the Properties inspector, click the folder icon to the right of the Src text box to identify the correct image file.**

   The Select Image Source dialog box appears. You can type the correct filename and path in the text box or browse to find the image.

   You fix links to pages just as you fix links to images, except you type the name of the correct file into the Link text box or click the folder icon next to it to find the file in your site folder.

4. **Click the filename and the Select button; then click OK.**

   The link automatically changes to reflect the new filename and location. If you replace an image, the image file reappears on the page.

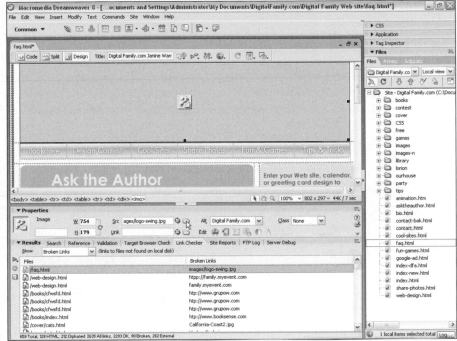

Figure 3-4:
Use the
Browse
button in the
Properties
inspector to
fix a broken
link by
identifying
the correct
filename.

If the link that you correct appears in multiple pages, Dreamweaver prompts you with a dialog box asking whether you want to fix the remaining broken link references to the file. Click the Yes button to automatically correct all other references. Click the No button to leave other files unchanged.

Testing Your Work with the Site Reporting Feature

Before you put your site online for the world to see, checking your work using the Dreamweaver Site Reporting feature is a good idea. You can create a variety of reports, and even customize them, to identify problems with external links, redundant and empty tags, untitled documents, and missing Alt text. You can easily miss things — especially when you work on a tight deadline — and what you miss can cause real problems for your viewers if you leave mistakes unfixed.

Before Dreamweaver added this great new feature, finding these kinds of mistakes was a tedious and time-consuming task. Now you can run a report that identifies these errors for you and use Dreamweaver to fix mistakes across your entire site automatically.

Follow these steps to produce a Site Report of your entire Web site:

1. **Select the site name from the drop-down list at the top of the Files panel and choose the site you want to work on from the list.**

   See Chapter 2 for step-by-step instructions for defining your site if you haven't done so already.

2. **Make sure all your open documents are saved by choosing File⇨ Save All.**

3. **From the Site menu, choose Site⇨Reports.**

   The Reports dialog box appears (see Figure 3-5).

4. **From the Report On drop-down list, choose Entire Current Local Site.**

   You can also choose to check only a single page by opening the page in Dreamweaver and then choosing Current Document from the Report On drop-down list. You can also run a report on selected files or on a particular folder. If you choose Selected Files, you must have already selected the pages you want to check in the Files panel.

5. **Select the type of report you want by putting check marks next to the report names in the Select Reports section.**

   Table 3-1 describes the kind of report you get with each option. You can select as many reports as you want.

The Workflow options in the Select Reports section are available only if you already enabled Check In/Out in the Remote Info section of the Site Definition dialog box and selected Maintain Design Notes in the Design Notes section of the Site Definition dialog box's Advanced tab. You can read more about the Site Definition dialog box in Chapter 2 and more about Design Notes and the Check in/Check Out feature in Chapter 4.

Figure 3-5:
You can select any or all the options in the Reports dialog box to run simultaneously, and you can run reports on a single page or on your entire site.

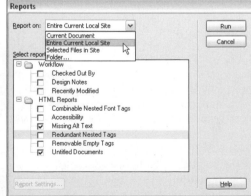

6. **Click the Run button to create the report(s).**

   If you haven't already done so, you may be prompted to save your file, define your site, or select a folder (see Chapter 2 for more information on defining a site in Dreamweaver).

   The Results panel opens (see Figure 3-6 displaying a list of problems found on a site). You can sort the list by different categories (filename, line number, or description) by clicking the corresponding column headings. If you run several reports at the same time, you can keep all the results tabs open at the same time.

Figure 3-6:
The Results panel displays a list of problems on your site.

▼ Results	Search	Reference	Validation	Target Browser Check	Link Checker	Site Reports	FTP Log	Server Debug
File	Line	Description
animation.htm	10	Warning: Missing "alt" attribute
animation.htm	5	Warning: Document uses default title 'Untitled Document'
asktheauthor.html	105	Warning: Missing "alt" attribute
asktheauthor.html	114	Warning: Missing "alt" attribute
asktheauthor.html	120	Warning: Missing "alt" attribute
asktheauthor.html	183	Warning: Missing "alt" attribute
asktheauthor.html	261	Warning: Missing "alt" attribute
bio.html	105	Warning: Missing "alt" attribute
bio.html	119	Warning: Missing "alt" attribute
bio.html	151	Warning: Missing "alt" attribute
Complete.	Complete.	

7. **Double-click any item in the Results panel to open the corresponding file in the Document window.**

   You can also right-click (Windows) or Control+click (Mac) on any line of the report and choose More Info from the drop-down list to find additional details about the specific error or condition.

8. **Use the Properties inspector or other Dreamweaver feature to fix the identified problem and then save the file.**

   Your changes aren't applied to your live site until you update your server. Use the Synchronize feature, described in Chapter 2, to update all your changes at once.

Table 3-1	Site Report Options
Report Name	*Results*
Checked Out By	Produces a list of files checked out of the site and identifies the person who checked them out.
Design Notes	Produces a list of Design Notes (see Chapter 4 for more on how to use Design Notes).
Recently Modified	Produces a list of files recently changed. You can set the time period for the report by clicking the Report Settings button.

(continued)

Table 3-1 *(continued)*

Report Name	Results
Combinable Nested Font Tags	Produces a list of all instances where you can combine nested tags. For example, `<font color= "#000000"><font size="2">Great Web Sites You Should Visit</font></font>` is listed because you can simplify the code by combining the two font tags into `<font color= "#000000" size="2">Great Web Sites You Should Visit</font>`.
Accessibility	Produces a list of possible accessibility issues in a wide variety of categories. To set the report categories, click the Report Settings button.
Missing Alt Text	Produces a list of all the image tags that do not include Alt text. *Alt text* is a short alternative text description for an image tag. If the image isn't displayed for some reason (many people choose to surf with images turned off), the Alt text appears in place of the image. Alt text is also important to the blind because special browsers that read pages to site visitors can't interpret text that is part of an image, but can read the Alt text included in the image tag.
Redundant Nested Tags	Produces a list of all places where you have redundant nested tags. For example, `<center>Good headlines <center>are harder to write </center> than you might think </center>` is listed because you can simplify the code by removing the second center tag to make the code look like this: `<center>Good headlines are harder to write than you might think</center>`.
Removable Empty Tags	Produces a list of the empty tags on your site. Empty tags often occur if you delete an image or text section without deleting all the tags associated with it.
Untitled Documents	Produces a list of filenames that don't have a title. The title tag is easy to forget because it does not display in the body of the page. The title tag specifies the text that appears at the very top of the browser window and is also the text that appears in the Favorites list when someone saves your page in his or her browser. And if that's not enough reason to have a descriptive title, a good title tag is one key to getting good placement in many search engines as well.

Chapter 4

Coordinating Your Design Work

Strive for consistency in all your designs — except when you're trying to be unpredictable. A little surprise here and there can keep your Web site lively. But, generally, most Web sites work best and are easiest to navigate when they follow a consistent design theme. Case in point: Most readers take for granted that books don't change their design from page to page, and newspapers don't change headline fonts and logos every day. Books and newspapers want to make life easier for their readers, and consistency is one of the primary tools for making sure readers find publications familiar. Dreamweaver offers several features to help you develop and maintain a consistent look and feel across your site, whether you're working on a Web site by yourself or you're coordinating a team of developers.

In this chapter, you discover three of my favorite Dreamweaver features — templates, Library items, and the Tracing Image feature. Find out how they combine to make your design work faster and easier to manage. This chapter also introduces you to Design Notes, the Check In/Out feature, the History panel, and the Quick Tag Editor — tools that you can use for managing a team of designers, retracing your steps in Dreamweaver, and tweaking HTML tags respectively.

Templating Your Type

Many Web design programs boast about their HTML templates. Often what they really mean is the program includes some ready-made page designs. Dreamweaver takes this concept a few leaps further by providing template design features that enable you to create a predesigned page and specify which sections can and can't be altered. This is a valuable feature if you work with a team of people with varying skill levels, or if you have to create dozens of pages with the same basic layout. For example, if you're building a site for a real-estate company and you want to let the employees update the sales listings without messing up the page design, a template with locked regions can be an ideal way to allow sales staff to add new information without accidentally breaking anything.

Templates are best used when you're creating a number of pages that share the same characteristics, such as the same background color, column design, or image arrangement. For example, if you're creating a Web site for a bed-and-breakfast inn, such as the Inn on Tomales Bay featured in the examples in this chapter, you might create a template for all the pages where you want to show off the rooms in the Inn. In that case, you might create a room template design with a spot for a photo, descriptive text, and forward and back arrows so that visitors could easily move through the pages for all the rooms. As you create each new page, you would start with the template, changing only the photo, descriptive text, and links. Templates can save tons of time and help ensure that page designs are more consistent.

Dreamweaver's template feature has an additional functionality that enables you to make global changes to your site by changing just the template file. Here's how it works. If you create a series of pages with the same template, and then decide you want to alter the template design, the changes you make to the original template can automatically be applied to any or all the files created from the template. For example, if you need to change the logo for your bed-and-breakfast on all your pages, you can simply replace the logo on the original template and, using the automated update feature, apply that change to all the pages created with that template. This feature can be a huge timesaver when you need to make changes to several pages at once.

Dreamweaver 8 includes a wealth of ready-to-use templates; with this version, you even find Starter Pages, which include prewritten text to help you get started with common sites features, such as calendars and product pages. Templates, starter pages, and many other predesigned components in Dreamweaver give you a choice of many page layouts, cascading style sheet designs, framesets, and table-based layouts that can help you create a Web site quickly.

Creating Predesigned Pages with Dreamweaver's Design Files

Dreamweaver comes with a great collection of predesigned pages you can use to create Web sites with Cascading Style Sheets, frames, and complex page designs. Macromedia calls these *design files,* but they are essentially templates — predesigned pages you can customize with your own content. Using a template, or design file, to create a new page is similar to creating any other page in Dreamweaver with the added advantage that much of the work is already done for you.

Dreamweaver's design files do not include all the most advanced features of Dreamweaver templates, such as the capability to make global changes, unless you first save the files as custom templates (instructions for that are in the following section).

Among Dreamweaver's design files, you can find the following:

- ✔ **Framesets:** These page designs are specific to HTML frames, which enable you to display multiple pages on the screen at once. Chapter 7 has instructions for working with frames and frame templates.

- ✔ **Page Designs (CSS):** These files use Cascading Style Sheets to control layout and design.

- ✔ **Starter Pages:** These page designs include written content to give you a head start as you create common sections in a Web site, such as a calendar or product page.

- ✔ **Page Designs:** These are most useful as inner page designs around which you can place your standard header, footer, or navigation, and they use standard CSS formatting and tables to control layout and design.

In addition to the design files included in Dreamweaver, you can create custom templates. Step-by-step instructions are in the "Creating Your Own Templates" section later in this chapter.

To use one of Dreamweaver's design files to create a page, follow these steps:

1. **Choose File⇨New.**

   Alternatively, you can choose any of the options from the Create From Samples section on the Dreamweaver Start page.

2. **Choose a design file from any of the four collections available on the General tab: Framesets, Page Designs (CSS), Starter Pages, or Page Designs.**

   Dreamweaver's design files for the selected collection display in the New Document window. In the example shown in Figure 4-1, I chose the Page Designs from the Category list and then selected the Image: Slide Show from the Page Designs list.

3. **From the list of page designs in the middle of the New Document window, click to display a preview of a template.**

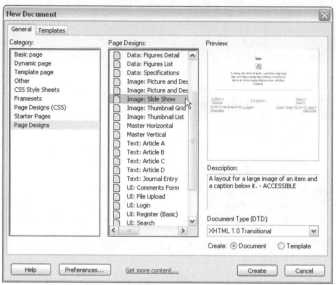

 4. **Choose whether you're creating a document or a template, and click the corresponding radio button from the bottom right of the New Document window.**

 5. **With the design file selected, click Create to create a new page.**

    A new page is created from the design file and opens in the main work area.

 6. **Choose File⇨Save to save the page before you make any changes.**

    Saving your pages before adding images or setting links is important. Make sure you save the new page within the main folder of the Web site you are creating.

    If you have not already completed the setup process for this site, see Chapter 2 to take care of this important preliminary step.

 7. **Click to select any text area, image, link, or other element on the page and replace it with your own images or text to customize the design.**

    In the example shown in Figure 4-2, I've replaced the blank image in the middle of the page with an image from the Inn on Tomales Bay and replaced the title and caption text. Creating additional pages with this same design file would allow me to easily create a slide show of images from this bed-and-breakfast inn.

 8. **Continue to edit the page, replacing images and filler text (Dreamweaver uses Latin as filler text), setting links, and making any other alterations or additions to the page.**

 9. **When you are done, use File⇨Save to save your changes.**

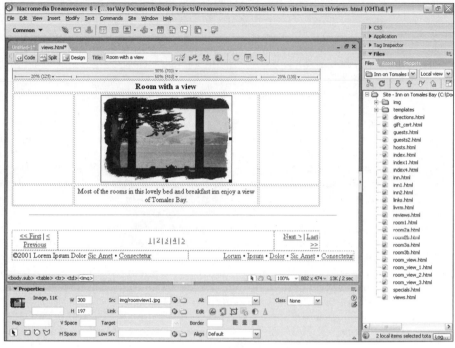

Figure 4-2:
You can edit a page created from a Dreamweaver design file much like you would edit any other page.

You can edit or replace anything in a Dreamweaver design file, and even alter the design to better fit your site.

Creating Your Own Templates

Creating a template is as easy as creating any other file in Dreamweaver. You can start by creating an HTML page as you would any other page (or modifying an existing page as you would edit any other page). The main difference is that when you save the file you save it as a template and the file is stored in a special Templates folder, which Dreamweaver automatically creates in the main folder for your Web site. Templates must be kept in this common folder for the automated features in Dreamweaver to work properly.

The template features work only if you define your Web site in Dreamweaver. If you haven't gone through the setup process to define your site yet, refer to Chapter 2.

Custom templates created in Dreamweaver have locked (noneditable) regions and unlocked (editable) regions. Use *editable regions* for content that changes, such as product descriptions or events in a calendar. Use locked regions for static, unchanging content, such as a logo or site navigation elements.

For example, if you're publishing an online magazine, the navigation options may not change from page to page, but the titles and stories do. To indicate the style and location of an article or headline, you can define *placeholder text* (an editable region, with all the size and font attributes already specified). When you're ready to add a new feature, you simply select the placeholder text and either paste in a story or type over the selected area. You do the same thing to create a placeholder for an image.

While you're editing the template itself, you can make changes to any part of the file, be it the editable or locked regions. While editing a document made *from* a template, however, you can make changes only to the editable regions of the document. If you go back and change a template after creating it, Dreamweaver gives you the option of having those changes updated in all the pages you created with that template.

You can create both *editable regions* and *editable attributes* in a Dreamweaver template. An editable region can be changed in files created from the template — you alter text, replace images, and even add tables, images, text, and so on. Editable attributes relate only to specific elements in a template. For example, you may want to make the attributes of an image editable to allow the alignment to be changed from left to right.

In a new template, all elements are locked by default except for two parts of the document head section, which is indicated by the `<HEAD>` `</HEAD>` tags. These tags enable you to change the title in any page created from a template, or to insert JavaScript if you use behaviors on the page. For the template to be of much use for building new pages, you must make areas in the body of the page editable as well. Remember that you can always go back to the template later to alter the design, make more areas editable, or lock areas so they can't be changed.

Creating a new custom template

To create a template that you can use to create new pages, follow these steps:

1. **In the Files panel on the right side of the work area, click the Assets tab and then click the Templates icon (see Figure 4-3).**

   The Templates panel opens. You don't have to have the Templates panel open to create a new template, but having it handy when you're working on templates is good because it provides a list of available templates as well as easy access to template editing and organizational functions.

Figure 4-3:
The
Templates
panel
displays a
list of all
available
templates in
the selected
site and
provides
access to
template
editing
functions.

2. **Choose File⇨New.**

The New Document window opens (see Figure 4-4).

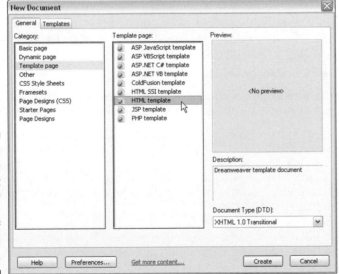

Figure 4-4:
The New
Document
window
includes a
variety of
template
options.

3. **From the Category list in the of the New Document window, choose Template Page.**

   The template options become visible in the Template Page list in the middle of the New Document window.

4. **Choose HTML Template.**

   You can choose from a variety of template options, including templates for ASP (Active Server Pages), ColdFusion, and PHP, all of which are used for creating dynamic sites, like those shown in Chapters 13, 14, and 15.

5. **Click the Create button.**

   A new blank template is created and opens in the main work area, and the New Document dialog box closes.

6. **Choose File⇨Save and name the template.**

   The new template is added to the Assets panel (refer to Figure 4-3).

7. **You can now edit this page as you edit any other HTML page, inserting images, text, tables, and so on.**

8. **Choose Modify⇨Page Properties to specify background, text, link colors, and other options that apply to the entire page.**

   This works just like any other Dreamweaver document.

9. **To create an editable region, select the content you want to affect, right-click (Windows) or Control+click (Mac), and choose Templates⇨ New Editable Region (as shown in Figure 4-5).**

   The New Editable Region dialog box opens.

10. **Give the new region a name. I recommend something that identifies the kind of content it is, such as *headline* or *photo_caption*.**

    The region you define as editable becomes an area that can be changed in any page created with the template. You can have multiple editable regions in one template, such as a photo that is an editable region and a photo caption that is a separate editable region. Areas that you don't mark as editable become locked and can be changed only if you modify the template itself.

11. **Click OK.**

    The editable region is enclosed in a highlighted area with a tab at the top left, indicating the name of the region.

12. **When you finish designing the page, choose File⇨Save to save your template.**

You can make an entire table or an individual table cell editable, and you can make entire rows editable. (For more about creating HTML tables, see Chapter 6.)

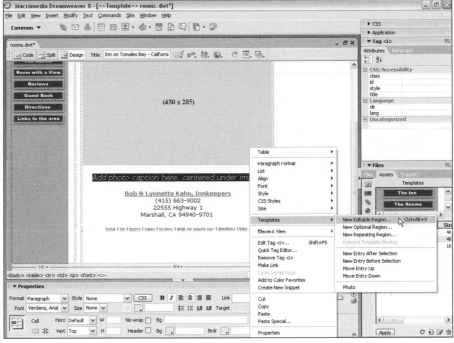

Figure 4-5:
You can
modify any
area of a
template to
make it
editable.

Saving any page as a template

Sometimes you get partway through creating a page before you realize you're
likely to want more pages like it and you should create a template so you don't
have to re-create the same page design multiple times. Similarly, you may have
a page that someone else created that you want to turn into a template. No
matter where the original page comes from, creating a template from an existing page is even easier than creating a new template from scratch.

To save a page as a template, follow these steps:

1. **Open the page that you want to turn into a template.**

   Choose File⇨Open and browse to find your file. Or, open the site in the
   Files panel and double-click the file to open it.

2. **Choose File⇨Save As Template.**

   The Save As Template dialog box appears (see Figure 4-6).

3. **Select a site from the Site drop-down list.**

   The menu lists all the sites that you have defined in Dreamweaver. If
   you're working on a new site or haven't yet defined your site, Chapter 2
   shows you how to define your site.

You can use the Save As Template option to save a page as a template into any defined site, which makes it easy to save a page design from one site as a template for another site.

4. **In the Save As text box, type a name for the template.**

In the example shown in Figure 4-6, I named the template *guests*.

Figure 4-6:
You can view all the templates in any defined site in the Save As Template dialog box.

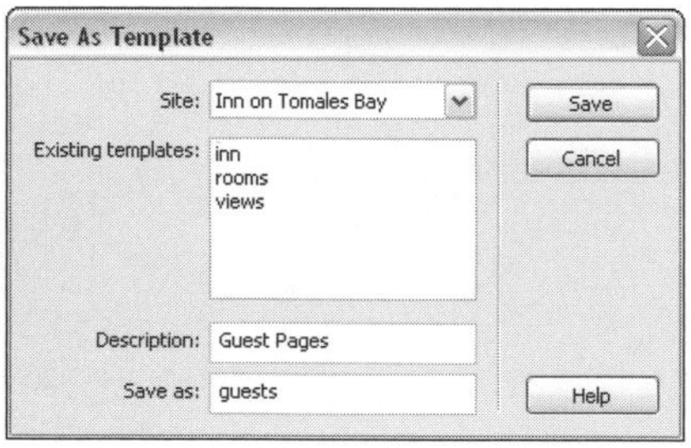

Save As Template		
Site: Inn on Tomales Bay		Save
Existing templates: inn rooms views		Cancel
Description: Guest Pages		
Save as: guests		Help

5. **Click the Save button.**

Notice that the file now has the `.dwt` extension, indicating that it's a template. You can now make changes to this template the same way you edit any other template.

6. **Decide if you want to update links or not.**

Because your original file was probably saved in a different directory from the templates, Dreamweaver offers to update all your links and keep them pointing to the correct destination. Unless you have a specific reason not to allow Dreamweaver to take care of the links for you, click Yes.

7. **Make any changes that you want and choose File⇨Save to save the page.**

Follow the steps in the earlier section, "Creating a new custom template," to create editable regions. Follow the steps in the next exercise to create editable attributes.

Making attributes editable

To create editable attributes in a template, follow these steps:

1. **In any Dreamweaver template, select an item you want to have an editable attribute.**

In the example shown in Figure 4-7, I selected a section of text, and I am in the process of making text attributes editable.

Figure 4-7:
Select
any text,
image, or
other page
element
and use
the Modify
menu to
make the
attributes of
that element
editable.

2. **Choose Modify➪Templates➪Make Attribute Editable, as shown in
   Figure 4-7.**

   The Editable Tag Attributes dialog box appears, shown in Figure 4-8.

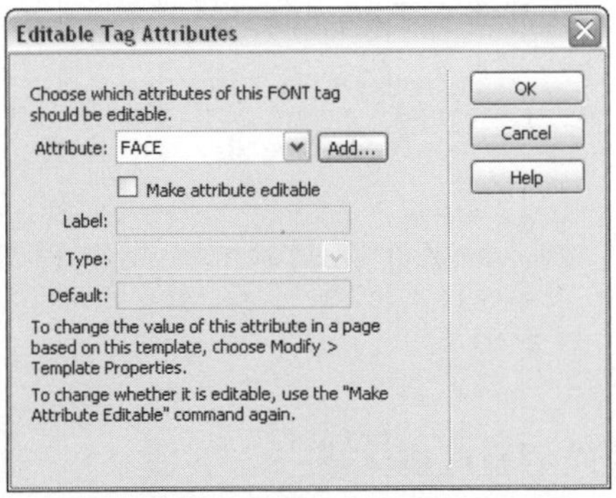

Figure 4-8:
Identify
which
attributes
you want
editable in
the Editable
Tag
Attributes
dialog box.

3. **From the Attribute drop-down list, choose the attribute you want to be
   editable.**

   If the attribute doesn't exist yet, click the Add button.

4. **Click to place a check mark in the Make Attribute Editable box and fill in the Label, Type, and Default options.**

   The attribute options vary depending on whether you select an image, text, or other element on the page. With these options, you can control whether or not an image can be changed and what specific attributes of the image tag may be altered when the template is used.

5. **Click OK.**

Using custom templates

After you create your own custom templates, you'll want to put them to use. You can use templates to create or modify all the pages in your Web site or use templates for specific sections. For example, in a site such as the Inn on Tomales Bay site, you could create one template for the pages that feature each of the rooms and another template for a slide show of photos from guests. Using a template to create a new page is similar to creating any other HTML page.

To use a template to create a page, follow these steps:

1. **Choose File⇨New.**

   The New Document window opens.

2. **Select the Templates tab at the top of the New Document window.**

   The New from Template dialog box opens, as shown in Figure 4-9, displaying all the templates from the sites you have defined in Dreamweaver.

3. **From the Templates For list on the left, choose the site that contains a template you want to use.**

   The templates in the selected site appear in the middle of the dialog box.

4. **Select the template you want to use from the Site list in the middle of the dialog box.**

   A preview of the selected template displays in the right side of the dialog box. In the example shown in Figure 4-9, I selected the Rooms template from the Inn on Tomales Bay Web site.

5. **Click the Create button.**

   A new page is created from the template and displays in the main work area.

6. **Edit any of the regions of the page that are editable using Dreamweaver's regular editing features.**

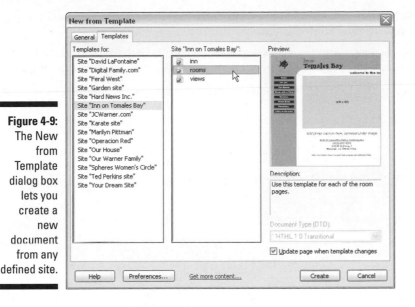

Figure 4-9:
The New
from
Template
dialog box
lets you
create a
new
document
from any
defined site.

Making Global Changes with Templates

One of the greatest advantages of using templates is that you can automatically apply changes to all the pages created with a template by altering the original template. For example, suppose you want to make a change to the layout of all your slide show pages after you've created a slide show using Dreamweaver's slide show template. First, you would open the slide show template, make the edits you want to the overall page design, and when you save the template, you can opt to automatically update all the pages created with that template. If you're making changes to many pages at once this can be a real timesaver. You can also choose to leave all the pages previously created with the template unchanged and to have only new pages created with the template reflect the changes.

To change a template and automatically update all the files in your site that use that template, follow these steps:

1. **Open an existing template.**

2. **Use Dreamweaver's editing features to make any changes you want to the template.**

3. **Choose File⇨Save.**

   The Update Template Files dialog box appears, shown in Figure 4-10.

4. **Click the Update button to modify all the pages listed in the Update Template Files dialog box.**

   Dreamweaver automatically changes all the pages listed in the Update Template Files dialog box to reflect the changes you made to the template.

   Choose the Don't Update button to leave these pages unchanged.

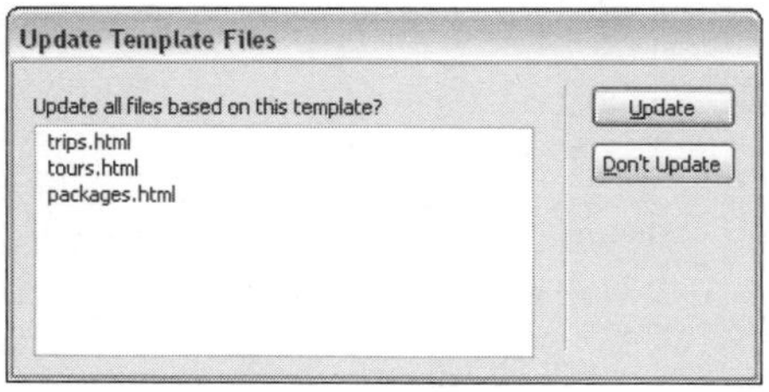

Figure 4-10:
You can
update all
the files
created with
a template
from the
Update
Template
Files dialog
box.

If you're not sure what template was used to create a page, you can open the template while you have the page open, make changes to the template, and update all the pages created with it by following these steps:

1. **Open a document that uses the template that you want to change.**

2. **Choose Modify⇨Templates⇨Open Attached Template as shown in Figure 4-11.**

   The template opens.

3. **Use Dreamweaver's regular editing functions to modify the template as you would edit any page or template.**

   For example, to modify the template's page properties, choose Modify⇨Page Properties.

4. **Choose File⇨Save.**

   The Update Template Files dialog box appears (refer to Figure 4-10).

5. **Click the Update button to modify all the pages listed in the Update Template Files dialog box. Click the Don't Update button to leave these pages unchanged.**

   If you chose Update, Dreamweaver automatically changes all the pages listed in the Update Template Files dialog box.

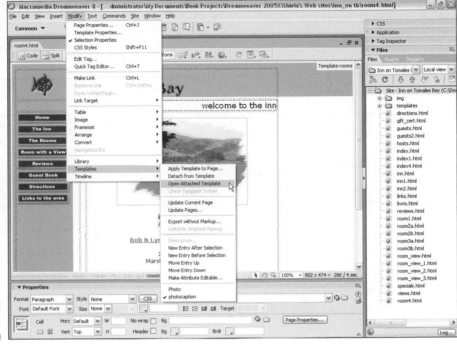

Figure 4-11:
You can
open an
attached
template
and auto-
matically
apply the
changes to
the pages
created
from that
template.

You can also apply changes to a template using the Update Pages option.
To do so, you have to first open the template, and then make and save your
changes without applying those changes to pages created with the template.
Then anytime later, you can choose Modify⇨Templates⇨Update Pages to
apply the update.

Attaching and Detaching Templates

You can apply a template to an existing page by attaching it, and you can
remove a template from a page by detaching it. When you apply a template
to an existing document, the content in the template is added to the content
already in the document. If a template is already applied to the page, Dreamweaver attempts to match editable areas that have the same name in both
templates and to insert the contents from the editable regions of the page
into the editable regions in the new template. This happens automatically if
all region names are the same.

Remove or detach a template from a page if you want to ensure that changes
to the original template don't affect the page created with the template.
Detaching a template also unlocks all regions of a page, making it completely
editable.

You can apply a template to an existing page by using any one of the following techniques:

- Choose Modify⇨Templates⇨Apply Template to Page and then double-click the name of a template to apply it to the page.
- Drag the template from the Template panel into the Document window.

If the editable regions don't match up, Dreamweaver asks you to match up inconsistent region names in a dialog box. After the region conflicts are resolved, click OK.

You can detach a template, or remove the template association from a file, by selecting Modify⇨Templates⇨Detach from Template. This action makes the file fully editable again, but any future changes you make to the template will not be reflected on the detached page.

Reusing Elements with the Library Feature

The Library feature is not a common feature in other Web design programs, so the concept may be new to you even if you've been developing Web sites for a while. The more experience you have with this feature, however, the more likely you are to appreciate its value and the time you can save using library items.

The Dreamweaver Library feature automates the process of inserting and updating elements that appear on multiple pages in a Web site. You can save any element as a Library item — for example, a logo or a row of images that serve as a site's navigation, or even a table with images and links. After you save it in the library, you can insert any item or collection of items into any page from the Library with drag-and-drop ease. And, if you ever need to change a Library item (by adding or changing a link, for example), you simply edit the stored Library item and Dreamweaver automatically updates the Library item on any or all the pages where it appears throughout the site.

A *Library item* is a snippet of code that can contain image references and links. Like templates, Library items are a great way to share the work of your best designers with less experienced ones. For example, one designer can create a logo and another the navigation elements, and then these can be placed in the Library and made available to the entire team. You have more flexibility with Library items than templates because they are elements you can place anywhere on any page, even multiple times. Libraries are not shared among sites, however, so each site you define must have its own collection of elements in its Library.

You can save any element from the body of a document as a Library item. That includes text, tables, forms, images, Java applets, and even multimedia files. Library items can also contain behaviors, but special requirements exist for editing the behaviors in Library items. (For more on behaviors, see Chapter 9.)

Library items cannot contain their own style sheets because the code for styles can only appear as part of the Head area of an HTML file. (For more on style sheets, see Chapter 8.)

Creating and using Library items

The following sections show you the steps for creating a Library item, adding one to a page, and editing and updating a Library item across multiple pages. For these steps to work properly, you must do them in sequential order. Before creating or using Library items, you must first define a site or open an existing site. If you're not sure how to do this, see Chapter 2.

Creating your Library item within an existing page works well because you can see how the item looks before you add it to the Library. You can, of course, edit an item after it's in the Library, but it may not look just as it will on a Web page. For example, Library items don't include <BODY> tags when they are saved in the Library, so link colors display as default blue when viewed in the library, even if the link colors have been changed to purple in all the pages in a site.

Creating a Library item

To create a Library item that you can use on multiple pages on your site, follow these steps:

1. **Open any existing file that has images, text, or other elements on the page that you want to save as a Library item.**

   Alternatively, you can create a new page and insert only the element you want to save to the library.

2. **From this page, select an element or collection of elements that you want to save as a Library item, such as the row of images used for your site navigation.**

3. **Choose Modify➪Library➪Add Object to Library.**

   The Assets tab of the Files panel opens and displays the Library. Your new Library item displays as "Untitled."

4. **Name the element as you would name any file in the Finder on a Mac or in Explorer on a PC.**

   When you name a Library item, you automatically save it to the Library. You can then easily apply the item to any new or existing page in your site. The Library section of the Assets panel lists all Library items, as shown in Figure 4-12.

Adding a Library item to a page

You can easily add elements from the Library to your pages by simply dragging them from the Assets panel to the page. When you add a Library item to a page, the content is inserted into the document and a relationship is established between the content on the page and the item in the library. This is important as it enables you to edit the Library item later and apply the changes to all pages where the item appears, but it also means that you can not edit the item on the page where it is inserted. You must edit Library items from within the Library, as you see in the following section.

To add a Library item to a page, follow these steps:

1. **Create a new document in Dreamweaver or open any existing file.**

2. **From the Files panel, choose the Assets tab and then select the Library icon.**

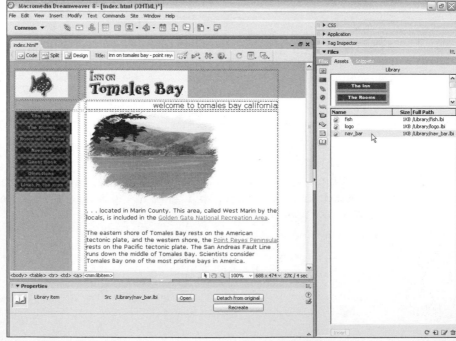

Figure 4-12: The Assets panel displays all Library items, and you can use drag and drop to save and insert Library items to and from pages.

The Library opens in the Assets panel (refer to Figure 4-12).

3. **Drag an item from the Library to the Document window.**

   Alternatively, you can select an item in the Library and click the Insert button.

   The item automatically appears on the page. After you insert a Library item on a page, you can use any of Dreamweaver's formatting features to position it on the page.

Highlighting Library items

Library items are highlighted to distinguish them from other elements on a page. You can customize the highlight color for Library items and show or hide the highlight color in the Preferences dialog box.

To change or hide Library highlighting, follow these steps:

1. **Choose Edit⇨Preferences (Windows) or Dreamweaver⇨Preferences (Mac).**

   The Preferences dialog box appears.

2. **Select Highlighting from the Category section on the left.**

3. **Click the color box to select a color for Library items. Check the Show box to display the Library highlight color on your pages.**

   Leave the box blank if you don't want to display the highlight color.

4. **Click OK to close the Preferences dialog box.**

Making global changes with Library items

One of the biggest timesaving advantages of the Dreamweaver Library feature is that you can make changes to Library items and automatically apply those changes to any or all the pages where the Library item appears.

To edit a Library item, follow these steps:

1. **From the Files panel, choose the Assets tab and then select the Library icon.**

   The Library opens in the Assets panel (refer to Figure 4-12).

2. **Double-click any item listed in the Library to open it.**

   Dreamweaver opens a new window where you can edit the Library item.

   Because the Library item is just a snippet of code, it won't have a `<BODY>` tag in which to specify background, link, or text colors. Don't worry over this — the Library item acquires the right settings from the tags on the page where you insert it.

3. **Make any changes you want to the Library item as you would edit any element in Dreamweaver.**

   For example, you can change a link, edit the wording of text, change the font or size, and even add images, text, or other elements.

4. **Choose File⇨Save to save changes to the original item.**

   The Update Library Items dialog box opens, displaying a list of all pages where the Library item appears.

5. **Click the Update button to apply the changes you made to the Library item on all the listed pages. If you don't wish to apply the changes to the pages where the Library item appears, choose the Don't Update button.**

   The Update Pages dialog box appears and shows the progress of the updating. You can stop the update from this dialog box, if necessary.

If you want to create a new Library item based on an existing one without altering the original, follow Steps 1 through 3, and in place of Step 4, choose File⇨Save As and give the item a new name.

Editing one instance of a Library item

If you want to alter a Library item on a specific page where you have inserted it, or if you want to make changes to just a couple of pages, you can override the automated Library feature by detaching it, or breaking the link between the original in the Library and the item inserted into the page.

After you break a connection, you can no longer update that page's Library item automatically.

To make a Library item editable, follow these steps:

1. **Open any file that contains a Library item and select the Library item.**

   The Properties inspector displays the Library item options shown in Figure 4-13.

2. **Click the Detach from Original button.**

   A warning message appears, letting you know that if you proceed with detaching the Library item from the original, you can no longer update this occurrence of it when the original is edited.

3. **Click OK to detach the Library item.**

Figure 4-13:
The
Properties
inspector
features a
Detach from
Original
button,
making it
easy to
break the
link between
an element
on a page
and a cor-
responding
Library item.

Using a Tracing Image to Guide Your Layout

The Macromedia Tracing Image feature is unique in the world of Web design tools, although the concept dates back to the earliest days of design. The Tracing Image feature enables you to use a graphic as a guide to your page design, much like an artist who creates a sketch and then paints the final picture over the sketch.

The Tracing Image feature is ideal for people who like to first create a design in a program such as Photoshop or Fireworks and then model their Web page after it. By using the Tracing Image feature, you can insert an image into the background of your page for the purpose of tracing over it. Then you can position layers or create table cells on top of the tracing image, which makes exactly re-creating your design in HTML easier. You can use JPG, GIF, or PNG images as tracing images, and you can create them in any graphics application that supports these formats.

Although the tracing image appears in the background of a page, it doesn't take the place of a background image and will not display in a browser.

To add a tracing image to your page, follow these steps:

1. **Create a new page or open any existing page in Dreamweaver.**

2. **Choose Modify⇨Page Properties.**

   The Page Properties dialog box opens, as shown in Figure 4-14.

3. **Select Tracing Image from the Category list on the left of the dialog box.**

   The Tracing Image options display on the right.

4. **Click the Browse button to locate the image you want to use as a tracing image.**

   The Select Image Source dialog box appears.

5. **Click the image you want to trace from.**

6. **Click OK.**

7. **Set the opacity for the tracing image with the Transparency slider.**

   Lowering the transparency level causes the tracing image to appear faded, which makes distinguishing between the tracing image and content on the page easy. You can set the transparency level to suit your preferences, but somewhere around 50 percent seems to work well with most images.

8. **Click OK.**

   A tracing image appears in the Document window, as shown in Figure 4-15.

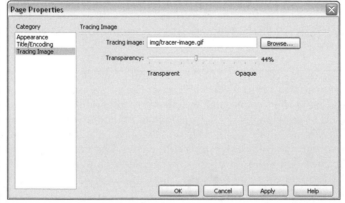

Figure 4-14: The Page Properties dialog box lets you set a tracing image to use when laying out your HTML page.

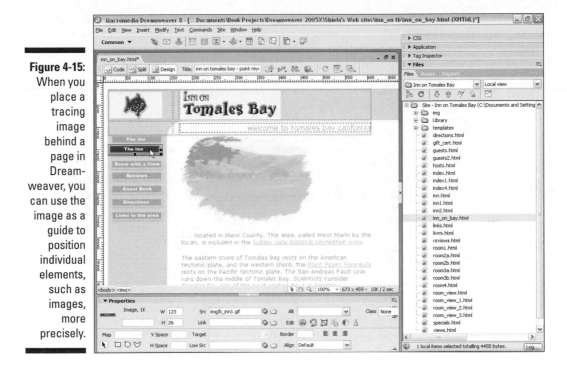

Figure 4-15:
When you place a tracing image behind a page in Dreamweaver, you can use the image as a guide to position individual elements, such as images, more precisely.

You have a few other options with the Tracing Image feature. Choose View⇨ Tracing Image to reveal the following options:

- ✔ **Show:** Hides the tracing image if you want to check your work without it being visible but don't want to remove it.

- ✔ **Align with Selection:** Enables you to automatically line up the tracing image with a selected element on a page.

- ✔ **Adjust Position:** Enables you to use the arrow keys or enter X, Y coordinates to control the position of the tracing image behind the page.

- ✔ **Reset Position:** Resets the tracing image to 0, 0 on the X, Y coordinates.

- ✔ **Load:** Enables you to add or replace a tracing image.

Making the Most of Dreamweaver's Site-Management Features

In Chapter 2, I introduce you to Dreamweaver's Manage Sites dialog box and some of the options in the Site Definition dialog box, such as the Local Info dialog box where you do the initial site setup for any Web site. In the following sections, I explain the rest of the options available from the Site Definition dialog box. If you're the only person working on a Web site, you don't need the features described in the next three sections.

Using a Testing Server

The Testing Server option enables you to specify a development server, a necessary step if you are creating a Web site using the Dreamweaver features with a database. You find more information about how to do this in Chapters 13, 14, and 15. If you're not creating a site using a database or a programming language (for example PHP or ASP), you don't need to make any changes to this dialog box.

Using Check In/Out

The Check In/Out feature is designed to keep people from overwriting each other's work when more than one person contributes to the same Web site (a valuable feature if you want to keep peace on your Web design team). When a person working on the Web site checks out a file, other developers working on the site are unable to make changes to that page. When you check out a file, you see a green check mark next to the filename in the Files panel. If someone else checks out a file, you see a red check mark next to the file name.

To use the Check In/Out feature, check the Enable File Check In and Check Out option at the bottom of the Remote Info dialog box. The dialog box expands to expose other options. If you want files checked out whenever they are opened, check the Check Out Files When Opening option (see Figure 4-16).

Keeping the peace with version control

Version control systems enable you to better manage changes and prevent different team members from overwriting each other's work. If you already use these programs, you'll be glad to know that you can integrate both Visual SourceSafe and systems that use the Web DAV protocol with Dreamweaver. This way, you can take advantage of the Dreamweaver site-management features and still protect your code-development process. If you don't know about these programs, visit the Microsoft site (http://msdn.microsoft.com/ssafe/) to find out more about Visual SourceSafe.

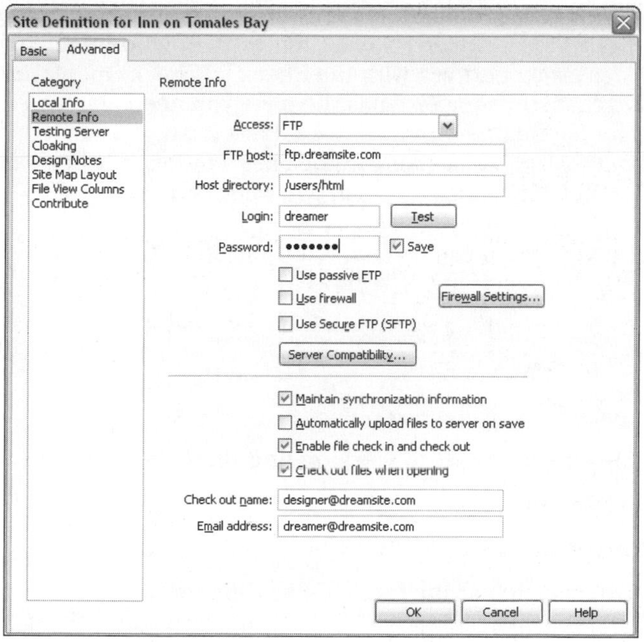

Figure 4-16:
The Check In/Out feature helps you keep track of who is working on a page when more than one person is contributing to a site.

Using this feature, you can track which files a particular person is working on. But if you want to use this tracking mechanism, check the Check Out Files When Opening option and then fill in the name you want associated with the files (presumably your name or nickname if you prefer) in the Check Out Name field and then include your e-mail address in the Email Address field. (The Email Address field is needed for Dreamweaver's integration with e-mail, which facilitates communication among developers on a site. See the next section for more information about integrated e-mail.)

Staying in touch with integrated e-mail

Dreamweaver features integrated e-mail as another handy tool for collaborative Web design when you use the Dreamweaver Check In/Out tool (described in the previous section). In conjunction with the e-mail program you already use, integrated e-mail gives you easy access to the e-mail addresses of other members of your team when you need them.

When you work on a site with a team of people, finding that someone else has already checked out the page you want to work on is common. Until that person checks the file back in, doing the work you need to do to the page is impossible. In the Dreamweaver Site Definition dialog box, each developer types his or her e-mail address with the Check In/Check Out feature. Then, when you find that someone else has the page you need, you can easily fire off an e-mail telling that person to check it back in so you can work on it, just by clicking that person's name in the Files window. (Bribes can be more effective than threats, especially when you offer chocolate.)

Developers on your team can use the following steps to associate their e-mail addresses with their version of Dreamweaver as part of the Check In/Check Out setup:

1. **Choose Site⇨Manage Sites.**

   The Manage Sites dialog box opens.

2. **Select the site you want to work on and then click the Edit button.**

   The Site Definition dialog box opens.

3. **Click the Advanced tab.**

4. **In the Category list at the left, choose Remote Info.**

   The Remote Info page appears (refer to Figure 4-16).

5. **Select the Enable File Check In and Check Out check box.**

6. **Select the Check Out Files When Opening check box.**

7. **Enter your name in the Check Out Name text box.**

   Nicknames are okay as long as everyone on the team knows your silly name.

8. **Enter your e-mail address in the Email Address text box.**

9. **Click OK to save your changes. Click the Done button in the Manage Sites dialog box.**

   The Manage Sites dialog box closes.

Using Design Notes

If you sometimes forget the details of your work or neglect to tell your colleagues important things about the Web site you're all working on, the Dreamweaver Design Notes feature may save you some grief.

Design Notes are ideal if you want to hide sensitive information from visitors, such as pricing structures or creative strategies, but make it available to members of your development team. Information saved as a Design Note in Dreamweaver can travel with any HTML file or image, even if the file transfers from one Web site to another or from Fireworks to Dreamweaver.

Essentially, Design Notes enable you to record information (such as a message to another designer on your team) and associate it with a file or folder. Design Notes work a lot like the *comment tag* (HTML code that enables you to embed text in a page that won't display in a browser) but with a bit more privacy. Unlike the comment tag, which is embedded directly in the HTML code of a page (and can be seen if someone views the source code behind a page on the Web), Design Notes are never visible to your visitors. The only way for a visitor to view Design Notes is to deliberately type the path to your notes subdirectory and view the notes files directly. You can even explicitly block this from being allowed, but only if you have administrative access to your server. To be even more secure, you can keep the notes on your hard drive and prevent them from ever being uploaded to your server — though, of course, your team members won't see your witty remarks.

To access the Design Notes page, choose Design Notes in the Category list in the Site Definition dialog box (see Figure 4-17). The settings on this page enable you to control how Dreamweaver uses Design Notes:

- **Maintain Design Notes:** Select this option to ensure that the Design Note remains attached to the file when you upload, copy, or move it.

- **Upload Design Notes for Sharing:** Choose this option to include Design Notes when you send files to the server via FTP.

- **Clean Up:** This button enables you to delete Design Notes no longer associated with files or folders in your site.

When you create graphics in Macromedia Fireworks, you can save a Design Note for each image file that is also available in Dreamweaver. To use this integrated feature, create a Design Note in Fireworks and associate it with the image. Then when you save the Fireworks image to your local Web site folder, the Design Note goes with it. When you open the file in Dreamweaver, the Design Note displays when you right-click the image (Control+click on the Mac). This feature is a great way for graphic designers to communicate with other members of the Web development team.

To activate the Design Notes feature, follow these steps:

1. **Choose Site⇨Manage Sites.**

   The Manage Sites dialog box opens.

2. **Select the site you want to work on and then click the Edit button.**

   The Site Definition dialog box opens.

3. **Select the Advanced tab.**

4. **In the Category list at the left, choose Design Notes.**

   The Design Notes page appears (refer to Figure 4-17).

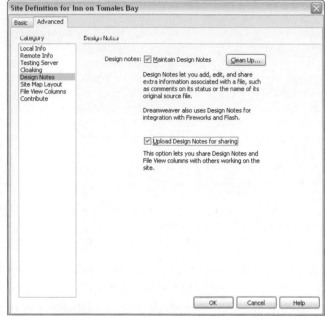

Figure 4-17:
The Design
Notes page
lets you
include
Design
Notes when
sending files
to the Web
server.

5. **Select the Maintain Design Notes option.**

   With this option selected, whenever you copy, move, rename, or delete a file, the associated Design Notes file is also copied, moved, renamed, or deleted with it.

6. **If you want your Design Notes to be sent with your files when they are uploaded to your server, select the Upload Design Notes for Sharing option.**

   If you're making notes only to yourself and don't want them to be associated with the page when you upload it to the server, deselect this option and Design Notes is maintained locally but not uploaded with your file.

7. **Click OK in the Site Definition dialog box; then click the Done button in the Manage Sites dialog box.**

   The Manage Sites dialog box closes.

To add Design Notes to a document, follow these steps:

1. **Open the file you want to add a Design Note to and choose File⇨ Design Notes.**

   The Design Notes dialog box opens (see Figure 4-18). You need to have a file checked out to add or modify a Design Note, but not to read a note.

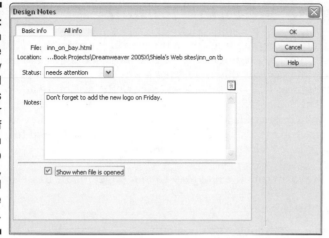

2. **Choose the status of the document from the Status drop-down list box.**

   Your options are Draft, Revision 1, Revision 2, Revision 3, Alpha, Beta, Final, and Needs Attention. You can choose any status, and you should set a policy with your design team about what each status means and how you use these options to manage your development.

3. **Type your comments in the Notes text box.**

4. **Click the Insert Date icon (icon of a calendar page just above the Notes text box) if you want to insert the current local date.**

   The current date is inserted automatically.

   You can also select the Show When File Is Open check box. If this box is selected, the Design Notes displays whenever the file is opened so that it can't be missed.

5. **Click the All Info tab in the Design Notes dialog box.**

   On the All Info tab, you can add other information that may be useful to developers of your site. For example, you can name a key designer (in the Name field) and define the value as the name of that person or the priority of the project (in the Value field). You also may define a field for a client or type of file that you commonly use.

6. **Click the plus (+) button to add a new information item; click the minus (–) button to remove a selected item.**

7. **Click OK to save the notes.**

   The notes you entered are saved to a subfolder named *notes* in the same location as the current file. The filename is the document's filename, plus the extension .mno. For example, if the filename is art.htm, the associated Design Notes file is named art.htm.mno. Design Notes are indicated in Site View by a small yellow icon that looks like a cartoon bubble.

Activating Site Map Layout

If you have trouble keeping track of all the files in your Web site and how they link to one another, you're not alone. As Web sites get larger and larger, this task becomes increasingly daunting. That's why Dreamweaver includes a Site Map Layout feature — to help you keep track of the structure and hierarchy of your site. This is not a Site Map like those you often see on Web sites that links to the main pages of a site. The Dreamweaver Site Map Layout is never visible to your visitors; it's a site-management feature designed to help you visually manage the files and folders in your site.

To create a site map from the Site Map Layout page, follow these steps:

1. **Choose Site⇨Manage Sites.**

   The Manage Sites dialog box opens.

2. **Select the name of the site you want to work on.**

3. **Click the Edit button.**

   The Site Definition box opens.

4. **Make sure the Advanced tab at the top of the Site Definition dialog box is selected and the Advanced options are visible.**

5. **Select the Site Map Layout option from the Category list at the left of the Site Definition dialog box.**

   The Site Map Layout options display in the right side of the Site Definition dialog box, as shown in Figure 4-19.

6. **Click the Browse button (the icon that resembles a file folder) next to the Home Page text box and browse to find the main folder of your Web site. Note, if you already filled out the Local Info page for your site, this field is already filled in.**

   This text box specifies the location of the home page of the Web site and the main site folder. This information is essential because it shows Dreamweaver where the Web site begins and ends.

7. **Specify the number of columns you want to display per row in the site map.**

   If you're not sure what you want for these settings, start with the default value of 200. You can always come back and change these settings later if you don't like the spacing of the icons in your site map.

8. **In the Column Width text box, set the width of the site map's columns in pixels.**

   Again, start with the default 125 if you're not sure how wide you want this to display.

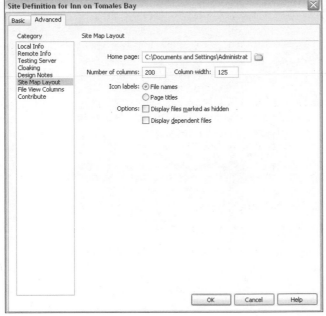

Figure 4-19:
The Site
Map Layout
options
enable you
to specify
how the Site
Map
navigation
window
appears.

9. **In the Icon Labels section, click to put a check mark in the box next to File Names or Page Titles to specify if you want the filename or the page title as the label for each page in the site map.**

   You can manually edit the displayed filename or page title after you generate the site map.

10. **In the Options section, you can choose to hide certain files, meaning that they won't be visible in the Site Map window.**

    If you select the Display Files Marked as Hidden option, files you have marked as hidden display in italic in the site map.

    If you select the Display Dependent Files option, all dependent files in the site's hierarchy display. A *dependent file* is an image or other non-HTML content that the browser loads when loading the main page.

11. **Click OK.**

    The Site Map is automatically generated.

12. **To view the Site Map, open the Files panel on the right side of the screen and select Map View from the drop-down list in the top-right corner (see Figure 4-20).**

    The Site Map displays in the Files panel using icons to represent each file and link in the site.

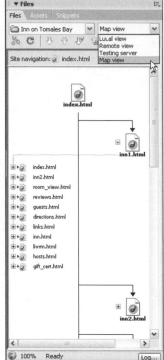

Figure 4-20:
The site
map
provides a
visual
reference to
the
structure,
hierarchy,
and links in
a Web site.

Using the File View Columns option

You can use the File View Columns category in the Site Definition dialog box (see Figure 4-21) to customize how file and folder options display in the expanded Files panel. This can be useful for sorting or grouping files in novel ways, for example, by adding a *section*, *department*, *season*, or *version* column. You can customize File View Columns in the following ways:

- ✔ You can add up to 10 new columns by clicking the small plus sign at the top of the dialog box and entering the name, association, and alignment of each new column.

- ✔ You can reorder or realign the order that columns display in by selecting the name of the column and then clicking the up or down arrows in the top right of the dialog to move it up or down the list.

- ✔ You can hide any columns except the filename column by selecting the column name and clicking to remove the check mark in the Show box.

✔ You can designate which (if any) columns are shared with other developers who have access to the site by selecting the column name and clicking to remove the check mark in the Enable Column Sharing box.

✔ You can delete any of the custom columns (you can not delete default columns) by selecting the column name and clicking on the minus sign at the top of the dialog box.

✔ You can rename custom columns as you would edit a filename.

✔ You can associate Design Notes with custom columns by selecting the column name and using the drop-down list next to Design Notes.

Enabling Contribute features

Macromedia Contribute is a program that was created so that people who don't know much about Web design can easily contribute to a Web site. Think of Contribute as sort of a Dreamweaver Light, except that it doesn't work very well as a stand-alone program. Contribute was designed to work on sites designed in Dreamweaver, and a number of features have been carefully integrated to make that collaboration work smoothly. If you're working with other developers of a site who use Contribute, make sure you check the box next to Enable Contribute Compatibility in the Contribute category of the Site Definition dialog box.

Figure 4-21: You can change the display options for the Files panel in the File View Columns category available from the Site Definition dialog box.

Remembering Your History

You can keep track of what you're doing and even replay your steps with the History panel. The History panel also lets you undo one or more steps and create commands to automate repetitive tasks.

To open the History panel, shown in Figure 4-22, choose Window⇨History. As soon as you open a file, the History panel starts automatically recording your actions as you do work in Dreamweaver. You can't rearrange the order of steps in the History panel, but you can copy them, replay them, and undo them. Don't think of the History panel as an arbitrary collection of commands; think of it as a way to view the steps you've performed, in the order in which you performed them. This is a great way to let Dreamweaver do your work for you if you have to repeat the same steps over and over again. It's also a lifesaver if you make a major mistake and want to go back one or more steps in your development work.

Here's a rundown of how you can put the History panel to use:

- ✓ **To copy steps you already executed:** Use the Copy Steps option as a quick way to automate steps you want to repeat. You can even select steps individually, in case you want to replay some (but not all) your actions exactly as you did them.

- ✓ **To replay any or all the steps displayed in the History panel:** Highlight the steps you want to replay and click the Replay button in the bottom of the History panel.

- ✓ **To undo the results of the replayed steps:** Choose Edit⇨Undo Replay Steps.

- ✓ **To apply steps to a specific element on a page:** Highlight that element in the Document window before selecting and replaying the steps. For example, if you want to apply bold and italic formatting to just a few words on a page, you can replay the steps that applied bold and italics to selected text.

Figure 4-22:
The History panel keeps track of what you do, making undoing and repeating any or all your steps easy.

Repeating your steps with Recorded Commands

You can automate repeat tasks using Dreamweaver's Recorded Commands feature, available from the Commands menu. Simply start the record option, execute any series of actions in Dreamweaver, stop, and save them. Then you just replay the recording to repeat the actions automatically.

To use the Recorded Commands option, choose Commands⇨Start Recording and then carefully execute a series of steps that you want to be able to repeat. When you complete the steps you want to record, choose Commands⇨Stop Recording and name the command to save it. To play the actions back, choose Commands⇨Play Recorded Command and select your new command. Then kick back and watch the action, or better yet, take a break and get out of your office for a change.

You can also set the number of steps displayed in the History panel by choosing Edit⇨Preferences (Windows) or Dreamweaver⇨Preferences (Mac) and selecting General from the Category list on the left. The default is 50 steps, more than enough for most users. The higher the number, the more memory the History panel uses.

Using the Quick Tag Editor

If you're one of those developers who likes to work in the Dreamweaver WYSIWYG editing environment but still wants to look at the HTML tags once in a while, you'll love the Quick Tag Editor.

The Quick Tag Editor, as the name implies, lets you quickly access HTML tags and enables you to modify, add, or remove an HTML tag without opening the HTML Source window. That means that while you're in the middle of working on a page in Design view, you can view the HTML tag you are working on without switching over to Code view. You can use the Quick Tag Editor to insert HTML, edit an existing tag, or wrap new tags around a selected text block or other element.

The Quick Tag Editor opens in one of three modes — Edit, Insert, or Wrap — depending on what you selected on the page before you launched the editor. Use the keyboard shortcut Ctrl+T (Windows) or ⌘+T (Macintosh) to change modes while the Quick Tag Editor is open.

You can enter or edit tags in the Quick Tag Editor just as you would in Code view, without having to switch back and forth between Code view and Design view.

To enter or edit tags in the Quick Tag Editor, follow these steps:

1. **With the document you want to edit open, select an element or text block.**

   If you want to add new code, simply click anywhere in the file without selecting text or an element.

2. **Choose Modify⇨Quick Tag Editor.**

   You can also press Ctrl+T (Windows) or ⌘+T (Macintosh).

   The Quick Tag Editor opens in the mode that is most appropriate for your selection, as shown in Figure 4-23. For example, if you click an image or formatted text, it displays the current tag so that you can edit it. If you don't select anything, or if you select unformatted text, the Quick Tag Editor opens with nothing in it, and you can enter the code you want to add. Press Ctrl+T (⌘+T) to switch to another mode.

   If you want to edit an existing tag, go to Step 3. If you want to add a new tag, skip to Step 4.

3. **If you selected an element formatted with multiple HTML tags or a tag with multiple attributes, press Tab to move from one tag, attribute name, or attribute value to the next. Press Shift+Tab to move back to the previous one.**

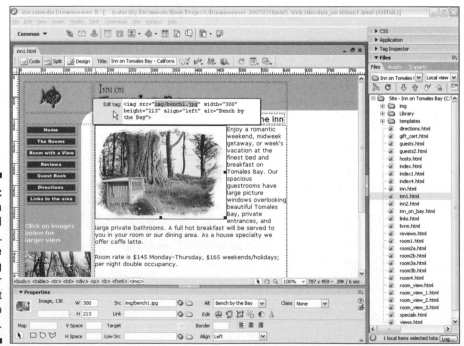

Figure 4-23:
You can view and edit HTML tags in the Quick Tag Editor without switching to Code view.

If you aren't sure about a tag or attribute, pause for a couple of seconds and a drop-down list appears automatically, offering you a list of all the tags or attributes available for the element you are editing. If this Hints list doesn't appear, choose Edit⇨Preferences⇨Code Hints (Windows) or Dreamweaver⇨Preferences⇨Code Hints (Mac) and make sure that the Enable Code Hints option is selected.

4. **To add a new tag or attribute, simply type the code into the Quick Tag Editor.**

   You can use the Tab and arrow keys to move the cursor where you want to add code. You can keep the Quick Tag Editor open and continue to edit and add attribute names and values as long as you like.

5. **To close the Quick Tag Editor and apply all your changes, press Enter (Windows) or Return (Mac).**

Chapter 5

Adding Graphics

*N*o matter how great the writing may be on your Web site, the graphics always get people's attention first. And the key to making a good first impression is to use images that look great, download quickly, and are appropriate to your Web site.

If you're familiar with using a graphics-editing program to create graphics, you're a step ahead. If not, you find pointers throughout this chapter, and you discover how to find preexisting graphics to use on your Web site. You also find out how to bring graphics into Dreamweaver and how to edit them without leaving the Web design environment. To help you get the most out of the images for your site, you find information about choosing an image-editing program and keeping image file sizes small.

If your images are ready and you want to dive into placing them on your pages, jump ahead to the "Inserting Images on Your Pages" section and find out how to place and align images, create image maps, and set a background image in Dreamweaver. You also discover some of Dreamweaver's newest features, which enable you to crop images and even adjust contrast and brightness without ever launching an external image-editing program.

Getting Great Graphics

You want your Web graphics to look good, but where do you get them? If you have some design talent, you can create your own images with Photoshop, Fireworks, or any other image program (you find descriptions of the most popular programs in the section "Creating your own images," later in this chapter). If you're not an artist, you may be better off gathering images from *clip art collections* (libraries of ready-to-use image files) and using royalty-free or stock photography, as described in this section. If you have a scanner, you can also scan in existing photographs or logos.

To create textures for backgrounds and buttons on your site, try scanning fabrics, handmade papers, and other textured objects. You can scan anything you can put against the glass of your scanner, even medals, coins, and other things you may have around the house or office. (Just be careful not to scratch the delicate glass on the scanner.)

Dreamweaver doesn't have any image-creation capabilities of its own, and only limited editing tools, so you need to use an image-editing program such as Photoshop to create or edit images. If you bought Macromedia Studio, you're in luck because it includes Fireworks (a great image editor for Web graphics). No matter what program you use to create and edit your images, you can set Dreamweaver's preferences to launch that program when you choose to edit an image from within Dreamweaver. If you have Macromedia Studio, the association is automatically set when you install the program. If you want to use a different image editor, choose File⇨Preferences, choose the Category File Types/Editors, and use the Browse button to add your software program.

Buying royalty-free clip art and photographs

If you don't want the hassle of creating your own images (or if you lack the artistic talent), you may be happy to find many sources of clip art available. Royalty-free images, which include clip art and photographs, are generally sold for a one-time fee that grants you all or most of the rights to use the image. (Read the agreement that comes with any art you purchase to make sure that you don't miss any exclusions or exceptions. For example, you may have to pay extra to use an image for commercial purposes.) You can find a wide range of CD-ROMs and Web sites full of clip art, photographs, and even animations that you can use on your Web site. (Speaking of animations, nowadays, you can even find Web sites that sell Flash files, animations, buttons, and other artistic elements that you can edit and integrate into your Web site. For more info on how to add multimedia to your Web site, see Chapter 12.) Many professional designers buy clip art images and then alter them in an image program — such as Macromedia Fireworks, Adobe Illustrator, or Adobe Photoshop — to tailor them for a specific project or to make the image more distinct.

Here are some clip art suppliers:

- **Getty Images, Inc.** (`www.gettyimages.com`): Getty Images is the largest supplier of royalty-free digital imagery on the Web, specializing in photographs and illustrations of a wide variety of subjects, including film footage. Pay for images and footage as you go.

- **Stockbyte** (`www.stockbyte.com`): Stockbyte is a great source for international royalty-free photos. You can purchase photographs in a variety of qualities, as you need them.

- **Photos.com** (`www.photos.com`): Photos.com is a subscription-based service for royalty-free stock photography and photo objects. A 1- to 12-month subscription gives you unlimited access and use of its collection.

- **iStockphoto.com** (`www.istockphoto.com`): An innovative variation of the fee-for-use model, iStockphoto lets you trade your own photographs for stock images.

- **Web Promotion** (`www.webpromotion.com`): A great source for animated GIFs and other Web graphics. Artwork on this site is free provided you create a link back to Web Promotion on your Web site, or you can buy the artwork for a small fee.

- **Fonts.com** (`www.fonts.com`): If you're looking to enhance your font collection, which is a good idea if you want to create distinctive Web graphics with text, you can preview and purchase a huge number of fonts at Fonts.com. You can search this site by font name or using descriptive keywords. Keywords help if you need a specific font but don't know its name.

Creating your own images

The best way to get original images is to create your own. If you're not graphically talented or inclined, consider hiring someone who can create images for you. If you want to create your own images for use in Dreamweaver, Fireworks is a good program to start with because it's tightly integrated with Dreamweaver and has a similar interface.

The last few years have seen a tremendous advancement in the features and capabilities of specialized Web graphics programs as well as increased competition between application vendors. In the future, expect even more changes because two of the biggest competitors — Adobe and Macromedia — are working on merging into one company and both Fireworks and Photoshop may change as a result). Most professional designers strongly prefer Adobe

Photoshop, although I have to say I've been quite impressed with Photoshop Elements, which is a "light" version, but offers many of the same features for a fraction of the cost. (If you're designing images for print, you need Photoshop; but for the Web, Elements is a surprisingly complete, low-cost alternative.) For vector-based graphics (a good choice for illustrations), Adobe Illustrator is the favorite.

The following is a list of the most popular image-editing programs on the market today. Unless otherwise indicated, all the following image programs are available for both Mac and Windows:

- **Macromedia Fireworks (www.macromedia.com/software/fireworks):** Fireworks was one of the very first image-editing programs designed specifically to create and edit Web graphics. Fireworks gives you everything you need to create, edit, and output the best-looking Web graphics, all in one well-designed product. Besides sharing a common interface with Dreamweaver, Fireworks also integrates extremely well with Dreamweaver to speed up and simplify the process of building a Web site. In Chapter 11, you discover some of the special features of Fireworks and Dreamweaver that help you to work with these two programs.

- **Adobe Photoshop (www.adobe.com/products):** Adobe calls Photoshop the "camera of the mind." This is unquestionably the most popular image-editing program on the market and a widely used standard among graphics professionals. With Photoshop, you can create original artwork, correct color in photographs, retouch photographs, scan images, and do much more. Photoshop has a wealth of powerful painting and selection tools in addition to special effects and filters to create images that go beyond what you can capture on film or create with other illustration programs. And Photoshop includes everything you need for creating and editing Web graphics.

- **Adobe Photoshop Elements (www.adobe.com/products):** If you're not designing images for print use, and you don't need all the bells and whistles offered in the full-blown version of Photoshop, Photoshop Elements is a remarkably powerful program — for about a sixth of the cost of Photoshop. Elements is especially well suited for Web graphics output and is easier to learn than Photoshop.

- **Adobe Illustrator (www.adobe.com/products):** Illustrator is one of the industry standards for creating vector-based graphics, ideally suited for illustrations. Adobe integrates all its design programs so you can drag and drop illustrations that you create in Illustrator right into other Adobe programs, such as Photoshop or InDesign. Illustrator also comes with an export feature that enables you to export your illustrations in GIF or JPEG format with a browser-friendly palette of colors so that your illustrations look great on the Web.

- ✓ **CorelDRAW Essentials (`www.corel.com`):** Another competitor in the graphics market, CorelDRAW offers features and capabilities similar to those of Adobe Photoshop for a fraction of the price. The Essentials package comes with CorelDRAW and Corel PHOTO-PAINT and includes a generous clip art and royalty-free photography collection. For less than the cost of Photoshop, you can get the complete CorelDRAW Graphics Suite.

- ✓ **Paint Shop Pro (`www.corel.com`):** Also by Corel, Paint Shop Pro is a full-featured painting and image-manipulation program available only for Windows. Paint Shop Pro is similar to Photoshop, but on a more limited scale because it doesn't offer the same range of effects, tools, and filters. However, it costs less than Photoshop and may be a good starter program for novice image-makers.

- ✓ **Macromedia Freehand (`www.macromedia.com/software/freehand`):** Macromedia Freehand is an illustration program used widely both on the Web and in print. Freehand has many excellent Web features, including support for Web file formats such as GIF, PNG, and JPEG, as well as vector formats such as Flash (.SWF) and Shockwave FreeHand (.FHC). Thirty-day trial versions are available for free on the Macromedia Web site.

- ✓ **MicroFrontier Color It! (`www.microfrontier.com`):** This low-cost, easy-to-use graphics program is available only for the Macintosh and is a great tool for beginners, as well as those on a tight budget. Although it's much more limited than many of the other programs in this list, it provides enough features to create basic banners and buttons for a small business Web site. A demo version is available for free from the MicroFrontier Web site.

Understanding the Basics of Web Graphics

Because having a basic understanding of graphics formats and how they work on the Web is so important, the following sections give you an overview of what you need to know about graphics as you create them or place them on your pages.

The most important thing to keep in mind when placing images on a Web page is that you want to optimize your images to keep your file sizes as small as possible. You may ask, "How small is *small?*" In fact, this is one of the most common questions people ask about Web graphics. The answer is largely subjective — remember that the larger your graphics files are, the longer people have to wait for them to download before they can see them. You may have the most beautiful picture of Mount Fuji on the front page of your Web site, but if it takes forever to download, most people aren't going to be patient enough to wait to see it. Also remember that when you build pages with multiple graphics, you have to consider the cumulative download time of all the graphics on the page. So smaller is definitely better.

Most Web pros consider anything from about 75K to 150K a good maximum *cumulative* size for all the elements on a given page. With the increasing popularity of DSL and cable modems, many Web sites are starting to become a bit more graphics-heavy. However, anything over 150K is pushing the limits, especially if you expect people with dialup modems (56K and under) to stick around long enough to view your pages.

To make determining the total file size of the images on your page easy, Dreamweaver includes this information in the status bar of the current Document window, as shown in Figure 5-1. This number indicates the total file size of all the images and HTML on your page as well as the expected download time at a given connection speed. (You can set your own connection speed by choosing Edit⇨Preferences⇨Status Bar⇨Connection Speed. On a Mac, choose Dreamweaver⇨Preferences⇨Status Bar⇨Connection Speed).

Achieving small file sizes requires using compression techniques and color reduction — tasks that you can achieve using any of the graphics programs mentioned in the preceding section. Whatever program you use, you should understand that you can reduce image sizes to varying degrees and that the challenge is to find the best balance between small file size and good image quality. If you really want to find out the best ways to create graphics for the Web, read *Web Design For Dummies* by Lisa Lopuck (Wiley Publishing, Inc.). It has a fantastic section on designing Web graphics.

Use GIFs for animations and transparency

GIF is the most widely accepted Web file format that can have transparent pixels to create a transparency effect. (The PNG format does also, but its support is spotty.) GIFs can also have multiple frames, so you can create small, animated loops with this format. Animated ads on the Web, generally referred to as *banners,* are sometimes made in GIF.

Designers frequently create a GIF that just consists of words because it allows them to use nonstandard fonts with perfect anti-aliasing and whatever colors and effects they want without worrying about whether the end user has the font installed. GIF is the ideal format for this because it offers more control over color compression, whereas JPEG compression can make the small lines and curves in text fuzzy.

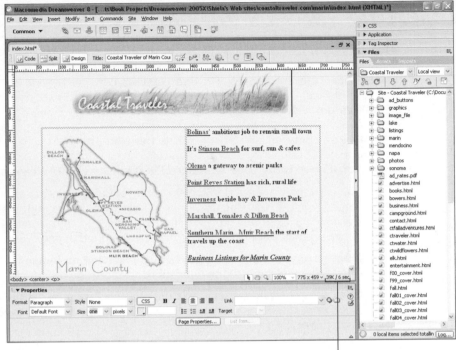

Total download size and estimated download time.

One of the most common questions about images for the Web concerns when you use GIF and when you use JPEG. The simple answer:

Use	*For*
GIF	Line art (such as one- or two-color logos), simple drawings, animations, images with a transparent background, and basically any image that has no gradients or blends
JPEG	Colorful, complex images (such as photographs), images containing gradients or color blends, and so on

That said, sometimes the best thing to do is just experiment with both formats and see which yields the best results. In time, you'll get a knack for which is the best format to use, depending on the type of image you're working with.

Inserting Images on Your Pages

Dreamweaver makes placing images on your Web pages easy.

Before inserting any images into your page, saving your page is important. After you save, Dreamweaver knows the directory location of the page and can then properly create the image links.

To place an image on a Web page, follow these steps:

1. **Open an existing page or choose File⇨New to create a new page.**

   You can create a basic HTML page or any of the template or other options available in the New Document dialog box. With the exception of the dynamic page options (covered in Chapters 13, 14, and 15), the insert image options work the same no matter what kind of page you create.

2. **Make sure you save your page before inserting an image by choosing File⇨Save and saving it to your main site folder.**

3. **Click the Insert Image icon on the Common Insert bar at the top of the work area (the icon looks like a small tree) and choose Image from the drop-down list.**

   The Select Image Source dialog box appears, as shown in Figure 5-2.

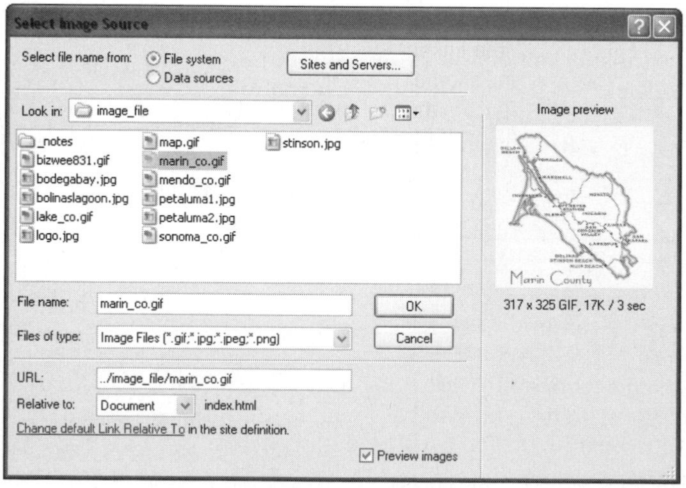

Figure 5-2:
You can locate and preview the image you want to place in the Select Image Source dialog box.

4. **In the Select Image Source dialog box, browse to locate the image you want to insert.**

   Alternatively, you can insert images simply by choosing Insert⇨Image, which also brings up the Select Image Source dialog box, or by dragging and dropping image files from the Files panel right onto your Dreamweaver document.

Dreamweaver only lets you insert images in valid Web graphics file formats, such as GIF or JPEG.

5. **Double-click the image to insert it or click once and then click OK.**

The image automatically appears on your page.

When you insert an image file onto a page, you create a link from the page to the image, much as you do when you create a link from one page to another. As a result, if your images and the pages they are linked to are not in the same relative location on your hard drive as they are on your server, you break the links and your images do not appear on your pages (instead you get that ugly broken GIF image). The best way to make sure your images and files stay where they're supposed to in relation to one another is to save them all in one main site folder and identify that folder using Dreamweaver's Site Setup features covered in Chapter 2.

How an image appears on a Web page

The HTML tag that you use to place images on a Web page is similar to the link tag that you use to create hyperlinks between pages. Both tags instruct the browser where to find something. In the case of the link tag, the path to the linked page instructs the browser where to find another URL. In the case of an image tag, the path in the tag instructs the browser to find a GIF or JPEG image file. The path describes the location of the image in relation to the page on which it appears. For example, `images/baby.gif` is a path that instructs a browser to look for an image file called `baby.gif` in the images directory. This path also implies that the images directory is in the same directory as the HTML file containing the link. Whenever you see a forward slash in HTML, it signifies a directory (or folder) that contains other files or folders.

Trying to determine the path can get a little complicated. Fortunately, Dreamweaver sets the path for you, but you need to take care of two important steps before Dreamweaver can do this properly:

1. **Save your page.**

When you save a page, Dreamweaver automatically remembers the exact location of the page in relation to the image. Saving the file is essential because the path always indicates the location of an image relative to the page containing the link (this is called a *relative link*). If you forget to save your file beforehand, Dreamweaver always prompts you to save the file before completing the link. If you don't save the file, Dreamweaver inserts an absolute link that references the image's location on your hard drive, but this link isn't valid on any other machine or when you upload your Web site. An *absolute link* to your hard drive works on your machine, but not on your Web server — or any other machine, for that matter.

2. **Define your site and identify your main Web site folder using the Site Setup features covered in Chapter 2.**

Aligning Images on a Page

After you place an image on your Web page, you may want to center or align it so that text can wrap around it. In the following two sections — "Centering an image" and "Aligning an image with text wrapping" — you find out the steps to accomplish both these goals.

Centering an image

To center an image on a page, follow these steps:

1. **Click to select the image that you want to center.**

   The Properties inspector changes to display the image properties.

2. **From the icons for alignment options in the Properties inspector, shown in Figure 5-3, click the Align Center icon.**

   The image automatically moves to the center of the page.

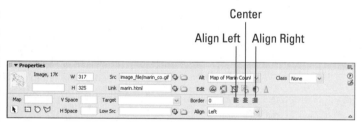

Center

Align Left | Align Right

Figure 5-3:
Use the alignment icons in the Properties inspector to center an image.

Aligning an image with text wrapping

To align an image to the right of a page and wrap text around it on the left, follow these steps:

1. **Insert the image immediately to the left of the first line of the text (see Figure 5-4).**

   The easiest way to do this is to place the cursor just before the first letter of text; then choose Insert⇨Image.

   Don't put spaces or line breaks between the image and the text.

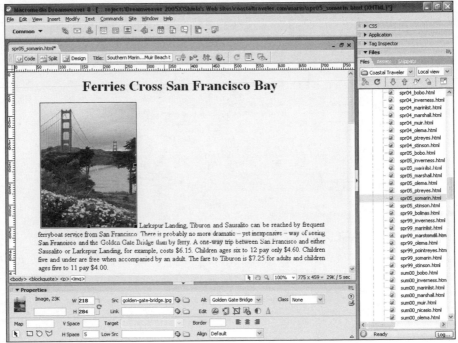

Figure 5-4:
To wrap text around an image, first place the image immediately to the left of the text with no spaces between the text and image.

2. **Click to select the image.**

The Properties inspector changes to display the image attribute options.

3. **In the Properties inspector, choose Right from the Align drop-down list.**

The image aligns to the right and the text automatically wraps around it, as shown in Figure 5-5.

To align the image to the left of the page with text wrapping around on the left, follow Steps 1 and 2, and then in Step 3, choose Left from the Align drop-down list instead of Right.

To prevent text from running up against an image, click the image, find V and H spacing on the Properties inspector, and enter the amount of space you want (the space is measured in pixels). Five to ten pixels is usually enough to add space around the image and prevent the text from bumping up against its edge. If you want to add space to only one side of an image, it's a bit more work, but you can more precisely control spacing with CSS (covered in Chapter 8). You can also use an image-editing program to add a transparent border to the edge of a GIF or add a few pixels that match the background to a JPEG.

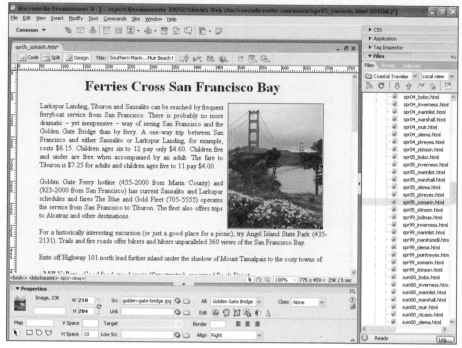

Figure 5-5:
The Align
drop-down
list in the
Properties
panel aligns
an image.

Creating complex designs with images

The alignment options available in HTML enable you to align your images vertically or horizontally, but you can't do both at once. Also, the alignment options don't really enable you to position images in relation to one another or in relation to text with much precision. For example, if you try to center an image that is positioned up against a text block, the text gets centered, too. One way to get around this limitation is to create HTML tables and then combine and merge cells in the table to control positioning. See Chapter 6 to find out how you can make table borders invisible and use them to create complex layouts. You can also use layers (Chapter 9) and Cascading Style Sheets to position elements on a page (Chapter 8).

Image Editing in Dreamweaver

New features in Dreamweaver enable you to do minor image editing inside Dreamweaver without opening Fireworks or any other graphics-editing program. These tools are available from the Properties inspector when an image is selected (see Figure 5-6).

You also find two buttons that enable you to use Macromedia Fireworks to edit images. The Edit button launches Fireworks and opens the selected image in the main window of the program, which makes using all the Fireworks editing features easy. Macromedia's careful integration of these programs means that when you save changes to the image in Fireworks, they are reflected in the page in Dreamweaver. A new button, just to the right of the Edit button, is designed to make optimizing an image fast and easy, which makes downloading faster. Chapter 10 covers both the Edit and Optimize in Fireworks features in greater detail.

Figure 5-6:
Use the
Crop,
Brightness
and
Contrast,
and
Sharpen
tools to edit
an image.

Brightness and Contrast

Crop | Sharpen

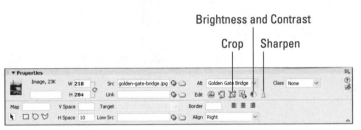

Before you get carried away editing your images, remember that Dreamweaver is primarily a Web-page creation application and not really designed to edit graphics. Although these tools can be useful, they shouldn't take the place of doing serious work on your graphics in an actual graphics application, such as Fireworks or Photoshop.

When you do use the tools for cropping, adjusting brightness and contrast, and sharpening an image, beware that you are changing the actual image (not just a copy of it). Make sure you're happy with these changes before you save the page you're working on. You can use the undo feature in Dreamweaver to revert back several steps, but after you save the page, you can't undo changes to an image. To protect your original image, considering saving a copy before editing it.

Cropping an image

Essentially, cropping an image is trimming it. To crop a graphic or photo, follow these steps:

1. **In the Document window, select the image you'd like to crop by clicking it.**

   The Properties inspector changes to display the image's properties.

2. From the Edit icons, click the Crop tool.

A dialog box appears warning you that cropping changes the original image.

Don't make the change if you're concerned about needing to keep the entire image available. If you're concerned, the best thing to do may be to make a copy of the image and apply your cropping to the copy.

3. Click OK.

A dotted line with handlebars appears in the image.

4. Outline the area of the image you want to keep with the handlebars.

Any part of the image that is darkened, as shown in Figure 5-7, is deleted when the crop completes.

5. Double-click inside the box, or press Enter (Return on a Mac).

The image is cropped.

You can undo cropping by choosing Edit⇨Undo, but remember that, after you save the page, changes permanently apply to the image and cannot be undone.

Dotted crop line

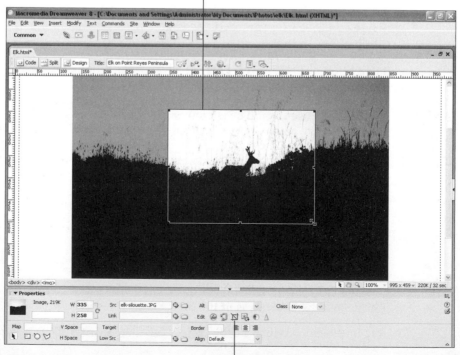

Figure 5-7: The Crop tool lets you edit your photo inside Dreamweaver. This example shows how you define the area to keep during a crop.

Crop tool

Adjusting brightness and contrast

Adjusting an image's brightness allows you to change the overall amount of light in an image. Contrast controls the difference between the light and dark areas of an image. To adjust brightness and contrast, follow these steps:

1. **In the Document window, select the image you want to alter.**

   The Properties inspector shows the image properties.

2. **From the Edit tools, click the Brightness and Contrast icon (a circle with light and dark halves).**

   A dialog box appears, indicating that changes you make are made to the original file.

3. **Click OK.**

   The Brightness/Contrast dialog box appears.

4. **Adjust the brightness and contrast settings of the image with the sliders.**

   Make sure to select the Preview check box if you want to see how the changes affect the image as you move the sliders around.

5. **Click OK.**

   The settings take effect permanently when you save the page.

Sharpening an image

When you apply sharpening to an image, you increase the distinction between areas of color. The effect can be one of increased definition to the shapes and lines in an image. To sharpen an image, follow these steps:

1. **In the Document window, select the image you want to sharpen.**

   The Properties inspector shows the image properties.

2. **From the Edit tools, click the Sharpen icon (a blue cone).**

   A dialog box appears, indicating that your change is made to the original file.

3. **Click OK.**

   The Sharpen dialog box appears.

4. **Adjust the sharpness of the image with the slider.**

   Make sure you select the Preview check box if you want to see how the changes affect the image as you move the slider.

5. Click OK.

The image is sharpened and changes are made permanently when you save changes to the page.

Using the Transparent GIF Trick

You may find it strange that I suggest you place an invisible image on a Web page, but that's exactly what I show you how to do in this section. A small, transparent GIF is a powerful element in Web page design because you can use it to control the exact position of other elements on a page. You'll notice that some other programs, such as Fireworks, also utilize transparent GIFs to force page elements into place more precisely. In Fireworks, transparent GIFs are automatically generated, and you can often recognize them because they use names such as `transparent.gif`, `clear.gif`, or `spacer.gif`. Regardless of the name, they all perform the same function.

To create your own transparent GIF, simply create a new document in any image editor with the background set to Transparent. Then don't add anything to the image before saving it as a GIF with the Transparent option selected. The result is an image that is invisible, but very useful for spacing purposes.

If you don't want to create your own transparent GIF or you just want to practice the following steps, you can download a free transparent GIF from my Web site at `www.DigitalFamily.com/free` (just look at the bottom of the page for the image that doesn't appear to be there, but is displayed under the Transparent GIFs headline and outlined so you can find it).

Some Web designers recommend that you create a single-pixel graphic for this purpose, but I find that a 10 x 10-pixel image works best because it's easier to select after you place it on your page in Dreamweaver. Remember, even if the clear GIF is 10 x 10 pixels, you change the height and width to any size because HTML enables you to specify any height and width for an image regardless of its actual size. Thus, you can alter the image attributes for height and width to adjust your transparent GIF to be larger or smaller depending on how much space you want between other visible elements on your page.

Dreamweaver makes using the transparent GIF trick easy because you have easy access to the height and width attributes in the Properties inspector. You may also need to specify the alignment of the image to achieve the desired effect.

To use a transparent GIF between images, text, or other elements on a page, follow these steps:

1. **Click to insert your cursor wherever you want the transparent GIF on your page — between two images or within a block of text, for example.**

2. **Choose File⇨Insert and browse to select your transparent GIF.**

3. **Click OK.**

   The transparent GIF is inserted on your page and automatically selected.

4. **With your transparent GIF still selected, alter the height and width (the H and W fields in the Properties inspector) until it is the size of the space you want to create.**

   The transparent GIF automatically adjusts to the height and width specified.

When you select a transparent GIF you can see the outline of the image while it's selected. Notice that as soon as you deselect the image, it becomes invisible in Dreamweaver. You can always reselect it by clicking in the area until the cursor highlights it. Just beware that selecting it can be tricky because it's not visible, especially if you make it very small. For this reason, I recommend resizing the GIF as soon as you place it on the page while it's still highlighted.

Creating a Background

Background images can bring life to a Web page by adding color and fullness. Used cleverly, a background image helps create the illusion that the entire page is one large image while still downloading quickly and efficiently. The trick is to use a small background image that creates a dramatic effect when it *tiles* (repeats) across and down the page (see Figure 5-8).

Background images are often called *tiles,* because they repeat like tiles across a kitchen floor. However, if you use a long, narrow image as a background or a large image that's small in file size, you can create many effects beyond a repeating tile.

Beware that certain backgrounds (such as the one shown in Figure 5-9) can make reading text that's placed on top of them hard. Choose your background images carefully and make sure your background and your text has plenty of contrast — reading on a computer screen is hard enough.

As you work with backgrounds, you may find another use for a transparent GIF. If you place a graphic on top of a patterned background, you end up with a rectangular area around the graphic that obscures the patterned background, as shown in Figure 5-10. To allow the background to be visible around, say, a headline, you can create your headline graphic on top of a color similar to the dominant color used in the background. When you save the GIF, set that color to be transparent. Placed on the page, the headline looks as if it's floating on top of the pattern (see Figure 5-11).

You may find that you need to change the color of text to make it stand out better against a background. Notice that in Figure 5-10 the black text looks good against the white background of the GIF, but after I made the GIF transparent, I saw that white text was easier to read against the dark green background pattern and changed the text color accordingly.

To insert a background image on a Web page, follow these steps:

1. **Choose Modify⇨Page Properties.**

   The Page Properties dialog box appears, as shown in Figure 5-12.

2. **Click Appearance from the Category list on the left.**

Figure 5-10: Normal GIFs and JPEGs always have a rectangular shape that looks bad on top of a patterned background.

Figure 5-11:
After the white around the title is set to be transparent, it floats on top of the background.

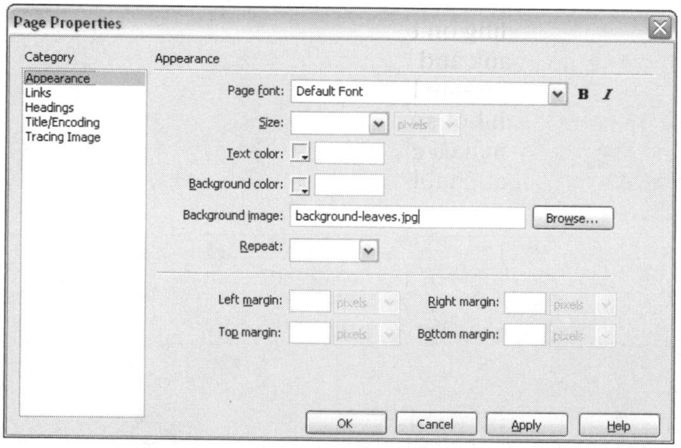

Figure 5-12:
The Page Properties dialog box enables you to set a background image, as well as a background color, among other things.

3. **Click the Browse button to the right of the Background Image text box.**

   The Select Image Source dialog box opens.

4. **Browse to find the image that you want to use as your background image.**

When you insert an image in your Web site, you want to make sure that the image is in the same relative location on your hard drive as it is on your server. If you plan to use your background tile throughout your site, you may want to store it in a common images folder where you can easily link to the image from any page in your site. See Chapter 3 for details on organizing image files.

5. **Double-click the filename of your background image to select it.**

   The Select Image Source dialog box disappears.

6. **Click OK in the Page Properties dialog box to finish.**

   Note that if you click the Apply button, you see the effect of the background tile being applied to the page, but the Page Properties dialog box stays open.

 If you don't want a background image to tile, choose the No-Repeat option from the Repeat drop-down list in the Page Properties dialog box and the image appears only in the top-right of the document.

Creating Image Maps

Image maps are popular on the Web because they enable you to create hot spots in an image and link them to different URLs. A common use of an image map is a geographic map, such as a map of the United States, that links to different locations, depending on the section of the map selected. For example, if you have a national bank and want customers to find a local branch or ATM machine easily, you can create hot spots on an image map of the United States and then link each hot spot to a page listing banks in that geographic location. Dreamweaver makes creating image maps easy by providing a set of simple drawing tools that enable you to create hot spots and set their corresponding links.

To create an image map, follow these steps:

1. **Place the image you want to use as an image map on your page.**

2. **Select the image.**

   The image properties display in the Properties inspector.

3. **To draw your hot spot, choose a shape tool from the Image Map tools in the lower-left of the Properties inspector (see Figure 5-13).**

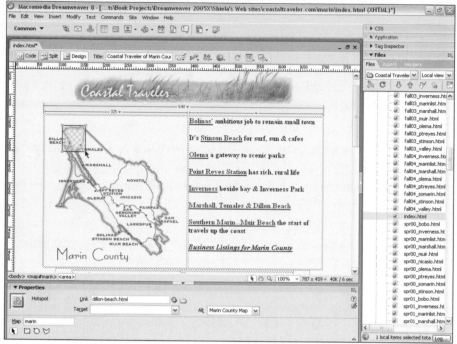

Figure 5-13:
Select any
image to
display the
image map
tools in the
Properties
inspector.

The shape tools include a rectangle, a circle, and an irregular polygon that allow you to draw regions on your images, called *hot spots,* each with a specific link.

4. **With the shape tool selected, click and drag over an area of the image that you want to make *hot* (link to another page). Here's how the different hot spot tools work:**

   • **Rectangle:** As you click and drag, a light blue highlight appears around the region that you're making hot; this highlighted area indicates the active region. If you need to reposition the hot area, select the Pointer Hotspot Tool (black arrow) from the lower-left corner of the Properties inspector and then select and move the region to the location you want. You can also resize it by clicking and dragging any of the corners.

   • **Circle:** The circle tool works much like the rectangle tool — just click and drag. To resize a circle hot spot, select the Pointer Hotspot Tool, and click and drag one of the small square boxes on its edges.

   • **Polygon:** The polygon tool functions a little bit differently; to make a polygon selection (such as one of the state of California in a U.S.

map), you click the tool once for each point of the polygon shape you want to draw. The shape automatically connects the points as you click. When you're done, switch to another map tool or click outside the image. You can change the size of the polygon or move any of its points by using the Pointer Hotspot Tool.

5. **To link a selected hot area, click the Folder icon next to the Link text box (at the top of the Properties inspector).**

   The Select File dialog box opens.

6. **Browse to find the HTML file that you want to link to the hot spot on your image.**

7. **Double-click the file to which you want to link.**

   The hot spot links to the selected page and the Select File dialog box automatically closes. You can also type the path directly in the Link text box if you know it, so you don't have to find it on your hard drive.

8. **To add more hot spots, choose an image and a shape tool, and repeat Steps 4 through 7.**

9. **To give your image map a name, type a name in the Map text field, just above the shape tools.**

   Giving your map (and all the hot spots it includes) a name helps to distinguish it in the event that you have multiple image maps on the same page. You can call the map anything you want, with the exception that you can't include spaces or special punctuation.

   When you finish, you see all your image map hot spots indicated by a light blue highlight.

At any time, you can go back and edit the image map by clicking and highlighting the blue region on your image and dragging the edges to resize the hot spot or by entering a new URL to change the link.

Part III
Advancing Your Site

The 5th Wave   By Rich Tennant

Well, there's your Web page, Crypto. Designed like you asked. But personally, I think it has too many spinning spirals and blinking lights. It makes...hard reading. Make...tired... look...at...lose...all... con...cen...tra...tion...

Perfect!

CRYPTO THE HYPNOTIST

In this part . . .

To create the most advanced designs in HTML, you need to use tables, frames, Cascading Style Sheets (CSS), or layers. This part introduces you to all of these design options and helps you decide which features offer the best options for your Web site. If you choose tables, Chapter 6 walks you through the steps to create tables for data and design. It also covers nested tables, merged cells, and so much more. Chapter 7 covers how to divide a page with frames, when this option is warranted, and how to target links so your pages work as you intend. In Chapter 8, you discover the power and design control that can only be achieved with CSS. As CSS becomes increasingly well supported on the Web, designers are taking the leap and enjoying the rewards. In version Dreamweaver 8, Macromedia has worked hard to give you the best tools to use these advanced design features.

Chapter 6

Coming to the HTML Table

· ·

· ·

Many people find the limitations of basic HTML frustrating. Professional designers get especially annoyed when they discover that they don't have the design control they're used to in print — they can't align elements as precisely as they want, can't layer images so they overlap, or can't adjust the line spacing in text.

Although more recent developments in CSS and layers provide far better design control than the early days of HTML, you still can't do everything you can do in print. Worse yet, you risk losing some of your audience when you use the latest CSS and layer options because, as you discover in the sidebar "Choosing between tables and layers," not everyone on the Internet uses the latest browser.

For this reason, HTML tables have long been the most common way to work around these limitations because using tables make it possible to create complex designs without sacrificing audience. That's changing as more and more people are equipped with browsers that can handle CSS and layers, but today many people still use tables to do Web-page design.

This chapter helps you appreciate how tables work for layout and what you can do with them that you can't do with basic HTML formatting. If you have ever used a desktop publishing program, such as QuarkXPress or Adobe InDesign, you have probably used text and image boxes to lay out pages. Layers work almost exactly like text boxes in a page-design program — tables achieve a similar effect, but with a little more effort. With tables, you place images and text in table cells and, by merging and splitting cells, you can create almost any page design you could want. For example, you can use a table to align two columns of text side by side with a headline across the top like the format you might see in a newspaper. Because you can make the borders of a table invisible, you can prevent the table itself from displaying. You still don't get the design control you're used to in a desktop publishing program, but with a little ingenuity, you can create complex page designs despite the limitations.

This chapter is designed to show you how to create HTML tables for everything from columnar data to complex page designs. Tables are a bit complicated to create and not as precise as you might like them to be, but Dreamweaver has a number of tools that make creating tables easier.

Creating Tables in Layout Mode

Tables are made up of three basic elements: rows, columns, and cells. If you have ever worked with a spreadsheet program, you're probably familiar with what tables are all about. Tables in HTML differ from spreadsheet tables mainly in that they're used for more complex alignment of data, which requires lots of merging and splitting cells. Back in the days when you had to design Web pages in raw HTML code by hand, even simple tables were difficult to create. The code behind an HTML table is a complex series of <TR> and <TD> tags that indicate table rows and table data cells. Figuring out how to type those tags so that they create a series of little boxes on a Web page was never an intuitive process. If you wanted to merge or split cells to create rows or columns with varying amount of cells, you faced a truly complex challenge.

Thank the cybergods that you have Dreamweaver to make this process easy. Using Dreamweaver, you can modify both the appearance and the structure of a table by simply clicking and dragging its edges. You can add any type of content to a cell, such as images, text, and multimedia files — even a smaller table. Using the Properties inspector, you can easily merge and split cells, add color to the background or border, and change the vertical and horizontal alignment of elements within a cell. And, you can easily alter your table if you change your mind about how you want the table to look after you have built it.

The easiest way to work with tables in Dreamweaver is to switch to Layout mode and use the special Layout Cell and Layout Table tools described in the following steps. With these tools, available only in Layout mode, Dreamweaver makes table creation much more intuitive. You can even switch between the two modes, Standard and Layout, to take advantage of all Dreamweaver's table features.

Layout mode provides a special view of your page elements designed to assist in the construction and editing of tables. In this mode, you can *draw* cells anywhere on a page and then drag the edges of a table to change its size. Figures 6-1 and 6-2 show the same table in Layout mode and Standard mode. You can tell the difference in modes by the way the table displays in Dreamweaver or by checking the Layout Mode and Standard Mode icons on the Layout Insert bar at the top of the work area.

Choosing between tables and layers

More and more pages on the Web are designed with layers, and you can expect to see that trend continue. As Internet users upgrade their browsers and newer browsers support layers better and better, their advantages are quickly outweighing the limitations.

Layers are much easier to control than tables, especially in Dreamweaver where you can simply click and drag to place them wherever you want on a page. You can put any element in a layer, including images, text, and multimedia files. You can even stack layers on top of each other, and you get down-to-the-pixel design control, which is far better than what you get with tables.

So why doesn't everyone use layers? Because if your visitors use older browsers (Netscape or Internet Explorer 4.0 and earlier) layers won't display in their browsers, meaning any text or images you place in a layer do not appear as you intended. Even newer browsers aren't always consistent about how they display layers, so some of your visitors may have unpredictable results, such as elements where you didn't intend them or misalignment of text and images. Thus, what you gain in design control with layers, you may lose twice over for someone using an old browser. For this reason, some designers still prefer tables, and they continue to be an important design tool on the Web.

Ultimately, you have to base your decision on whether to use layers or tables on what you know about your audience. Depending on your server, you may be able to check the log statistics and see what versions of browsers your visitors use (your service provider or system administrator may be able to give you this information). On many major sites, less than 3 percent of visitors are still using browser versions older than 4.0; but your audience may be different, and you have to decide what percentage of visitors you're willing to give up to gain the advantage of using layers.

If your goal is to have decent design control and the *most* universally recognized Web pages, tables are your safest option. If your goal is to design the most advanced site possible, then you should move on to CSS and layers, covered in Chapters 8 and 9. If you want the best of both worlds, design a page that uses both layers and tables to achieve the greatest design control yet still have a page that degrades gracefully for older browsers.

You have one other option in Dreamweaver. You can create your page design using layers and then use Dreamweaver's automated Layers to Tables conversion option to create a second set of pages with tables. Then you can add a behavior (also covered in Chapter 9) to your site that determines what browser version each of your visitors is using and directs each one to the appropriate page. This is a pretty cool trick, but you should know that the conversion process is not a perfect science (because you can do things with layers that you can't do with tables), and you add a lot more work to your site development and maintenance.

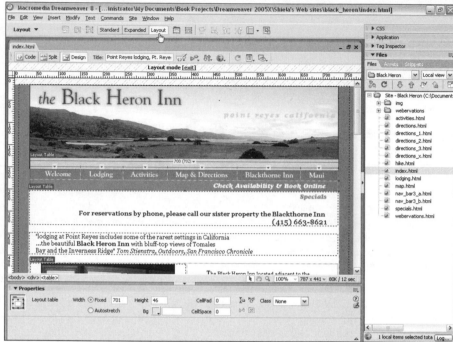

Figure 6-1:
Table Layout mode enables you to create tables and cells in Dreamweaver with drag-and-drop ease.

Figure 6-2:
Notice that the Properties inspector provides more table editing options in Standard mode. You can create and edit tables in either mode and even switch back and forth between them.

These steps show how to create a table in Layout mode with a long cell across the top and two smaller cells below it (like the table shown in Figures 6-1 and 6-2):

1. **Create a new HTML page (or open an existing page).**

   To create a new page, choose File⇨New and then select Blank Page from the Category list and HTML from the Basic Page list.

2. **Switch to Layout mode by choosing View⇨Table Mode⇨Layout Mode.**

   The Table layout options become visible on the Layout Insert bar at the top of the screen, as shown in Figures 6-1 and 6-2.

   You can also switch to Layout mode using the Layout Insert bar, available from the Insert bar drop-down list at the top of the screen.

   When you switch to Layout mode, you may see a message describing how to use the Layout Table and Layout Cell buttons when you first select this option. The message has some useful tips, but if you click the Don't Show Me This Message Again check box, you can avoid seeing it the next time. Click OK to close it.

3. **Click the Draw Layout Cell button, located on the Layout Insert bar.**

   The cursor changes to a crosshair when you move the mouse over the document area, indicating that you're ready to draw a table cell.

4. **With the mouse pointer on the document, click and drag to draw a rectangular shape anywhere on the page for your first table cell (see Figure 6-3).**

   The cell is drawn, and its surrounding table structure is automatically generated. A grid representing the table structure and other table cells appears.

5. **Draw another cell anywhere on the page by clicking the same Draw Layout Cell button again and then clicking and dragging to create the new cell.**

   Again, other cells are automatically generated to position the new cell where you have drawn it. You can draw as many new cells as you want.

   To continue drawing cells without having to go back each time and re-select the Draw Layout Cell tool, press the Ctrl key (⌘ on Mac) while you draw cells to retain the tool.

6. **Click to select any of the cells on the page and enter text, an image, or any other element.**

   You can enter anything in a table cell that you can enter on a Web page.

Figure 6-3:
When you
use Layout
mode to
draw a table
cell, such as
the cell
highlighted
in this
figure, the
table
structure
and
additional
cells are
auto-
matically
generated
around it.

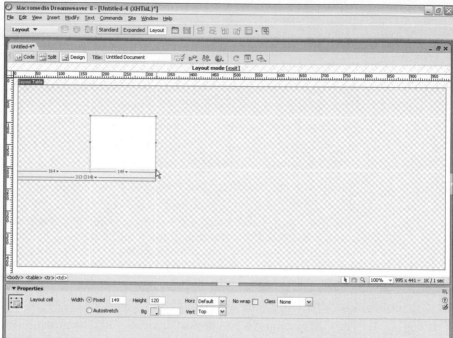

7. Click to select the border of any cell and drag to move it to a new location. To resize a cell, click one of the small boxes at the corners or middle of each table side and drag to enlarge or reduce the cell.

Depending on where you started drawing table cells, Dreamweaver may create table cells around the cells you created to maintain their positions on the page. For example, in the table shown in Figure 6-3, although I have one new cell, Dreamweaver fills in the gaps by automatically creating more cells.

A table's default position is the upper-left corner of a page, so in order to maintain the position of the cell I drew, Dreamweaver had to create additional cells to the top and left of the cell.

HTML doesn't allow you to place things anywhere on a page unless you use table cells (or layers) to control their placement. Empty cells that Dreamweaver creates to fill space in a table merely act as *spacer cells* and don't display in the browser as long as the table border is set to 0. In this way, a table creates the illusion that page elements can be positioned independently on any part of the page.

Designers often wonder how wide to make a table. My best advice is to design your pages for an 800 x 600 screen resolution because that's the most common size in use on the Web (believe it or not, a lot of people still have only 15-inch monitors). If you're creating a table that you want to cover the entire display area, a safe bet is to make your table 740 to 760 pixels wide and center it in the middle of the page. That leaves a little room on each side to prevent sideways scrollbars from appearing.

Editing Tables in Layout Mode

One wonderful advantage of working with tables in Layout mode is that you can use the layout grid to edit, move, and resize any of the rows, columns, and cells in the table. This capability enables you to use the grid as a true design guide for creating any kind of layout you want.

Tables are much easier to edit in Layout mode because you can click and drag to create cells wherever you want on the page and Dreamweaver automatically fills in the rest of the table needed to position the cells for you. That means you don't have to manually create spacer cells or do lots of merging or splitting to get cells where you want them on a page. This feature is still not as precise as layers, but it comes close.

You also have the flexibility to create *nested* tables (tables drawn within tables) for even more control over your layout. To create a nested table, simply click the Draw Layout Table button (available on the Layout Insert bar at the top of the work area) and begin drawing a new table inside an existing table cell. For more information on nested tables, see the section "Using nested tables: Tables within tables," later in this chapter.

Using Expanded Table mode to select sells

A third option for table editing is Expanded Table mode. To access this view, choose View⇨Table Mode⇨Expanded Tables Mode. This view makes selecting inside and around tables easier (without this option, it can be tricky to select specific cells within a table, especially if you're not really adept with your mouse). If you're in a hurry or working on lots of cells, this view makes it a lot easier to select and adjust table elements.

Changing Table Options in Standard Mode

Layout mode works best for creating and editing the overall *structure* of your table. When you're ready to start editing the *contents* of the table and its individual cells, you may prefer Standard mode because the Properties inspector provides more editing options in this mode. Using Layout mode, you can change some table attributes, but by using Standard mode, you can change all HTML table attributes, including the number of rows and columns as well as height, width, border size, and spacing.

When you select a table or cell, the attributes display in the Properties inspector, at the bottom of the work area. Click the border of any table to select it, and the Properties inspector displays the table options shown in Figure 6-4. To view all the options, click the expander arrow in the lower-right corner of the Properties inspector.

If you're having trouble selecting the table (sometimes selecting the entire table and not just an individual cell is tricky), simply place your cursor anywhere inside the table and choose Modify➪Table➪Select Table.

Figure 6-4:
The Properties inspector provides access to the attributes for a selected table.

The Properties inspector gives you access to the following table options for customizing the appearance of your table:

- ✔ **Table Id:** Provides a text area where you can enter a name or table.

- ✔ **Rows:** Displays the number of rows in the table. You can alter the size of the table by changing the number. Be careful, though: If you enter a smaller number, Dreamweaver deletes the bottom rows — contents and all.

✔ **Columns:** Displays the number of columns in the table. You can alter the size of the table by changing the number. Again, if you enter a smaller number, Dreamweaver deletes the columns on the right side of the table — contents and all.

✔ **W (Width):** Displays the width of the table. You can alter the width by changing the number. You can specify the width as a percentage or a value in pixels. Values expressed as a percentage increase or decrease the table's size relative to the size of the user's browser window.

✔ **H (Height):** Displays the height of the table. You can alter the height by changing the number. You can specify the height as a percentage or a value in pixels. Values expressed as a percentage increase or decrease the table's size relative to the size of the user's browser window. This table attribute is recognized only by version 4.0 browsers and above.

Table dimensions expressed as a percentage enable you to create a table that changes in size as the browser window is resized. For example, if you want a table to always take up 75 percent of the browser window, no matter how big the user's monitor or display area, set the size as a percentage. If you want a table to always be the same size — that is, to remain the same size regardless of the browser window size — choose pixels rather than percentages for your table dimensions.

✔ **CellPad:** Specifies the space between the contents of a cell and its border.

✔ **CellSpace:** Specifies the space between table cells.

✔ **Align:** Controls the alignment of the table. Options are left, right, and center.

✔ **Border:** Controls the size of the border around the table. The larger the number, the thicker the border. If you want the border to be invisible, set the border to 0.

✔ **Class:** Provides easy access to style sheet options. (See Chapter 9 for more on CSS.)

✔ **Clear and Convert:** The icons in the lower-left area of the Properties inspector (click the expander arrow in the lower-right corner to view them) provide these formatting options:

  • **Clear Row Heights** and **Clear Column Widths** enable you to remove all height and width values at one time.

  • **Convert Table Heights to Pixels** and **Convert Table Heights to Percents,** and **Convert Table Widths to Pixels** and **Convert Table Widths to Percents** enable you to automatically change Height and Width settings from percentages to pixels. Pixels specify a fixed width; a percent setting means the browser automatically adjusts the specified percentage of the browser display area.

✔ **Bg Color:** Controls the background color. Click the color square next to this label to open the color palette. Click to select a color from the box or click the color wheel at the top-right corner to choose any color. Also note that when you click the color square, the cursor changes to an eye-dropper, enabling you to pick up a color by clicking anywhere on the page. You can apply this option to a single cell by placing your cursor in a particular cell before specifying the color or to the entire table by selecting the table.

✔ **Bg Image:** Enables you to select a background image. Specify the file-name or click the folder icon to locate the image. You can apply this option to a single cell or to the entire table. Note that because many older browsers don't support background images in single cells, the image may not display for all viewers.

✔ **Brdr Color:** Controls the border color of the entire table. Click the color square next to this label and select a color from the box that appears, or use the color wheel at the top-right corner to choose any color. Also note that when you click the color square, the cursor changes to an eye-dropper, enabling you to pick up a color by clicking anywhere on the page.

You can also apply formatting options and change the attributes of any ele-ments, such as text, images, and multimedia files, that you have placed within a table cell. To do so, click to select the element and then use the options in the Properties inspector to make any desired changes, just as you would if the element were not in a table cell.

Merging and splitting table cells

Sometimes, the easiest way to modify the number of cells in a table is to *merge* cells (combine two or more cells into one) or *split* cells (split one cell into two or more rows or columns). Using this technique, you can vary the space in table sections and customize their structures. For example, you may want a long cell space across the top of your table for a banner and then mul-tiple cells underneath it so that you can control the spacing between columns of text or images. The following two sets of steps show you how to merge and split cells in a table.

You can merge and split cells only in Standard mode.

To merge cells, create a new HTML page and follow these steps:

1. **Choose Insert⇨Table and create a table with four rows and four columns, a 75 percent width, and a border of 1. Skip header and accessibility. Click OK, and the table appears on the page.**

2. **Highlight two or more adjacent cells by clicking and dragging the mouse from the first cell to the last.**

You can merge only cells that are adjacent to one another and in the same row or column.

3. **Click the Merge Selected Cells icon in the lower-left region of the Properties inspector to merge the selected cells into a single cell.**

   The cells are merged into a single cell by using the Colspan or Rowspan attributes. These HTML attributes make a single cell merge with adjacent cells by spanning extra rows or columns in the table.

To split a cell, follow these steps:

1. **Click to place the cursor inside the cell you want to split.**

2. **Click the Split Selected Cell icon in the lower-left region of the Properties inspector.**

   The Split Cell dialog box appears.

3. **Select Rows or Columns in the dialog box, depending on how you want to divide the cell.**

   You can split a cell into however many new rows or columns you want.

4. **Type the number of rows or columns you want to create.**

   The selected cell is split into the number of rows or columns you entered.

Controlling cell options

In addition to changing table options, you can control options for individual cells within a table. When you select a cell, which you do by clicking the cursor anywhere inside the cell area, the Properties inspector changes to display the individual properties for that cell (see Figure 6-5). The Properties inspector is where you find the controls to merge and split cells, as well as to change the alignment of the contents of a particular cell.

Make sure the table fits the contents

Be aware that table cells automatically adjust to accommodate whatever you insert into them. For example, if you create a cell that is 100 pixels wide and then insert a 300-pixel-wide image, the table cell has to adjust to fit the image. This can cause problems if the overall size of the table is not set large enough to accommodate all the objects within the table cells. As you build your tables, be aware of the size of the images and multimedia files you are inserting into cells or you may have unpredictable results. For example, if you set a table to a total width of 400 pixels and then insert 600 pixels worth of images, the table may not display the same in all browsers.

Figure 6-5:
When you
select an
individual
cell, the
Properties
inspector
provides
access to
attributes
for the
selected
cell within a
table.

You can also change multiple cells at the same time. For example, suppose that you want to have some, but not all, the cells in your table take on a certain color background and style of text. You can apply the same properties to multiple cells by selecting more than one cell at a time. To select adjacent cells, press the Shift key while clicking to select cells. To select multiple cells that are not adjacent, press the Ctrl key (the ⌘ key on the Mac) and click each cell you want to select. Any properties you change in the Properties inspector apply to all selected cells.

If you're having trouble selecting an individual cell because it contains an image, click the image and then use either the ← or → key on your keyboard to move the cursor and deselect the image, which activates the Properties inspector and displays the options for that cell.

When one or more cells are selected (they have to be adjacent for this to work), the top half of the Properties inspector controls the formatting of text and URLs within the table cells. The lower half of the Properties inspector provides these table cell attribute options (refer to Figure 6-5):

- **Merge Cells:** Merges two or more cells. To merge cells, you must first select two or more cells by clicking and dragging or by pressing either the Shift or Ctrl key while selecting multiple cells.

- **Split Cells:** Splits one cell into two. When you select this option, a dialog box lets you specify whether you want to split the row (you split the cell horizontally) or the column (you split the cell vertically). You can then specify the number of columns or rows, which controls how many times the cell divides. Note that you can apply the Split Cell option to only one cell at a time.

- **Horz:** Controls the horizontal alignment of the cell contents.

- **Vert:** Controls the vertical alignment of the cell contents.

- **W:** Controls the width of the cell.

- **H:** Controls the height of the cell.

- **No Wrap:** Prevents word wrapping within the cell. The cell widens to accommodate all text as you type or paste it into a cell. (Normally, the excess text just moves down to the next line and increases the height of the cell.)

- **Header:** Formats a cell's contents by using a Header style, which makes the text bold and centered by default.

- **Bg (Image):** Allows you to specify a background image for the cell.

- **Bg (Color):** Allows you to specify a background color for the cell.

- **Brdr (Color):** Allows you to change the border color of the cell.

Formatting tables with color schemes

One of the best reasons for using tables is to present lots of data in a clear and structured way. Tables accomplish this task because the use of rows and columns allows the reader to follow along easily when lots of data is represented. One way to make your data even more presentable and attractive is to colorize the rows and columns in the table. In the preceding section, you find out how to change the attributes of individual cells. This section explains how to use the Format Table feature to select predefined table formats with color schemes designed to enhance your presentation. Professional designers created these color schemes, so you can be sure that they look good on your Web page.

To use the Format Table feature, open an existing document or create a new HTML page, insert a simple table of any size, and follow these steps:

1. **Select an existing table in the document.**

2. **Make sure that you're in Standard mode. (Choose View⇨Table Mode⇨ Standard Mode.)**

3. **Choose Commands⇨Format Table.**

   The Format Table dialog box appears, as shown in Figure 6-6.

4. **Select one of the schemes by scrolling the list or modify any of the parameters to create your own scheme.**

5. **Click OK.**

   The color scheme applies to the table.

Figure 6-6:
Figure 6-6:
The Dream-
weaver
Format
Table
dialog box
provides a
variety of
previously
created
color
schemes to
enhance the
look of your
tables.

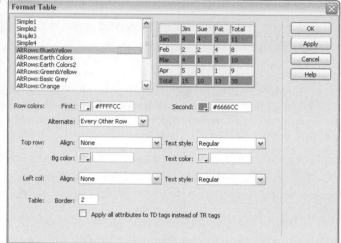

You can also modify any of the attributes in the Format Table dialog box to create your own color schemes.

Using low-contrast color schemes in tables is considered the most effective way to present content. (Just look at the Intuit Quicken software, E-Trade, and Amazon for examples of real-life illustrations.) High-contrast colors in tables are usually reserved for site menus and submenus or other elements you want to call more attention to.

Formatting multiple columns in a table

When you're working with lots of cells in a table, you may want to format multiple cells in the same way. Dreamweaver makes that task easy, whether you want to align numbers, make the headings bold, or change the color scheme. But before you start planning how to line up all your numbers perfectly, be aware that you don't have as much control in HTML as you have in a program such as Excel, where you can align numbers to the decimal point. You can, however, align the content of columns to the left, right, or center. Thus, if you use the same number of digits after the decimal point in all your numbers, you can get them to line up. For example, if one price is $12.99 and another is $14, express it as $14.00; then, when you right-align, the numbers line up properly. (If your columns are still not lining up the way you want them to, consider using a monospace font, which lines up better.)

The steps in this section explain how to create a table in Standard mode and align all the data cells to the right so that the numbers or other content align consistently. You can also use these steps to align the contents of table cells to the left or center and to apply other formatting options, such as bold or italic. In these steps, I insert the data into the table after I create the table in Dreamweaver.

If you want to import data from a table you have created in a program such as Word or Excel, see the section, "Importing Table Data from Other Programs," later in this chapter. If you're working with a table that already has data in it and just want to format or align the cells, go directly to Step 7.

If you're starting from scratch, create a new, blank HTML page and follow these steps from the beginning:

1. **Make sure that you're in Standard mode. (Choose View⇨Table Mode⇨ Standard Mode.)**

2. **Click to place the cursor where you want to create a table.**

   In Standard mode, tables are automatically created in the top, left area of the page, unless you insert them after other content. If you want a columnar table somewhere else on the page, consider creating a table in Layout mode as described earlier in the chapter and then inserting a nested table inside a cell for your columnar data.

3. **Click the Insert Table icon on the Insert bar.**

   Alternatively, you can choose Insert⇨Table. The Insert Table dialog box appears.

4. **In the appropriate boxes, type the number of columns and rows you want to include in your table.**

   Remember you can always add or remove cells later using the Properties inspector.

5. **Specify the width, border, cell padding, and cell spacing; then click OK.**

   The table automatically appears on the page.

6. **Click to place the cursor in a cell, and then type the data you want in that cell. Repeat for each cell.**

   Alternatively, you can use Edit⇨Paste Special to insert columnar data from another program, such as Excel.

7. **Select the column or row for which you want to change the alignment.**

   Place the cursor in the first cell in the column or row you want to align; then click and drag your mouse to highlight the other columns or rows that you want to change.

8. **Right-click (Windows) or Ctrl+click (Mac) in any cell in the highlighted column or row.**

   A pop-up menu appears, as shown in Figure 6-7. Alternatively, you can use the Properties inspector to change selected items.

9. **From the pop-up menu, choose Align and then choose Left, Center, Right, or Justify from the submenu.**

   This option enables you to change the alignment of all highlighted cells in the column or row at one time. If you're working with financial data, choose Align⇨Right, which produces the best alignment for numbers. You can also apply other formatting options, such as bold or italic, to selected cells and their contents by choosing the option from the pop-up menu or the Properties inspector.

If you want to format one cell in a column or row differently from the others, click to place the cursor in just that cell and then click one of the formatting options in the Properties inspector. You can also choose to align multiple cells that aren't *contiguous* (they don't touch each other) by pressing and holding the Ctrl key in Windows while you click the cells you want to select. On the Mac, you press and hold the Command key (⌘) while you click to select particular cells. Any options you change on the pop-up menu or in the Table Properties inspector apply to all selected cells.

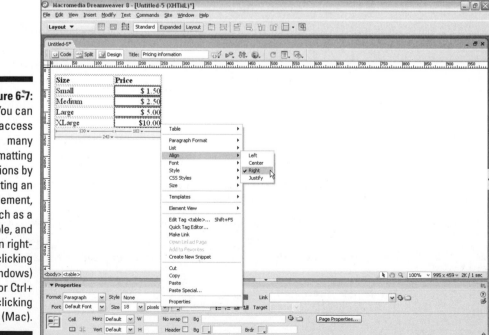

Figure 6-7:
You can access many formatting options by selecting an element, such as a table, and then right-clicking (Windows) or Ctrl+clicking (Mac).

Sorting Table Data

When you're working with lots of columnar data, you want to be able to sort that data, just as you do in a spreadsheet program, such as Excel. In this newest version of Dreamweaver, you can now sort data even after it's formatted in HTML (something you couldn't easily do before). You still don't have as many options as you do in Excel. For example, you can't sort different rows individually, but you can sort an entire table based on any row you specify.

To use the Sort Table Data feature, create a new, blank HTML page, add a table with several rows and columns, and add some content (I explain how in the preceding section). You may also open an existing page with a table of columnar data. Then, follow these steps:

1. **Select the table you want to sort.**

   Place the cursor in any cell of the table you want to sort.

2. **Make sure that you're in Standard mode. (Choose View⇨Table Mode⇨ Standard Mode.)**

3. **Choose Commands⇨Sort Table.**

   The Sort Table dialog box appears, as shown in Figure 6-8.

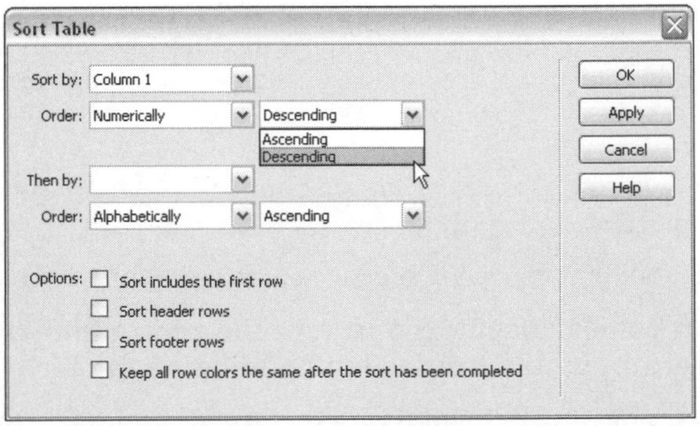

Figure 6-8: You can use the Dreamweaver Sort Table Data feature to sort cell contents alphabetically or numerically, even after they're formatted in HTML.

4. **Specify which column you want to sort by; then, choose Alphabetically or Numerically, and Ascending or Descending.**

   You can set up one or two sorts to happen simultaneously and opt whether to include the first row and whether to keep the TR (Table Row) attributes with a sorted row.

5. **Click OK.**

   The selected cells are sorted, just like they are in a program such as Microsoft Excel. (Pretty cool, huh?)

Importing Table Data from Other Programs

Manually converting financial data or other spreadsheet information can be tedious. Fortunately, Dreamweaver includes a special feature that enables you to insert table data created in other applications, such as Microsoft Word or Excel. To use this feature, the table data must be saved from the other program in a *delimited* format, which means that the columns of data are separated by either tabs, commas, colons, semicolons, or another type of delimiter. Most spreadsheet and database applications, as well as Microsoft Word, enable you to save data in a delimited format, often called CSV because that's the file extension they're given. Consult the documentation for the application you're using to find out how. After the data is saved in a delimited format, you can import it into Dreamweaver.

To import table data into Dreamweaver after it has been saved in a delimited format in its native application, create a new, blank HTML page and follow these steps:

1. **Choose File⇨Import⇨Tabular Data or choose Insert⇨Table Objects⇨ Import Tabular Data.**

   The Import Tabular Data dialog box appears (see Figure 6-9).

2. **In the Import Tabular Data text box, type the name of the file you want to import or use the Browse button to locate the file.**

3. **From the Delimiter drop-down list, select the delimiter format you used when you saved your file in the other application.**

   The delimiter options are Tab, Comma, Semicolon, Colon, and Other. You should have made this choice when you exported the data from the original program in which you created it, such as Excel. If you don't remember what you chose, you can always go back and do it again. You must select the correct option in order for your data to import correctly.

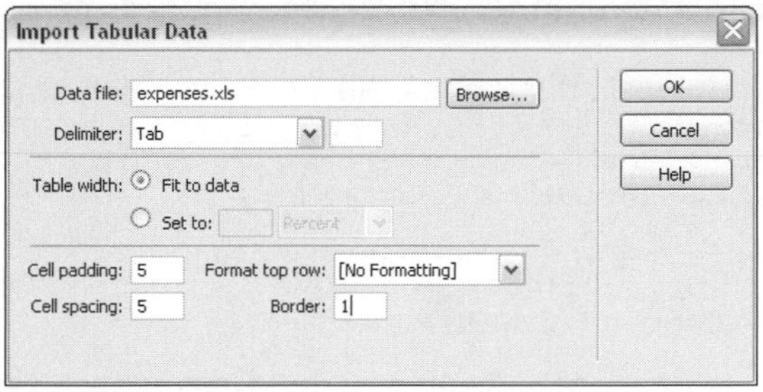

Figure 6-9:
You can
import
tabular data
into Dream-
weaver
from other
programs,
such as
Excel.

Import Tabular Data

Data file: expenses.xls   [Browse...]   [OK]

Delimiter: [Tab ▾] [ ]   [Cancel]

Table width: ◉ Fit to data   [Help]
         ○ Set to: [ ] [Percent ▾]

Cell padding: [5]   Format top row: [No Formatting] ▾

Cell spacing: [5]   Border: [1]

4. **Select the table width.**

   If you choose Fit to Data, Dreamweaver automatically creates the table to fit the data being imported. If you choose Set, you must specify a percent or pixel size.

5. **Specify the cell padding and cell spacing only if you want extra space around the data in the table to be created.**

6. **Choose an option from the Format Top Row option only if you want to format the data in the top row of the table.**

   Your options are bold, italic, or bold italic.

7. **Specify the border size.**

   The default is 1, which puts a small border around the table. Choose 0 if you don't want the border to be visible. Choose a larger number if you want a thicker border.

8. **Click OK to automatically create a table with the imported data.**

Dreamweaver also enables you to export data from a table into a delimited format. This capability is useful if you want to export data from a Web page so that you can import it into another program, such as Word or Excel, or into a database program, such as FileMaker or Access. To export data from Dreamweaver, place the cursor anywhere in the table and choose File⇨ Export⇨Table. In the Export Table dialog box, choose from the options on the Delimiter drop-down list (you can choose Tab, Space, Comma, Semicolon, or Colon). From the Line Breaks drop-down list, specify the operating system (you can choose Windows, Mac, or Unix).

Using Tables for Spacing and Alignment

As you get more adept at creating Web pages, you may find that HTML tables are a crucial part of creating almost any design that requires more than basic alignment of elements on a page. Using tables, you can get around many of the limitations of basic HTML and accomplish some of these design feats:

- Evenly spaced graphical bullets (little GIF files that can take the place of bullets) next to text

- Text boxes and fields properly aligned in a form

- Images placed wherever you want them on a page

- Columns of text that don't span an entire page

- Myriad intricate layouts that are impossible to accomplish without using tables or layers (for more on layers, see Chapter 9)

In the rest of this chapter, I show you how to use tables to create a variety of page designs, including a few of the ones I just listed.

When you use a table for design control, turn off the border so that it's not visible in the design. You do that by typing **0** (zero) in the Border text box in the Properties inspector with the table selected.

Using tables to design forms

Creating text boxes and drop-down lists for HTML forms is easy in Dreamweaver, but if you want all the fields to line up well, you may want to use tables to help with the formatting. In Chapter 12, you find step-by-step instructions for creating a variety of forms; for now, I assume that you have already created a form and want to align the text boxes evenly. I use a simple form with just a few questions as an example, but you can use this technique to align any form elements.

To use a table to align form elements, such as text boxes, evenly on your page, follow these steps:

1. **Open a page that has an HTML form on it (or create a new HTML form).**

   See Chapter 13 to find out how to create HTML forms.

2. **Click to place the cursor where you want to start formatting your form.**

3. **Choose Insert⇨Table.**

   The Insert Table dialog box appears.

4. **Type the number of columns and rows you want in your table.**

   I set the table to three rows and two columns.

5. **Set the width to whatever is most appropriate for your design and click OK.**

   Remember, up to 760 pixels is a good width if you are designing for an 800 by 600 screen resolution, which many designers consider the best size to reach the most users.

6. **Enter** 0 **for the border.**

   When you set the border to 0, the edges of your table change from solid lines to dotted lines so that you can still see where the borders are while you're working in Dreamweaver. When you view the page in a browser, as shown in Figure 6-10, the border of the table is invisible.

7. **Click OK.**

   The table automatically appears on the page.

8. **You need to copy the data from your form into the table. Using the Cut and Paste commands from the Edit menu, cut the text preceding the form's first text field and paste it into the cell in the upper-left corner of the table.**

   Alternatively, you can select the text and then click and drag it into each table cell.

   In my example in Figure 6-11, I cut the words *Who are you?* and pasted them into the first table cell.

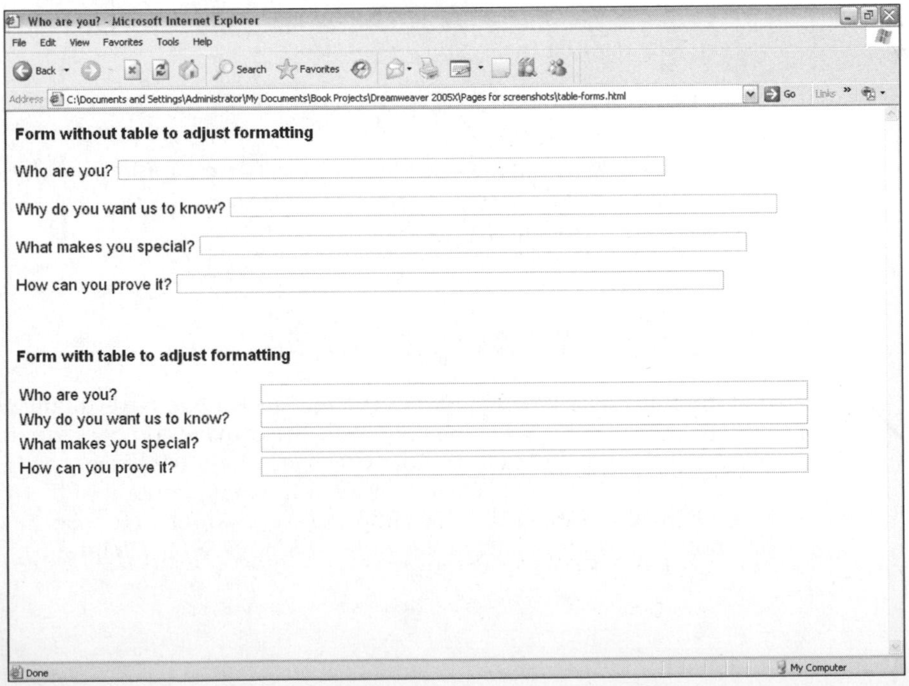

Figure 6-10:
When the form fields in the table display in the browser, they line up evenly; with the border set to 0 you can't even tell it's there.

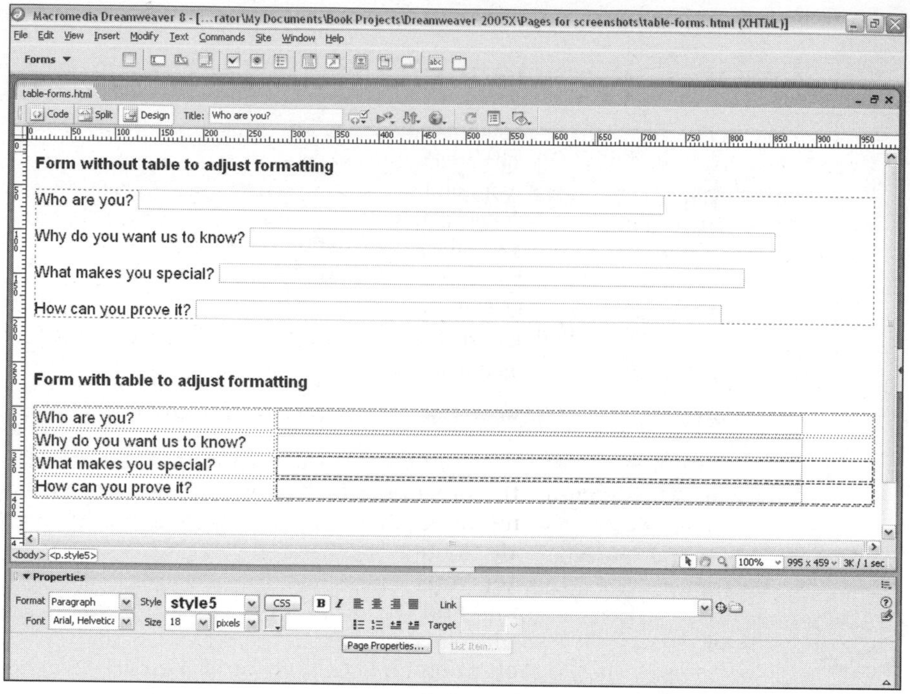

Figure 6-11:
You can use
a table to
better align
form data
and
elements.

9. **Select the first text field (the empty box where users type their responses) and copy and paste (or click and drag) the field into the desired cell of the table.**

10. **Repeat Steps 8 and 9 until you have moved all form elements into table cells.**

11. **Click the vertical column divider line between the first and second columns and drag it to the left or right to create the alignment you want for your form.**

Aligning a navigation bar

A common element on Web pages is a *navigation bar,* a row of images or text with links to the main sections of a Web site. Navigation bars are usually placed at the top, bottom, or side of a page, where users can easily access them but where they're out of the way of the main content of the page. Designers sometimes use HTML frames (see Chapter 7) to insert a navigation bar, but most prefer using tables or layers (covered in Chapter 9).

Vertical alignment solves common problem

If you're having trouble getting the contents of adjacent cells to line up with each other, setting Vertical alignment to Top may solve your problem. A common frustration when you're building tables is that you have two or more rows side by side with text in one and images in the another and you want the top of the image and the top of the text to line up. Often they don't because they are different lengths, and the table is trying to adjust the contents to best use the space within their respective cells. The solution is simple: Select all the cells you want to align, and in the Properties inspector, change Vertical alignment to Top. Seemingly like magic, all the content jumps right to the top of the cells and lines up perfectly. This is such a common problem, I routinely set the Vertical alignment of table cells to Top.

In the last example in the preceding section, you see how to create a table in Standard mode by using the regular table tools. In this section, you discover how to use Layout mode to build a table, similar to the way you do at the beginning of this chapter. You can use either mode for creating the table featured in this section, but I find Layout mode is easier to use because you can simply drag cells into place instead of having to calculate where to merge and split cells to create such a complex design. To use Layout mode to create a table that positions a navigation bar across the top of a Web page, like the one featured in Figure 6-12, follow these steps:

1. **Switch to Layout mode by choosing Layout from the drop-down list on the Insert bar and clicking the Layout icon, or choose View⇨Table Mode⇨Layout Mode.**

   The table layout options become visible on the Layout Insert bar.

2. **Select the Draw Layout Table button from the Layout Insert bar, and create a table by clicking in the upper-left region of the display area and dragging to fill the entire page.**

3. **Click the Draw Layout Cell button on the Layout Insert bar to select the tool for drawing table cells.**

   Visualizing how you want your table to look is helpful before you start drawing cells in the next step. The structure is dictated by the shape and size of your navigation bar and other elements that need to be on the page. (Figure 6-12 shows an example of a common design with the navigation bar across the top of the page, just below a banner with the site's logo.)

4. **Click and drag your mouse on the page to draw the size and shape of each of the cells you need to contain your navigation bar and other page elements.**

   Figure 6-12 shows a page that was created using multiple tables. Notice that the table that holds the navigation elements includes a separate cell for each graphic in the navigation row.

To continue drawing cells without having to go back each time and re-select the Draw Layout Cell tool, press the Ctrl key (⌘ on Mac) to retain the tool while you draw cells.

5. **When you're done creating all the cells you want in the table, click the Standard Mode icon on the Layout Insert bar to return to Standard mode.**

6. **Click to place the cursor in the table cell in which you want to insert a navigation bar image and choose Insert⇨Image. Use the Browse button to locate the image you want to insert into the table cell.**

7. **Double-click the filename of the image.**

    The image automatically appears in the table cell. Repeat this step to insert multiple images.

    As you can see in Figure 6-12, you can insert a series of images to create a row of buttons that runs across the top of the page. Similarly, you can create a table to hold images that run down the right or left side of a page. You can also use text in place of images by simply entering the text you want in each of the table cells.

8. **Select the table and make sure that the Border option is set to 0 in the Properties inspector.**

    This step makes your table invisible so that the border doesn't display in a browser.

Figure 6-12:
Layout mode makes it easy to build a table that you can use to create almost any page design.

Using nested tables: Tables within tables

Placing tables within tables, called *nested tables,* can help you create extremely complex designs. You create nested tables by inserting a table within a cell of another table. In the days when you had to write your own code, this task was daunting. Dreamweaver now makes nesting tables easy, enabling you to create complex designs without ever looking at the HTML code.

The best Web designs communicate the information to your audience in the most elegant and understandable way and are easy to download. To make sure that your designs don't get too messy, remember these guidelines:

- ✔ A table within a table within a table is nested three levels deep. Anything more than that gets hairy.

- ✔ Pages that use nested tables take longer to download because browsers have to interpret each table individually before rendering the page. For some designs, the slightly longer download time is worth it, but in most cases you're better off adding or merging cells in one table, as I explain in the section "Merging and splitting table cells," earlier in this chapter. One situation that makes a nested table worth the added download time is when you want to place a table of financial or other data in the midst of a complex page design.

To place a table inside another table, follow these steps:

1. **Click to place the cursor where you want to create the first table.**

2. **Choose Insert⇨Table.**

   The Insert Table dialog box appears.

3. **Type the number of columns and rows you need for your design.**

4. **Set the Width option to whatever is appropriate for your design and click OK.**

   The table is automatically sized to the width you set.

5. **Click to place the cursor in the cell in which you want to place the second table.**

6. **Repeat Steps 2 through 4, specifying the number of columns and rows you want and the width of the table.**

   The new table appears inside the cell of the first table.

7. **Type the information that you want in the nested table cells as you would enter content in any other table.**

Chapter 7

Framing Your Pages

● ●

● ●

*N*o one wants to be "framed," whether that means being falsely accused of something you didn't do or trapped in the HTML frameset of a Web site with no escape. Appreciating not only the best way to create frames, but also the best way to use them to enhance site navigation is important if you don't want to leave your visitors feeling stuck in your pages.

Many experienced Web designers say you should never use frames. I take a more open approach — I don't *recommend* frames, but I think you should decide for yourself. Besides, I can think of a few instances when frames come in quite handy, such as when you want to bring in content from another Web site and still maintain your own navigation and logo. Of course, you should do this only with permission from the other site (see the sidebar later in this chapter, "Resist using frames when you link to other people's Web sites").

To help you make the most of this HTML design feature, this chapter not only covers how to build HTML framesets in Dreamweaver, but also discusses when frames are most useful and when you should avoid them. Frames add a wide range of design possibilities, but they can also create confusing navigation systems and can be very frustrating to viewers. As you go through this chapter, consider not only how to create frames, but also whether they are really the best solution for your Web site project.

Appreciating HTML Frames

Frames add innovative navigation control because they enable you to display multiple HTML pages in one browser window and control the contents of each framed area individually. Web developers commonly use frames to create a design with two or more sections within one browser window. Each section consists of a different HTML page, and you can place links in one section that, when selected, display information in another page in a different section within the same browser window.

Web pages that use frames, such as the one shown in Figure 7-1, are split into separate sections — or individual *frames*. All the frames together make up a *frameset*. Behind the scenes, each frame of the frameset is a separate HTML file, which makes a page with frames a little complicated to create, even with Dreamweaver. If you choose to create your frame files in a text editor, you have to juggle multiple pages, working on each frame one at a time, and you can see what you create only when you preview your work in a browser. The visual editor in Dreamweaver makes creating frames a lot easier because you can view all the HTML files that make up the frameset at the same time and can edit them while they display in the way in which they appear in a browser.

As a navigational feature, frames enable you to keep some information constant, while changing other information in the same browser window. For example, you can keep a list of links visible in one frame and display the information each link brings up in another frame, as the site shown in Figure 7-1 does.

Figure 7-1:
This Southwest Scenes Web site uses frames to keep navigation buttons on the left and the banner at the top, while changing the content in the main part of the page.

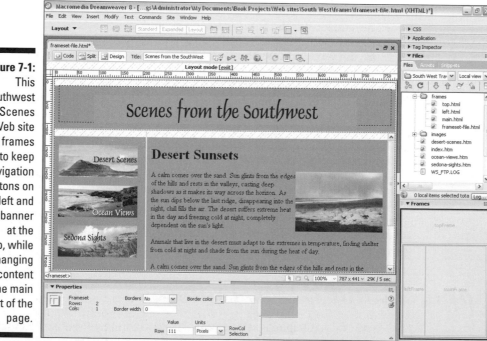

You can create as many frames as you want within a browser window. Unfortunately, some people overuse them and create designs that are so complex and broken up that they're neither aesthetically appealing nor easily navigable. Putting too many frames on one page can also make a site hard to read because the individual windows are too small. This has led many Web surfers to passionately hate frames. And some sites that rushed to implement frames when they were first introduced have since either abandoned frames or minimized their use.

Here's a list of guidelines to follow when using frames:

- ✔ **Don't use frames just for the sake of using frames.** If you have a compelling reason to use frames, then create an elegant and easy-to-follow frameset. But don't do it just because Dreamweaver makes creating them relatively easy.

- ✔ **Limit the use of frames and keep files small.** Remember that each frame you create represents another HTML file. Thus, a frameset with three frames requires a browser to fetch and display four Web pages, and that may dramatically increase download time.

- ✔ **Turn off frame borders.** Browsers that support frames also support the capability to turn off the border that divides frames in a frameset. If you turn the borders off, your pages look cleaner. Frame borders, shown in Figure 7-1, are thick and an ugly gray in color, and they can break up a nice design. You can change the color in the Properties inspector, but I still recommend that you only use them when you feel that they're absolutely necessary. I show you how to turn off frame borders in the "Changing Frame Properties" section toward the end of this chapter.

- ✔ **Don't use frames when you can use CSS or tables instead.** Tables are easier to create than frames and provide a more elegant solution to your design needs because they're less intrusive to the design. I include lots of information on creating tables in Chapter 6, and you find coverage of CSS — an increasingly popular design option — in Chapter 8.

- ✔ **Don't place frames within frames.** The windows get too darned small to be useful for much of anything, and the screen looks horribly complicated. You can also run into problems when your framed site links to another site that's displayed in your frameset. The sidebar "Resist using frames when you link to other people's Web sites" later in this chapter provides many more reasons to limit using frames inside of frames.

- ✔ **Put in alternate <NOFRAMES> content.** The number of users surfing the Web with browsers that don't support frames becomes smaller every day. Still, showing them *something* other than a blank page is a good idea. I usually put in a line that says, "This site uses frames and requires a frames-capable browser to view." <NOFRAMES> content can also be read by search engines, which may otherwise fail to catalog the content within framed pages.

Understanding How Frames Work

Frames are a bit complicated, but Dreamweaver helps make the whole process somewhat easier. When you create a Web page with frames in Dreamweaver, you need to remember that each frame area is a separate HTML file, and Dreamweaver saves each frame area as a separate page. You also want to keep track of which file displays in which of the frames so that you can aim links properly.

Figure 7-2 shows a simple frameset example with three frames, each containing a different HTML page and different text *(Page 1, Page 2,* and *Page 3)* so that I can clearly refer to them in the following numbered steps.

In addition to the files that display in each frame, you need to create a separate HTML file to generate the frameset. This page doesn't have a <BODY> tag, but it describes the frames and instructs the browser how and where to display them. This gets a little complicated, but don't worry: Dreamweaver creates the frameset HTML file for you. I just want to give you a general understanding of all the files that you're creating so that the following steps make more sense.

To help you understand how this works, take a look at the example in Figure 7-2. In this document, you see three frames, each displaying a different HTML page. The fourth HTML file that makes up the frame page *contains* the other frames but doesn't show up in the browser. This file is the frameset file, and it describes how the frames display, whether they are on the left or the right side of the page, the top or bottom, and how large they are. The frameset file also contains other information, such as the name of each frame, which is used to specify which frame a link opens into or *targets.* You find out more about linking frames in the "Setting Targets and Links in Frames" section later in this chapter.

Creating a frame in Dreamweaver

When you create a frame page in Dreamweaver, realizing that the file you are starting with is the *frameset* file is important — the file doesn't show up in the browser but merely instructs the browser how to display the rest of the frames and which pages to use as content for each frame. When you edit the *content* of any of the frames in the frameset, you do not actually edit the frameset file, but the files that populate the framed regions within the frameset. Normally you have to edit the files separately, but Dreamweaver makes designing with frames easier by letting you edit the content of each frame in the *context* of the frameset as it looks in a browser. If you can grasp this concept, you've come a long way toward understanding how frames work and how to use Dreamweaver to create and edit them. If it hasn't sunk in yet, read on and it will.

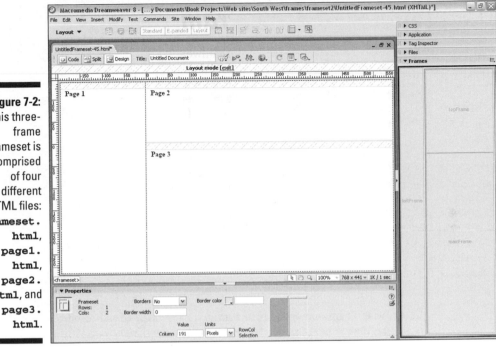

Figure 7-2:
This three-
frame
frameset is
comprised
of four
different
HTML files:
`frameset.`
`html,`
`page1.`
`html,`
`page2.`
`html,` and
`page3.`
`html.`

Creating a frame by using the Split Frame command

You can create frames in two ways in Dreamweaver. The first way is achieved by splitting a single HTML file into two sections, which then become individual frames. When you do that, Dreamweaver automatically generates an untitled page with the <FRAMESET> tag and then additional untitled pages display in each of the frames within the frameset. Suddenly, you're managing several pages, not just one. This concept is important to understand because you have to save and name each of these pages as a separate file, even though Dreamweaver makes you think you're working on only one page that's broken into sections.

Always save your HTML files first before inserting anything into them; however, the opposite is true when you work with frame files in Dreamweaver. Wait until after you create all the frames in your frameset and *then* save them one at a time; otherwise, tracking your files gets a bit too complicated and confusing. I explain more in the section, "Saving files in a frameset," later in this chapter; but first, you create a simple framed page.

To create a simple frameset in Dreamweaver, such as the one shown in Figure 7-2, follow these steps:

1. Choose File⇨New.

The New Document window opens, as shown in Figure 7-3.

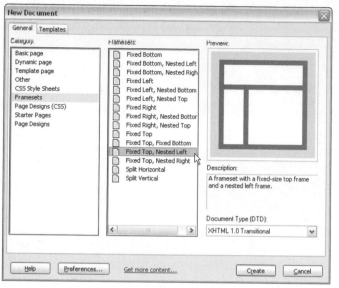

Figure 7-3:
Dreamweaver includes a long list of predefined framesets to make creating new frames easier.

2. **Choose Framesets from the Category list, and then select the Fixed Top, Nested Left option from the Framesets list.**

3. **Click the Create button.**

   The frameset automatically appears.

4. **Click and drag any of the bars dividing the frames to adjust the size of the frame area.**

5. **To edit each section of the frameset, click inside the frame that you want to work on and edit it like any other HTML page.**

   Remember, always save your files before setting links or inserting images and other files.

   You can type text, insert images, create tables, and add any other features just as you do to any other page.

   To save your files, continue with the instructions in the section "Saving files in a frameset," later in this chapter.

Creating a frame by using the Frames icon on the Layout Insert bar

Another way to create frames is with the Frames icon (which has a drop-down list), shown at the top of Figure 7-4. The Layout Insert bar (available by selecting Layout Bar from the drop-down list at the top of the work area) includes the Frames icon, which displays several predefined frames sets from a drop-down list. You can create a frameset in Dreamweaver simply by selecting any of these options from the Frames drop-down list. Figure 7-4 shows the Layout Insert bar with the Frames icon selected and an option applied to a new document from the drop-down list.

To create a framed page using the Frames icon on the Layout Insert bar, follow these steps:

1. **Choose File➪New➪Basic Page to create a new page.**

2. **From the Layout Insert bar, click the Frames icon and select the design that most closely approximates the type of frameset you want to build from the drop-down list (refer to Figure 7-4).**

   Don't worry if it isn't exactly the design you want; you can alter it later.

3. **Modify the frameset as needed.**

   You can further modify your frameset by clicking and dragging the borders of the frames to resize them.

   You can also split frames by choosing Modify➪Frameset and then choosing to split the frame left, right, up, or down.

To save your files, continue with the instructions in the next section "Saving files in a frameset."

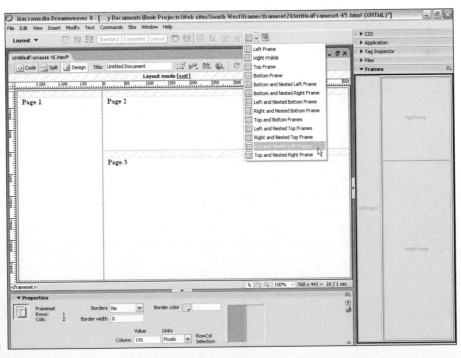

Figure 7-4:
The Layout Insert bar contains predefined framesets that you select from the drop-down list by clicking the Frames icon.

Saving files in a frameset

As I mention earlier, you shouldn't save your frameset file until *after* you add all your frames; otherwise, keeping track of your files gets very complicated. Remember, frames in HTML consist of at least two HTML files, even if it appears as if you are only working on one file.

When you are ready to save, Dreamweaver gives you multiple save options for saving all the files. You can either save everything all at once, or you can save each frame and frameset individually. The example in the previous section, "Creating a frame in Dreamweaver," is composed of four separate HTML files, and each needs to be named and saved to your hard drive. To save all the files in the frames document you create, follow these steps:

1. **Choose File⇨Save All.**

   The Save As dialog box appears, asking you to name the file and designate a folder to save it in. This is the first of several Save As dialog boxes you see (how many depends on how many frames your document contains).

2. **Enter a name for the file.**

   Dreamweaver suggests a name, but you can choose your own. The first file you save represents the *frameset* file (the file that holds all the other frames in place). You can tell this by looking at the Dreamweaver Document window behind the Save As dialog box: The entire document has a thick dotted highlight around it representing the frameset.

3. **Browse your hard drive to locate the desired folder for the HTML files and click the Save button.**

   The first frameset file saves, and a new Save As dialog box appears for the next one. For each frameset file, you need a distinct name. I like names such as `frame1.html`, `frame2.html`, or `leftframe.html`, `rightframe.html`. It doesn't matter too much, but such names can help you distinguish the frame files later. After you save all the frames, the Save As dialog box disappears.

Carefully name the files that you save in a way that helps you keep them in order and know which is which. Notice that as you are prompted to save each file, Dreamweaver indicates which frame area it is by highlighting it with a dark border on-screen behind the dialog box. You may find your task easier by choosing filenames that make sense and that help you to identify which area they represent.

After you save and name your documents the first time, choosing Save All saves any and all the files in your frameset without prompting you separately for each frame. Choosing Save All is a good way to make sure that all the pages in your frameset save whenever you edit a frames-based document.

Resist using frames when you link to other people's Web sites

I understand that most people don't want to lose viewers to another site when they create a link, but that's the nature of the Web. If your site is designed well, you shouldn't have to worry about losing people. Instead, you should show them around your informative site and then politely help guide them to other resources they may find of interest — and let them go. If you link to another site and target that link within your frames, you keep users captive and usually leave them annoyed with you for taking up valuable browser space and making it harder to navigate the site they've followed your link to visit. By displaying content from other sites within one or more of the frames in your site, you risk doing yourself far more harm than good.

If you insist on using frames when you link to another site, do so discretely by placing a small, narrow frame across the bottom of the screen or the left side — not a wide band across the top, and certainly not more than one frame that still contains information from your site. Not only is this rude and ugly, but some people have been sued by sites who charged that using frames when they linked misled visitors into thinking the content belonged to them when it didn't.

Another reason not to use frames when you link to someone else's site is that other sites use frames, too. If you link a site that uses frames into a site that uses frames, you quickly create a mess of frames within frames that makes navigation confusing at best. Not everyone knows you can get out of frames by right-clicking a link in Windows or clicking and holding a link on a Mac and choosing Open Frame in Separate Window. Now that you know this trick, at least you can get out of a framed situation if you ever find yourself trapped in one.

Sometimes, you may not want to save all the files at once. To save an individual frame displayed in a frameset without saving all the other frames, place your cursor in any of the frames and choose File⇨Save Frame just as you save any other individual page. Dreamweaver saves only the file for the frame in which your cursor is located.

To save only the page that defines the frameset, make sure the entire frameset is selected (you can do this by clicking in the upper-most left corner of the Workspace), and then choose File⇨Save Frameset. If you have not selected the entire frameset, the Save Frameset option doesn't appear on the File menu. *Remember:* This page doesn't display in any of the frames; it simply defines the entire display area, specifying which of the other pages displays in each frame, as well as the position and size of the frames.

As you continue to work on your frame page, remember that whenever you make a change in one of the content frames, you edit content in a *different* file from the one you started with (the frameset file). You may get confused as to which file you need to save when working in this manner. Don't worry — this is what confuses a lot of people about using frames in Dreamweaver. When you edit the content in one of the frames, make sure that your cursor is still in that frame when you choose File⇨Save Frame so that you save the page that corresponds to the frame you are working on. To be safe, you can always choose File➪Save All Frames in order to save all changes to all files in the frameset, including the frameset file itself. The Save All command is also useful when you make changes to several of the frames and want to save all the changes with just one command.

Setting Targets and Links in Frames

One of the best features of frames is that you can change the contents of each frame separately within the Web browser. This feature opens a wide range of design possibilities that improves navigation for your site. One very common way to use a frameset is to create a frame that displays a list of links to various pages of your site and then opens those links into another frame on the same page. This technique makes keeping a list of links constantly visible possible and makes navigation a lot simpler and more intuitive.

Setting links from a file in one frame so that the pages they link to open in another frame is like linking from one page to another, and that's essentially what you're doing. What makes linking within a frameset distinctive is that, in addition to indicating which page you want to open with the link, you have to specify which frame section it *targets* (opens into).

But before you can set those links, you need to do a few things: First, you need to create some other pages that you can link to (if you haven't done so already). Creating new pages is easy. Choose File➪New ➪HTML Page to create additional pages and then save them individually. If your pages already exist, you're more than halfway there; it's just a matter of linking to those pages.

The other thing you have to do before you can set links is to name each frame so that you can specify where the linked file loads. If you don't, the page just replaces the frameset altogether when someone clicks the link, and this defeats the purpose of using frames in the first place.

Naming frames

Naming a *frame* is different from naming the *file* that the frame represents. You find out how to name the files in the previous section "Saving files in a frameset;" you do that just as you name any other file you save. The *frame name* is like a nickname that allows you to distinguish your frames from one another on a page and refer to them individually — this becomes important when you set links and want to target a link to open in a particular area of the frameset. The *filename* is the actual name of the HTML file for the frame. The *frame name* is the nickname that you refer to when you want to set links.

You can see the names of your frames in the Frames panel, shown in Figure 7-5. If you're happy with the names that Dreamweaver automatically assigned to your frames, you can skip the following steps. If you want to change the names of the frames in your frameset or assign your own name as you create a new frame, follow these steps:

1. **Open an existing frameset or create a new one.**

   See the "Creating a frame in Dreamweaver" section, earlier in this chapter, if you don't know how to create a frameset.

2. **Choose Window⇨Frames to open the Frames panel at the right of the work area.**

   The Frames panel opens, as shown in Figure 7-5.

   The Frames panel is a miniature representation of the frames on your page that enables you to select different frames by clicking within the panel.

3. **Click to place your cursor in the area of the Frames panel that corresponds to the frame that you want to name.**

   As displayed in Figure 7-5, you can see that I selected the top frame. You can click to select any of the frames in the panel.

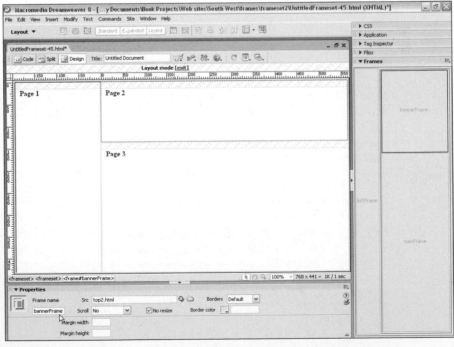

Figure 7-5:
The Frames panel is a miniature representation of the framed page that provides access to frame properties, such as frame names.

The Properties inspector displays the properties for that particular frame. You can make any changes to the frame's properties by altering the properties in the Properties inspector after selecting the frame. You can also select the entire frameset by clicking the border around all the frames in the Frames panel. The Frames panel allows you to select only one frame or frameset at a time.

4. **In the Frame Name text box on the left side of the Properties inspector, type a name for the frame.**

   Dreamweaver assigns names automatically when you save the files in a frameset. In the example shown in Figure 7-5, Dreamweaver assigned the names topFrame, mainFrame, and leftFrame. You can leave these names as is or change them to anything else in the Properties inspector (just don't use spaces or special characters in the names).

   In the example, I changed the topFrame to bannerFrame. You should name your frames in a way that makes sense to you and helps you remember what they are so you can better target them (which you can find info on in the "Setting links to a target frame" section that follows).

5. **Choose File⇨Save Frameset to save the frameset page after changing any of the names.**

   The frameset is the file you don't see in the display area that describes the other frames and contains information such as frame names.

   Remember, you can save any individual frame by placing your cursor in the frame and choosing File⇨Save, or you can save all the files in your frameset (including the frameset page) by choosing File⇨Save All Frames. Refer to the "Saving files in a frameset" section, earlier in this chapter, for more information on saving frames.

Now that you identified or changed the names of your frames, you're ready to start setting links that target frames. Don't close these files yet — you want to use them to follow the steps in the next section to set links.

I like to save my work on a regular basis so that I never lose more than a few minutes of work if my system crashes or the power goes out. Beware, however, that when you work with frames, you need to save all your pages to save your work. You can save each page separately by choosing File⇨Save Frame to save only the frame that the cursor is currently located in. To save all your pages at once, simply choose File⇨Save All to save all the pages in the frameset.

Setting links to a target frame

Setting links in a frameset requires some preliminary work. If you jumped to this section without creating a frameset or naming your frames, you may want to refer to the sections earlier in this chapter. If you already have a frameset, have named the frames, and just want to find out how to set links, this section is where you want to be.

Setting links in a frameset is like setting any other links between pages, except that you need to specify the target frame, meaning the frame where the linked page will display when a user clicks on the link. For example, if you want a link in the left frame to control what's in the main frame, you need to specify the main frame as the target in the link. If you don't specify a target, the link opens in the same frame the link is in. Because the most common reason to use frames is to keep navigation links in one frame and open their corresponding pages in another, you probably want to target a frame when you set a link.

If this seems confusing, don't fret. After you try the following steps, it should become clear how targets work in framesets:

1. **Open an existing frame set or create a new frameset.**

   In Figure 7-6, you see that I am using the Scenes from the Southwest Web site, which I created to use as an example in this chapter.

2. **Highlight the text or click to select the image you want to serve as the link.**

   In my example, I selected Sedona Sights. Note that this works the same whether you are creating a link with text or an image.

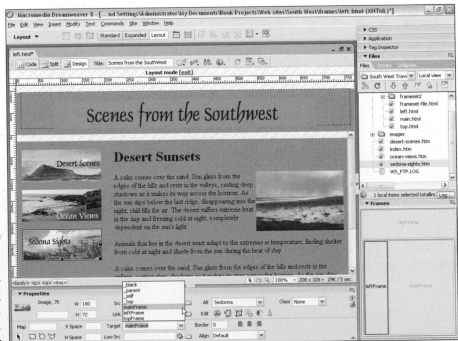

Figure 7-6:
Use targets to specify where a link opens in a frameset.

3. **In the Properties inspector, enter any URL in the Link text box or use the Browse button to select the page you want to link to.**

   In my example, I used the Browse button to set a link to the file named `Sedona-sights.html`.

4. **From the Target drop-down list in the Properties inspector, choose the name of the frame that you want the link to open into.**

   In my example, I selected the *mainFrame* frame as the target. You should choose the name that corresponds to the frame where you want your linked page to open. Notice that Dreamweaver conveniently lists all the frames you named in your document in the Target drop-down list, which I have open in Figure 7-6.

   The result, as shown in Figure 7-7, is that when the frameset displays in a browser and a user clicks the graphic that says Sedona Sights in the left frame, the page named `sedona-sights.html` displays in the main frame area.

   You can't test your links until you preview your work in a browser, and you have to save your work before you preview it.

Figure 7-7:
The selected link opens the page and targets the main frame area. In this example, the Sedona Sights page opens.

Comparing target options

You have many options when you target links in a frameset. As shown in the preceding section, "Setting links to a target frame," you can specify that a linked page open in another frame within your frameset. But in addition, you can set linked pages to open in the same frame as the page with the link, to open a completely new page with no frames, and even to open a second browser window and display the page without affecting the original framed design. Table 7-1 provides a list of target options and what they mean. You can find all these options in the Target drop-down list of the Properties inspector.

The Target drop-down list in the Properties inspector is activated only when you select a linked image or section of text. There must be a link in the Link field of the Properties inspector before you can set a target.

Table 7-1	Understanding Frame Target Options
Target Name	*Action*
_blank	Opens the linked document into a fresh new browser window.
_parent	Opens the linked document into the parent frameset of the page that has the link. (The *parent* is the frameset or frame that contains the frame with the link.)
_self	Opens the linked document in the same frame as the original link, replacing the current content of the frame. This is the default option and usually does not need to be specified.
_top	Opens the linked document into the outermost frameset, replacing the entire contents of the browser window.

Changing Frame Properties

As you get more sophisticated in using frames, you may want to further refine your frames by changing properties, which enables you to turn off frame borders, change the frame or border colors, limit scrolling, and so on. To access these options in Dreamweaver, choose Window⇨Frames, click inside the Frames panel in the area that corresponds to the frame that you want to change, and then use the Properties inspector to access the options I describe in the following four sections. Figure 7-8 shows the Properties inspector as it appears when you select a frameset in the Frames panel.

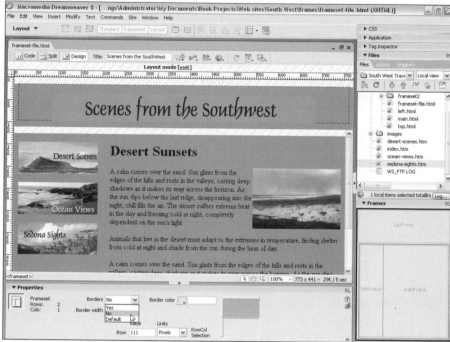

Figure 7-8:
The selected frames or framesets and their properties are visible in the Properties inspector.

TIP

If you don't see the margin height and width options, make sure that you click the expander arrow in the bottom-right corner of the Properties inspector. Clicking this arrow causes all available properties to display for the selected item.

Changing frame borders

I think the best thing that you can do with a frame border is to turn it off. You can turn the borders off for your site by choosing No from the Borders drop-down list in the Properties inspector for either the frameset or any of the individual frames in the frameset. Your other options include Yes, which forces the borders to be visible, and Default, which usually means Yes. In case of individual frames, however, the Default option inherits the settings for the parent frameset.

You can make global border settings by using the Properties inspector and applying the settings to the frameset. To select the frameset so that its properties are visible in the inspector, click the border that encloses the frameset in the Frames panel. Figure 7-8 shows a frameset selected in the Frames panel and its corresponding properties displayed in the Properties inspector.

If you choose to keep your borders visible, you may want to customize the color by clicking the Border Color square in the Properties inspector and then choosing a color from the color palette.

If you select a specific border, the Properties inspector also enables you to specify the border width. Simply enter a value in pixels in the Border Width text field to change the width of the selected border.

Frame border colors are not well supported by all browsers and may not display as you intend. Most designers simply turn off frame borders, but if you do keep them make sure that your design still looks okay if the borders are thick and grey, which is the default. Many browsers, including recent ones, don't display a different border color.

Changing frame sizes

The easiest way to change the size of a frame is to select the border and drag it until the frame is the size that you want. When you select the border, the Properties inspector displays the size of the frame, enabling you to change the size in pixels or as a percentage of the display area by entering a number in the Row or Column text boxes. If you specify 0 width for your frame borders, you may not see them on the page in order to drag and resize them. If this is the case, you can view the borders by choosing View⇨Visual Aids⇨ Frame Borders, and Dreamweaver indicates the borders with a thin gray line that you can easily select.

Changing scrolling and resizing options

Scrolling options control whether a viewer can scroll up and down or left and right in a frame area. As shown in Figure 7-9, the scrolling options for frames are Yes, No, Auto, and Default. As a general rule, I recommend leaving the Scroll option set to Auto because a visitor's browser can then turn scrolling on if necessary. That is, if the viewer's display area is too small to see all the contents of the frame, the frame becomes scrollable. If all the contents fit within the visible boundaries, the scroll arrows don't display.

If you set this option to Yes, the scroll arrows are visible whether they're needed or not. If you set it to No, they won't be visible, even if that means your viewer can't see all the contents of the frame — a sometimes dangerous proposition because there's no easy way to scroll. Default leaves it up to the browser. In most browsers, the Default option results in the same display as the Auto option, but Default yields unpredictable results. As a general rule, using Auto is best so the scroll bar is visible only if needed.

Figure 7-9:
The Scroll
Options list
in the
Properties
inspector
controls
frame-
scrolling
options.

Also notice the No Resize option in Figure 7-9. If you place a check mark in this box, a visitor to your site can't change the size of the frames. If you leave this box unchecked, your user can select the border and drag it to make the frame area smaller or larger, just as you can when you develop your frames in Dreamweaver. Generally, I like to give viewers control, but I often check the No Resize option because I want to ensure that my viewers don't alter the design, especially because some viewers may do so accidentally.

Setting margin height and width

The Margin Width and Margin Height options enable you to specify the amount of margin space around a frame. Normally in a browser window, a small margin is visible between the edge of the window and any content, such as images or text. That's why you can't normally place an image on your page flush against the edge of the browser. With frames, though, you can actually control the size of the margin or even eliminate the margin altogether.

I generally recommend that you set the margin to at least two pixels and make the margin larger if you want to create more space around your content. If you want to get rid of the margin altogether, set it to zero and any images or text in the frame appears flush against the edge of the frame or browser window if the frame touches the edge of the browser. If the frame touches another frame, you can use this technique to create the impression of seamless images across frames.

Chapter 8

Cascading Style Sheets

*T*he biggest boon for Web designers in recent years is the advent of *Cascading Style Sheets (CSS),* a way to extend HTML and give yourself greater style control over every part of your page. CSS is especially useful for formatting the look of frequently used elements, like headlines and subheads, that you use again and again in your pages. For example, if you want all main headlines to be Arial, bold, and centered, you can create a single style with those options and apply only that style rather than all three individual HTML tags. You can then create style sheets that work simultaneously across multiple pages or your entire site.

Cascading Style Sheets also enable you to lay out your pages — and they're much more powerful than using tables to position elements. CSS is rapidly becoming the preferred method of designing pages. Forward-thinking designers find the power of CSS more than pays back the learning curve required to get started.

If you haven't jumped on the CSS bandwagon yet, this chapter is designed to help you appreciate the benefits and introduce you to these timesaving features so that you can begin using CSS in your page designs right away. Macromedia believes strongly in CSS and has added new features to Dreamweaver 8 that make accessing and understanding style sheets easier.

In this chapter, you see how Cascading Style Sheets work and how they're implemented in Dreamweaver. You're also introduced to the most advanced CSS capabilities, and you gain a glimpse into the future of Web design. In Chapter 9, you find more detailed instructions about using CSS and layers to control page layout.

Checking Browser Compatibility

Although CSS has been around for a while, many designers have resisted using it because early browsers (such as Netscape and Internet Explorer 4.0) poorly implemented it. That's all changing now that most of the users of the Internet have upgraded to more advanced browsers and these modern browsers are doing an increasingly good job of rendering CSS pages. The newest versions of Firefox, Netscape, Internet Explorer, Safari, and Opera all offer very good (though. at times. inconsistent and incomplete) support for CSS. To help you watch out for inconsistencies, Dreamweaver offers several features designed to help manage browser differences (the end of Chapter 9 covers these features).

Unless you need to reach the widest possible audience and expect that some viewers may be using ancient browsers, such as Netscape 4 and earlier, you shouldn't have to worry much about browsers that can't render CSS. Even in cases where you do need to reach those archaic holdouts, CSS is designed to degrade gracefully: You may lose your fancy formatting, but at least viewers can still see your content. (The exception is layers, as described in Chapter 9, which older browsers don't always display.)

You do need to worry about browsers that interpret and understand CSS differently. For example, you find significant differences between how the increasingly popular Mozilla Firefox browser and Microsoft Internet Explorer implement CSS. Be sure to include enough time for testing in all the browsers you expect your visitors to use so that you can clear up any problems before publishing your pages on your site.

Appreciating Cascading Style Sheets

The concept of style sheets has been around long before the Web. Word processing programs, such as Microsoft Word, have long used style sheets to control text formatting. Using style sheets in a word processor, for example, you could create specific style definitions — such as Heading, Body, and Footer — and apply those styles to sections of text. The timesaving benefits of this approach are enormous because you need to define complex styles only once and then can apply them with a single click anywhere in your document. The concept is exactly the same with Web documents and Cascading Style Sheets.

The most powerful aspect of CSS, as you see in the section "Using External Style Sheets," is its capability to make global style changes across an entire Web site. Suppose that one fine day you decide that all your headlines should be purple rather than blue. If you weren't using CSS, changing all your headlines would be a huge undertaking — a matter of opening every Web page in your site and making changes to the font tags around your headlines. With

CSS, you can simply open the style sheet and make changes to the style that controls all the headlines. Save the style sheet, and voila! Your headlines are now all automatically purple. If you ever have to redesign your site (and believe me, every good site goes through periodic redesigns), you can save hours or even days of work if you have created your design with CSS.

Benefits of CSS

CSS is a continually developing technology with a remarkably broad scope, and not all its capabilities are included in Dreamweaver 8. Nonetheless, you gain many, many advantages by using CSS in Dreamweaver. The following partial list shows some of what you can do:

- ✔ Designate specific fonts.
- ✔ Define font sizes based on percentages, pixels, picas, points, inches, millimeters, and other precise measurements.
- ✔ Set bold, italic, and underline properties.
- ✔ Set text color and background color for text blocks and other objects.
- ✔ Change link colors and remove link underlining.
- ✔ Create mouseover effects on links.
- ✔ Indent and justify text.
- ✔ Transform text into upper-, lower-, and mixed-case.
- ✔ Create customized bullets.
- ✔ Control margins and borders around text.
- ✔ Redefine how existing HTML tags display.
- ✔ Precisely position elements on a page.
- ✔ Add borders to blocks of text and images.
- ✔ Flow text around images and other text.

Are style sheets making you crazy?

If you choose to format text or other elements on your pages without using style sheets, you may be frustrated with some of Dreamweaver's automated style sheet features, which try to create style sheets for you and can alter styles when you apply formatting manually. Don't fret, you can turn off these automated CSS features in Dreamweaver by choosing Edit⇨Preferences, and then unchecking the Use CSS instead of HTML Tags option in the General panel.

Using CSS with templates

Templates, as described in Chapter 4, are ideally suited for use with CSS because they're geared toward a collaborative work environment. With Dreamweaver, you can use both internal and external styles sheets in a template. In fact, using external style sheets makes a great deal of sense when using templates because the formatting of the page is separated from its content. To save a page with CSS info as a template, just choose File⇨Save As Template. Any template you create that contains internal styles or links to external styles automatically updates whenever its style sheet changes.

With templates, both the link code at the head of the page and any internal styles are locked regions by default. Users are prevented from editing the style sheet definitions, but they have an ideal way to manage the look and feel of a site via formatting specifications that cannot be modified from a document that uses a template.

Looking at the code behind CSS

A *Cascading Style Sheet* is basically a list of rules defining the behavior of an HTML document. HTML already contains a bunch of rules about the behavior of different tags, but without CSS, you can't alter those rules — they're kind of like the grammar rules in a language.

CSS, however, enables you to create your own rules and override the rules of HTML, which are quite limited in terms of page design. These new rules determine how a browser displays certain page elements. Imagine if you could invent a bunch of new words and grammar rules for the English language. Now imagine that everyone else could do that too. Communication could get confusing pretty quickly, right?

What keeps the communication from breaking down with CSS is that every time you invent new rules, you include the equivalent of a dictionary entry and grammar guide that goes along with each document. This is the style sheet.

CSS styles reside in the <HEAD> area of an HTML page if they apply to only that page, or in a separate file if you create an external CSS that applies to multiple pages. A style sheet consists of lines of code that are grouped into rules. A style sheet can contain any number of rules, and each rule contains a selector and a declaration block composed of one or more properties and a corresponding value. If this stuff is starting to sound a little confusing, don't worry. You find step-by-step directions later in this chapter, and Dreamweaver hides most of the technical stuff behind the scenes (unless you like to look at the code).

To give you an idea of what CSS looks like, Figure 8-1 illustrates the various components of a style sheet.

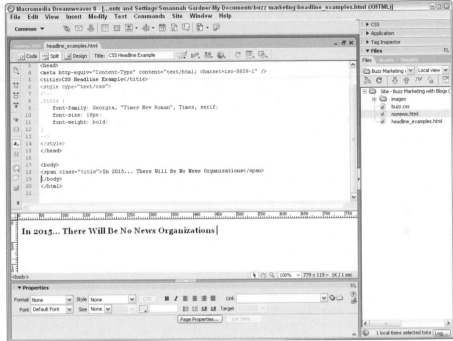

Figure 8-1:
A style
sheet
embedded
in an HTML
document.

After looking over Figure 8-1, you may be thinking that CSS looks kind of complicated. Well, to be perfectly honest, it is. In fact, I want you to know that you can't read only this chapter on CSS and become proficient enough to write your own CSS code. Even experienced Web designers face a steep learning curve in becoming proficient with CSS. What I can tell you in this chapter is how Dreamweaver handles CSS so that you can implement it quickly and easily.

This chapter gives you the introduction you need to use style sheets effectively, but if you really want to learn all the details of style sheets, I suggest that you explore some other, more complete resources on CSS, such as *CSS Web Design For Dummies,* by Richard Mansfield (published by Wiley Publishing, Inc.).

If you happen to know some CSS already, and you're advanced enough to be able to hand-code CSS, Dreamweaver includes a cool feature named Code Hints. Code Hints offer autocomplete options for filling in code that speed up the manual coding process. Code Hints work only in Code view and activate as you type new CSS declarations. You can also force the list of Code Hints to appear by pressing Ctrl+spacebar (or ⌘+spacebar on the Mac).

"So what's all this about cascading?"

The term *cascading* refers to the way in which conflicts in CSS rules are resolved. Because styles can be attached to documents in multiple ways, and the properties can be invoked in multiple ways, the browser must interpret these style rules in a certain order. This hierarchical order works in kind of a top-down fashion, in much the same way water cascades over rocks as it flows down a stream.

The benefits of this cascading process become apparent when you define multiple style choices in your style sheet. Cascading Style Sheets enable you to define a variety of presentation possibilities that are rendered in the browser. CSS is set up this way to help compensate for the many variables that affect how pages display on the Web, such as differences among computer platforms, screen resolutions, and browser versions. When you define the design of your page by creating CSS rules, items first in the list receive lower priority. As the browser *cascades* down the list, the later rules receive greater priority, so that a style rule very close to a page element usually takes precedence over a rule in an external style sheet. This concept becomes clearer as you become more familiar with how CSS operates. (You find out what happens when you apply conflicting styles in the section "Conflicting styles," later in this chapter.)

Advanced capabilities of CSS

When designers are introduced to CSS, they often get excited about the capability to control and format text in ways that were never possible with straight HTML. But the CSS fun doesn't stop there! Besides helping you to format your text, CSS also encompasses a host of other geeky techniques that enable you to control the layout and appearance of page elements. CSS forms the basis of layers (which you can read more about in Chapter 9), even though you wouldn't know it without looking closely at the code on your page. *Layers* are an advanced CSS implementation that enable you to precisely position objects on your page, stack them one on top of the other, and even add interactivity to elements. Interactive effects with layers can be programmed by using DHTML (*Dynamic HTML*) and JavaScript to create complex animations and transitions on your pages.

Chapter 9 covers Cascading Style Sheets and Dynamic HTML in greater detail. Dynamic HTML is made possible through scripting languages that use the Document Object Model to create dynamic effects and global styles. Think of Cascading Style Sheets as HTML on steroids. Think of Dynamic HTML as HTML on rocket fuel.

Working with the CSS Panel

The CSS panel has two panes when in the All mode: All Rules and Properties. The All Rules pane shows all the styles defined for the page you have open, whether the styles are internal or contained in an external style sheet. If you select one of the page's styles, its properties are shown in the Properties pane, where you can easily add, edit, and remove existing styles (see Figure 8-2).

When you first open this panel, you need to click the plus sign (+) (or triangle on the Mac) that is next to the <STYLE> tag in the CSS panel to see the styles associated with the page. (If you don't see a style tag or any styles, no styles are associated with the page.)

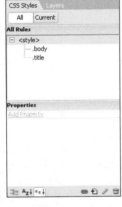

Figure 8-2:
The new CSS panel, showing all the styles associated with the open document.

Click the Current button to show the Current mode. Use the Current mode to see only the style of an item currently selected in your open document. This mode has three panes: Summary for Selection, Rules, and Properties (see Figure 8-3). In the Summary for Selection pane, you see the rules currently defined for this style. In the Rules pane, you see all the rules that influence the currently selected element; this pane is exceptionally useful when you have created a complicated layout. In the third pane, you can edit, add, or delete properties of the current rule.

New CSS Rule   Edit Style Sheet

Attach Style Sheet   Delete CSS Rule

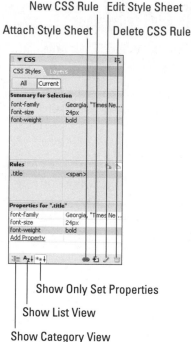

Figure 8-3:
The new
CSS panel,
showing
the style
of an item
selected in
the open
document.

Show Only Set Properties

Show List View

Show Category View

On the left-hand side of the panel, you see the Show Category View, Show List View, and Show Only Set Properties icons. These apply to the Properties panel in both the Current and All modes. Here's how to use these:

- ✔ **Show Category View:** In the category view of the Properties view, Dreamweaver displays all the properties available to use for a rule, organized by the category to which they belong. For example, all the font properties are grouped into a Font category.

- ✔ **Show List View:** In the list view, Dreamweaver displays all the properties available to use for a rule, organized alphabetically.

- ✔ **Show Only Set Properties:** When you define a new rule, you set certain properties, but of course you can set many more. In this view, Dreamweaver displays only those properties you defined for this rule.

The second set of icons, on the bottom-right of the CSS panel, includes icons that are useful no matter what mode the panel is in. From left to right, these icons represent Attach Style Sheet, New CSS Rule, Edit Style Sheet, and Delete CSS Rule (this one resembles a trash can). The easiest way to start a new style sheet is to create a new style. Click the second icon on the bottom left (New CSS Rule) of the CSS panel.

When you click the New CSS Rule icon, the New CSS Rule dialog box opens, as shown in Figure 8-4, and displays the following options:

Figure 8-4:
The New
CSS Rule
dialog box.

✔ **Name:** Although the first field in this box is Name, when you first bring it up, its title changes, depending on which CSS type you select by using the three radio buttons in the Selector Type area. Read the description for each of the CSS types in the following bullets to see how to fill out the Name field.

✔ **Selector Type:** These three radio button options allow you to define the type of style you want to create:

• **Class** enables you to define a new style that you can apply to any section on a page by using the Class attribute. When you select this option, you must also fill in the name of the class in the Name field above it. All custom style names must begin with a period (.), which Dreamweaver automatically inserts as you name the style.

• **Tag** enables you to create a style that adds to or changes the formatting associated with an existing HTML tag. When you select this option, the Name field asks for a tag name. Clicking the Tag drop-down list allows you to select from a huge list of HTML tags (the default one is the <BODY> tag). For more information on this option, see the section, "Redefining HTML tags," later in this chapter.

• **Advanced** enables you to define other types of styles, which usually consist of a kind of hybrid that combines a custom style with a specific HTML tag. The most common of these are the a: styles, which apply only to the <A> tag and enable you to do tasks such as change the color of a link when the mouse hovers over it. When you select this option, the Selector field asks for the selector name. Choices in the pop-up list are a:active, a:hover, a:link, and a:visited.

✔ **Define In:** This option lets you choose whether your style sheet exists within the current document or in a separate file. When you select a new style sheet file, you're creating an external style sheet. If you select This Document Only, you're creating an internal style sheet, in which defined styles are available only for the page you're working on.

After you click OK in the New CSS Rule dialog box, another dialog box appears in which you define the different rules for the style. I explain the CSS Rule Definition dialog box in the "Defining CSS Rules" section, later in this chapter.

Creating Style Sheets in Dreamweaver

When you start creating and using Cascading Style Sheets, you use one of the most complex and advanced Dreamweaver features. Consequently, creating style sheets takes a little more time to grasp than does applying basic HTML tags and modifying their attributes. Still, Dreamweaver makes defining style sheets much easier than writing them by hand — a task much closer to writing programming code than to creating HTML tags.

To help you get the hang of using Dreamweaver to create style sheets, you find detailed descriptions of all the panels and dialog boxes that define CSS rules throughout this chapter. If you want to understand every option or have a particular question about an option as you create your style sheets, refer to the "Working with the CSS Panel" section.

Choosing the right style

You can create two types of style sheets with CSS and Dreamweaver: internal and external. An *internal style sheet* stores its rules within the HTML code of a page and applies only to that page. An *external style* is a text file you create and store outside your HTML page. You can then reference it as a link within as many HTML documents as you like. In this way, you can apply style sheets to an entire Web site or to any page that links to the external style sheet, which also means that you can have many different pages referencing the same style sheet. You create these two kinds of style sheets in almost the same way, as you see later in this chapter.

You can also define three different kinds of CSS styles to use in either an internal or external style sheet:

✔ **Classes:** A *class* is a completely new set of formatting attributes you can apply to any text selection. Don't worry much about the technical terms because I get into them in more detail as you read on. For now, just know that when you define a class, you give it a name, and then you use that name to apply the style to any element on the page. By creating a class you make up your own HTML tag with formatting rules you can define yourself.

✔ **Tags:** You can change how *existing* HTML tags are rendered by the browser; in this case, you're overriding the existing rules or adding additional formatting to an existing rule. For example, you could redefine the H2 heading tag by specifying that the tag also applies the font face Arial and the color blue. When you alter an existing tag, you change the way all instances of that HTML tag manifest throughout your page — or throughout your Web site.

✔ **Advanced:** This third kind of style relates to specific, preexisting attributes of tags that can be modified with CSS. In Dreamweaver, you can use these advanced styles to change attributes of the <A> tag and to alter the appearance of sets of links on your page, depending on what is going on around them. This is especially useful when you have links displayed on different background colors making the default link colors inappropriate. A CSS selector of this kind is also referred to as a *pseudoclass* because it's a combination of the two preceding styles.

Creating a new style

In this section, you jump right into steps for creating and applying styles in Dreamweaver. In this section, you define a style for headlines using CSS. If you want to create a style for another element, follow these same steps and change the specific attributes as needed.

You can leave attributes unspecified if you don't want to use them. If you don't specify them, the browser uses its own default. For example, if you don't specify a font, the browser uses the default page font specified by the user in the browser preferences.

To define a new style, create a new document or open an existing HTML file, and follow these steps:

1. **Choose Text⇨CSS Styles⇨New.**

   The New CSS Rule dialog box appears. The new style is automatically named `.unnamed1`.

2. **In the Name text box, type a new name for the style.**

   Dreamweaver gives you a default name that begins with a period (.) because class names must *always* begin with a period. You can name the style anything you want as long as you don't use spaces or punctuation. Dreamweaver adds the initial period to the class name if you omit it. Because you're creating a headline style, I suggest you name this new style *.headline*.

This structure can be a little confusing because when you apply the style to an element on your page, the period (.) is not visible; it's only needed when you create the style.

3. **In the Selector Type category, make sure that the button next to Class is selected.**

4. **In the Define In area, select This Document Only to create an internal style sheet.**

An internal style sheet affects only the current page, not a group of HTML pages — you can find more details on this later in this chapter.

5. **Click OK.**

The CSS Rule Definition dialog box opens.

6. **For the Font choice, select a font set from the drop-down list or enter the name of a font in the Font field.**

To use fonts that aren't in the drop-down list, choose the Edit Font List option from the drop-down list to create new font options.

You generally should use a font set that specifies three or more fonts rather than just specify a single font in the font choices. A browser can only display a font if the font is installed on the user's computer. If a user doesn't have the font, the browser searches for the next font in the list you specified. If you only specify one font and the user doesn't have it, the browser's default font is used to display the text. By specifying multiple fonts, you have a better chance that your text displays close to the way you intend.

7. **From the Size drop-down list, choose the size you want for your headline.**

Large headlines commonly appear at 24 or 36 points. Notice that you can also specify sizes in pixels, picas, mm, and several other measurements.

Using precise CSS measurement units, such as pixels and points, for text is much more consistent across computer platforms than using HTML sizes, such as 1, 2, and 3. Still, because of the different screen resolutions between Macs and PCs, you don't achieve perfect size consistency between the two platforms, although you get much closer than by using HTML size formatting. Always check your designs on multiple platforms and multiple browsers if exact text formatting and appearance are critical. (See Chapter 9 for more on the Dreamweaver features for checking browser compatibility.)

8. **From the Style drop-down list, choose a font style.**

Each of these settings is optional. You can leave any or all the fields blank.

9. **From the Weight drop-down list, choose Bold to make your headline thicker and darker.**

10. **Ignore Variant and Case because these attributes aren't well supported by current browsers.**

11. **Click the color well and choose a color for the headline.**

    Sticking to the default color swatches in the color well is certainly the quickest way to choose a color, but you can also create custom colors by clicking the icon that looks like a rainbow-colored globe in the upper-right corner of the color well and selecting a color from the System Color Picker.

12. **Click OK when you finish.**

    Notice in Figure 8-5 that your new headline style is added to the list of styles in the CSS panel. If the style doesn't appear, click the plus sign (+) (or triangle on the Mac) next to the <STYLE> tag to reveal the rules in the current style.

After you create a style sheet and add rules to it, you can apply the styles to any Web page or selected text block using several different methods. See the next section for details.

Although the most common use of style sheets is text formatting, you can create styles for any element on a page. For example, you could create a style for images that controls alignment and other attributes.

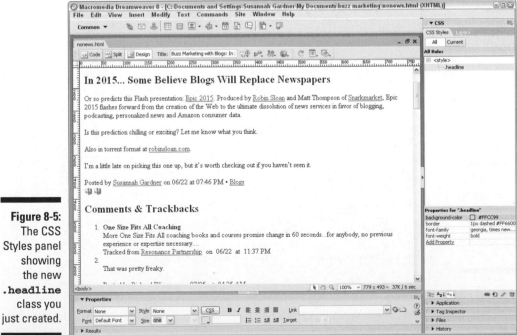

Figure 8-5:
The CSS Styles panel showing the new **.headline** class you just created.

Applying styles in Dreamweaver

Defining custom styles in Dreamweaver is the time-consuming part. Applying them after you defined them is the timesaving part. Applying them is easy: You simply select the text, or other element, you want to affect and choose the predefined style you want to apply to it.

To apply a style in Dreamweaver, follow these steps:

1. **Highlight the text, or other element, in an open document to which you want to apply a style.**

2. **In the Properties inspector, click the Style pop-up menu to reveal the list of styles associated with the document and select the one you want.**

   Notice that Dreamweaver allows you to preview the style when you select it with this method, as shown in Figure 8-6. After you choose a style, the selected text changes in the Document window (see Figure 8-7).

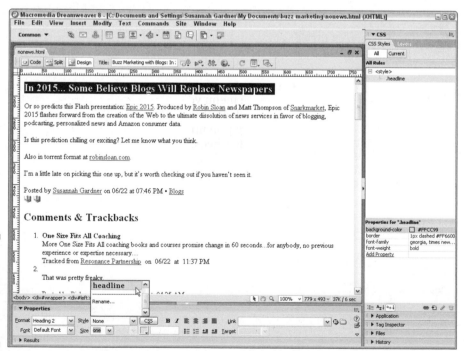

Figure 8-6:
Selecting a style with the Properties inspector.

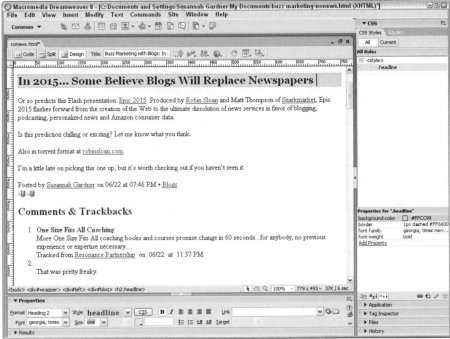

Figure 8-7:
After
applying the
`.headline`
style to
the page.

Another way to apply a style to a highlighted text selection is by choosing the
name of the style from the menu you see when you choose Text⇨CSS Styles
or right-click (Control+click on the Mac) the selected text and then choose
the style from the resulting pop-up menu. The method you choose depends
on your own personal preferences. I like to use the Properties inspector
because it's the only method that allows you to preview the way the style
appears before applying it.

When you apply a style at the code level, Dreamweaver generally adds a class
attribute to the tag surrounding the text to which you apply the style. This
class attribute is tied to the style you defined and causes the selected text to
take on the properties of the style. For example, if you have a section of text
that looks like this in Code view before attaching a style:

```
<P>This is my headline</p>
```

Dreamweaver adds a class attribute to the `<P>` tag, which associates it to the
`.headline` class. The resulting code looks like this:

```
<P class="headline">This is my headline</P>
```

In cases where no preexisting tags enclose the text, Dreamweaver adds the <SPAN> tag, which acts as a container for the style. A selection of text that starts out like this in Code view:

```
This is my headline
```

ends up like this after applying the style:

```
<SPAN class="headline">This is my headline</SPAN>
```

Removing styles in Dreamweaver

To remove a style from a selected text block, choose the None option from the Style drop-down list in the Properties inspector (as shown in Figure 8-8) or choose Text⇨CSS Styles. It's really that simple.

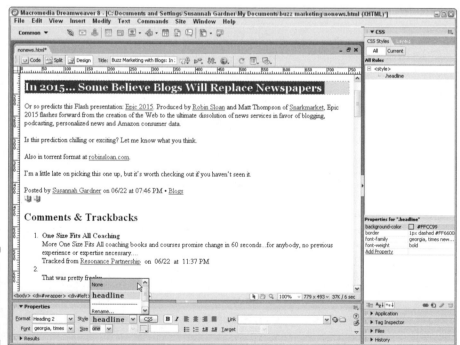

Figure 8-8:
Removing a style in Dream-weaver.

Redefining HTML tags

When you create a custom style, as I explain in the preceding section, you start a completely new style with its own, unique name, containing various rules that you define by using the CSS Rule Definitions options covered in the "Creating a new style" section, earlier in this chapter. When you redefine an HTML tag, however, you begin with an existing HTML tag — such as <B> (bold), <PRE> (for unformatted text), or <TABLE> (table) — and change the attributes associated with this specific tag. In this case, you don't need to apply the style because the style applies at the time you use the HTML tag, affecting *all* content that falls inside the tag. This distinction between creating a new class and redefining an existing tag is an important one.

You may ask "Why would I need such a feature?" or "What's the best scenario in which to use it?" In the preceding section, you find out how to create a new style class that you can *selectively* apply to any block of text on your page. In the case of redefined HTML tags, the new attributes apply to *all* instances of that tag. This feature can be quite powerful if used correctly, but it does require a little knowledge about HTML tags and how they work.

For example, every HTML page has a <BODY> tag. If you know that you want all the text on your page to appear in a specific font, you can redefine the <BODY> tag to inherit a specific font, and that saves you the time of having to apply a class to all body text. Because of the cascading nature of style sheets, you can still apply class styles to individual selections of text falling within the <BODY> tag that can further modify or even override the attributes initially defined for this tag.

To redefine an HTML tag, follow these steps:

1. **Create a new CSS rule.**

   You have several ways to call up the New Rule Style dialog box. Try clicking the New CSS Rule button in the lower-right portion of the CSS panel to call it up.

2. **In the Selector Type category in the New CSS Rule dialog box, select the Tag option.**

   Notice that when you select the Tag option, the name of the Name text box at the top changes to Tag.

3. **Click the Tag pop-up menu to reveal a comprehensive list of HTML tags and choose the tag you want from this list (see Figure 8-9).**

   If you're unsure of the meaning of any of these HTML tags, consult the Reference panel, available by choosing Window⊅Reference.

4. **Select the This Document Only option in the Define In field to create an internal style sheet.**

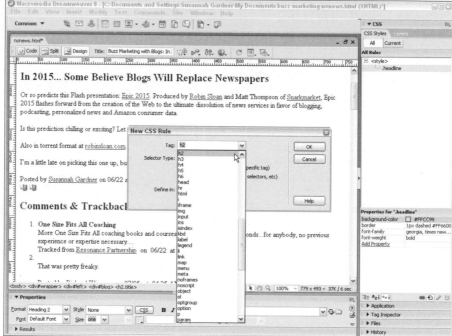

Figure 8-9:
The
Redefine
HTML Tag
option gives
you a list of
all HTML
tags you
can redefine
using CSS.

5. **Click the OK button, and then use the CSS style definition categories to define the new tag style.**

    Be aware that when you redefine an existing HTML tag, any text you have already formatted with that tag changes to reflect the new definition.

A good use of the Redefine HTML tag feature is to create style definitions for HTML header tags, such as H1, H2, and H3. This way, you can exercise greater control over the appearance of these headers and easily apply them by choosing Text⇔Paragraph Format. Using header tags also has an added benefit because search engines often give higher priority to keywords that appear in the H1 to H6 header tags.

Working with CSS selectors

The third type of style is the CSS selector. Dreamweaver refers to it as an *advanced selector*. CSS selectors allows you to affect various predefined attributes of a given HTML element or affect elements according to how they are placed in a document or positioned relative to other elements. The most common use of this type of style according to Dreamweaver is in conjunction with the <A> anchor tag: You can use it to change the appearance of links on your page. In HTML, the <BODY> tag already has certain attributes associated with it — such as link, visited, active, and hover — that affect the appearance of all hypertext links in the document. Using a CSS selector style allows you to access these attributes and change their qualities. For example, you can remove underlines from links and create mouseover effects using styles, as you can see in the next two sections.

Eliminating underlines from links

One of the most commonly used CSS techniques involves disabling the underline attribute of the anchor tag, <A>, so that hypertext links are no longer underlined in the browser. Many Web designers like to remove the underline because they think that it detracts from the design, and they consider underlined links old-fashioned. Instead, they use other, more modern ways of displaying links using CSS selector styles. This technique works in almost all modern Web browsers, including Netscape 4.0 and higher.

To disable underlining for hypertext links, follow these steps:

1. **Choose Text⇨CSS Styles⇨New (or click the New CSS Rule button in the CSS panel).**

   The New CSS Rule dialog box appears.

2. **Select the Advanced option in the Selector Type area.**

3. **Choose a:link from the Selector pop-up menu.**

4. **In the Define In area, select This Document Only.**

5. **Click OK.**

   The CSS Rule Definition dialog box opens.

6. **Make sure that the Type category is selected; then, check the None option in the Decoration area, as shown in Figure 8-10.**

7. **Click OK to apply the changes.**

After you click OK, active links are no longer underlined on the page when they display in a browser (as long as it's 4.0 or higher). Try creating a link on the page in Design mode, and you see that the link is no longer underlined. The link takes on the default blue color for hyperlinks, however, so that you know that it's still a link. If you want to change the blue color, you can use the CSS style definitions to change the color for the a:link selector.

Adding a little interactivity

To make your links interactive, you can further modify the <A> tag by adding an effect that underlines the link only when a viewer hovers the mouse over it. That way, your viewer instantly receives feedback that the link is indeed a hyperlink.

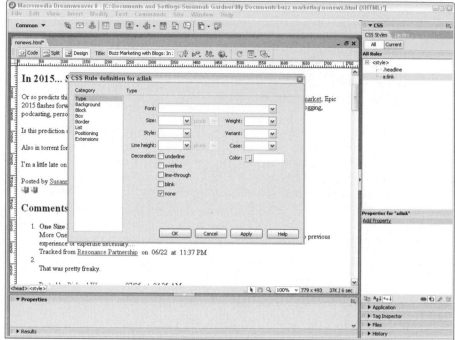

Figure 8-10:
Using CSS
to disable
the
underlining
of hypertext
links.

To display an underline when users mouseover a link:

1. **Choose Text⇨CSS Styles⇨New (or click the New CSS Rule button in the CSS panel).**

   The New CSS Rule dialog box appears.

2. **Select the Advanced option in the Selector Type area.**

3. **Choose a:hover from the Selector pop-up menu.**

4. **In the Define In area, select This Document Only.**

5. **Click OK.**

   The CSS Rule Definition dialog box opens.

6. **Make sure that the Type category is selected and check the Underline option in the Decoration section.**

7. **Click OK to apply the changes and then save your document.**

To preview the effects of the style changes you just made, you need to view the page in a Web browser because some interactive effects don't show up in

Dreamweaver Design view. Take a look at how your links now appear and how they interact with the user. This cool effect is much simpler to create than a rollover behavior. Try experimenting with different style sheet rules on the different anchor selectors to achieve exciting results.

For example, you can also cause the link, when it's moused over, to become bold rather than underlined or to change color. You can also apply any other CSS effect you can think of to enhance the appearance of your links. You can modify a:visited links to change the attributes of visited links and a:active links to change the attributes of links while they're being clicked. Remember that any styles you create in this way affect *all* links on your page unless you specifically apply a different class style to the individual link that overrides the selector style.

Dreamweaver features a quick way to alter the appearance of links in the Page Properties dialog box (see Figure 8-11). When you use this option, Dreamweaver automatically generates the CSS code to alter your link display. You don't have as much control with this option (you can change many more aspects of your link display if you set up the CSS yourself); but for quickly modifying link behavior (especially if all you want to do is get rid of underlining), this shortcut is a good one. Simply choose Modify⇨Page Properties and make your changes in the Links category. Later, you can add additional properties via the regular CSS tools.

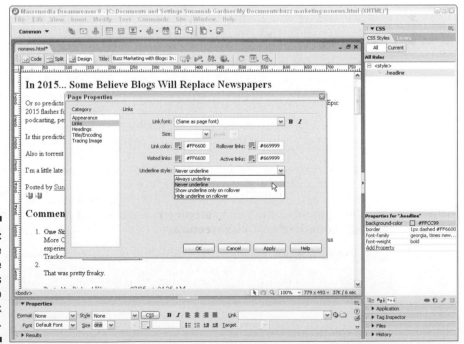

Figure 8-11:
Using the
Page
Properties
dialog box to
modify link
appearance.

Conflicting styles

Be careful when you apply more than one style to the same element (something that's easier to do than you may realize). This advice holds true for CSS styles as well as style attributes applied via HTML, such as font-styling properties. The styles may conflict, and because browsers aren't all consistent in the way in which they display styles, the results can be inconsistent and undesirable.

For the most part, Netscape and Internet Explorer display all attributes applied to an element, even if they're from different style rules, as long as the styles don't conflict. If they do conflict, browsers prioritize styles depending on how the styles have been defined and the order in which they appear. The method for determining this priority is what cascading is all about.

Here's an example to help you get the idea. You define a custom style named .headline with red text that's not bolded, and you apply it to a block of text on the page. Then you decide that you want that text to be bold, so you apply the bold tag independently by selecting it from the Properties inspector. You have now used two different types of styles. Because they don't conflict, all of them take effect, and your text becomes bold and red. If, however, you apply another color to the same block of text — blue, for example — using the Properties inspector, you have a conflict.

Understanding how browsers handle these conflicts is important. The basic guideline is that CSS rules get the highest priority, followed by HTML presentation attributes (for example, align, color, face, and bgcolor), followed by the browser default settings (font type and font size, for example). CSS rules always get the highest priority in any scenario, and internal style sheets get priority over external style sheets.

When two CSS styles conflict, priority is determined through the *order of cascade.* Although this concept can get complex, one guideline to follow is that the style that was listed most recently usually has priority. But instead of bending your brain to figure out how rules cascade, you generally should avoid creating styles that conflict. Either go back and redefine an existing style, apply regular HTML tags individually, or create a new style. Remember that you can use the Duplicate option by right-clicking (Control+click on a Mac) a style in the CSS panel to create a new style with the attributes of one that already exists, and then make minor alterations. (For more on editing existing styles, see the following section.)

In cases where you do end up with conflicting styles, the best practice is to view your page in a Web browser to see how the style looks to the user. Although Dreamweaver 8 has greatly improved its rendering of CSS, Dreamweaver still doesn't always replicate the browser display perfectly.

Editing an existing style

You can change the attributes of any style after you have created it by editing its style definitions. This capability is a major advantage of Cascading Style Sheets: You can make global changes to a page or even to an entire Web site by changing a style you applied to multiple elements through the use of an external style sheet. Be aware, however, that everything you defined with that style changes when you make your edit.

Remember that you can also create new styles by duplicating an existing style and then altering it. Then, you can apply that new style without affecting elements that are already formatted on your pages with the original version of the style.

To edit an existing style, follow these steps:

1. **Click the CSS button in the Properties inspector.**

   The CSS panel comes up.

2. **Click the All button to list all the styles in effect on the page you have open.**

3. **Select from the list of styles the style you want to change.**

   Dreamweaver displays the style definition in the Properties pane.

4. **Click the value of the attribute you want to edit and select or type your change.**

   The style sheet updates as soon as you make the edit. At the same time, all elements you defined with that style automatically change.

 Duplicating a style with a new name (style-disabled) and deleting the original one is a quick way to disable an unwanted style without losing the code. This way, you don't have to re-create it if you ever want it back.

You can undo your edit by pressing Ctrl+Z (Windows) or ⌘+Z (on a Mac), or by choosing Edit➪Undo Set Attribute before doing anything else.

Defining CSS Rules

When you choose to make a new style and select one of the three style options in the New CSS Rule dialog box, the CSS Rule Definition dialog box opens. It's where you decide how you want your style to look by selecting the attribute options, which in CSS are referred to as *rules*. This dialog box includes eight categories, each with multiple options you can use to define various rules to apply as part of your CSS declaration. In this section, I discuss each of these eight categories.

You don't have to make selections for all options in each category. In fact, usually you only select a few properties from one category. Any options you leave blank remain as the browser's default. For example, if you don't specify a text color, the text displays as black or whatever the default color is.

Note: Some options in the CSS Rule Definition dialog box aren't supported by all current browsers and are included for future compatibility. Some CSS properties aren't displayed here. Don't be frustrated by options in these categories that Dreamweaver doesn't display. If they aren't included in Dreamweaver, it's because they're fairly esoteric, advanced, or one of those properties that just isn't well-supported across current browsers. The good news is that Macromedia is looking ahead and building these options into Dreamweaver so that they're ready whenever these features are supported. Keep an eye on the Macromedia Web site, at www.macromedia.com, and the Macromedia CSS information site at www.macromedia.com/devnet/dreamweaver/css.html for changes and updates to Dreamweaver, as well as for news about changing standards and support for these CSS features. Always preview your work in your target browser(s) to make sure the properties you set are properly supported.

The Type category

After you name your style and specify the fields described in the "Creating a new style" section earlier in this chapter, click OK and the CSS Rule Definition dialog box appears (see Figure 8-12).

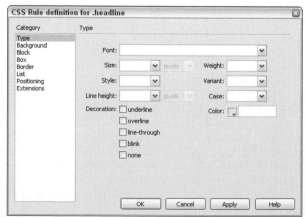

Figure 8-12:
The Type
category in
the CSS
Rule
Definition
dialog box.

When you choose Type from the Category list, the Type options are visible, and you have these formatting options:

- ✔ **Font:** Specifies a font, font family, or series of families. You can add fonts to the list by choosing Edit Font List from the drop-down list.

- ✔ **Size:** Defines the size of the text. You can choose a specific numeric size, and the pop-up menu to the right of this field allows you to choose the unit of measurement. You can also select from a list of relative values (xx-small, x-small, and so on) that the browser interprets in relation to other textual elements on the page.

- ✔ **Style:** Enables you to choose whether the text appears as normal, italic, or oblique. (Italic and oblique are rarely different in a Web browser, so stick with italic unless you have a specific reason not to.)

- ✔ **Line Height:** Enables you to specify the height of a line on which the text is placed (graphic designers usually call it *leading*).

- ✔ **Decoration:** Enables you to specify whether text is underlined, overlined (the line appears over the text rather than under it), or displayed with a strikethrough. You can also choose Blink, which makes the text flash on and off, or None, which removes all decorative effects.

   Use the Decoration options sparingly, if at all. Links are automatically underlined, so if you underline text that isn't a link, you risk confusing viewers. Overlined and strikethrough text can be hard to read. Use these options only if they enhance your design. And, by all means, resist the blink option; it's distracting and can make the screen difficult to read. (Overline and blink don't display in the Document window; you must preview your page in a Web browser to see these effects.)

- ✔ **Weight:** Enables you to control how bold the text displays by using a specific or relative boldness option.

- ✔ **Variant:** Enables you to select a variation of the font, such as small caps. Unfortunately, this attribute isn't yet supported by most browsers; for example, if you specify small caps the text may simply display in all caps.

- ✔ **Case:** Enables you to globally change the case of selected words, making them all uppercase or lowercase or with initial caps.

- ✔ **Color:** Defines the color of the text. You can use the color well (the square icon) to open a Web-safe color palette in which you can select predefined colors or create custom colors.

After you select the Type options for your style sheet, click OK to save the settings.

The Background category

The Background category in the CSS Rule Definition dialog box (see Figure 8-13) enables you to specify a background color or image for a style that you can then apply to a block of text or an area of your Web page.

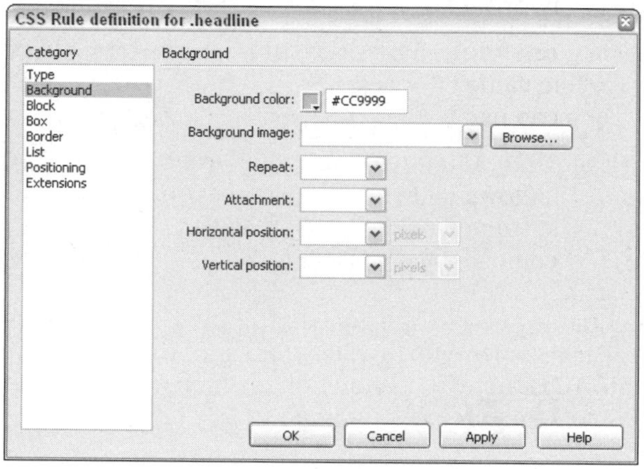

Figure 8-13:
The
Background
category in
the CSS
Rule
Definition
dialog box.

You can choose from these options:

- ✔ **Background Color:** Specifies the background color of an element, such as a table. You can use the color well (the square icon) to open a Web-safe color palette in which you can select predefined colors or create custom colors.

- ✔ **Background Image:** Enables you to select a background image as part of the style definition. Click the Browse button to select the image.

- ✔ **Repeat:** Determines how and whether the background image tiles across and down the page. In all cases, the image is cropped if it doesn't fit behind the element.

   The Repeat options are

   - • **No Repeat:** The background displays once at the beginning of the element.

   - • **Repeat:** The background image repeats vertically and horizontally behind the element.

   - • **Repeat-x:** The background repeats horizontally, but not vertically, behind the element.

   - • **Repeat-y:** The background repeats vertically, but not horizontally, behind the element.

✔ **Attachment:** This property determines how the background behaves when the page is scrolled.

   • **Fixed:** The background remains glued to one place in the viewing area and does not scroll out of sight even when the Web page is scrolled.

   • **Scroll:** The background scrolls along with the Web page. This is the default behavior for backgrounds.

✔ **Horizontal Position:** Allows you to align the image left, center, or right, or to set a numeric value to determine the horizontal placement of the background. You can use horizontal positioning only when the background doesn't repeat.

✔ **Vertical Position:** Allows you to align the image top, center, or bottom, or to set a numeric value to determine the vertical placement of the background. You can use vertical positioning only when the background doesn't repeat.

The Block category

The Block category (see Figure 8-14) defines spacing and alignment settings for tags and attributes.

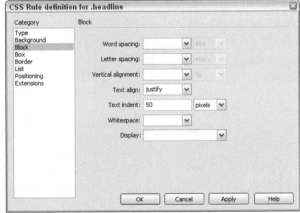

Figure 8-14:
The Block category in the CSS Rule Definition dialog box.

You can choose from these options:

✔ **Word Spacing:** Defines the amount of white space inserted between words in points, millimeters (mm), centimeters (cm), picas, inches, pixels, ems, and exs.

✔ **Letter Spacing:** Defines the amount of white space inserted between letters in points, millimeters (mm), centimeters (cm), picas, inches, pixels, ems, and exs.

✔ **Vertical Alignment:** This property aligns inline elements like text and images in relation to the elements that surround them. Note that you may have to preview the page in a browser to see these effects. Your options are baseline, sub, super, top, text-top, middle, bottom, text-bottom, or you can set a numeric value.

✔ **Text Align:** Left, right, center, or justify your text.

✔ **Text Indent:** Specifies how far the first line of text is indented. Negative numbers are allowed if you want the first line to stick out.

✔ **Whitespace:** This property tells the browser how to handle line breaks and spaces within a block of text. Your options are Normal, Pre (for preformatted), and Nowrap.

✔ **Display:** Indicates how to render an element in the browser. You can hide an element by choosing None.

The Box category

The Box category (see Figure 8-15) defines settings for tags and attributes that control the placement and appearance of elements on the page.

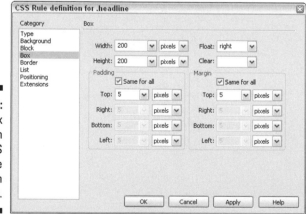

Figure 8-15:
The Box category in the CSS Rule Definition dialog box.

You can think of all HTML elements (even tags such as <A>) as boxes in terms of CSS layout. You can use the Box category properties to set positioning and spacing issues for these boxes:

✓ **Width, Height:** Enable you to specify a width and height that you can use in styles you apply to images, layers, or any other element that can have its dimensions specified. You can use pixels, points, inches, centimeters, millimeters, picas, ems, exs, or percentages for your measurements.

✓ **Float:** Enables you to align a boxed element to the left or right so that other elements, such as text, wrap around it.

✓ **Clear:** Prevents floating content from overlapping an area to the left or right, or to both sides. (This option doesn't currently display in Dreamweaver.)

✓ **Padding:** Sets the amount of space around an element to its edge. You can set padding separately for the top, right, bottom, and left. Padding is measured in pixels, points, inches, centimeters, millimeters, picas, ems, exs, and percentages.

✓ **Margin:** Sets the amount of space between the edge of an element and other elements on the page. You can set the margin separately for the top, right, bottom, and left. Padding is measured in pixels, points, inches, centimeters, millimeters, picas, ems, exs, and percentages.

For more on using the Box category for layout, see Chapter 9.

The Border category

The Border category defines settings — such as width, color, and style — for the borders of box elements on a page. Your options are Style, Width, and Color (see Figure 8-16). Many borders are not reproduced properly in Dreamweaver; use your browser to preview the results.

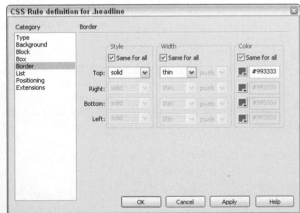

Figure 8-16:
The Border
category in
the CSS
Rule
Definition
dialog box.

The List category

The List category defines settings, such as bullet size and type, for list tags. You can specify whether bullets are disc, circle, square, decimal, lower-roman, upper-roman, upper alpha, lower alpha, or none. If you want to use a custom bullet, you can use the Browse button to locate an image to be used as the bullet. You can control the location of the list bullet in relation to the list item (see Figure 8-17).

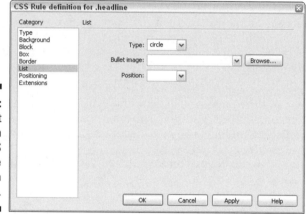

Figure 8-17:
The List category in the CSS Rule Definition dialog box.

The Positioning category

The Positioning category (see Figure 8-18) enables you to precisely position elements on a page. This style uses the tag specified for defining layers in the Layer preferences. The default in Dreamweaver for layers is the <DIV> tag. You can change it by editing the Layer preferences. The <DIV> tag is the most commonly supported, however, so you should try to stick with it. See Chapter 9 for more on layer preferences.

To understand how positioning works, it's important to know that positioning is done relative to something else, like another element on the page or the browser window. How you set up positioning to work depends on where your element is on the page, and what other elements it may be inside. Here are the Positioning options:

✔ **Type:** Enables you to specify the position of a layer as absolute, relative, or static:

  • **Absolute:** This positioning uses the top and left coordinates entered in the Placement text boxes to control the position of the layer relative to the upper-left corner of the Web page or to the element that contains this element.

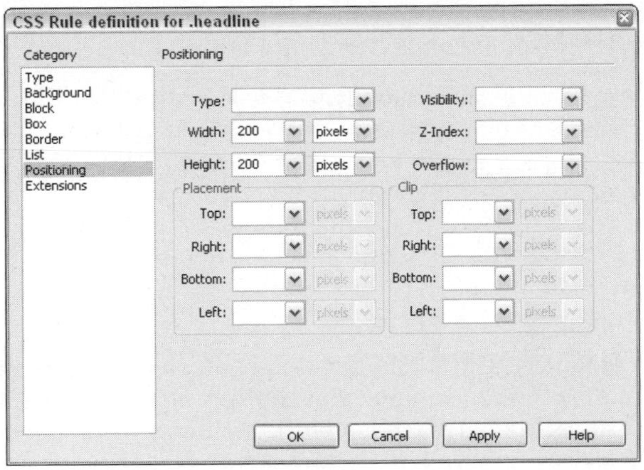

Figure 8-18:
The Positioning category in the CSS Rule Definition dialog box.

- **Relative:** This positioning uses a position relative to the point you insert it into the page.

- **Static:** This positioning keeps the layer in the place where you insert it on the page relative to the browser window. Scrolling the window doesn't have an effect on a static element, so be careful not to place it over other information.

✔ **Visibility:** Enables you to control whether the browser displays the element. You can use this feature, combined with a scripting language, such as JavaScript, to dynamically change the display of layers. Visibility is used to create a number of effects on a page because you can control when something is seen or not seen. For example, you can cause an element to appear on a page only when a user clicks a button, and then make it disappear when the button is clicked again.

The default is to inherit the original element's visibility value:

- **Inherit:** The layer has the visibility of the element in which it is contained.

- **Visible:** The layer is displayed.

- **Hidden:** The layer isn't displayed.

✔ **Width, Height:** Enables you to specify a width and height that you can use in styles you apply to images, layers, or any other element that can have its dimensions specified. You can use pixels, points, inches, centimeters, millimeters, picas, ems, exs, or percentages for your measurements.

✔ **Z-Index:** Controls the position of the layer on the *Z* coordinate, which is how it stacks in relation to other elements on the page. Higher-numbered layers overlap lower-numbered layers.

✔ **Overflow:** Tells the browser how to display the contents of a layer if the layer doesn't contain the entire contents. (This option does not currently display in the Dreamweaver Workspace.)

- **Visible:** Forces the layer to increase in size to display all its contents. The layer expands downward and to the right.

- **Hidden:** Cuts off the contents of the layer that don't fit. This option doesn't provide any scroll bars.

- **Scroll:** Adds scroll bars to the layer regardless of whether the contents exceed the layer's size.

- **Auto:** Makes scroll bars appear only when the layer's contents exceed its boundaries. (This feature does not currently display in the Dreamweaver Workspace.)

✔ **Placement:** Defines the size and location of an element layer within its containing element. For example, you can set the right edge of the element to line up with the right edge of the element that contains it. The default values are measured in pixels, but you can also use pc (picas), pt (points), in (inches), mm (millimeters), cm (centimeters), or % (percentage of the parent's value).

✔ **Clip:** When the content of an element overflows the space allotted and you set the Overflow property to scroll or auto, you can set the clip settings to specify which part of the layer is visible by controlling which part of the layer is cropped if it doesn't fit in the display area.

The Extensions category

Extensions (see Figure 8-19) include filters and cursor options:

✔ **Pagebreak:** Inserts a point in a page where a printer sees a page break. This option allows you to control the way the document is printed.

✔ **Cursor:** Defines the type of cursor that appears when a user moves the cursor over an element.

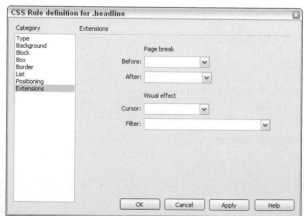

Figure 8-19: The Extensions category in the CSS Rule Definition dialog box.

> ✔ **Filter:** Enables you to apply to elements special effects such as drop shadows, motion blurs, and many others. These are only visible in Microsoft Internet Explorer.

Using External Style Sheets

The first part of this chapter focuses on using CSS only in the context of internal style sheets. Internal style sheet information is stored in the HTML code of the document you're working on and applies to only the current document. If you want to create styles you can share among documents, you need to use external style sheets. External style sheets enable you to create styles you can apply to pages throughout a Web site by storing the style sheet information in a separate text page that can be linked to from any HTML document.

External style sheets (also called *linked style sheets*) are where you can realize the greatest timesavings with CSS. You can define styles for common formatting options used throughout an entire site, such as headlines, captions, and even images, which makes applying multiple formatting options to elements fast and easy. Big news- and magazine-type Web sites often use external style sheets because they need to follow a consistent look and feel throughout the site, even when many people are working on the same site. Typing styles to HTML tags via an external style sheet is a foolproof way of making sure that everyone creating content for your Web site ends up with pages that look the same. Using external style sheets also makes global changes easier because when you change the external style sheet, you globally change every element to which you applied the style throughout the site.

Creating an external style sheet

You create external style sheets almost exactly the same way you create internal style sheets, except that external style sheets need to be saved as separate files. When you use Dreamweaver to create an external style sheet, Dreamweaver automatically links the style sheet to the page you're working on. You can then link it to any other Web page in which you want to apply the style definitions.

To create an external style sheet, follow these steps:

1. **Choose Text⇨CSS Styles⇨New.**

   The New CSS Rule dialog box appears.

2. **Select from the Selector Type category the type of style you want to create.**

   Remember that you have three options: Class, Tag, or Advanced.

3. **Fill out the Name field, or select an option from the Tag or Selector fields, depending on which selector type you chose in Step 2.**

4. **In the Define In area, select (New Style Sheet File).**

5. **Click OK.**

   The Save Style Sheet File As dialog box opens.

6. **Select a location in which to save the style sheet file and click Save. Name the file and be sure to use a `.css` extension to identify your file as a style sheet.**

   Dreamweaver automatically adds the `.css`; just make sure you don't delete it.

7. **Click Save.**

   The CSS Rule Definition dialog box opens.

8. **Define the new style rule specifying all formatting options you want applied with the new style.**

9. **Click OK to save the new style and close the dialog box.**

   Your new style is saved to your external style sheet and made available to link to any of the files in your Web site.

Linking to an external style sheet

After you set up an external style sheet, you may want to link it to additional Web pages. Begin by opening the page to which you want to attach the style sheet, and follow these steps:

1. **Choose Window⊅CSS Styles.**

   The CSS panel appears.

2. **Click the Attach Style Sheet icon in the CSS panel (the first button in the lower-right area).**

   The Attach External Style Sheet dialog box appears (shown in Figure 8-20), prompting you to select the location of the external style sheet. You can type the URL if it's a remote file on the Web like this line:

   ```
   http://www.mycompany.com/CSS/mystyle.css
   ```

   or use the Browse button to locate a file inside your site folder and Dreamweaver automatically sets the link for you.

   Notice that two options are available for linking to an external style sheet: Link and Import. Attaching a style sheet by linking it is the pure HTML way to handle attachment; importing is intended to allow one style sheet to call another.

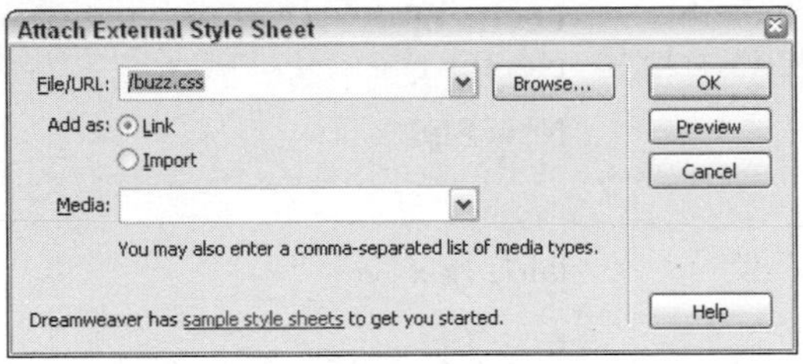

Figure 8-20:
Attach an
external
style sheet
with this
dialog box.

The Media drop-down list allows you to select a scenario for which to use the style sheet. For example, if you've created a style sheet that formats your page correctly for PDA display, select the Handheld option on this menu.

3. **After you select the external style sheet, click the OK button.**

The dialog box disappears, and the external CSS file automatically links to your page. Any styles you have defined in the external style sheet now appear in the CSS panel, and any redefined HTML styles or CSS selectors are automatically applied to the page. Because you have established a link on this page to the external style sheet, the styles in the external style sheet always appear in the CSS panel whenever you open this file (see Figure 8-21).

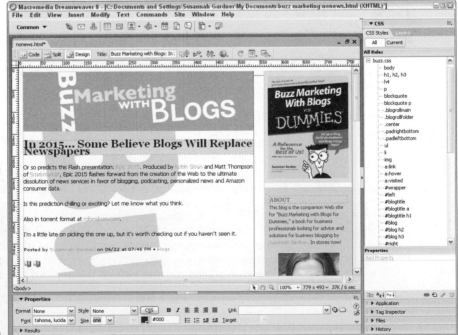

Figure 8-21:
External
style sheets
linked to the
current
document
appear in
the CSS
Styles
panel.

4. **To apply a style on your page, select the text to which you want to apply the style and apply the style in the same way you would with an internal style sheet.**

   For more on applying styles, see the section "Applying styles in Dreamweaver," earlier in this chapter.

Editing an external style sheet

You edit linked external style sheets exactly the same way as you edit internal style sheets using the CSS panel, which lists all styles in the document, whether they're internal or external. Use the Properties pane of the CSS panel to directly edit the rules for each style. Any changes you make to the external style sheet are automatically made, even though it's a separate document (as long as the style sheet exists locally on the computer). If you try to edit a remote CSS file from a linked page in Dreamweaver, you can't because Dreamweaver doesn't have edit privileges for the file.

If you want to edit a remote CSS file, you have to download the file to your hard drive before you can open it in Dreamweaver. In Dreamweaver, you can open .css files by either double-clicking them or choosing File⇨Open, both of which open the style sheet in Code view. Code view is the only view available for CSS files because they're text files and have no layout components. When you view an external style sheet this way, you can still use the CSS panel to edit the style sheet, even if the style sheet isn't linked to an HTML page. Be sure to save it when you finish editing it! Of course, if you prefer, you can also edit the code by hand directly in Code view. Figure 8-22 shows an example of a style sheet opened directly in Dreamweaver. Notice that the CSS panel displays all relevant style information and gives you access to the CSS editing tools.

When you finish editing an external style sheet, you need to upload it to your server before the styles apply to pages on your live Web site.

Applying ready-made external style sheets

Macromedia includes a bunch of sample style sheets for you to use to create new pages in your Web site. These come in the form of external styles sheets that have been created with some popular styles in mind to help you get better acquainted with style sheets and give you a jump-start in designing with them. You can either use these styles as is or modify them to suit your needs.

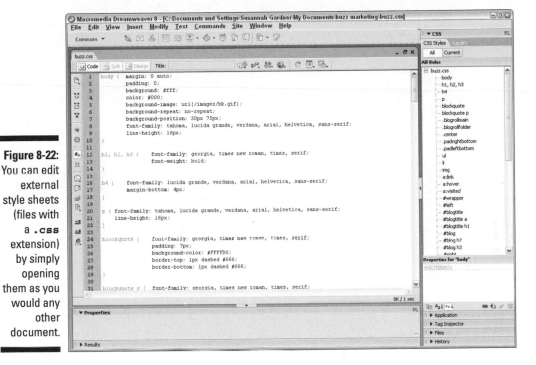

Figure 8-22:
You can edit external style sheets (files with a `.css` extension) by simply opening them as you would any other document.

To access the sample style sheets provided by Macromedia, follow these steps:

1. **File⇨New.**

   The New Document dialog box opens (see Figure 8-23).

2. **Select CSS Style Sheets from the Category list to display the list of CSS files, and try clicking any of the sample styles that are listed.**

   Notice that a preview of how the style appears displays on the right side of the dialog box when you click any of the sample styles.

3. **Select a style you like and click Create.**

   A new, untitled style sheet in Code view opens.

4. **To save the style sheet, choose File⇨Save (or Save As) and save it in the site directory where you plan to use it.**

   You can also modify the rules before saving the file if you want to customize your style sheet. If you do this, be sure to choose Save As instead of Save so that you don't overwrite the sample file.

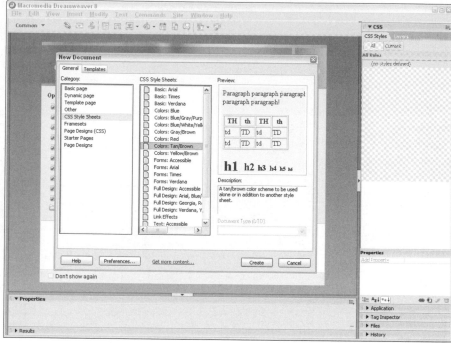

Figure 8-23:
You can access and preview the Macromedia-provided sample style sheets by creating a new CSS document.

Using Design Time Style Sheets

After you become savvy about using style sheets, you'll find that working with external style sheets affords the most power because you can link to them from multiple pages in your site rather than have to create a new internal style sheet for each page in your site. You also have the added advantage that you can easily alter your styles in just one place if you need to make changes after styles are applied. Even better, you can create multiple external style sheets as part of the design process and use a Dreamweaver feature called Design Time Style Sheets to switch back and forth between them as you work on your document.

One benefit of the Design Time Style Sheets feature is that you can view how different external style sheets affect your page without having to link to them. This feature is a great way to quickly switch back and forth between style sheets in a document and explore various what-if scenarios with the style sheets you create before you apply them. You may begin to like this feature because you can play around with and explore the full power of CSS.

After you decide that you like a particular style sheet, you can apply it to your page as you do any other style sheet. (See the section, "Applying Styles in Dreamweaver," earlier in this chapter for how to apply a style.)

Design Time Style Sheets affect only the appearance of styles in Dreamweaver. Because they're not real links, they show up only at runtime when a Dreamweaver document is open. Design Time Style Sheet info is also stored in a Design Note file. If you want to preserve your Design Time Style Sheet info, be sure that you don't delete the corresponding Design Note file.

To set up Design Time Style sheets, follow these steps:

1. **Choose Text⇨CSS Styles⇨Design-Time.**

   The Design Time Style Sheets dialog box appears (see Figure 8-24).

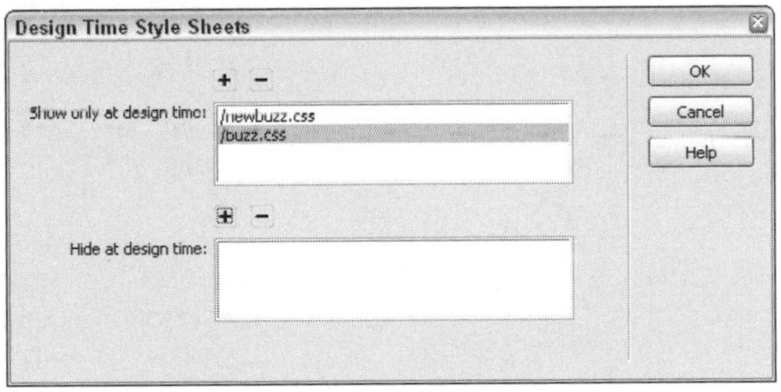

Figure 8-24:
Design Time
Style Sheets
let you view
or hide
multiple
style sheets
at runtime.

2. **To work with a specific style sheet, click the Add Item (+) button above the Show Only at Design Time field.**

   The Select File dialog box appears, and you can select a CSS file. Remember that CSS files usually end with a `.css` extension. You can also add multiple CSS files by clicking the Add button again to add a new CSS file.

3. **To hide a specific style sheet, click the Add Item (+) button above the Hide at Design Time field and select from the Select File dialog box the style you want to hide.**

4. **To delete a listed style sheet from either category, select the style sheet and click the Remove Item (-) button to delete it.**

Part IV
Making It Cool

The 5th Wave   By Rich Tennant

©RICHTENNANT

"Evidently he died of natural causes following a marathon session animating everything on his personal Web site. And no, Morganstern – the irony isn't lost on me."

In this part . . .

Dynamic HTML and multimedia make the Web sing, dance, and delight. In this part, you find a chapter dedicated to harnessing the power of Dynamic HTML and the design control of layers. You discover how Macromedia has integrated its image program, Fireworks, to work with Dreamweaver so that image creation and editing are seamless. And you find out how to add multimedia files, such as sound, video, and Flash animations, to your Web pages.

Chapter 9

Advanced HTML: CSS Layouts, DHTML, and Behaviors

. . . .

In This Chapter

▶ Positioning precisely with layers

▶ Looking at DHTML

▶ Using and applying behaviors

▶ Working with older Web pages

▶ Exploring extensions and the Extension Manager

▶ Converting to XHTML

. . . .

As the Web and those of us who use it mature in our experience and technical prowess, using complex HTML features, such as CSS layouts and Dynamic HTML, is becoming more common. Two powerful Dreamweaver features make creating advanced HTML and DHTML possible: layers and behaviors. Brace yourself, you're getting into some of the most complex Dreamweaver Web-design features in this chapter, but I think you'll find the power and precision of these options well worth the effort.

This chapter starts off by introducing Dreamweaver's Layers features, which enable precise positioning of text, images, and other elements on a page, using the `<DIV>` tag and CSS layouts. You also find step-by-step instructions for creating your own CSS layouts (a complex, but infinitely customizable way to create page layouts).

The rest of this chapter explains how to implement DHTML into your Web pages by applying behaviors to elements on your pages. Doing so allows you to add some of the most advanced design features and interactivity to your Web pages.

Working with Layers

Layers permit precise positioning of elements on an HTML page. Think of a layer as a container for other elements, such as images, text, tables, and even other layers. You can put this container anywhere on an HTML page, and even stack these containers on top of each other.

Using layers, you can position text blocks and images exactly where you want them on a page by placing them in a `<DIV>` tag and then specifying the layer's distance from the top and left sides of a page, or from another layer. This complexity and control is sorely missing from standard HTML. One of the greatest limitations of HTML is its inability to stack elements on top of each other. With layers, a positioning option called the Z index adds this capability, which allows you to layer text, images, and other elements.

Because a layer is a container, you can manipulate everything in it as a unit, such as moving a layer on top of another layer or making the entire layer visible or invisible.

Remember that pre-algebra teacher who was addicted to transparencies and the overhead projector? Layers work similarly to those transparencies: You can move layers around to position elements exactly where you want them, use the layers to overlap elements on a page, or turn the layers on and off to control visibility. If you're new to layers, you may want to check out the following sections and experiment a little with creating layers, adding images and other elements, and moving layers around.

Creating layers

To create a layer, follow these steps:

1. **Choose Insert⇨Layout Objects⇨Layer.**

    A box representing an empty layer appears at the top of the page outlined in blue (see Figure 9-1).

    Alternatively, you can click the Draw Layer button in the Layout Insert bar and then click and drag to create a new layer anywhere in the work area.

Layer not <LAYER>

The term *layers* can be confusing. Several years ago there was an actual `<LAYER>` HTML tag. However, it never became part of the HTML standard. In fact, today it's completely obsolete. Nonetheless, you may find tutorials and references to the `<LAYER>` tag.

Don't confuse the HTML tag with Dreamweaver layers, which are actually just absolutely positioned `<DIV>` tags controlled by CSS styles.

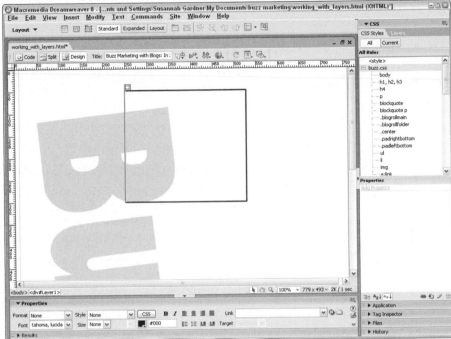

Figure 9-1:
You can
create a
layer
anywhere
on the page.

2. Click anywhere along the outline of the layer box to select it.

When you hold the mouse over the outline of the layer, the cursor turns to a four-pointed arrow (or a hand on the Macintosh). You also see eight tiny, square handles around the perimeter of the box.

3. Click and drag any of the handles to resize the layer.

Adding elements, resizing, and repositioning layers

To make a layer useful, you have to put something inside it. You can place pretty much anything within a layer that you can place in a document. To add images or text to a layer, follow these steps:

1. Click to insert your cursor inside the layer.

A blinking cursor appears inside the layer box.

2. Choose Insert⇨Image.

The Select Image Source dialog box appears.

3. **Click the filename of the image you want to insert.**

4. **Click OK.**

   The Image Tag Accessibility Attributes dialog box opens.

   If you don't want this box to open each time you insert an image, you can change the accessibility attributes by choosing Edit⇨Preferences (Windows) or Dreamweaver⇨Preferences (Mac).

5. **Fill in the Alternate text and Long description fields and click OK.**

   The image appears inside the layer.

6. **Select the image and use the Properties inspector to make any formatting changes to it.**

   Formatting images inside layers works the same way as on a regular HTML page. For example, using the Align Center icon centers the image in the layer. Find more information about formatting images in Chapter 5.

7. **Click inside the layer again to insert your cursor and enter some text (see Figure 9-2).**

Figure 9-2: You can insert images and text inside layers, just as you would insert them inside a document.

8. **Highlight the text and format it by using the text-formatting options in the Properties inspector or by choosing formatting options from the Text menu. Or, use the Style drop-down list in the Properties inspector to apply or define a style.**

   Formatting text inside layers is just like formatting text inside a regular Dreamweaver document. You can read more about formatting text in Chapter 2.

9. **Click the tab that appears in the upper-left area of the layer or anywhere along the border to select the layer.**

   You know that you have successfully selected the layer when you see the selection *handles,* the little black squares that appear at the corners and in the middle of each side.

10. **Click any handle and drag to resize the layer.**

    As a general rule, always size a layer so that its contents *just* fit within its boundaries. Positioning the layer on the page is then easier.

    Rather than drag to resize, you can type new measurements for the width (W) and height (H) directly into the Properties inspector (refer to Figure 9-2). The Properties inspector displays these options only when the layer is selected.

11. **To move a layer, click and drag the little tab (which appears in the upper-left area of the layer when it's selected).**

    Because layers use exact, or *absolute,* positioning, you can move them to any precise location on a page, and they display in that exact location in browsers that support layers, such as Netscape Navigator 4 and Internet Explorer 4 and later.

    The Properties inspector also displays the Layer coordinates when the layer is selected: L (for left), T (for top). In addition to using the click-and-drag method to move a layer, you can change a layer's position by entering a number in the position boxes, L (number of pixels from the left edge of the page), and T (number of pixels from the top of the page).

12. **Name your layer by typing a name in the Layer ID text box in the upper-left corner of the Properties inspector.**

    When you create a new layer, Dreamweaver automatically names your layers for you, starting with Layer1, Layer2, and so on. You should change the name to something more descriptive, especially if you're working with lots of layers on a page. Keeping track of them by name makes them much easier to manage. Remember that you must select the layer first in order for its properties to appear in the Properties inspector.

Stacking layers and changing visibility

A powerful feature of layers is their maneuverability: You can stack them on top of each other and make them visible or invisible. Later in this chapter, in the "Working with Behaviors" section, you find out how to use these features in combination with behaviors to create rollovers and other effects. To stack layers, simply drag one layer on top of another. Unlike images, layers give you complete layout control on the page by including the capability to over-lap one another. To overlap images, simply place each image within a sepa-rate layer and then move one layer so that it overlaps the other. To let you control which layer is on top, Dreamweaver provides two ways of changing the order of stacking: the Z index, available in the Properties inspector, and the Layers panel (see Figure 9-3), which you can access by choosing Window⇨Layers.

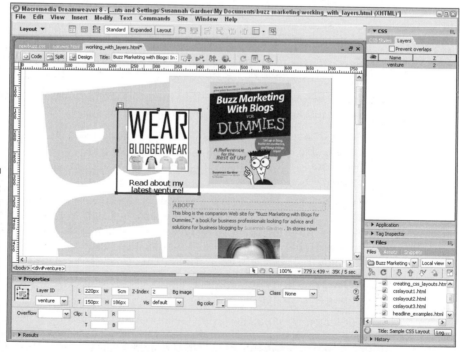

Figure 9-3:
The Layers panel changes the visibility and stacking order of your document's layers.

To stack layers and change their order and visibility, follow these steps:

1. **Open a page that has two or more layers on it.**

2. **Select the layer by clicking anywhere on the border outline of the layer.**

3. **Choose Window⇨Layers to open the Layers panel.**

   The Layers panel lists any layers that appear on your page. If you're familiar with layers in Adobe Photoshop or Macromedia Fireworks, you may
   find some similarities here, such as the eye icon to control layer visibility
   and the capability to drag layers around in the panel to reposition them.

4. **Reorder the stacking of the layers by changing the Z-Index number of
   the layers in the Properties inspector.**

   You can also change the Z-Index number in the Layers panel. The lowest
   number is the bottommost layer. To change the number, simply click to
   select it and type the new number.

   You can rename a layer by double-clicking the name in the Layers panel
   to select it and then typing a new name.

5. **Click the eye icon to the left of any layer in the Layers panel to turn
   the layer visibility on or off (refer to Figure 9-3).**

   If no eye appears, the visibility is set to default, which usually means *on*,
   except in the case of nested layers. (You can find out about nested
   layers in the next section.) If the eye is open, the layer is visible on the
   screen and in the browser. If the eye is closed, the layer is invisible; it's
   still there — it just isn't displayed on-screen or in the browser.

   If you want to prevent any of your layers from overlapping, check the
   Prevent Overlaps check box in the Layers panel.

Nesting layers: One happy family

Another way to position layers on a page is by nesting them. A *nested layer* is
essentially a layer that's invisibly tied to another layer and maintains a kind of
parent-child relationship with the first layer. The child layer uses the upper-
left corner of the parent layer as its orientation point for positioning rather
than the upper-left corner of the browser window because it's nested *within*
the parent layer. Even if the layers are on different areas of the page, they still
retain this parent-child relationship. When you move the first layer around on
the page, the nested layer moves along with it. You can also think of this scenario as an owner walking his dog on a leash — where the owner goes, the
dog has to follow, even though the dog can still move independently of its
owner within the confines of the length of the leash.

If you were to nest another layer into the child layer, that would then make
the child layer both a parent and a child. The new layer then uses the upper-
left corner of its parent layer as its orientation point. The first layer in the
nested chain still retains control over all the child layers, so they all move
when the parent moves.

Nested layers can be a great way to keep chunks of your layout working
together as you move them around the page. Rather than try to keep track of

loads of different layers and move each one individually, you can group them into more easily manageable *family units*. Furthermore, you can make a whole family visible or invisible by clicking the eye icon of the parent layer in the Layers panel if the child layer's visibility has been set to default (no eye icon in the Layers panel). When the child layer's visibility is set to default, it inherits the visibility of its parent layer. As you experiment with layers and start using lots of them on your page, understanding inheritance becomes essential. Be aware, though, that when a child layer is set to either visible (eye icon on) or invisible (eye icon off) in the Layers panel, it's unaffected by the visibility setting of its parent layer.

Make sure Dreamweaver's preferences are set to allow nesting. Choose Edit➪Preferences, and then in the Preferences dialog box, select the Layers category. Then select the check box labeled Nesting: Nest When Created within a Layer.

To create a nested layer, follow these steps:

1. **Choose Insert➪Layout Objects➪Layer.**

   A box representing the layer appears at the top of the page. Dreamweaver automatically names the layer Layer1.

2. **Place the cursor inside the first layer, and choose Insert➪Layout Objects➪Layer to create a second layer inside the first.**

3. **Position the second layer anywhere on the page by dragging the small tab in the upper-left corner of the layer box or clicking and dragging anywhere on the layer's border.**

   Visually, nested layers don't need to reside inside their parent layers; they can be placed anywhere else on the page or be stacked on top of each other.

4. **Choose Window➪Layers to open the Layers panel, if it isn't already open.**

   The Layers panel opens.

   In the Layers panel, you see that a nested layer displays underneath and slightly indented from its parent, and a line shows their relationship (see Figure 9-4).

Figure 9-4:
The Layers panel.

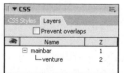

Setting layer options

Like other HTML elements, layers have many attributes you can set.
Dreamweaver makes these options available in the Properties inspector
whenever you select a layer.

This list describes the layer options and what they control:

- **Layer ID:** You can type your own descriptive name on this drop-down
  list in the upper-left corner of the Properties inspector. If you don't name
  a layer, Dreamweaver names it for you. Use only standard alphanumeric
  characters for a layer name (don't use special characters, such as
  spaces, hyphens, slashes, or periods).

- **L (Left):** This value specifies the distance of the layer from the left side
  of the page or parent layer. Dreamweaver automatically enters a pixel
  value when you create or move a layer by dragging and dropping it. You
  can also enter a numeric value in pixels or percents (positive or negative) to control the positioning.

- **T (Top):** This value specifies the distance of the layer from the top of the
  page or parent layer. Dreamweaver automatically enters a pixel value
  when you create or move a layer by dragging and dropping. You can also
  enter a numeric value in pixels or percents (positive or negative) to control the positioning.

- **W (Width):** Dreamweaver automatically specifies the width when you
  create a layer on a page. You also have the option of entering a numeric
  value to specify the width. You can change the px (pixels) default measurement to any of the following: pc (picas), pt (points), in (inches), mm
  (millimeters), cm (centimeters), or % (percentage of the page or parent
  layer's width). Don't put any spaces between the number and the measurement abbreviation.

- **H (Height):** Dreamweaver automatically specifies the height when you
  create a layer on a page. You also have the option of entering a numeric
  value to specify the height. You can change the default measurement of
  px (pixels) to any of the following: pc (picas), pt (points), in (inches),
  mm (millimeters), cm (centimeters), or % (percentage of the page or
  parent layer's height). Don't put any spaces between the number and
  the measurement abbreviation.

- **Z-Index:** This option determines the position of a layer in relation to
  other layers when layers are stacked. Higher-numbered layers appear on
  top of lower-numbered layers, and values can be positive or negative.

- **Vis:** This visibility setting controls whether a layer is visible or invisible.
  You can modify this setting with a scripting language, such as JavaScript,
  to dynamically change the display of layers.

You can choose from these visibility options:

- **Default:** The default option in most browsers is the same visibility property as the parent's value. If there is no parent layer, the default state is visible.

- **Inherit:** This option always uses the visibility property of the layer's parent.

- **Visible:** This option always displays the layer, regardless of the parent's value.

- **Hidden:** This option always makes the layer transparent (invisible), regardless of the parent's value. Even when it's hidden, all the content on a layer downloads when the page is viewed in the browser. You can dynamically control visibility by using the JavaScript behaviors covered in "Working with Behaviors" later in this chapter.

✔ **Bg Image:** With this option, you can select a background image for the layer in the same way that you would select a background image for a Web page. Click the folder icon to select an image or enter the name and path in the text box.

✔ **Bg Color:** Use this option to set a background color for a layer. Clicking the color square opens the color palette. If you want the layer background to be transparent, leave Bg Color blank.

✔ **Overflow:** These options determine how the contents of a layer display if they exceed the size of the layer.

You can choose from these Overflow options:

- **Visible:** If the layer has too much content, this option lets the content spill out over the edges of the layer — though this effect may not perform as expected in certain browsers. Making sure that content won't escape the confines of a layer is usually best. Be sure to preview the results in the browser to make sure you get the effect you want.

- **Hidden:** Clips off the edges of content that doesn't fit within the specified size of a layer. Be careful with this option; it doesn't provide any scroll bars.

- **Scroll:** Adds scroll bars to the sides of a layer regardless of whether its contents exceed the layer's size.

- **Auto:** Displays scroll bars only if the layer's contents don't fit within the layer's boundaries.

✔ **Clip:** This option controls which sections of the contents of a layer are cropped if the layer isn't large enough to display all its contents. You should specify the distance from the L (Left), T (Top), R (Right), and B (Bottom). You have to specify clips in pixels, or choose the Auto value.

Converting tables to layers: Precise positioning for older Web pages

If you want to achieve precise pixel-perfect positioning of elements on a Web page, layers are the easiest way to do it. You can achieve precision at a level impossible to obtain using regular HTML. Unfortunately, this wasn't always true. Back in the bad old days of browser versions 4.0 and earlier, layers were only wishful thinking.

So what happens if you want to work with a Web page created at that time, or better yet, bring that page into the world of CSS? If you're in this situation, you're sure to be pleased to find that Dreamweaver has a tool for you. Using this feature, you can convert a layout created years ago using older techniques into an HTML page that uses layers.

To convert a page that uses tables to one that uses layers and maintains the same page layout, choose Modify⇨Convert⇨Tables to Layers. Dreamweaver rebuilds the page using layers you can easily reposition with pixel-level precision.

You can go in the other direction, too, and convert layers into tables. Choose Modify⇨Convert⇨Layers to Tables, and the layers convert to a table structure that mimics the layers' positioning and uses table cells to control placement.

The Dreamweaver Layers to Table conversion feature isn't perfect because you can do things with layers that you can't do with tables. For example, you can't convert a page that contains nested or overlapping layers. Some designers use the Layers to Table conversion feature to create multiple pages and then direct visitors to the most appropriate design for their browsers, even if they have to alter the table version to make it look okay without all the DHTML features. Just make sure to use the Save As feature to save your converted page with a new name so that you have both versions.

Using CSS for Page Layout

Besides using CSS to format text, you can control visual formatting and lay out pages using the positioning features of CSS. Complex CSS layouts are becoming an increasingly popular alternative to complicated table layouts. Today's savvy Web designers are taking the time to learn how to make the most of CSS so that they can reap the benefits: quick design edits today, and faster Web site redesigns down the line. Should you abandon table layouts in favor of CSS? There's not a right or wrong answer here. Tables are still a valid layout technique, but they are harder to edit and update down the line. At the same time, remember that developing a really powerful CSS structure takes time and experience, not to mention a lot of testing in the browsers you expect your Web site visitors to use.

Take a look at examples of CSS-designed Web pages as you begin to explore the world of CSS for layout. Get started by visiting a site maintained by CSS guru Eric Meyer (www.meyerweb.com/eric/css/edge). You should also visit the CSS Zen Garden (www.csszengarden.com), a collaborative project that repurposes the same HTML code with CSS designs created by graphic designers. On these sites, you find lots of examples of CSS-designed pages and general tips about using CSS.

To use CSS for page layout, explore the Block, Border, and Positioning categories in the CSS Rule Definition dialog box, described in Chapter 8. Before you move on to these more complex topics, make sure you're familiar with the basic ones covered in Chapter 8.

The Box model

The key to understanding the way CSS works with page layout is to think in terms of the Box model. The *Box model* asserts that any element tag in an HTML document is handled by CSS as a container box. When you define a CSS rule and apply it to your page, you're creating a box on the page, not too unlike a cell in a table. This box acts as a container for your content and has attributes such as margin, border, and padding, for example.

Although you can use any CSS element for page layout purposes, the <DIV> tag is used most often to create page layouts. <DIV> stands for *div*ision, and these tags are quite simply containers that hold other content — in other words, to make a division on the page. Any content on a page that is surrounded by an opening and closing < DIV> tag becomes an object (also referred to as a box or layer) with properties such as border, margin, height, and width that you can manipulate using CSS.

Inline elements flow with text and don't contain begin and end lines. For example, the <B> and <IMG> tags are inline elements. You can place these elements one after another, and a new line break doesn't appear between each element. They simply flow with the text.

In contrast, a *block element* is one that interrupts the flow of the page, creating a box or block around which other page elements align. Some regular HTML tags are block elements, like the <P> tag, which creates a line break before and after it is used and doesn't allow anything to display alongside it. Using the <DIV> tag to create your block elements is handy, and that's, in fact, what it's intended to do.

Dreamweaver *layers*, discussed earlier in this chapter, are CSS block elements that have had absolute positioning attributes applied to them.

Using classes and ID selectors

You can implement CSS styles in one of three ways:

✔ **Define certain attributes for an HTML tag.** Anytime the tag is used, those attributes are applied.

✔ **Create a custom style with a unique name.** Apply the style to any existing element in the Web page by the addition of the Class attribute.

Use the <SPAN> tag on its own to apply a style:

```
<SPAN CLASS="HEADLINE">Headline text</SPAN>
```

Or, apply the style to an existing HTML tag:

```
<P CLASS="HEADLINE">Headline text</P>
```

✔ **Define certain attributes that are only used once in a Web page.** For example, when you create a copyright footer at the bottom of the page, its unique style is applied using the ID attribute.

You can apply the ID attribute to any tag, but it's frequently used with the <DIV> tag:

```
<DIV ID="COPYRIGHT">Copyright 2005</DIV>
```

Creating a CSS Layout

In this section, you find out how to create a custom CSS layout. This is more complicated than using Dreamweaver's layers option, but it provides you complete control.

In this section, you work with the <DIV> tag to create a sample layout. As you begin to master this technique, you're well on your way to designing any kind of CSS page layout. Figure 9-5 shows a Web page with CSS layout.

Starting with content

To get started, you need to start a new page and put some text on the page:

1. **Start a new document by choosing File⇨New.**

   The New Document window opens.

2. **Select Basic Page from the Category list and HTML from the Basic Page list. Click the Create button.**

   Your new document opens in the Document window.

3. **Type an identifying phrase at the top of your document. Press Enter (or Return) once to start a new paragraph.**

   In my example (refer to Figure 9-5), I typed "Logo would be here".

4. **Repeat Step 3 as many times as you need.**

   In my example (refer to Figure 9-5), I created two more blocks of text reading "Left-hand column" and "Main column."

5. **Choose File⇨Save and save your document.**

Creating and applying CSS rules

After you have boilerplate text in your template, you must create the styles that build and control the layout and apply them to the text.

Follow these steps to set up the bounding box shown as a dashed line (refer to Figure 9-1):

1. **Click and drag to select all the text in your document.**

2. **Choose Insert⇨Layout Objects⇨Div Tag.**

   The Insert Div Tag dialog box opens (see Figure 9-6).

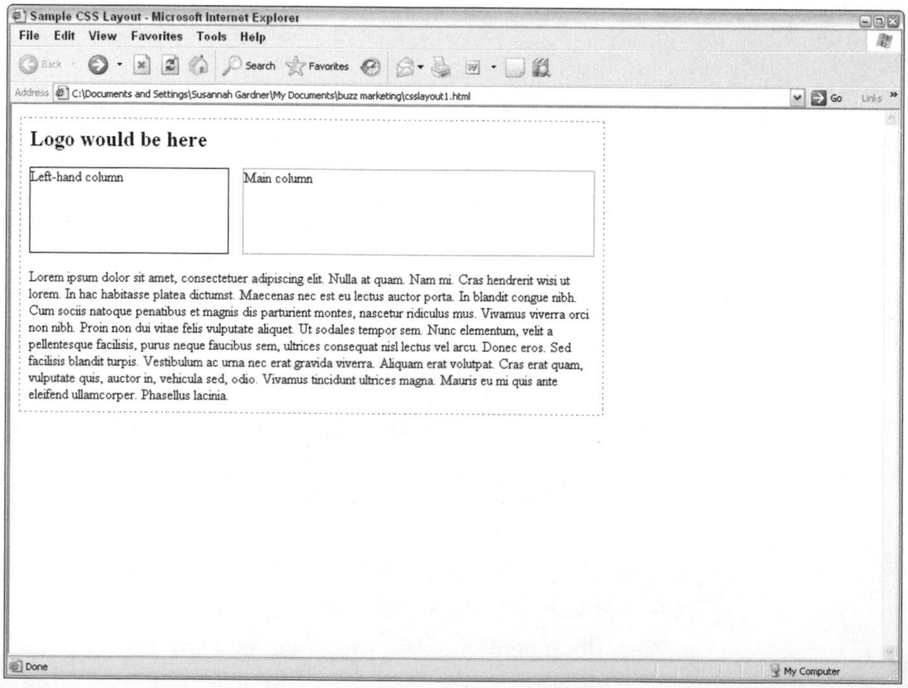

Figure 9-5:
You can use CSS to create this simple page layout.

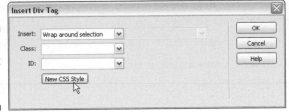

Figure 9-6:
The Insert
Div Tag
dialog box.

3. **Click the New CSS Style button.**

   The New CSS Rule dialog box opens (see Figure 9-7).

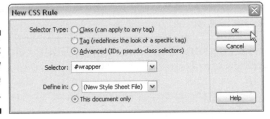

Figure 9-7:
The New
CSS Rule
dialog box.

4. **Select the Advanced radio button.**

5. **Type a name in the Selector field.**

   You can enter any name in the Selector field to identify the selector you're creating; just make sure you don't use spaces or special characters and always include the # sign, which is the way you indicate an ID selector in CSS.

   In my example, I used **#wrapper** as my name.

6. **Choose the This Document Only radio button, and click OK.**

   The CSS Rule Definition dialog box opens.

7. **Select the Box category and choose the following settings (see Figure 9-8):**

   • **Width:** 645 pixels

   • **Padding:** Enter 10 pixels in the field next to Top and check the Same for All box to apply padding to top, right, bottom, and left.

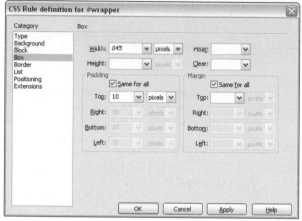

Figure 9-8:
The Box
category
of the
CSS Rule
Definition
dialog box.

8. **Select the Border category. Make sure the Same for All check box is selected for all attributes, and specify the following settings next to Top (see Figure 9-9):**

- **Style:** Dashed

- **Width:** 1 pixel (You first select Pixels from the drop-down list and then enter 1.)

- **Color:** #999999 (You can also use the color swatch to specify any hexadecimal color, just as you would set the color for the background or text on a Web page.)

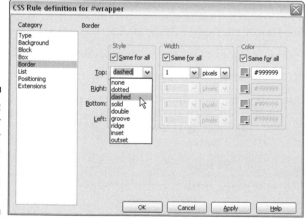

Figure 9-9:
The Border
category
of the
CSS Rule
Definition
dialog box.

9. **Click OK to close the CSS Rule Definition dialog box.**

10. **Click OK to close the Insert Div Tag dialog box.**

    The style is created and visible in the CSS panel, and it is applied to the text in the Document window.

Follow these steps to define a style for any additional columns:

1. **Click and drag to select the text you want in the column of your document.**

   In Figure 9-5, the text is `Left-hand column`.

2. **Choose Insert⇨Layout Objects⇨Div Tag.**

   The Insert Div Tag dialog box opens (refer to Figure 9-6).

3. **Click the New CSS Style button.**

   The New CSS Rule dialog box opens (refer to Figure 9-7).

4. **Select the Advanced radio button.**

5. **Type the name of your selector in the Selector field.**

   In my example, I used **#left** for the name.

6. **Choose the This Document Only radio button, and click OK.**

   The CSS Rule definition dialog box opens (as shown in Figure 9-10).

7. **Select the Box category and choose the following settings:**

   • **Width:** 225 pixels.

   • **Float:** Left.

8. **Select the Border category and choose the following settings, being sure that the Same for All check box is selected for each attribute:**

   • **Style:** Solid.

   • **Width:** 1 pixel (You first select Pixels from the drop-down list and then enter 1.)

   • **Color:** #000000 (You can also use the color swatch to specify any hexadecimal color, just as you would set the color for the background or text on a Web page.)

9. **Click OK to close the CSS Rule Definition dialog box.**

10. **Click OK to close the Insert Div Tag dialog box.**

    The style is created and visible in the CSS panel and is applied to the text.

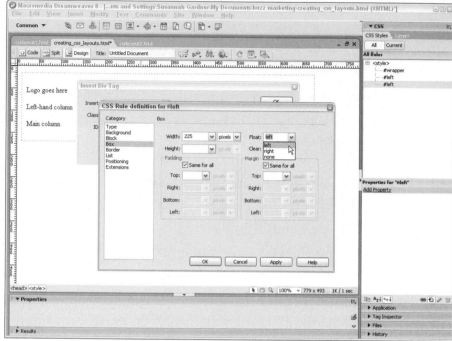

Figure 9-10:
Defining
the Float
attribute
in the
CSS Rule
Definition
dialog box.

The final style defines the main column (refer to Figure 9-5):

1. **Click and drag to select the text.**

   In this example, the text reads `Main column`.

2. **Choose Insert⇨Layout Objects⇨Div Tag.**

   The Insert Div Tag dialog box opens.

3. **Click the New CSS Style button.**

   The New CSS Rule dialog box opens.

4. **Select the Advanced radio button.**

5. **Type the name of your selector into the Selector field.**

   I used **#main** for my example.

6. **Choose the Define in This Document Only check box, and click OK.**

   The CSS Rule definition dialog box opens.

7. **Select the Box category and choose the following settings:**

   • **Width:** 400 pixels.

   • **Float:** Right.

8. **Select the Border category and choose the following settings, being sure that the Same for All check box is selected for each attribute:**

   - **Style:** Solid.

   - **Width:** 1 pixel (You first select Pixels from the drop-down list and then enter 1.)

   - **Color:** #FF0099 (You can also use the color swatch to specify any hexadecimal color, just as you would set the color for the background or text on a Web page.)

9. **Click OK.**

10. **Click OK to close the Insert Div Tag dialog box, making sure that its name appears in the ID field.**

    The style is created and visible in the CSS panel, and it is applied to the text.

Congratulations! You have a reasonably complex CSS layout in front of you. Now you need to understand a couple of strategies that are at work here:

✔ The Float attribute aligns an element in a Web page to the left or right and flows other elements around it. Text wraps to the right of an element floated left, just as it does when you use the Align attribute with the `<IMG>` tag. To make your layout resemble Figure 9-5 exactly, use the Enter (or Return) key to add space below the first line of text and then type some additional text.

✔ By creating a `<DIV>` tag that contains the two smaller columns and setting the Padding attribute, you create the effect of white space between the borders and the content in the `<DIV>` tag.

You can experiment using this layout by adding text and other HTML, not to mention other CSS styles. A `<DIV>` tag can contain any content you put into a Web page, so get creative!

Although this layout method may seem complicated, it is incredibly powerful and loads quickly in a browser because little actual HTML code is generated. This style of layout relies on positioning the block elements in relation to each other, influenced by any margin and padding settings you choose. (Take a peek at the Code view to see just how little code was generated.)

All about DHTML

Dynamic HTML *(DHTML)* has received so much hype and attention that you would think you could do anything with it, including your laundry. Well, DHTML isn't quite powerful enough to take over your domestic duties, but it does add a range of functionality to a Web page that has been impossible with HTML alone. In fact, DHTML is kind of like HTML on steroids. DHTML is really about using advanced scripting techniques to create dynamic content, which is impossible with HTML alone. *Dynamic content* means that you can create and alter page content *after* the page has been loaded in a browser. JavaScript has been used by designers to add dynamic effects to Web pages for a while, but with DHTML you can affect the attributes of HTML tags, which means that you can create many more kinds of effects and make them happen more quickly.

The biggest drawback of DHTML is the same as you find with any reasonably complex Web technology: Because browsers aren't consistent about support, some cool things you can do with DHTML don't work in all browsers. Testing in all the browsers you think your Web site visitors might use is important. However, Dreamweaver includes features to make it easier than ever to design pages that work in various browsers.

DHTML is, however, much more complicated to write than regular old HTML. Even HTML frames, which are complex by many Web design standards, look relatively simple when compared to JavaScript and the kind of code you have to write in order to create DHTML. This area is where Dreamweaver shines: Macromedia has implemented a series of tools that let you create DHTML effects without having to be a JavaScript programmer.

Working with Behaviors

Some of the coolest features used on the Web today are created by using Dreamweaver behaviors, which use a scripting language called JavaScript. These behaviors are really just built-in scripts — some of which use DHTML and some of which don't — that provide an easy way to add interactivity to your Web pages. You can apply behaviors to many elements on an HTML page and even to the entire page itself. Writing JavaScript is more complex than writing HTML code, but not as difficult as writing in a programming language such as C, C++, or Java. (No, Java and JavaScript are not the same. Read Chapter 11 for more on Java applets and how they differ from JavaScript.) Dreamweaver takes all the difficulty out of writing JavaScript behaviors by giving you an easy and intuitive interface that doesn't require you to ever touch the complicated code behind the scenes.

Using the behaviors options, you can make images change when viewers pass their cursors over them (a rollover), or make a layer draggable by the person viewing the Web page. Combining the power of behaviors with layers opens up a range of tricks that look great on a page and load quickly.

Consider this slightly corny example: If you tickle someone, that person laughs. Dreamweaver would call the tickling an *event* and the laughter an *action*. The combination is a Dreamweaver *behavior*.

You may already be familiar with the rollover behavior, when one image is switched for another. In a rollover, putting your mouse over an image is the *event*. The *action* is the switching of the original image for another. Rollovers are especially common in navigation; mousing over a navigation button causes it to be highlighted. You can use behaviors to affect text, images, and — you guessed it — layers.

If you have always wanted to add cool interactive features, such as making something flash or pop up when users move their cursors over an image or click a link, you're going to love the *behavior* feature in Dreamweaver. To fully appreciate what Dreamweaver can do for you, you may want to switch to Code view after attaching a behavior, just to see the complex code required to create behaviors. If you don't like what you see, don't worry: Go back to Design view and you can continue to let Dreamweaver take care of the code for you (I just wanted you to see how lucky you are that Dreamweaver takes care of all that for you).

When you use behaviors in Dreamweaver, you use dialog boxes to set up interactive effects. You can attach behaviors to a page, a link, an image, or almost any other element on a page by simply selecting the element and choosing the behavior you want from the Behaviors tab in the Tag panel.

The following sections show you how to use behaviors to open a new window or create a rollover. At least 20 behaviors are built into Dreamweaver so I can't cover all of them here, but after you see how to apply a couple of them, you should have the idea of how to use the rest. After you have the idea, spend a little time experimenting with behaviors so you get an idea of all the cool things you can do with them.

Using a behavior to open a new browser window

You can use behaviors in Dreamweaver to create many interactive features, such as opening a new browser window when someone clicks a link. This is a great way to make supplemental information available without losing the original page a visitor was viewing. Although the following steps provide instructions for a specific behavior, you can use these steps to apply any other behavior to a selected image or other element.

To add a behavior to a selected image (or any other element) on a page, follow these steps:

1. **Select an image on a page by clicking it.**

   You can select any image, text, or layer on a page and apply a behavior to it the same way.

To attach a behavior to the entire page, click the <BODY> tag in the tag selector on the far-left side of the status bar, at the bottom of the Document window.

2. **Create a link for the image or text you are working with.**

Most actions, such as a browser opening or an image rollover, occur because the user clicks or moves a mouse over the text or image that triggers the event. For the user to know this is possible, be sure to make the text or image a link, so that the user's mouse cursor changes, giving him the clue to click.

Don't worry if you don't want the behavior to actually be a link that opens a new Web page when clicked; you can "trick" the browser into making the element appear to be a link:

- Type **javascript:void(0);** in the Link box in the Properties inspector for the text, image, or layer you're working with. This code makes the element a link, but means that the browser doesn't open a new Web page when the link is clicked. This trick only works for users who have not disabled Javascript in their browsers.

- Enter the number sign (#) in the Link box in the Properties inspector. The browser reloads the same page instead of going to a new one.

3. **Choose Window⇨Behaviors to open the Behaviors panel.**

4. **Click the plus sign (+) and choose the behavior you want from the pop-up menu.**

You can choose any behavior listed on the pop-up menu. In Figure 9-11, I selected the Open Browser Window behavior.

A dialog box opens specific to that behavior where you can specify the properties for the selected behavior.

If a behavior is grayed out, that means it can't be associated with the element you have selected. For example, the Drag Layer behavior can only be applied to a layer so it's grayed out if you've selected an image or text.

5. **Specify the parameter options to control how you want the behavior to work.**

The Open Browser Window behavior creates an action so that when someone clicks the image to which you applied this behavior, a new browser window opens. This dialog box enables you to set the properties to specify how the new browser window displays. (For example, you can restrict the size of the new browser window, like the one shown in Figure 9-12.)

In the example shown in Figure 9-12, the URL to Display field is where you enter the address of the page you want to open in the new browser window. Setting a window width and height gives you the capability to specify the size of the new window. You can also decide which attributes that window should have. Check the box next to Navigation Toolbar,

Location Toolbar, Status Bar, Menu Bar, Scrollbars As Needed, or Resize Handles, if you want the new browser window to include any of these features. Finally, you can name the new window, which is important if you want to target that same window and load additional pages into it.

Figure 9-11:
Selecting a behavior from the Behaviors panel.

6. **After you specify the parameters for the behavior, click OK.**

   The dialog box closes, and the new behavior now appears in the Behaviors panel.

Figure 9-12:
Select a behavior from the Behaviors panel, and a dialog box offers you different options for controlling the behavior.

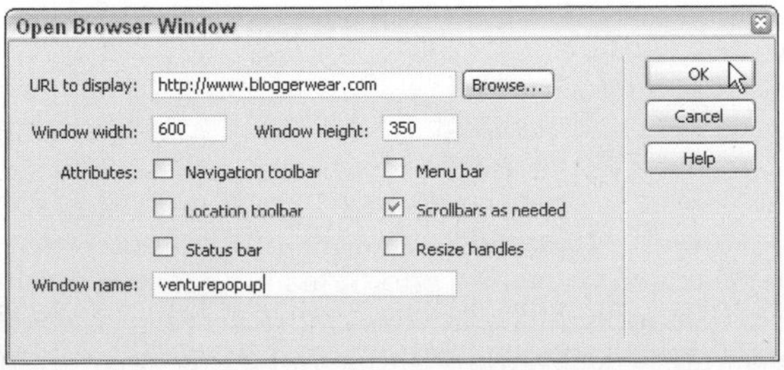

7. **To change the event that triggers your behavior, select the current event from the left side of the Behaviors panel.**

   The Events drop-down list opens, from which you can select various events to trigger the behavior.

   The most commonly used event is the `onClick` event, which in this case would cause the new browser window to open when a user clicks the image. For more information about events and what each one accomplishes, see the section "Choosing the best event for a behavior" later in this chapter.

8. **To test the action, choose File⇨Preview in Browser, and then select the browser in which you want to test your work.**

   Whatever browser you choose opens the page so that you can see how it really looks in that browser. Click the image to test whether a new browser window opens (see Figure 9-13).

Figure 9-13: The Open Browser Window behavior lets you control the size and attributes of the new window that you can open above the main window.

If you're using behaviors, try to avoid starting your filenames with a number or using a slash mark, which is never a good idea for a filename but is particularly problematic when applying behaviors (more so with JavaScript than with Dreamweaver). Your safest option is to avoid using slashes anywhere in the name or numbers at the beginning of a filename (you can use numbers anywhere else in the name).

Adding new behaviors to Dreamweaver

If you know how to write JavaScript, you can add your own behaviors to the list of choices in Dreamweaver. You can also find new behaviors created by Macromedia and by other developers, many of which you can download for free and then add to Dreamweaver. You can also purchase a range of extensions. You can find instructions for creating and adding new actions in the Dreamweaver Exchange section of the Macromedia site at www.macromedia.com/exchange/dreamweaver.

To go to this site and try out new behaviors, click the plus sign (+) in the Behaviors panel and choose the Get More Behaviors option at the bottom of the pop-up menu. This action launches your default Web browser and connects you to the Dreamweaver Exchange section of the Macromedia Web site if you're online.

Adding a rollover image behavior

Rollover images are now some of the most commonly used interactive elements on Web sites. With rollovers, you can swap one image with another when the mouse passes over it, giving users visible feedback as they interact with your site. You have surely seen this effect used on Web site navigation menus. Again, I include this example because it's a common behavior, but you can follow these same steps to apply many other behaviors in Dreamweaver.

Because rollover images are so popular on the Internet, Dreamweaver includes a special rollover option. To create a rollover using that feature, choose Insert➪ Image Objects➪Rollover Image and enter the names of the two images in the dialog box. However, using the Behavior dialog box to create a rollover effect gives you more options about how the rollover images display and what a user must do to trigger the effect.

To create a rollover (swapping) image in Dreamweaver, follow these steps:

1. **Click to place your cursor on the page where you want the rollover to appear.**

   Rollover effects require at least two images: one for the initial state and one for the rollover state. You probably should make a special set of images to use with your rollover behavior. They both should be the same dimensions, or else you get some strange scaling effects.

2. **Choose Insert➪Image Objects➪Rollover Image to open the Insert Rollover Image dialog box.**

   The Insert Rollover Image dialog box appears, as shown in Figure 9-14.

Insert Rollover Image

Image name:	bloggerbutton
Original image:	bloggerwear.gif Browse...
Rollover image:	bloggerwear_over.gif Browse...
	☑ Preload rollover image
Alternate text:	Get Bloggerwear!
When clicked, Go to URL:	http://www.bloggerwear.com Browse...

OK   Cancel   Help

3. **Name your image in the Image Name field of the dialog box.**

   For you to be able to apply a behavior to an element, such as an image, the element must have a name so that the behavior script can reference it. Names also enable you to swap images other than the one you're pointing at by using their names as a reference ID. The name can be the same as the filename, but can also simply be descriptive.

4. **Specify the first image you want visible in the Original Image text box. (Use the Browse button to easily locate the image.)**

5. **Enter the image you want to have visible when visitors move their cursors over the first image in the Rollover Image text box. (Use the Browse button to easily locate the image.)**

6. **Check the Preload Rollover Image check box if you want the image to load into the browser's cache even before it becomes visible to a visitor.**

   If you don't choose to do this step, the image is downloaded when a visitor puts the mouse over the original image. This option should almost always be turned on.

7. **In the When Clicked, Go To URL section, enter a URL or browse to locate another page on your site that you want to link to.**

   If you don't specify a URL, Dreamweaver automatically inserts the # (anchor tag reference).

8. **Click OK.**

   The images are automatically set up as a rollover.

9. **Click the globe icon at the top of the page to preview your work in a browser where you can test to make sure that the rollover works.**

Choosing the best event for a behavior

Events, in interactive Web-speak, are things a user does as she interacts with your Web page. Clicking an image is an event, as is loading a page in the browser or pressing a key on the keyboard. You can probably think of many more. Different browser versions support different events (the more recent the browser version, the more events are available), and you can select the types of browsers you want to support. To see the list of available behaviors for specific browsers, click the plus (+) sign in the Behaviors panel, choose Show Events For, and select the type of browsers your users use. You should always provide support for as many browsers and browser versions as possible.

Likewise, some events are available only for certain kinds of objects in your page. This list describes some of the more commonly used events, ones that the majority of Web users can experience (using Netscape Navigator and Internet Explorer 4.0 and later):

- ✔ **onAbort:** Triggered when the user stops the browser from completely loading an image (for example, when the user clicks the browser's Stop button while an image is loading).

- ✔ **onBlur:** Triggered when the specified element stops being the focus of user interaction. For example, when a user clicks outside a text field after clicking in the text field, the browser generates an onBlur event for the text field. onBlur is the opposite of onFocus.

- ✔ **onChange:** Triggered when the user changes a value on the page, such as choosing an option from a pop-up menu, or when the user changes the value of a text field and then clicks elsewhere on the page.

- ✔ **onClick:** Triggered when the user clicks an element, such as a link, button, or image.

- ✔ **onDblClick:** Triggered when the user double-clicks the specified element.

- ✔ **onError:** Triggered when a browser error occurs while a page or image is loading. This event can be caused, for example, when an image or URL can't be found on the server.

- ✔ **onFocus:** Triggered when the specified element becomes the focus of user interaction. For example, clicking in or tabbing to a text field of a form generates an onFocus event.

- ✔ **onKeyDown:** Triggered as soon as the user presses any key on the keyboard. (The user doesn't have to release the key for this event to be generated.)

- ✔ **onKeyPress:** Triggered when the user presses and releases any key on the keyboard; this event is like a combination of the onKeyDown and onKeyUp events.

- ✔ **onKeyUp:** Triggered when the user releases a key on the keyboard after pressing it.

- ✔ **onLoad:** Triggered when an image or the entire page finishes loading.

- ✔ **onMouseDown:** Triggered when the user presses the mouse button. (The user doesn't have to release the mouse button to generate this event.)

- ✔ **onMouseMove:** Triggered when the user moves the mouse while pointing to the specified element and the pointer doesn't move away from the element (stays within its boundaries).

- ✔ **onMouseOut:** Triggered when the pointer moves off the specified element (usually a link).

- ✔ **onMouseOver:** Triggered when the mouse pointer moves over the specified element. Opposite of onMouseOut.

- ✔ **onMouseUp:** Triggered when a mouse button that has been pressed is released.

- ✔ **onMove:** Triggered when a window or frame is moved.

- ✔ **onReset:** Triggered when a form is reset to its default values, usually by clicking the Reset button.

- ✔ **onResize:** Triggered when the user resizes the browser window or a frame.

- ✔ **onScroll:** Triggered when the user scrolls up or down in the browser.

- ✔ **onSelect:** Triggered when the user selects text in a text field by highlighting it with the cursor.

- ✔ **onSubmit:** Triggered when the user submits a form, usually by clicking the Submit button.

- ✔ **onUnload:** Triggered when the user leaves the page, either by clicking to another page or by closing the browser window.

Attaching multiple behaviors

You can attach multiple behaviors to the same element on a page (as long as they don't conflict, of course). For example, you can attach one action that is triggered when users click an image and another when they move their cursors over the image. You can also trigger the same action by using multiple events. For example, you can play the same sound when a user triggers any number of events.

To attach additional behaviors to an element, click the plus sign again in the Behaviors panel and select another option from the pop-up menu. Repeat this process as many times as you want.

Editing a behavior

You can always go back and edit a behavior after you create it. You can choose a different event to trigger the behavior, choose a different action, or remove behaviors. You can also change parameters you have specified.

To edit a behavior, follow these steps:

1. **Select an object with a behavior attached.**

2. **Choose Window⇨Behaviors to open the Behaviors panel.**

   Here are some options you can choose in the Behaviors panel:

   - **Change a triggering event:** Choose a different event from the Events drop-down list in the Behaviors panel.

   - **Remove a behavior:** Click the action in the Behaviors panel to select it and then click the minus sign at the top of the pane. The behavior disappears.

   - **Change parameters for an action:** Double-click the gear icon next to the action and change the parameters in the dialog box that opens.

   - **Change the order of actions when multiple actions are set:** Select an action and then click the Move Event Value Up or Move Event Value Down buttons to move it to a different position in the list of actions.

Ensuring That Your Pages Work in Older Browsers

You may love all the Dreamweaver features described in this chapter because they make creating dynamic, interactive elements for your Web pages easy. However, don't forget that older browsers may have trouble handling some of the more advanced features you can create. As each day passes, older browsers are less of an issue because fewer people are using them, although browser support is certainly still a problem. Even newer browsers don't support all DHTML in quite the same way.

Figuring out which browser to target when you start working with behaviors can be frustrating. One solution (besides not using behaviors) is creating two versions of pages that use behaviors and adding a Check Browser behavior that can redirect visitors to the page that works best for them.

The Check Browser action is implemented from the Behaviors panel. This action automatically sends users to different URLs depending on the version of browsers they're using, so you can create a fancy version of your site for new browsers and a simpler version for older browsers. Because this action even allows you to send Netscape and Internet Explorer users to different URLs, you can design different pages for each browser's capabilities, as shown in Figure 9-15. Here's the best way to use this action: Select the <BODY> tag by using the HTML tag selector on the document's status bar, and then choose the Check Browser action in the Behaviors panel (click the plus sign to access the list of actions).

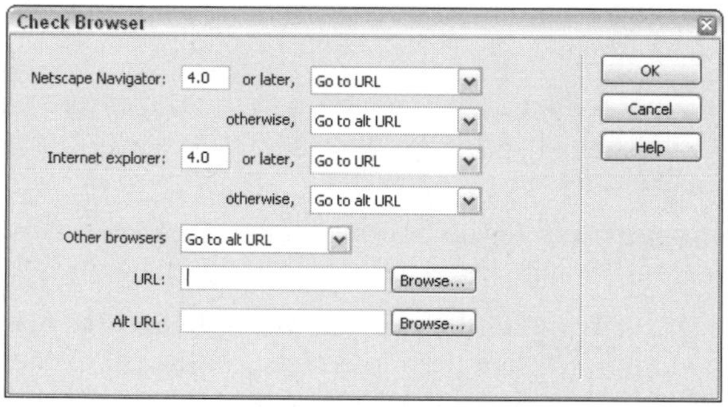

Figure 9-15:
The Check Browser dialog box lets you direct users to different URLs based on which browsers they're using.

Check Browser

Netscape Navigator:	4.0	or later,	Go to URL
		otherwise,	Go to alt URL
Internet explorer:	4.0	or later,	Go to URL
		otherwise,	Go to alt URL
Other browsers	Go to alt URL		
URL:			Browse...
Alt URL:			Browse...

OK Cancel Help

Applying this behavior to your page causes a browser-detect script to determine the type of browser your visitor uses when the page first loads. After the page loads, the visitor is either directed to a different URL based on that detection or kept on the same page. For example, you can send all visitors using Netscape 4.0 and older to one page in your site and users of Internet Explorer 5.0 to another page. To ensure that users of the oldest browsers see the simple page rather than try to interpret fancy code, you should insert this behavior in the basic version of the page and then redirect newer browsers to the alternative fancy pages. The only problem with this solution, of course, is that you have to create more than one site — one for older browsers and one or more for the newer browsers — and that can turn into lots more work.

If you have an audience that is using some of the less common browsers — like Safari or Opera — this solution may not work for you. Remember that testing your pages in the browser you think your site's visitors use is the only way to be sure you create pages that work for them.

Using Extensions and the Extension Manager

Extensions let you easily add new features to Dreamweaver by simply downloading them from a Web site or creating your own new extensions, which you can share with others. Extensions are similar to behaviors except that they're even more powerful.

For example, you can use extensions to add a list of all the state zip codes or country codes to your page, instantly embed QuickTime movies and other multimedia files, or connect to back-end databases with a simple menu command. The idea behind extensions is that anyone with a little bit of scripting ability can create new ways to customize Dreamweaver and share his creations with the Dreamweaver community. The place to find out more about extensions and to download them (mostly for free) is the Macromedia Exchange for Dreamweaver site at www.macromedia.com/exchange/dreamweaver.

After you log into Macromedia Exchange (membership is free), you're welcome to download and install any of the scores of extensions — their number grows every day as developers continually create new ones. You can search for extensions by category or simply browse the ever-growing list.

To install an extension, download it first from the Macromedia Exchange site or any other source (many sites now have free extensions on the Web) and then use the Extension Manager, a utility included in Dreamweaver, to install the new extension. Extensions you download from the site are saved as files on your computer with an .mxp extension. The Extension Manager makes installing and removing these files in Dreamweaver a breeze.

TIP

Extending Dreamweaver with the Extension Manager

One of the reasons Dreamweaver is so popular is because you can customize the program so extensively using the Extension Manager. Dreamweaver has hooks throughout the program where you can add your own extensions. You can download a wide array of extensions from www.Macromedia.com and many others created by third-party developers.

Search the Web and you can find extensions for blogging, for photo galleries, for obscure programming languages, for Flickr.com, and more. You also find slideshow behaviors and templates for all manner of sites.

To run the Extension Manager and install an extension, follow these steps:

1. **Choose Help⇨Manage Extensions.**

   The utility launches.

2. **Choose File⇨Install Extension in the Extension Manager; then browse your drive to select the new extension.**

   After the installation is complete, you see brief instructions on how to use the extension.

3. **Unless the instructions require you to restart Dreamweaver, simply switch to Dreamweaver, and you're ready to use your new extension.**

Converting to XHTML and Beyond

The Dreamweaver Convert feature enables you to convert an HTML page into one of several flavors of XHTML, as well as some variations on the HTML standard. The eXtensible Markup Language is increasingly important on the Web, and if you work with XML, you may appreciate that Dreamweaver is supporting XML development.

XML isn't a markup language — it's a meta-markup language you can use to store and organize data so that you can tailor it to meet a broad range of needs. XML is a subset of SGML, but it retains much more of the power of SGML than HTML did, while still being streamlined enough to be efficient on the Web. Because XML doesn't have a fixed set of tags and elements, XML enables developers to define the elements they need and apply those elements where they need them. That's what the X in XML is all about: It's *eXtensible*. You can adapt it to fit your content, whether you're a stockbroker, publisher, or astronomer.

XML is built on a solid foundation of rules and standards, and it's officially endorsed by the W3C (World Wide Consortium — the Internet police), so it has the potential to solve many of the problems caused by conflicting standards in other formatting options now available. The rules dictate such crucial issues as where tags appear, which names are legal, and which attributes can be attached to which elements. These strict standards make it possible to develop XML parsers that can handle any XML document without limiting the ultimate flexibility of the kind of content or how it's displayed. The XML standards also feature rules for syntax and link checking, comparing document models, and datatyping, as well as checking to see whether a document is well formed and valid. And, XML uses Unicode as its standard character set, so it supports the broadest range of languages, special characters, and symbols, including Arabic, Chinese, and Russian.

One of the most significant differences between XHTML and HTML is that XHTML can be used to describe the type of content, and not just focus on specific formatting for a Web browser. That enables content to be stored and shared in a way that makes publishing in multiple formatting styles easy. For example, rather than describe a headline as font size 5, Helvetica, bold, you can simply describe the headline as a headline. XML then allows you to apply a style sheet (or multiple style sheets) to that content so that the headline and body can be formatted on the fly. You do this with Cascading Style Sheets and the XML Extensible Style Sheets. The separation of the formatting from the content description is what enables the same content to be sent efficiently to a wide range of partners, each of whom can apply its own formatting or to a broad range of viewing devices, such as Web browsers, handheld devices, and cell phones, which require different formatting.

If you want to know more about XML, consider reading *XML For Dummies,* 4th Edition, by Ed Tittel (published by Wiley Publishing, Inc.).

If you are coding for a particular level of XML- or HTML-compliance, you can set Dreamweaver to create every new document in that format by setting the New Document preferences. Choose Edit⇨Preferences and look for the New Document category.

Chapter 10

Roundtrip Integration: Fireworks and Dreamweaver

In This Chapter
▶ Fireworks as an image-editing program
▶ Using other image editors besides Fireworks
▶ Optimizing graphics without leaving Dreamweaver
▶ Inserting and editing Fireworks HTML

*I*n this chapter, you discover some of the special features that make Dreamweaver work so well with Fireworks, the Macromedia image-creation and -editing program. Fireworks, specially designed for developing images for the Web, is a great complement to Dreamweaver. Much of the information in this chapter also applies, however, to other image-editing programs, such as Adobe Photoshop.

If you don't have Fireworks, you can download the free, 30-day trial from www.macromedia.com/fireworks/. Because Dreamweaver offers very limited graphics capabilities, you need Fireworks (or programs like it — see the list of options in Chapter 5) to create images from scratch or to edit existing images and prepare them for use on the Web.

Fireworks was one of the first image-editing programs designed specifically for the special needs of the Web, and it's ideally suited to creating images for use on the Internet. Using Fireworks, you can automate your workflow, *optimize* graphics (compress and prepare them for Web use), and create sophisticated animations, fancy *rollovers* (images that change when you hover the mouse pointer over them), and special effects in a fraction of the time these tasks used to take. Fireworks can even generate HTML and create Web pages all by itself! More important for you, Fireworks integrates especially well with Dreamweaver, enabling roundtrip graphics editing back and forth between the two programs. Normally, when you work with Dreamweaver and another graphics editor, it takes many steps between creating images and getting them into a Web page — one of the most time-consuming parts of building and maintaining a Web site. *Roundtrip graphics editing* gives you lots of short-cuts, making the trips back and forth between the two programs much quicker and easier.

Dreamweaver to Fireworks: Image Editing

Suppose that a client suddenly wants the logo on a Web page to be a different color. Normally, you have to launch an image-editing program, track down the logo, open it, edit it, save it, switch back to Dreamweaver, and then import the logo again to your page. Using the special integration features between Dreamweaver and Fireworks, though, greatly simplifies the entire process — a few clicks of the mouse can replace all those other time-consuming tasks.

This section show you how to select an image in Dreamweaver, automatically open the image in Fireworks, edit the image, and update it back in Dreamweaver with just a few mouse clicks.

To launch Fireworks directly from Dreamweaver and edit an existing image, follow these steps:

1. **In an open document, select a GIF or JPEG image you want to edit.**

2. **In the Properties inspector, click the Edit in Fireworks button, as shown in Figure 10-1.**

   The Find Source dialog box appears, asking whether you want to use an existing document as the source of the file you selected.

Figure 10-1:
The Properties inspector displays an Edit in Fireworks button (look for the FW) when you select an image.

3. **Click one of the options in the Find Source dialog box:**

   Yes: Select a different file from the optimized image file on your page. For example, you can select the original file from which you exported the optimized Web version of the graphical image on your page. It may be a PNG file or a Photoshop file, for example. (For more on PNG files, see the "PNG: Portable Network Graphics files" sidebar, later in this chapter.)

   No: Opens the GIF or JPEG that you selected in Dreamweaver and are using on the Web page.

Because the GIF or JPEG image used on your Web page was probably optimized earlier for Web use, editing it again often degrades the image quality. Going back to the original, pre-optimized version of the graphical image gives you the option to start again from scratch. Keep in mind that each time a GIF or JPEG is saved, it gets compressed and loses some data and quality. If you need to make an additional edit, using the original image and saving a new GIF or JPEG produces a better-looking file.

After clicking the Yes or No button, the image document opens in Fireworks.

4. **Make the edits you need to make to the image within Fireworks.**

   You can edit the image by using any of the tools in Fireworks, or change the optimization settings for the file in the Optimize panel.

5. **When you finish editing the image, click the Done button in the upper-left corner of the Fireworks Document window (see Figure 10-2).**

Figure 10-2:
Clicking the Done button in Fireworks automatically updates the image in Dreamweaver.

Dreamweaver becomes the active window and the image automatically updates on the page, reflecting recent edits without requiring any other action on your part, other than saving the document.

WARNING!

After you click the Done button in Fireworks, you can't undo any changes you make to the image files by choosing the Undo command. The changes are permanent.

Using an Image Editor Other Than Fireworks

When you click the Edit in Fireworks button in the Properties inspector (see Step 2 in the preceding section), Dreamweaver tries to launch Fireworks as its default editing application. But what if you don't use Fireworks or don't own a copy? Fear not: You can achieve a somewhat less-automated workflow with almost any other graphics editor. You just need to change your preferences in Dreamweaver to specify which program you prefer to use instead of Fireworks.

PNG: Portable Network Graphics files

Fireworks uses the PNG *(Portable Network Graphics)* format as its native file format. PNG is similar to the PSD format, used by Adobe Photoshop, in that it retains the highest possible quality for the graphical image without suffering any of the degradation in image quality that usually occurs with a GIF or JPEG. The Portable Network Graphics format was created long before Fireworks. The PNG format is one of the few formats, in addition to GIF and JPEG, that a Web browser can display. Because the PNG format allows for the many extra features that Fireworks offers, Macromedia chose it as the native format for Fireworks.

The PNG file format was originally created as a potential replacement for the GIF format because PNGs offered far greater image quality, compression levels, and numerous other features lacking in GIFs. PNG files offer a multitude of improvements over GIFs, including resolution up to 48 bits (as opposed to 8 bits in GIF), better compression, built-in *gamma correction* (the capability to adjust to the different brightness levels between PC and Mac monitors), and greater levels of transparency.

So, why are we all still using the GIF format? Although PNG files represent a marked improvement over GIF files, many of its most useful features simply aren't well supported by some browsers.

For more information about PNG files, take a look at the PNG home page at www.libpng.org/pub/png/ or the W3C PNG page at www.w3.org/Graphics/PNG.

To designate a different application as the Dreamweaver external image editor, follow these steps:

1. **On the Dreamweaver menu bar, choose Edit⇨Preferences (Windows) or Dreamweaver⇨Preferences (Mac) and select the File Types/Editors category.**

   The Preferences dialog box for File Types/Editors appears, as shown in Figure 10-3.

Figure 10-3: You can specify other image editors besides Fireworks.

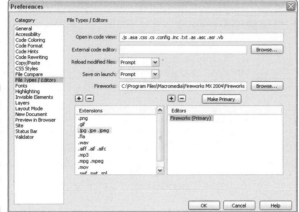

2. **Select an image format from the Extensions list.**

   For each file format, you can specify one or more external editors, in addition to a primary editor.

3. **In the Editors list on the right, click the plus sign (+) to add an editor for all your image files in the specified format.**

   The Select External Editor dialog box appears, asking you to find the program to assign as the editor for this file type.

4. **Browse your drive until you locate the graphics application you want to assign; then click the Open button.**

   After you click the Open button, the application appears in the list of image editors on the right.

5. **Click the Make Primary button to make it your primary editor.**

   You can add as many editors to the list as you want, but you can assign only one primary editor for each file type.

6. **Repeat Steps 2 through 5 for any other graphics extensions you want to assign to other graphics editors.**

7. **Click OK.**

Clicking the Edit button opens the assigned application. You can also select an alternative image-editing application when you right-click the image and open the Edit With menu.

Although you can use graphics applications other than Fireworks, none except Fireworks includes the Done button, which updates the image in Dreamweaver. If you use another application, you need to save the edited graphical image and import the image into Dreamweaver again manually.

Dreamweaver to Fireworks: Optimizing an Image

Suppose that the logo on your page looks fine, but is taking too long to download and needs to be compressed a bit more. The latest version of Dreamweaver puts immediate access to the Fireworks Optimize dialog box in the Properties inspector.

To optimize an image in Fireworks from within Dreamweaver, follow these steps:

1. **Select the image in Dreamweaver.**

2. **Click the Optimize in Fireworks button in the Properties inspector (see Figure 10-4).**

Adobe Photoshop and ImageReady

Although Fireworks does the whole roundtrip thing with Dreamweaver and using Fireworks rather than another image editor makes more sense, many Web designers use Adobe Photoshop and its integrated Web application, Adobe ImageReady.

Because Photoshop and ImageReady can do many of the same functions as Fireworks (image slicing, optimization, rollovers, and animation), many designers reason: "Why spend time finding out how to use a new program and figuring out how to do what I already know how to do (and perhaps, do *well*) in another program?" Seamless integration with Dreamweaver is certainly a big benefit, and Fireworks is less expensive than Photoshop. However, both are excellent programs, and the choice is up to you.

Figure 10-4:
The
Optimize in
Fireworks
button
is in the
Properties
inspector.

The Find Source dialog box appears, asking whether you want to use an existing document as the source of the file you selected.

The default setting for this command is for Dreamweaver to ask about source files each time you launch Fireworks. You can change this setting by choosing Always Use Source PNG or Never Use Source PNG from the Fireworks Source Files drop-down list in the same dialog box.

3. **Click the Yes or No button in the Find Source dialog box:**

> **Yes:** Allows you to select a different file from the optimized image file on your page, such as the original file from which you exported the optimized Web version of the graphical image used on your page.

> **No:** Opens the file used on your Web page and displays the optimization dialog box within Fireworks.

Whichever option you click, the image opens in the Fireworks Optimize dialog box.

4. **Apply new optimization settings on the Options tab of the Fireworks Optimize dialog box (see Figure 10-5).**

You can change the number of colors in the file or change its quality settings to achieve a smaller file size and then preview the changes within the Fireworks preview panel. You can also crop the image, but you can't make any other image edits in this window.

5. **Click the Update button.**

The file automatically updates in Dreamweaver with the changes you just applied. If you selected a PNG file to edit (you clicked the Yes button in the Find Source dialog box), the original PNG file isn't altered — only the optimized GIF or JPEG file is. If you cropped your image first, click the Reset Size button.

After you click the Update button in Fireworks, you cannot undo any changes you make to the image files by choosing the Undo command. The changes are permanent.

Figure 10-5:
You can optimize an image with the Fireworks Optimize dialog box without leaving Dreamweaver.

TIP

The coolest Fireworks optimization feature by far has to be the Optimize to Size Wizard. Click the button with a vise icon on it at the bottom of the Options tab and type the target file size. Then the wizard tries to compress the file enough to achieve the size you specify; the image usually suffers a decrease in quality or in the number of colors used. Although the settings usually require a bit more tweaking after you run this command, the wizard does a great job of doing the groundwork.

Inserting Fireworks HTML

One of the niftiest Fireworks features is that you can automatically generate HTML files when you're cutting up images for your Web designs. This feature works well for slicing large graphics into pieces and generating tables to hold the pieces together. For example, you can use Fireworks to create a navigation bar, and then slice that bar to create a separate graphic for each navigation item. The only question is, after you generate this HTML code from Fireworks, how do you get it to your Dreamweaver page? Because Fireworks generates an HTML page, you can simply open that page in Dreamweaver, of course. But if you want to put that HTML directly into an existing Web page, you can easily insert the HTML and its associated images with just the click of a button.

To insert a Fireworks-generated table with sliced images into a Dreamweaver document, follow these steps (I assume in this example that you know how to use Fireworks to slice up images and generate HTML tables and that you have already exported an HTML file from within Fireworks):

1. **With a document open and the cursor placed at the point where you want to place the HTML, choose Insert⇨Image Objects⇨Fireworks HTML.**

   The Insert Fireworks HTML dialog box appears (see Figure 10-6).

Figure 10-6: You can insert Fireworks HTML directly into Dream-weaver.

2. **Click the Browse button to select the HTML file to import; click OK when you locate it.**

   Dreamweaver inserts the table and its associated images from the Fireworks document into Dreamweaver (see Figure 10-7).

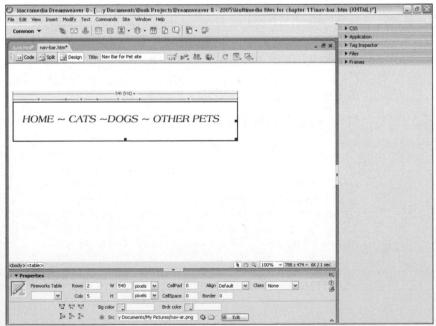

Figure 10-7: The Properties inspec-tor for Fireworks-generated HTML gives a visual indication of the source PNG file.

If you're interested in finding out more about Macromedia Fireworks, check out *Fireworks MX Bible,* by Joseph W. Lowery and Derren Whiteman, both published by Wiley Publishing, Inc.

Editing Fireworks HTML

After you insert Fireworks HTML into Dreamweaver, some special options become available in the Properties inspector, allowing you to easily edit the images and their associated code in Fireworks. If you refer to Figure 10-7, you see that the Properties inspector adds a few items that appear only when you insert a Fireworks HTML table. One item is an indicator of the source PNG file for the images, and the other is an Edit button, which lets you edit the table in Fireworks.

To edit an existing Fireworks table in Dreamweaver, follow these steps:

1. **Select the table in the Dreamweaver document.**

   Fireworks-generated HTML imported into Dreamweaver becomes an object with special attributes that display in the Properties inspector when you select the object (refer to Figure 10-7).

2. **Click the Edit in Fireworks button in the Properties inspector to launch Fireworks.**

   You're asked to find the original PNG file corresponding to the inserted HTML and images if Fireworks can't find it automatically. After you locate the PNG file, the image appears within a Fireworks Document window.

3. **Make any edits or adjustments to the Fireworks document.**

4. **Click the Done button in the upper-left corner of the Fireworks Document window (see Figure 10-8).**

   The HTML code and graphics regenerate and automatically update in Dreamweaver!

Figure 10-8:
Clicking the Done button in Fireworks automatically updates the code in Dreamweaver without any further work.

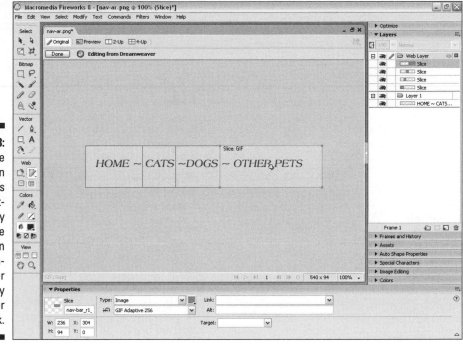

Chapter 11

Showing Off with Multimedia

• •

• •

*N*ow that more than 30 percent of Internet users have DSL lines, cable modems, or even faster connections, multimedia has become an important part of many Web sites. Those of us who have become spoiled with CD-ROMs and music videos are often less than satisfied with flat, text-based Web sites.

Not all Web sites warrant multimedia; if your goal is to provide information in the fastest way possible to the broadest audience, text is still the best option. But if you want to provide a richer experience for your users, to show rather than just tell, or to entertain as well as inform, adding sound, video, and animation is the way to go.

Although you can't use Dreamweaver to create audio or video files, in this chapter you find out how to use Dreamweaver to add a wide range of multimedia file types to your Web pages so your visitors can view them. I also include a primer of the various kinds of multimedia options.

The most complicated aspects of working with multimedia on the Web are choosing the best format and editing multimedia files in sound, video, or other multimedia-editing programs. As you see in this chapter, adding multimedia files to your pages once they're created is relatively easy (similar to adding image files or creating links, but with more options controlling how and when they play).

Understanding Multimedia Players

When you add sound, video, or any other kind of multimedia to a Web site, you should know that your visitors may need a special *player* (sometimes with an associated *plug-in*) to play or view your files.

Players are small programs that work alone or in cooperation with a Web browser to add support for non-browser functions, such as playing sound, video, and animation files. Some of these programs come with plug-ins, which are small applications that can plug into a browser and extend its capabilities.

Some of the best-known multimedia players and plug-ins include the Flash Player, Windows Media Player, Real Networks RealPlayer, and Apple QuickTime. Some have become so popular that they are built into the latest browsers or operating systems.

The problem is that if your visitors don't have the player required to view your multimedia file, they have to download and install it; otherwise they see some sort of broken icon that represents the content on your site and not your cool multimedia file. Many visitors are scared off by the idea of down-loading something new off the Internet, others are just plain annoyed by the requirement, and some really can't do it at all (for example, many companies make it impossible for employees to download and install software for secu-rity reasons).

Creating warnings for multimedia files

Because multimedia files require special play-ers, it's a good idea to include a warning mes-sage any time you add video, audio, or other multimedia files to your Web site. The message should include an explanation of the type of file you're using, the size of the file, how long it may take to download, and what kind of player is required to view it.

You may want to include a warning, such as one of the following examples, with a video file:

To play this video file, click the above image. The video clip is 30 seconds long and shows our cool widget in action. If you're using a modem connection, the video may take a minute or two to download and play. If the video does not appear to be playing or if you receive an error message, you may not have the necessary software to play the video.

To play this 30-second video file, click the image. Using a modem, the video takes about 90 seconds to download. If the video does not play, you may need to install Windows Media Player, free for Macintosh and Windows.

You can use Dreamweaver to place any of these multimedia file types in your Web pages, but it's up to you to choose the format that's best for your audience. You can find literally hundreds of plug-ins available for Web pages. Some have become very common, such as those used for playing sound and video. Others are more obscure, such as specialized plug-ins that display three-dimensional worlds and 360-degree images.

Don't risk losing your viewers unless you have a compelling reason. You should never make your visitors download a special plug-in just to see your logo spinning around, for example. Unless you're offering something of value, such as an interactive game or a three-dimensional map for example, you probably should avoid any multimedia options that require special plug-ins.

Working with Macromedia Flash

Flash has clearly emerged as the favorite technology for creating animations and a wide variety of interactive features on the Web. You can even integrate sound and video into Flash, making it a common choice for combining formats.

One of the things that makes Flash so popular, so flexible, and so fast on the Internet, is that it uses *vector graphics.* That means the graphics in Flash are based on mathematical descriptions instead of thousands of dots, and those equations take up far less space than bitmapped animations do. And, because vector graphics provide a description of something instead of a physical representation, they can be scaled up or down in size without affecting the image quality or the size of the file that's downloaded. This capability to scale makes Flash ideally suited for the many different monitor sizes used by Web viewers, as well as the tiny displays on cell phones and other hand-held devices. You can even project Flash graphics on a wall or movie screen without losing quality, although any photographs or video files integrated into a Flash file may lose quality at higher resolutions.

Flash files use the file extension .swf, and you can insert them into any Web page. In the following sections you find out more about adding Flash files, buttons, and text to your Web site. If want to know how to create Flash files, check out *Macromedia Flash 8 For Dummies,* by Gurdy Leete and Ellen Finkelstein (published by Wiley Publishing, Inc.).

On the downside, Flash may or may not print as you would hope and may cause accessibility problems for the disabled. It's also usually more work to update, and may not be read by search engines as they crawl your site. But if you've got the talent, the time, and the staff, it's definitely one of the coolest ways to build a Web site.

Adding Flash Buttons and Text with Dreamweaver

Dreamweaver features the capability to create and edit simple Flash files from within Dreamweaver and includes predesigned Flash options you can add to your pages, even if you don't have Macromedia Flash. Though you can't create complex Flash animations with Dreamweaver, these built-in features enable you to create graphical text objects and cool Flash buttons. Dreamweaver has a large library of existing Flash objects that you can use.

Even better, because the Macromedia Flash Objects architecture is extensible, you can download new Flash styles from the Macromedia Exchange Web site by clicking the Get More Styles button in the Insert Flash Button dialog box. Clicking this button launches your Web browser and connects you to the Macromedia Exchange site, where you can download more buttons (you must have a live Internet connection). See Chapter 15 for more details on Macromedia Exchange.

Creating Flash text with Dreamweaver

With the Flash text object, you can create and insert a Flash (.swf) text movie into your document. Flash text movies enable you to utilize a vector-based text graphic in the font of your choice. (*Vector-based* means that the images are made up of coded instructions to draw specific geometric shapes.) The great advantage to using Flash text is that you can use any fonts you want without worrying about whether your audience have the same fonts on their computers. You can also set a rollover effect without the need to create separate images, and the size of the text can scale up or down without any effect on image quality or file size.

To insert a Flash text object, follow these steps:

1. **Open any existing page in Dreamweaver, or create and save a new document.**

   You must save the document before inserting a Flash text object.

2. **Select Common from the Insert bar, if it isn't already selected.**

3. **From the Media drop-down list on the Common Insert bar, choose Flash Text, as shown in Figure 11-1.**

   Or you can choose Insert➪Media➪Flash Text.

   The Insert Flash Text dialog box appears, as shown in Figure 11-2.

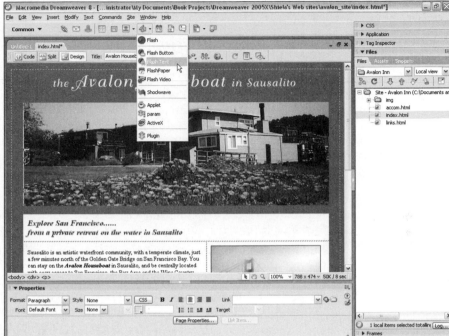

Figure 11-1:
The Media drop-down list provides quick access to the Flash Text option.

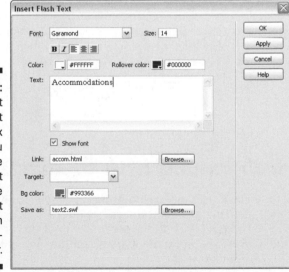

Figure 11-2:
The Insert Flash Text dialog box lets you create and edit interactive Flash text within Dreamweaver.

4. **Select the options, including font, style, size, color, alignment, and background color:**

   • **Font and Font size:** Select any font you have available on your hard drive and specify the size in which you want it to display. The size of the font determines the size of the box around the Flash text. To see the text previewed in your font of choice, check the Show Font box. Use the formatting options below the Font box to specify the alignment of the text and if it should display in bold or italic.

   • **Color:** This option indicates the color of the text.

   • **Rollover Color:** This option indicates the color that the text changes to when the user rolls the mouse over the text.

   • **Link, Target:** Use the Link box to specify the page or file that opens when the viewer clicks the link, and Target to specify where the linked page opens.

   • **Bg Color (background color):** If you make this option the same as the background color of the Web page on which you're placing the text, the text appears to float on the page. If you specify a different color, a box appears around the text filled with this color. If you don't specify a color, the background is white, not transparent.

   • **Save As:** Because you're creating a Flash file when you use this option, you need to name the new file. Always save the file with the `.swf` extension. Use the Browse button (the small folder icon) to specify where you want to save the Flash file on your hard drive.

5. **Click OK.**

   You can also click the Apply button to preview the Flash text in your Dreamweaver document before clicking OK.

   The dialog box closes and the Flash text is inserted on the page. To edit the text again or change any of the options, double-click the Flash text to open the dialog box.

Creating Flash buttons with Dreamweaver

Even more exciting than Flash text are Flash buttons. *Flash buttons* are pre-designed graphics that you can customize and use as interactive buttons on your Web sites. Like Flash text, Flash buttons are made up of vector graphics, and you can scale and resize them without any degradation in quality.

To insert a Flash button, follow these steps:

1. **Open any existing page in Dreamweaver, or create and save a new document.**

   You must save the document before inserting a Flash button.

2. **Select Common from the Insert bar, if it isn't already selected.**

3. **From the Media drop-down list on the Common Insert bar, choose Flash Button.**

   Or choose Insert⇨Media⇨Flash Button.

   The Insert Flash Button dialog box appears, as shown in Figure 11-3.

Figure 11-3:
The Insert
Flash Button
dialog box
lets you
create
and edit
interactive
Flash button
graphics
within
Dream-
weaver.

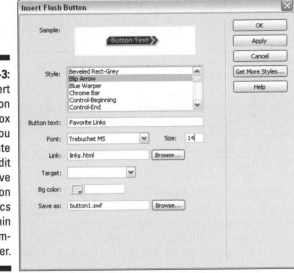

4. **In the Style field, scroll to select the type of button you want to use.**

   The selected button displays in the Sample field at the top of the dialog box.

5. **Customize your button by entering the text you want to display on the button, selecting a font, and so on.**

   Enter the text you want to use in the Button Text field or leave it blank if you don't want any text on the button. Select the other text options, including font, style, size, color, and alignment.

   Select the link, target, and background colors in the appropriate fields, if you want the button to serve as a link.

Because you are creating a Flash file when you use this option, you need to name the new file. Always save the file with the .swf extension. Use the Browse button (the small folder icon) to specify where you want to save the Flash file on your hard drive.

6. **When you're done setting the options, click OK to insert the button.**

   You can also click the Apply button to preview the button in your Dreamweaver document before clicking OK.

   The dialog box closes, and the button is inserted on the page. To edit the button again or change any of the options, double-click the button to open the dialog box.

Preview the button in a browser to see any rollover effects built into the Flash file, or select it and click Play in the Properties inspector.

Inserting Flash files

Flash files, often called Flash *movies* even when they don't include video, are also easy to insert into a Web page using Dreamweaver, but you need a program such as Macromedia Flash to create them first. In this section, I assume you have a completed Flash file (an animation or other Flash movie), and you want to add it to your Web page.

Because Macromedia released the Flash file format as an open standard, you can create Flash files with a variety of vector-editing programs, including Adobe Illustrator, which has an Export to SWF option.

You link to a Flash file much as you do an image, but because Flash can do so much more than a still image, you have a variety of settings and options to control how your Flash file plays.

Before you start, make sure to save the Flash file you want to insert in the main folder for your Web site. I recommend creating a multimedia folder in your main Web site folder for audio and other multimedia files, just as most designers create an image folder for image files.

To add a Flash file to a Web site, open an existing page, or create a new document and save the file, and then follow these steps:

1. **Click to insert the cursor where you want the Flash file to display on your Web page.**

2. **Select Common from the Insert bar, if it isn't already selected.**

3. **From the Media drop-down list on the Common Insert bar, choose Flash.**

   You can also choose Insert⇨Media⇨Flash.

   The Select File dialog box appears.

4. **Browse your drive to locate the Flash file that you want to insert in your page. Click to select the file.**

5. **Click OK.**

   After you click OK, the dialog box closes and the code is inserted into your document.

Dreamweaver displays Flash as a gray box the size of the Flash file. To play the file, click to select it and then click the green Play button on the right side of the Properties inspector (shown in the upcoming Figure 11-4). Your Flash file should also play when you preview the page in a browser.

Setting options for Flash

Like most HTML tags, the tags that link Flash and other multimedia files to Web pages have *attributes,* which define how a file plays within a browser, controlling such actions as whether an animation plays automatically when a page is loaded or if a visitor must click a link for the animation to begin. Dreamweaver automatically sets some of these options, such as the height and width of the Flash file, and you may want to specify some of the others.

If you don't see all the options in the Properties inspector, click the expander arrow in the lower-right corner to display the more advanced options.

You can set these Flash options in the Properties inspector, shown in Figure 11-4:

- ✔ **Name field:** Use the text field in the upper-left corner of the Properties inspector, just to the right of the F icon, if you want to type a name for your file. You can leave this field blank or name the file whatever you want. Dreamweaver doesn't apply a name if you leave the field blank. You only have to provide a name for scripting.

- ✔ **W (Width):** Use this option to specify the width of the file. The file is measured in pixels.

- ✔ **H (Height):** Use this option to specify the height of the file. The file is measured in pixels.

- ✔ **File:** Dreamweaver automatically fills in this field when you insert a Flash file with the filename and path. You risk breaking the link to your flash file if you alter this field.

- ✔ **Edit:** Click this button to open a Flash file with the Macromedia Flash program, where you can edit it. Note that you can only edit the source Flash file. After saving Flash files for Web use with the .swf extension, you can't edit them again.

- ✔ **Src (Source):** This text field enables you to identify the source file you used to create the .swf file inserted into a page. After this option is set, clicking the Edit button automatically opens the source file in Flash and provides a Done button to integrate changes back into Dreamweaver. Because the programs are integrated, any changes you make in Flash automatically reflect in Dreamweaver when you use this option.

✔ **Reset Size:** You can change the display size of a Flash file by clicking a corner and dragging it. Clicking this button reverts the Flash file to its original size. Unlike images, video, and many other file types, you can resize Flash files without affecting image quality or proportion because they are vector based.

✔ **Class:** Use the drop-down list to apply any style sheets defined for the document.

✔ **Loop:** Checking this box causes the Flash file to repeat (or *loop*). If you don't check this box, the Flash movie stops after it reaches the last frame.

✔ **Autoplay:** Checking this box causes the Flash movie to play as soon as it downloads to the viewer's computer. If you don't check this box, whatever option you have set within the Flash file itself (such as onMouseOver or onMouseDown) is required to start the movie. You can also apply a behavior elsewhere in the document to start play (Chapter 9 covers Dreamweaver behaviors).

✔ **V Space (Vertical Space):** If you want blank space above or below the file, enter the number of pixels.

✔ **H Space (Horizontal Space):** If you want blank space on either side of the file, enter the number of pixels.

✔ **Quality:** This option enables you to prioritize the anti-aliasing options of your images versus the speed of playback. *Anti-aliasing,* which makes your files appear smoother, can slow down the rendering of each frame because the computer must first smooth the edges. The Quality parameter enables you to regulate how much the process is slowed down by letting you set priorities based on the importance of appearance versus playback speed.

You can choose from these Quality options:

  • **Low:** Anti-aliasing is never used. Playback speed has priority over appearance.

  • **High:** Anti-aliasing is always used. Appearance has priority over playback speed.

  • **Auto High:** With this somewhat more sophisticated option, playback is set to begin with anti-aliasing turned on. However, if the frame rate supported by the user's computer drops too low, anti-aliasing automatically turns off to improve playback speed. This option emphasizes playback speed and appearance equally at first but sacrifices appearance for the sake of playback speed, if necessary.

  • **Auto Low:** Playback begins with anti-aliasing turned off. If the Flash player detects that the processor can handle it, anti-aliasing is turned on. Use this option to emphasize speed at first but improve appearance whenever possible.

✔ **Scale:** Specify this option only if you change the file's original Height and Width size settings. The Scale parameter enables you to define how the Flash movie displays within those settings.

The following options in the Scale drop-down list enable you to set preferences for how a scaled Flash movie displays within the window:

- **Default (Show All):** This option enables the entire movie to display in the specified area. The width and height proportions of the original movie are maintained and no distortion occurs, but borders may appear on two sides of the movie to fill the space.

- **No Border:** This option enables you to scale a Flash movie to fill a specified area. No borders show up, and the original aspect ratio is maintained, but some cropping may occur.

- **Exact Fit:** The Flash movie is exactly the width and height that are set, but the original aspect ratio may not be maintained, and the movie may look squished.

✔ **Align:** This option controls the alignment of the file on the page. This setting works the same for plug-in files as for images.

✔ **BgColor:** This option sets a background color that fills the area of the file. This color displays if the specified height and width are larger than the file and during periods when the movie isn't playing, either because it's loading or has finished playing.

✔ **Play button:** Click the green Play button to play a Flash file in Dreamweaver.

✔ **Parameters:** This button provides access to a dialog box where you can enter parameters specific to your Flash files.

Finding Flash resources online

One of the best places to learn more about creating Flash files is on the Internet, where a wide range of Web sites offer everything from pre-designed Flash files you can easily customize to tips and tricks for getting the most out of this award-winning technology. You may find these Web sites useful if you want to learn more about Flash.

✔ **Macromedia** (www.macromedia.com): You find loads of tips and tricks for creating and using Flash files (as well as many inspiring examples of Flash in action).

✔ **Swish** (www.swishzone.com): If you're looking for an alternative to Macromedia Flash, Swish is a great little program that's more reasonably priced and capable of creating Flash files.

✔ **Flash Kit** (www.flashkit.com): You find a wide range of resources for Flash developers.

✔ **Flash Arcade** (www.flasharcade.com): This site has some of the best interactive games created in Flash.

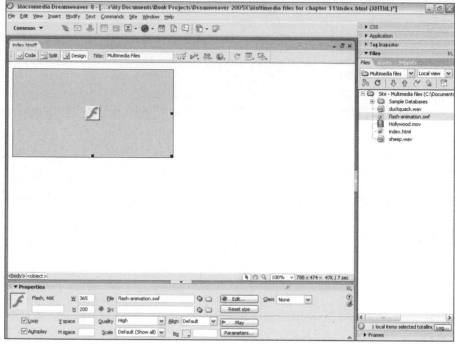

Figure 11-4:
After you insert a Flash file into a Web page, the Properties inspector enables you to specify many options for how to play the file.

Working with Video on the Web

As bandwidth has grown on the Web, the use of video files has grown more dramatically than almost any other multimedia file type. Adding a video file to a Web page is relatively easy; the hard part is choosing the right format and optimizing your video so it downloads quickly and still looks good. Optimizing video is beyond the scope of this book, but I do include some general information about different video file types to help you make more informed decisions about the kind of video files you add to your pages with Dreamweaver.

You can save video in a number of video formats. Unfortunately, no single video format works for everyone on the Web. That's because you need a video player to view video on the Web and not everyone has a player, let alone one that plays all video formats. These days, most new computers come with pre-installed video and audio players that play the most common file formats. If you use a Windows computer, you probably have Windows Media Player on your computer. If you use a Mac, you probably have QuickTime. Both video players can handle multiple video formats, so anyone with a relatively new computer can likely view video in common formats.

If your visitors don't have the player that they need to view your video files, you can instruct them on how to download a player. Most multimedia players are free and relatively easy to install. That's why I recommend that you make it a habit to include instructions for downloading the best player for the video whenever you add a video file to your Web pages. See the earlier sidebar "Creating warnings for multimedia files" for a couple examples.

You can set a video file to play automatically when visitors open a page (assuming they have the right player), but I recommend that you require your visitors to click a link or make some other action before you start playing a video. I like to give visitors an idea of what to expect so they know it's worth the wait before they find they are in the middle of downloading a big video file. (You find instructions for linking to and embedding video in the section later in this chapter called, "Adding Multimedia Files to Your Web Page.")

Beware that many people surf the Web in their offices, in libraries, and in other locations where unexpected sound can be jarring, disruptive, or worse. Always give people a warning before you play video or audio and always give them a way to turn it off quickly when necessary if you want your visitors to come back and watch more.

Comparing popular video formats

How do you know which format to use? According to many Web designers, the most widely supported option for video these days is Windows Media. Most PC computers come with the Windows Media player preinstalled, and a version is available for Mac users as well. Other Web designers prefer

---

Streaming media plays faster

Windows Media, RealMedia, and QuickTime are the most popular formats in large part because they support streaming. To *stream* multimedia means to play a file while it's downloading from the server. This is valuable because video and audio files can take a long time to download.

Here's how streaming works. When you click a link to a video file, your computer begins to download it from the server. The server calculates how much of the file to send and which particular parts of the file you're requesting (if you're listening to the middle of a radio show, for example). If you're using a player that supports streaming, the video or audio file begins to play as soon as the enough of it downloads successfully to assure an uninterrupted experience. If you don't use streaming, the entire file must download before playing. Although it can take the same amount of time to download the entire file, streaming can greatly reduce the time your visitor needs to start viewing a video online.

RealMedia and RealAudio formats from RealNetworks because they say these formats provide better streaming and quality options. The biggest challenge with RealMedia is that it requires special software on the Web server. (Check with your Internet hosting service for rates and support.) QuickTime is another popular format, especially among Mac users, and you can get video down to the smallest file sizes without losing quality.

You can convert video from one file format to another relatively easily using most video-editing programs. For example, you can open a video in AVI format in a program such as Adobe Premier Elements (a good video editor for beginners) and then choose File⇨Export to convert it to any dozen formatting and compression options. For example, you could convert an AVI file to the Windows Media format with the compression setting for a 56K modem or into the QuickTime format with the compression setting for a cable modem. Editing video can get complicated, but converting a video file is relatively easy once you understand the conversion options. (For more video software options, see the "Comparing video-editing programs" sidebar.)

The following sections provide a brief description of the most common digital video formats.

Windows Media Video

Defined by Microsoft and popular on the PC, this video format supports streaming and plays with Windows Media Player as well as many other popular players.

   ✔ File extension: `.wmv, asx`
   ✔ Web site: `www.microsoft.com/windows/windowsmedia`

RealVideo

RealNetworks designed this file format to play in RealPlayer (available for Mac and PC). RealMedia provides optimization well suited to low-speed and high-speed connections, but requires special software on your Web server for streaming.

   ✔ File extension: `.rm, rv`
   ✔ Web site: `www.real.com`

MPEG

Pronounced *em-peg*, video in the MPEG (*Moving Picture Experts Group*) format can be optimized to download much faster than formats with similar quality, such as AVI. MPEGs can play on most video players, including Windows Media Player, RealPlayer, and dedicated MPEG players.

   ✔ File extension: `.mpeg, mpg`
   ✔ Web site: `www.mpeg.org`

QuickTime

Based on the MPEG standard, Apple developed QuickTime. The QuickTime player is built into the Macintosh operating system and is used by most Mac programs that include video or animation. QuickTime is a great format for video on the Web and supports streaming, but it's used primarily by those who favor Macs (although QuickTime files can be viewed on Windows computers as well).

- ✔ File extension: `.qt, mov`
- ✔ Web site: `www.quicktime.com`

AVI

Created by Microsoft, AVI (Audio Video Interleave) is one the most common video formats on Windows computers and can play on most common video players. AVI is fine if you're viewing video on a CD or on your hard drive where the file doesn't have to download, but these files are generally too big to use on the Internet. If your files are in AVI, you should convert them to one of the other formats before adding them to your Web site. Otherwise, you force your visitors to download unnecessarily large video files.

- ✔ File extension: `.avi`
- ✔ Web site: No one site about AVI exists, but you can find information if you search for AVI at `www.microsoft.com`.

Working with Audio on the Web

Audio works much like video on the Web. You can link to a sound file or you can embed the file into your page, and either way, your visitors need to have the right player to hear it. You find instructions for both in the following section "Adding Multimedia Files to Your Web Page."

The following sections provide a brief description of the most common digital audio formats:

MP3

By far the most successful audio compression format, MP3 comes from the same family as MPEG and supports streaming audio. Most music you can download from the Internet is in MP3 format, and it is clearly the first choice of most Web developers.

- ✔ File extension: `.mp3`
- ✔ Web site: `www.mp3.com`

Comparing video-editing programs

Anyone who's had to sit through someone else's amateur home movies knows why video editing software is so crucial. Too many blurry, shaky images, stomach-wrenching zooms, and abrupt pans, and you find yourself clutching the arms of your chair and hoping you don't have to sit through much more.

Even professionals fall prey to these common mistakes, which is why most pros shoot at about a 20:1 ratio — that is, they expect to have to shoot 20 minutes of tape to capture 1 usable minute of video. Be kind to your audience and do what the pros do — *ruthlessly* cut your video down to only the very best moments, and arrange segments so that they have a logical beginning, middle, and end.

Every program listed in this chapter lets you perform basic editing and cutting as well as create fade-ins. The programs also support the addition of special features, such as opening titles, voiceovers, and music tracks. As you go up the price scale, you add features for creating special effects, slow motion, fast motion, and even filters that can make your video look like a scratchy sepia-toned 1920s-era silent movie.

The following are some of the most popular video editing programs on the market today:

✔ **Adobe Premiere:** This high-end video-editing program is comparable to the Hollywood standard, Final Cut Pro, but it's not quite as expensive and it works on a PC. To use this program effectively, you need a very fast computer, gigabytes of available hard drive space, and a lot of free time.

✔ **Adobe Premiere Elements:** This new "lite" version of Adobe Premier is much better suited to a home user. It costs about $600 less (retailing for about $100) and the menus and options are much simpler to learn.

Unless you've managed to get your mitts on a $30,000 high-definition video camera, Premiere Elements is more than enough for your needs.

✔ **Pinnacle Studio Plus:** This program is aimed at the "prosumer" market, meaning it's designed for people who have some familiarity with shooting and editing video and want a lot of features but aren't professionals and don't have a company expense account to cover their costs. Studio Plus does the basics, capturing video and allowing you to cut and paste scenes, dub audio, and create titles. It also includes some special effects (such as slow motion, burring, and stretching an image) and even a blue screen feature, which lets you film against a blue background and then combine video files to create movies of things that aren't possible, such as your hamster dunking a basketball as skillfully as Michael Jordan.

✔ **Ulead VideoStudio Pro:** "Lite" versions of Ulead's products are often bundled with capture cards or other hardware and provide basic video-editing features. Ulead also produces MediaStudio, which is an audio program. You can add plug-ins that enable VideoStudio to work with high-definition video and do basic retouching of the images.

✔ **iMovie:** Part of the Apple iLife suite and an excellent video-editing program, iMovie is available only for the Macintosh. Many Macs now come with iLife already installed, so if you have a newer Mac you probably already have this editing program. Acclaimed for its intuitive interface, iMovie is fully integrated with the rest of iLife, which includes iPhoto, and works seamlessly with Mac's DVD and CD creation software.

Windows Audio

Microsoft's Windows Audio format supports streaming and can play with Windows Media Player, as well as many other popular players. It also offers digital rights management functionality.

- File extension: `.wma`
- Web site: `www.microsoft.com/windows/windowsmedia`

RealAudio

RealNetworks designed this streaming file format it plays in RealPlayer (available for Mac and PC). RealAudio is especially popular among radio stations and entertainment sites.

- File extension: `.ra`
- Web site: `www.real.com`

Ogg Vorbis

One of the newest audio formats on the Web, Ogg Vorbis is an open source format and is not patented. According to developers, it is constantly being improved by programmers who volunteer to work on it, but you may not get much direct support for this file type. Ogg Vorbis is the only audio format for the Web that offers surround sound for those who have multiple speakers.

- File extension: `.ogg`
- Web site: `www.vorbis.com`

WAV

This file format is popular in digital media because it offers the highest sound quality possible. But audio files in this format are often too big for use on the Web, averaging 10MB for a minute of audio (in comparison, an MP3 file that is five times longer can be less than one-third the size). Although WAV files are commonly used on the Internet because of their nearly universal compatibility, I recommend that you convert WAV files (especially for long audio clips) to one of the other audio formats.

- File extension: .wav
- Web site: No official Web site exists for WAV files, but you can find some documentation at `www.microsoft.com` if you search for WAV.

Adding Multimedia Files to Your Web Page

Because you need a player, or *plug-in*, to play multimedia files, you use Dreamweaver's plug-in options to embed audio, video, and other multimedia files into a Web page. You also have the option of linking to an audio or video file. (Dreamweaver offers more sophisticated options for inserting Flash files, covered earlier in this chapter.)

Embedding a file

When you embed a file into a Web page, it can automatically begin to play when the page loads (as long as your visitor has the necessary player).

To use Dreamweaver to embed a video or audio file into a Web page, follow these steps:

1. **Click to insert the cursor where you want the file to display on your Web page.**

   If you're inserting a sound file, the play, pause, and stop controls display wherever you insert the file.

2. **Select Common from the Insert bar, if it isn't already selected.**

3. **From the Media drop-down list on the Common Insert bar, choose Plugin. (The icon looks like a puzzle piece.)**

   You can also choose Insert➪Media➪Plugin.

   The Select File dialog box appears.

4. **Browse your drive to locate the sound or video file you want inserted in your page and click to select it.**

5. **Click OK.**

   The dialog box closes, and the file is automatically inserted on the page. You see a small icon that represents the file (the icon looks like a puzzle piece).

6. **Click the icon to open the file options in the Properties inspector.**

   The options for the file you have embedded appear in the Properties inspector.

   7. **Click the Preview button (the icon that looks like a globe at the top of the work area) to open the page in a browser where you can best test your multimedia file.**

      Dreamweaver launches your specified Web browser and displays the page. If you have the necessary player and you have the file set to auto-play, your file automatically displays when the page launches.

Linking to a file

 Many people like to have multimedia files, such as video, pop up in a new browser window. To do this, create an HTML file and embed your multimedia file in it. Then use the Open Browser Window behavior in Dreamweaver to create a pop-up window that displays your multimedia page. For more on how to work with Dreamweaver behaviors, see Chapter 9.

To use Dreamweaver to link to a video, audio, or other multimedia file, follow these steps:

   1. **Click to select the text, image, or other element you want to use to create a link.**

      This works just like creating a link to another page.

 If you're linking to a video file, a good trick is to take a single still image from the video and insert that into your Web page. Then create a link from that image to the video file.

   2. **In the Properties inspector at the bottom of the page, click the Browse button just to the right of the link field.**

      The Browse button looks like a small file folder.

   3. **Browse your hard drive to find the video or audio file you want to link to.**

      As with any other file you link to, make sure you've saved your audio or video files into your main Web site folder.

   4. **Click to select the file you want to link to.**

   5. **Click OK.**

      The dialog box closes, and the link is automatically created.

   6. **Click the Preview button (the icon that looks like a globe at the top of the work area) to open the page in a browser where you can test the link to your multimedia file.**

      Dreamweaver launches your specified Web browser and displays the page. If you have the necessary player, the file downloads, your player launches, and then your file automatically plays.

Setting options for multimedia files

When you select an embedded multimedia file, such as a sound or video file, the Properties inspector displays the options for the file, as shown in Figure 11-5. The following describes those options:

- **Name text field:** Use the text field in the upper-left corner of the Properties inspector, just to the right of the plug-in icon, if you want to type a name for your plug-in file. You can leave this field blank or provide any name you want. Dreamweaver doesn't provide a name if you leave this field blank. This name identifies the file only for scripting purposes.

- **W (Width):** Specify the measurement of the file in pixels.

- **H (Height):** Specify the measurement of the file in pixels.

  For most plug-ins, the height and width tags are required, but Dreamweaver doesn't automatically insert them. Instead, you need to note the size of the file in the program used to create it, or take a best guess and preview your file in a browser to ensure it displays properly. If you're adding a sound file, the height and width specify the size of the control buttons.

- **Source:** This option specifies the name and path to the file. You can type a filename or click the folder icon to browse for the file. This field is automatically filled in when you embed the file.

- **Plg URL:** This option enables you to provide a URL where viewers can download the plug-in if they don't already have it.

- **Align:** This option enables you to specify how the element aligns on the page. Alignment works just as it does for images.

✔ **Class:** Use the drop-down list to apply any style sheets defined for the document.

✔ **Play button:** Click the green Play button to preview the media file. The media plug-in must be installed in Dreamweaver (in the Configuration/ Plugins folder) for it to preview in Dreamweaver.

✔ **V Space (Vertical Space):** If you want blank space above and below the plug-in, enter the number of pixels you want.

✔ **H Space (Horizontal Space):** If you want blank space on either side of the plug-in, enter the number of pixels you want, or use a percentage to specify a portion of the browser window's width.

✔ **Border:** This option specifies the width of the border around the file when it is displayed.

✔ **Parameters:** Click this button to access a dialog box in which you can enter additional parameters specific to the type of multimedia file you inserted.

Working with Java

Java is a programming language, similar to Basic, C, or C++, that you can use to create programs that run on a computer. What makes Java special is that it can run on any computer system and can display within a browser.

If you create a program in another programming language, you usually have to create one version for the Macintosh, another for the PC, and a third for Unix. But Java, created by Sun Microsystems, is platform-independent so that developers can use it to create almost any kind of program — even complex programs, such as sophisticated games or even a word processing program — that work on any type of computer without the user having to customize the code for each platform.

Another advantage of Java is that these programs (often called *applets*) can run within a Web browser, allowing the program to interact with different elements of the page or with other pages on the Web. This capability has made Java quite popular on the Internet because it provides a way to add sophisticated capabilities to Web pages irrespective of the operating system the Web browser is running on. You can embed Java applets in Web pages, you can use Java to generate entire Web pages, or you can run Java applications separately after they download.

Inserting Java applets

To insert a Java applet in your Web page, follow these steps:

1. **Click to insert the cursor where you want the applet to display on your Web page.**

2. **Select Common from the Insert bar, if it isn't already selected.**

3. **From the Media drop-down list on the Common Insert bar, choose Applet (the icon looks like a little coffee cup).**

   Alternatively, you can choose Insert⇨Media⇨Applet.

   The Select File dialog box appears.

4. **Use the Browse button to locate the Java applet file you want to insert on the page.**

5. **Click to highlight the filename, and then click OK to close the dialog box.**

   Dreamweaver doesn't display applets in the Dreamweaver work area. Instead, you see an icon that represents the applet. To view the applet on your Web page (the only way to see the applet in action), preview the page in a browser, such as Navigator 4.0 and later or Internet Explorer 4.0 and later, that supports applets.

6. **Select the Applet icon to open the Properties inspector.**

   You can set many options in the Properties inspector. If you want to know more about these options, read on.

JavaScript is not Java

JavaScript, a scripting language that many people often confuse with Java, has little in common with Java other than its name and some syntactic similarities in the way the language works. JavaScript is much simpler than Java with far fewer capabilities. Unlike Java, you can write JavaScript directly into HTML code to create interactive features. You can't use it, however, to create standalone applets and programs, as you can use Java. You don't get the complex functionality of Java, but

JavaScript is much easier to use and doesn't require a plug-in.

JavaScript is often used in combination with other multimedia elements on a page, such as images or sound files, to add greater levels of interactivity. Dynamic HTML also uses JavaScript and is covered in Chapters 8 and 9. In those chapters, you can read about how to use Dreamweaver to apply behaviors and other features using JavaScript with HTML.

Setting Java parameters and other options

Like other file formats that require plug-ins or advanced browser support, Java applets come with the following options (see Figure 11-6):

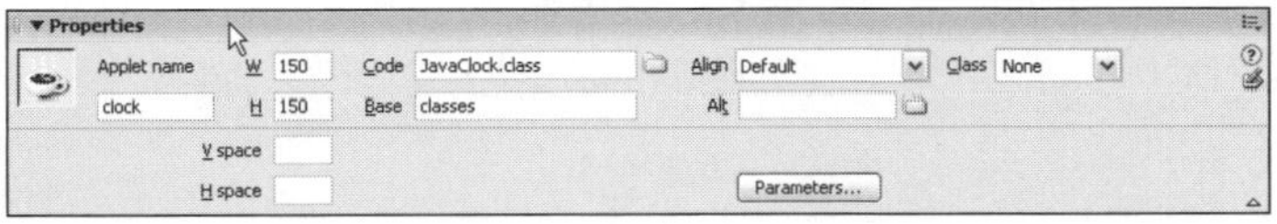

Figure 11-6:
The Properties inspector lets you specify options for Java applets.

▶ **Applet Name:** Use this field in the upper-left corner if you want to type a name for your applet. Dreamweaver doesn't apply a name if you leave this field blank. This name identifies the applet for scripting.

▶ **W (Width):** This option specifies the width of the applet. You can set the measurement in pixels or as a percentage of the browser window's width.

▶ **H (Height):** This option specifies the height of the applet. You can set the measurement in pixels or as a percentage of the browser window's height.

▶ **Code:** Dreamweaver automatically enters the code when you insert the file. Code specifies the content file of the applet. You can type your own filename or click the folder icon to choose a file.

▶ **Base:** Automatically entered when you insert the file, Base identifies the folder that contains the applet. Most browsers aren't set up for automatic install, so you can type your own directory name. This folder is necessary for applets consisting of multiple files.

▶ **Align:** This option determines how the object aligns on the page. Alignment works just as it does for images.

▶ **Alt:** This option enables you to specify an alternative file, such as an image, that displays if the viewer's browser doesn't support Java. That way, the user doesn't see just a broken file icon. If you type text in this field, the viewer sees this text; Dreamweaver writes it into the code by using the Alt attribute of the <APPLET> tag. If you use the folder icon to select an image, the viewer sees an image; Dreamweaver automatically inserts an <IMG> tag within the <APPLET> and </APPLET> tags of the applet.

✔ **V Space (Vertical Space):** If you want blank space above or below the applet, enter the number of pixels you want.

✔ **H Space (Horizontal Space):** If you want blank space on either side of the applet, enter the number of pixels you want.

✔ **Parameters:** Click this button to access a dialog box in which you can enter additional parameters for the applet.

✔ **Class:** Use this drop-down list to access style sheets created with CSS.

You can find lots more information in *Java 2 For Dummies,* by Barry Burd (published by Wiley Publishing, Inc.).

Using ActiveX Objects and Controls

Microsoft ActiveX objects and controls are reusable components similar to miniature applications that can act like browser plug-ins. Because they work only in Internet Explorer on the Windows platform, they're useful for only certain audiences. As a result, no clear standard for identifying ActiveX objects and controls exists. Still, Dreamweaver supports using ActiveX and provides some flexibility so that you can set the parameters for the ActiveX control you use, if you decide to use them.

✔ **Name text field:** Use the text field in the upper-left corner of the Properties inspector, just to the right of the ActiveX icon, if you want to type a name for your ActiveX object. You can leave this field blank or name it whatever you want. Dreamweaver doesn't provide a name if you leave it blank. This name identifies the ActiveX object only for scripting purposes.

✔ **W (Width):** You can specify the measurement of an ActiveX object in pixels or as a percentage of the browser window's width.

✔ **H (Height):** You can specify the measurement of an ActiveX object in pixels or as a percentage of the browser window's height.

✔ **ClassID:** The browser uses the ClassID to identify the ActiveX control. You can type any value or choose any of these options from the drop-down list: RealPlayer, Shockwave for Director, and Shockwave for Flash.

✔ **Embed:** Checking this box tells Dreamweaver to add an <EMBED> tag within the <OBJECT> tag. The <EMBED> tag activates a Netscape plug-in equivalent, if available, and makes your pages more accessible to Navigator users. Dreamweaver automatically sets the values you have entered for ActiveX properties to the <EMBED> tag for any equivalent Netscape plug-in.

- ✔ **Src:** This option identifies the file that's associated with the <EMBED> tag and used by a Netscape plug-in. You must check the Embed box for this field to become active.

- ✔ **Align:** This option specifies how the object aligns on the page. Alignment works just as it does for images.

- ✔ **Parameters:** Click this button to access a dialog box in which you can enter additional parameters for the ActiveX controls.

- ✔ **V Space (Vertical Space):** If you want blank space above or below the object, enter the number of pixels you want.

- ✔ **H Space (Horizontal Space):** If you want blank space on either side of the object, enter the number of pixels you want.

- ✔ **Base:** This option enables you to specify a URL for the ActiveX control so that Internet Explorer can automatically download the control if it's not installed on the user's system.

- ✔ **ID:** This option identifies an optional ActiveX ID parameter. Consult the documentation for the ActiveX control you're using to find out which parameters to use.

- ✔ **Data:** This option enables you to specify a data file for the ActiveX control to load.

- ✔ **Alt Img:** This option enables you to link an image that displays if the browser doesn't support the <OBJECT> tag.

Chapter 12

Forms Follow Function

• •

• •

*T*he most powerful and interactive Web sites rely on HTML forms to collect data from users. Whether HTML forms appear as simple text boxes that provide quick access to search engines or as long registration forms that collect valuable consumer information from visitors, forms are a crucial element of interactivity.

To understand how Web forms work, think of the elements that make up a job application on paper. You can fill in your address in little rectangles and check off boxes. You can reproduce these traditional information-gathering elements from paper forms in HTML with equivalent tags that enable site visitors to submit information to your Web server for processing and storage. Some of the elements you can create include check boxes, radio buttons, and editable text boxes with different characteristics.

However, to collect the information from a Web form after a visitor fills it out, a CGI program of some sort needs to reside on your server. Creating or installing such a program requires programming skills that go beyond HTML and generally beyond the scope of this book. In this chapter, you find out how to create all the form elements, but you have to work with a programmer or check with your system administrator to find out what kinds of scripts may be available on your server if you want to process the data collected in the form.

You also need to create forms if you want to build a dynamic site using Dreamweaver's most advanced features, which Chapters 13, 14, and 15 cover. In this chapter, you find out how to create the HTML forms in Dreamweaver.

Whether you want to create a simple guest book or a complicated online shopping cart system, you need to know how to set up the text areas, radio buttons,

Understanding how CGI scripts work

Common Gateway Interface (CGI) scripts are programs written in a programming language such as Perl, Java, C++, ASP, or PHP. They work in tandem with your Web server to process the data submitted by a user. Think of CGI scripts as the engine behind an HTML form and many other automated features on a Web site. These scripts are much more complex to create than HTML pages, and these languages take much longer to figure out than HTML. CGI scripts reside and run on the server and are usually triggered by an action a user takes, such as clicking the Submit button on an HTML form.

A common scenario with a script may go like this:

1. A user loads a page, such as a guest book, fills out the HTML form, and clicks the Submit button.

2. The browser gathers all the data from the form and sends it to the Web server in a standard format.

3. The Web server takes the incoming data and hands it off to the CGI script, which unpacks the data and does something with it, such as places the data in an e-mail message, and sends the message to a specified e-mail address, or adds the data to a database.

4. The CGI script sends instructions or a block of HTML back to the browser via the Web server to report on the outcome of the script, such as a Thank You page.

In Dreamweaver, you can easily create HTML forms and the Submit buttons that go with them (you can even use the code editor in Dreamweaver to write CGI and other scripts), but you have to know a programming language in order to do so. If you know Perl, PHP, or ASP, writing most simple CGI scripts isn't that hard. But if you don't know one of these programming languages, you're probably better off hiring someone else to do it for you or downloading ready-made scripts from the Web. If you search the Web for CGI scripts, you can find that many programmers write them and give them away for free. Be aware, however, that when you download a program, you run the risk of creating a security risk for your server (so look for trustworthy scripts with good reviews and support). You also have to install any scripts you get on your server and almost always have to alter the programming code at least a little to tailor them to work with your unique system. You may also need to contact your Internet service provider (ISP) to help you load the script on the server because many commercial service providers don't give you access to do it yourself.

Many ISPs make basic CGI scripts (such as guest-book forms and simple shopping cart systems) available to customers as part of membership. These scripts would be tested and supported at least minimally by the ISP. You may find changing ISPs worth the hassle if your ISP doesn't now offer the scripts you want. Most ISPs that offer CGI scripts provide instructions for using them on their Web sites. These instructions include the location of the script on the server. You must include this information in your HTML form so that the Submit button triggers the proper script. You can find more information about setting your HTML form to work with a script in the section, "Creating HTML Forms," later in this chapter.

and drop-down lists that make up an HTML form. Fortunately, Dreamweaver makes creating forms easy by including a special Forms Insert bar at the top of the screen to provide quick access to common form elements.

Appreciating What HTML Forms Can Do for You

Forms follow function, to paraphrase the old saying. On the Web, functions require forms because forms are an integral part of interactive features. By using forms, Web designers can collect information from users — information that they can then use in a variety of ways. Forms are commonly used to create shopping cart systems, guest books, contact forms, search engines, chat rooms, and discussion areas.

Creating HTML Forms

The basic elements of HTML forms — radio buttons, check boxes, and text areas, for example — are easy to create with Dreamweaver, as I demonstrate in this main section. Remember that your form doesn't work unless it links to a script. Although Dreamweaver doesn't provide any scripts, it does make linking your HTML forms to a script or database easy. You need to know where the script resides on the server to set this link. The name and location of the script depend on your server, but for the purposes of showing you how to link to a script with Dreamweaver, assume that the script you need to link to is named `guestbook.pl` (the `.pl` indicates that the script was written in Perl) and that the script is on the server in a folder named cgi-bin (a common name for the folder that holds these kinds of scripts).

Setting up secure commerce systems

Shopping cart systems use HTML forms to collect data from visitors, such as the number of widgets they want to buy and the address to deliver the widgets. You can sell millions of widgets over the Internet, but if you want to do it profitably, you have to set up a secure transaction system to process the orders and confirm payment information.

Most shopping cart systems on the Internet link to a secure transaction system. These systems are usually connected to a financial verification system that can immediately verify a credit card to approve or deny a charge and transfer funds to the appropriate bank account (yes, that should be *your* bank account) for the amount of the transaction. To make this process easier for businesses, many ISPs now offer complete e-commerce solutions, designed to help you coordinate all these requirements. Check the Web site of your Internet service provider to find out more. E-commerce systems are available also at Yahoo! (`http://store.yahoo.com/`) and at Costco (`www.costco.com`), in the Business Services section. To find out more about how secure transactions work and how to set up your own system, visit `www.verisign.com`.

The following steps walk you through linking any form to this sample script. To use these steps with a different script, simply change the name of the script and the name of the directory location to reflect your system. Start with an open page — either a new page or one to which you want to add a form:

1. **Choose Insert⇨Form⇨Form.**

   You can also click the Form icon on the Forms Insert bar, as shown at the top of Figure 12-1. The Forms Insert bar displays all the common form elements.

   An empty form container is created in your document and is displayed as a rectangle outlined by a red dotted line, like the one shown in the Document area of the figure. This dotted line is used by Dreamweaver to indicate that an area is defined as a form in the HTML code.

   You can control the display of invisible elements, such as form containers, by choosing Edit⇨Preferences (Windows) or Dreamweaver⇨ Preferences (Mac) and in the Invisible category, checking or unchecking the Form Delimiter box.

2. **Click the red outline to select the form and display the form options in the Properties inspector (refer to the bottom of Figure 12-1).**

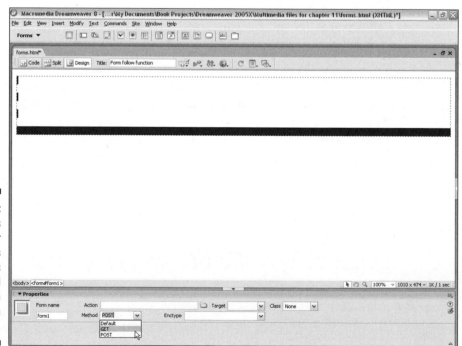

Figure 12-1:
The Forms
Insert bar
provides
easy access
to all
common
form
elements.

3. **Type a name in the Form Name text box.**

   You can choose any name for this field as long as you don't use spaces, special characters, or punctuation. Scripting languages, such as JavaScript, use the name to identify the form.

4. **Type the directory name and the name of the script in the Action text box.**

   Using the sample script I describe earlier, you can type **/cgi-bin/ guestbook.pl** to specify the path to the Perl script in the cgi-bin folder. You can use the Browse button in the Properties inspector to set this link only if you have a copy of the script on your computer in the same relative location in which it resides on the server. If you're not the programmer, or you don't know much about the script, you probably have to ask your system administrator or Internet service provider for this information. (ISPs that offer scripts for Web clients often include instructions with this information on their Web sites.)

   Notice that the path to the script I include in the example starts with a forward slash, indicating that the cgi-bin folder resides at the root level on the site. You could also use the full URL, starting with http://.

5. **In the Properties inspector, use the Method drop-down list box to choose Default, Get, or Post (refer to Figure 12-1).**

   The Get and Post options control how the form works. The option you use depends on the kind of CGI script you use on your server. Get this information from your system administrator, programmer, or Internet service provider.

These are just the preliminary steps you need to create a form. When you establish the boundaries of a form, as represented by the dotted red line that appears after Step 1, Dreamweaver creates the code that goes in the background of your form and enables it to interact with a script on your server. The rest of this chapter shows you how to add various form elements, such as text boxes, radio buttons, and drop-down list boxes.

You can use CSS get rid of the auto margin spacing around a form. Chapter 8 covers Cascading Style Sheets.

Comparing radio buttons and check boxes

Radio buttons and check boxes make filling in a form easy for viewers of your site. Rather than make users type a word, such as *yes* or *no,* you can provide radio buttons and check boxes so that users can simply click boxes or buttons.

What's the difference between radio buttons and check boxes? *Radio buttons* enable users to select only one option from a group. Thus, radio buttons are good for either/or options or situations in which you want users to make only one selection. *Check boxes,* on the other hand, enable users to make multiple choices, so they're good for "choose all that apply" situations when users can make multiple choices, or for approval situations: "Check this box if . . ."

Creating radio buttons

To create radio buttons on a form, follow these steps:

1. **Click your form to select it.**

   If you haven't yet created a form, follow the steps in the section "Creating HTML Forms," earlier in this chapter.

2. **Click the Radio Button icon on the Forms Insert bar.**

   You can also choose Insert⇨Form⇨Radio Button. Either way, a radio button appears inside the form's perimeter.

3. **Repeat Step 2 until you have the number of radio buttons you want.**

4. **Select one of the radio buttons on the form to reveal the radio button's properties in the Properties inspector, as shown in Figure 12-2.**

Figure 12-2: Radio buttons are best for multiple-choice options when you want to restrict users to only one choice.

5. **Type a name in the Radio Button text box.**

   All radio buttons in a group should have the exact same name so that the browser associates them with one another and prevents users from being able to select more than one. If you want users to be able to choose more than one item from a list, use check boxes, as described in the following section.

6. **Type a name in the Checked Value text box.**

Each radio button in a group should have a different Checked Value name so that the CGI script can distinguish them. Naming them for the thing they represent is usually best — *yes* when the choice is yes and *no* when it's no. If you're asking users about their favorite ice cream flavors, for example, use as values the flavor each button represents. This name is usually included in the data you get back when the form is processed and returned to you (it can be returned in an e-mail message or sent directly to a database). How the data is returned depends on the CGI script or other programming used to process the form. If you're looking at the data later, interpreting it is easier if the name is something that makes sense to you.

7. **Choose Checked or Unchecked next to Initial State.**

These two buttons determine whether the radio button on your form appears already selected when the Web page loads. Choose Checked if you want to preselect a choice. You should only set one radio button option to be preselected and remember the user can always override this setting by choosing another radio button.

8. **Select the other radio buttons (from the Forms Insert bar) one by one and repeat Steps 5 through 7 to specify the properties in the Properties inspector for each one.**

If your form is complete, jump ahead to the "Finishing off your form with Submit and Reset buttons" section, later in this chapter.

Creating check boxes

To create check boxes, follow these steps:

1. **Click your form to select it.**

If you haven't yet created a form, follow the steps in the section "Creating HTML Forms," earlier in this chapter.

2. **Click the Check Box icon on the Forms Insert bar.**

You can also choose Insert⇨Form⇨Check Box.

3. **Repeat Step 2 to place as many check boxes as you want.**

4. **Select one of the check boxes on your form to reveal the check box properties in the Properties inspector, as shown in Figure 12-3.**

Figure 12-3:
Check
boxes are
best for
multiple-
choice
options that
enable
users to
select more
than one
option.

5. **Type a name in the Checkbox text box.**

   You should use a distinct name for each check box because users can select more than one check box and you want to ensure that the information submitted is properly associated with each individual check box.

6. **Type a name in the Checked Value text box.**

   Each check box in a group should have a different Checked Value name so that the CGI script can distinguish them. Naming them for the thing they represent is usually best. As with radio buttons, the Checked Value is usually included in the data you get back when the form is processed and returned to you. If you're looking at the data later, interpreting it is easier if the name is something that makes sense to you.

7. **Choose Checked or Unchecked next to Initial State.**

   This option determines whether the check box appears already selected when the Web page loads. Choose Checked if you want to preselect a choice. A user can always override this preselection by clicking the text box again to deselect it.

8. **Select the other check boxes (from the Forms Insert bar) one by one and repeat Steps 5 through 7 to set the properties in the Properties inspector for each one.**

If your form is complete, jump ahead to the "Finishing off your form with Submit and Reset buttons" section, later in this chapter.

Adding text fields and text areas

When you want users to enter text, such as a name, e-mail address, or comment, you need to use a text field. To insert text fields, follow these steps:

1. **Click the form to select it.**

   If you haven't yet created a form, follow the steps in the section, "Creating HTML Forms," earlier in this chapter.

2. **Click the Text Field icon on the Forms Insert bar.**

   You can also choose Insert➪Form➪Text Field. A text field box appears.

3. **On the form, click to place your cursor next to the first text field and type a question or other text prompt.**

   For example, you may want to type Address: next to a text box where you want a user to enter an address.

4. **Select the text field on your form to reveal the Text Field properties in the Properties inspector, as shown in Figure 12-4.**

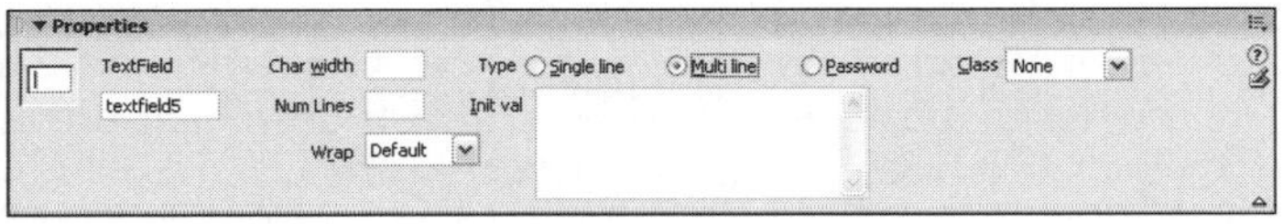

Figure 12-4:
Use the Text Field option to create form fields in which users can enter one or more lines of text.

5. **Type a name in the TextField text box.**

   Each text area on a form should have a different text field name so that the CGI script can distinguish them. Naming them for the thing they represent is usually best. In Figure 12-4, you can see that I named the Address option Address. Many scripts return this name next to the contents of the text field a visitor enters at your Web site. If you're looking at the data later, you can more easily interpret it if the name corresponds to the choice.

6. **In the Char Width box, type the number of characters you want to be visible in the field.**

   This setting determines the width of the text field that appears on the page. Determine the size by the amount of information you expect users to enter.

7. **Type the maximum number of characters you want to allow in the Max Chars box.**

   If you leave this field blank, users can type as many characters as they choose. I usually limit the number of characters only if I want to maintain consistency in the data. For example, I like to limit the State field to a two-character abbreviation. Again, you determine the size to make it by the amount of information you expect users to enter.

You can set the Char Width field to be longer or shorter than the Max Chars field. You can choose to make them different if you want to maintain a certain display area because it looks better in the design, but you want to enable users to add more information if they choose to. That way, if users type more characters than can display in the area, the text scrolls so that users can still see the end of the text they're typing.

8. **Next to Type, click to select the button next to Single Line, Multi Line, or Password:**

   • Choose **Single Line** if you want to create a one-line text box, such as the kind I created for the Name and Address fields shown in Figure 12-4.

   • Choose **Multi Line** if you want to give users space to enter text. (Note that if you choose Multi Line, you also need to specify the number of lines you want the text area to cover by typing a number in the Num Lines field, which appears as an option when you choose Multi Line.)

   • Specify **Wrap** to control how the user's data displays if he exceeds the length of the text field. Selecting Off or Default prevents the user's text from wrapping to the next line.

   • Choose **Password** if you're asking users to enter data that they might not want to display on-screen. This type of field causes entered data to appear as asterisks and disables copying from the field.

9. **In the Init Val text box, type any text you want to display when the form loads.**

   For example, you can include the words `Add comments here` on the form in the text field under Comments. Users can delete the Init Value text or leave it and add more text to it.

10. **Select the other text areas one by one and repeat Steps 5 through 9 to set the properties in the Properties inspector for each one.**

If your form is complete, jump ahead to the "Finishing off your form with Submit and Reset buttons" section, later in this chapter.

Firefox, Netscape, Safari, and Microsoft Internet Explorer don't display text fields in forms equally. The differences vary depending on the version of the browser, but the general result is that a text field displays with different dimensions in one browser than in another. Slight differences exist with color, scroll bars, and shape in the case of check boxes. Unfortunately, this problem has no perfect solution, but you should test all your forms in all browsers and create designs that look okay even when the text fields display differently.

Creating drop-down lists

When you want to give users a multiple-choice option but don't want to take up lots of space on the page, drop-down lists are an ideal solution. To create a drop-down list using Dreamweaver, follow these steps:

1. **Click your form to select it.**

   If you haven't yet created a form, follow the steps in the section "Creating HTML Forms," earlier in this chapter.

2. **Click the List/Menu icon on the Forms Insert bar.**

   You can also choose Insert⇨Form⇨List/Menu. A drop-down list appears.

3. **Click to place your cursor next to the List field and enter a question or other text prompt.**

   In Figure 12-5, I use the example What is your favorite sport?.

4. **Select the field that represents the list on your page to reveal the List/ Menu properties in the Properties inspector, as shown at the bottom of Figure 12-5.**

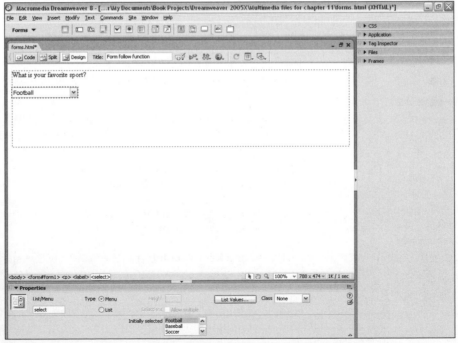

Figure 12-5: The List/Menu option enables you to create a drop-down list of options that doesn't take up lots of room on your page.

5. Type a name in the List/Menu text box.

Each list or menu on a form should have a different name so that you can differentiate the lists when you sort out the data.

6. Next to Type, choose Menu or List.

This step determines whether this form element is a drop-down menu or a scrollable list. If you choose List, you can specify the height and control how many items are shown at a time. You can also specify whether a user can select more than one item. If you choose Menu, these options aren't available.

7. Click the List Values button in the upper-right of the Properties inspector.

The List Values dialog box opens (see Figure 12-6), and you can enter the choices you want to make available. Click the plus sign (+) to add an item label; then type the label text you want in the text box that appears in the dialog box. Item labels display on the menu or list on the Web page in the order in which you enter them. Use the minus sign (–) to delete a selected option. Press the Tab key to move the cursor to the Value side of the dialog box, where you can enter a value. Values are optional, but if present, they are sent to the server instead of the label text. This provides a way of including information that you don't want to display on the drop-down menu. For example, if you enter `football` as a label on the left, you can enter `American` as a value on the right to distinguish American football from soccer, which is often called football in other parts of the world. If you don't enter a value, the label is used as the submitted data when the form is processed.

Figure 12-6:
Use the List Values dialog box to create the options in a List form field.

8. Click OK to close the dialog box.

If your form is complete, jump ahead to "Finishing off your form with Submit and Reset buttons," section later in this chapter.

Unless you have a CGI script or other program connected to this form, it isn't executed, even if you have created the form itself correctly.

Finishing off your form with Submit and Reset buttons

For your users to be able to send their completed forms to you, you need to create a Submit button, which, when clicked, tells the user's browser to send the form to the CGI script that processes the form. You may also want to add a Reset button, which enables users to erase any information they have entered if they want to start over.

Many developers don't use the Reset button because they find it confusing and because visitors can always leave a page before hitting the Submit button if they choose not to complete a form.

These buttons are easy to create in Dreamweaver. To create a button, follow these steps:

1. **Click your form to select it.**

    If you haven't yet created a form, check out the steps in the section "Creating HTML Forms," earlier in this chapter. I suggest that you also enter a few fields, such as radio buttons or text fields. There's not much point in having a Submit button if you don't collect any data that needs to be submitted.

2. **Click the Button icon on the Forms Insert bar.**

    You can also choose Insert⇨Form⇨Button.

    A Submit button appears, and the Form Properties inspector changes to reveal button properties. You can change it to a Reset button or other kind of button by altering the attributes in the Properties inspector, as shown in the remaining steps.

3. **Select the button you just added to display the button properties in the Properties inspector, as shown in Figure 12-7.**

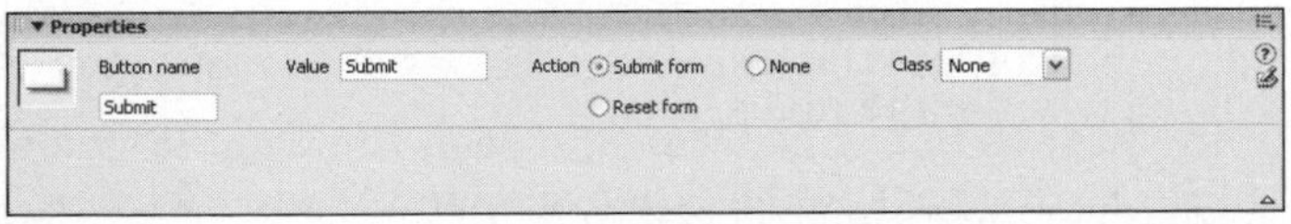

Figure 12-7:
Submit and Reset buttons enable users to submit their information or clear forms.

4. **Click either the Submit Form or Reset Form button next to Action.**

   A Submit button invokes an action, such as sending user information to an e-mail address. A Reset button returns the page to the way it was when the page loaded. There is also a None option, which creates a button that doesn't do anything.

5. **In the Label text box, type the text you want to display on the button.**

   You can type any text you want for the label, such as Search, Go, Clear, or Delete.

There you have it! Now that you know how to use Dreamweaver to create the basic elements of HTML forms, you can develop more intricate forms for your Web site. *Remember:* None of these forms works without a CGI script or other program behind it to execute when the user enters the information.

Using jump menus

Many designers use jump menus as navigational elements because they can provide a list of links in a drop-down list without taking up lots of room on a Web page. You can also use a jump menu to launch an application or start an animation sequence.

To create a jump menu, follow these steps:

1. **Click your form to select it.**

   If you haven't yet created a form, follow the steps in the section "Creating HTML Forms," earlier in this chapter. Note that you don't need a Submit button to make a jump menu work, although adding one may make the action step clear to users.

2. **Click the Jump Menu icon on the Forms Insert bar.**

   You can also choose Insert⇨Form⇨Jump Menu.

   The Insert Jump Menu dialog box opens.

3. **In the Text field, under Menu Items, type the name you want to display in the drop-down list.**

   Click the plus sign (+) to add more items. As you type items in the Text field, they display in the Menu Items list, as shown in Figure 12-8.

4. **Use the Browse button to locate the page you want to link to or enter the URL for the page in the When Selected, Go to URL field.**

   You can link to a local file or enter any URL to link to a page on another Web site, and you can use the Browse button to specify the URL you want to link to.

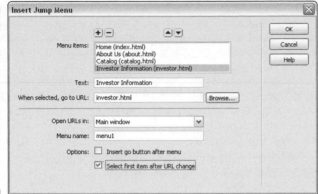

Figure 12-8:
When you
create a
jump list,
items you
type in the
Text field
display in
the Menu
Items drop-
down list.

5. **Use the Open URLs In field to specify a target if you're using frames.**

   If you're not using frames, the default is Main Window. Then, when the user selects an option, the new page replaces the page he is viewing.

6. **Use the Menu Name field if you want to enter a unique identifier for this menu.**

   This option can be useful if you have multiple jump menus on a page. You can use any name you want, but you can't use spaces, special characters, or punctuation.

7. **Use the Insert Go Button After Menu option if you want to force users to click a button to activate the selection.**

   If you don't add a Go button, the linked page loads automatically as soon as the user makes a selection. The Go button is really just a Submit button — it's just usually labeled a Go button on a jump menu.

Choosing other form options in Dreamweaver

As though all the features I describe earlier in this chapter aren't enough, Dreamweaver includes a few specialized form options for facilitating interactivity, adding images, and even adding hidden fields. You can use each of these options:

✔ **File Field icon:** Enables you to add a Browse button to a form so that users can upload files from their local computers to your server. The button enables users to upload images or text files, but it works only if your server is set up to handle this kind of upload from a browser. Check with your system administrator if you're not sure.

A File field is useful if you're creating a system like the one at the online service at www.MyEvent.com. It has a "Build your own Web site" system that enables anyone to create an individual site without needing a program like Dreamweaver. Many Web sites now provide this service to users. The sites are generally template-based systems that walk readers through a series of forms where they choose designs and enter text that they want to appear on their Web pages. Most people want to be able to add more than just text to their sites — they want to add their own images, such as logos and photos. That's where a File field becomes necessary. By using this form option, you can enable readers to browse their own hard drives for a file and then automatically upload it to your server, where it can be linked to their pages.

The complex File Field feature requires a sophisticated CGI script and special server access to work. If you aren't a programmer, you may need assistance to use this option on your site.

✔ **Image Field icon:** Makes adding an image to your form simple and easy. You can use images to create more attractive or interesting buttons.

✔ **Hidden Field icon:** Inserts data that isn't displayed to users but can be used by a script or other application that processes the form. Most scripts have a few hidden fields that are necessary for full functionality.

Making your forms look good

The best way to get your form fields to line up nicely is to use an HTML table. You may want to use a table to align a form by putting all your text in one row of cells and all your text fields in an adjacent row. You may also want to place all your radio buttons in the cells on the left and the text they correspond to in the cells on the right. (Chapter 6 shows you how to create HTML tables and how to use them to align information in your forms.) You can also use images and table border to make tables look better.

Part V
Working with Dynamic Content

The 5th Wave   By Rich Tennant

"Games are an important part of my Web site. They cause eye strain."

In this part . . .

The most sophisticated and technically complicated Web sites are created using databases to dynamically generate Web pages, ideal for content-heavy Web sites. Although creating a Web site with these advanced features is far more complex than what you find in earlier parts of this book, the rewards can be worth the trouble. In this part, you discover the benefits of creating a dynamic site, find out how to work with a database on the Web, and follow step-by-step instructions to build a simple database-driven site.

Chapter 13

Building a Dynamic Web Site: Getting Started

· ·

In This Chapter

▶ Defining a dynamic Web site

▶ Going over the basic terminology

▶ Setting up a Data Source Name

· ·

*T*he most sophisticated Web sites on the Internet, such as Amazon.com or CNN.com, were created using complex programming and databases. Combining a database that records information about users with the capability to generate pages automatically is what enables Amazon to greet you by name when you return to its site, track your orders as you buy books, and even make recommendations based on your previous purchases.

Static Web sites, which you can build using the instructions in Chapter 12, work well for many Web sites (including my own at www.JCWarner.com). But for anyone creating a really large, content-heavy site, such as a magazine or newspaper Web site, or large e-commerce sites where you need to track inventory and want users to be able to search through products, dynamic Web sites are a better choice.

Before you even start down this path, let me warn you of two things. First, creating a database-driven Web site is far, far more complex than creating the kinds of Web sites described in the earlier chapters of this book. And second, the most sophisticated sites on the Web, such as Amazon and CNN, use highly customized systems that require teams of very experienced programmers to create (and are far beyond what you can do with Dreamweaver's dynamic site features).

That said, Dreamweaver does include basic database development features that you can use to create dynamic Web sites. In this chapter and the two that follow, you find an introduction to these features and instructions for creating a basic, database-driven site.

A description of the more advanced Dreamweaver database features is beyond the scope of this Dummies book. If you want to use Dreamweaver's most advanced database features, you find more information in *Dreamweaver MX 2004 Bible*, written by Joseph Lowery (published by Wiley Publishing, Inc.).

This chapter begins by introducing you to what a dynamic Web site and a database are and the many ways in which, through a dynamic Web site, you can display and edit information contained within a database. You also discover what you need to have in place in order to create a dynamic Web site. In Chapters 14 and 15, you find step-by-step directions for creating various dynamic features on a real-world Web site.

Understanding the Dynamic Web Site

A *dynamic* Web site is usually connected to a *database,* which delivers different data to each Web site visitor based on his or her requests. Many dynamic Web sites also have Web pages that permit an administrator or a site visitor to make changes to the information that is displayed through a series of simple steps without ever leaving the Web browser. A good example of a dynamic Web site is a search engine. You type what you want to find into a search field and when you submit your request, you get instant results with information that is relevant (ideally, anyway!) to your search request.

If you want to add just a simple search engine to a Web site, see Chapter 17 for tips about using Google's free search engine features on any Web site.

A dynamic Web site has many advantages besides the capability to create a site-wide search. Suppose that you have a Web site where you sell 657 different kinds of candy. On a *static* Web site, you would have to create 657 pages, one for each candy product. With a database-driven site, you create just *one* page that contains special code to describe where to display the product name, image, description, and any other pertinent information on the page. Then you enter all your product information into a database (if it's not in one already), and the special code in the page design communicates with the database, collecting each product's information and creating a page on the fly for each product as visitors request that product.

Not only can this kind of system save lots of time (because you don't have to create all those individual pages), dynamic Web sites also enable you to make changes and updates with less effort. And you can even display the same product information in multiple page designs, in different combinations, and even on different sites with much less effort.

These sites are usually set up so that the Web site can be administered through a Web browser, allowing staff with little or no technical skills to easily add or remove products and make changes to existing products. They simply enter or edit information in a form using a Web browser and click Submit, and they can make changes to the database. Once updated, that new information appears instantly the next time a product page is loaded for a visitor.

Usually, you would limit the capability to make these changes to a few people on your staff. You don't necessarily want your customers making price changes or altering product descriptions, but you may want your sales staff to be able to easily make changes, even when they're out in the field. You can control this situation by setting up different levels of password access to your site. That way, customers can search for certain information, and staff members with special access and the right passwords can search for even more information and make changes to it. The system you use to do both these tasks is essentially the same, but you set up different levels of access to make it all work this way.

Beware, however, that before a non-technical staff person can easily make changes and updates to a dynamic site, someone who is technically savvy has to do a significant amount of setup work to create the dynamic system. Again, this kind of Web site system only makes sense if you're creating a very large, complex, and data-rich Web site. A programmer could spend much more time setting up even a simple database site than it takes to create quite a few static Web pages.

Talking the Talk: Key Concepts

If you're sure that you want to create a dynamic Web site and that the basic database features in Dreamweaver are up to the task for you, then read on. You can do some very cool things with a database-driven site, even if you're not creating the next Amazon. Before jumping into your first dynamic Web site, however, the following pages are designed to help you become familiar with a few key concepts that play an integral role in dynamic Web site development.

Exploring a database

A *database* is a collection of information compiled in one or more *tables*. Each table has multiple *fields* (also called *columns*) and individual *records* in rows. What? Okay, picture a mail-order catalog, such as Pottery Barn. (Indulge me — it's my favorite.)

The catalog itself is the *database*. It contains a collection of information about various products. Each product is a *record* in the database. In this case, all particular products have an item number, price, and a color — and each of those is a *field*. A *record* in a database consists of one complete set of all fields in a table. Taking it a step further, within the catalog, the various products are organized in categories often because they have something in common (furniture, rugs, bedding, wall décor). Each category is a *table* — a grouping of various records from a database that have something in common.

This type of table isn't the same kind discussed in Chapter 6, where you find out how HTML tables are used to format information, much as you would use a spreadsheet program, such as Excel. Database tables aren't used for formatting; they're for grouping and organizing content.

How it works on the Web

Databases on the Web work in much the same way. Suppose that you go to www.penpal.net to find a new pen pal. If you're a registered member, you can search by location, gender, and age: Starting on the search page, you can click the <u>Search by Country</u> link. On the next page, you can choose France and click the Search button. The following page lets you choose age range, and the next page lets you choose gender. You might choose Ages 21-29, and on the last page you can choose a specific age and gender, a 25-year-old male for example. After you click male, a list of potential pen pals who match your requirements appears right before your eyes (see Figure 13-1).

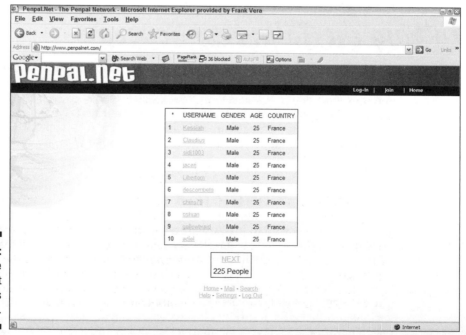

Figure 13-1:
The
Penpal.net
results
page.

When you submit your criteria, some specific code on that page matched your information with information in a database that lists other people looking for a pen pal. It looked through every record (individual person), trying to find records (pen pals) with fields that match your request. If you want, you could also list yourself as a potential pen pal for others to find you by entering your information and adding it to the database directly from your Web browser!

Database applications

Various applications are made specifically for creating and managing data, including Microsoft Access, SQL Server, MySQL, FoxPro, and Oracle. Novices most commonly use Access to create small databases (MDB files). Access is also commonly used to communicate visually with bigger databases, such as Microsoft SQL Server.

I created the examples in this book in Microsoft Access 2000 running with the Windows XP Professional operating system. If you want to dig deeper into the world of databases, consider purchasing *Database Development For Dummies* and *SQL For Dummies*, both written by Allen G. Taylor; *Access 2003 For Dummies,* written by John Kaufeld; or *Oracle8i For Dummies,* written by Carol McCullough-Dieter (all published by Wiley Publishing, Inc.).

Plugging in the data

Now that you have the database basics covered, you need to provide a way for the Web site and the database to communicate. In the next section, I show you how to set up a Web server and an application server step-by-step so that you can get started.

Setting up the Web server

While working with Web sites that are *static* (the content is entered by hand and isn't permanently altered by, or customized for, the person viewing the site), you may be used to previewing pages directly from your local hard drive. It's not that simple when the content is dynamic because Dreamweaver adds some special code that the server needs to process before the content is published to the viewer. Having a Web server is crucial when you're working with a dynamic Web site, because you need to test your work along the way to make sure that you get the results you're shooting for.

A *Web server* is both a piece of computer hardware on which a Web site is stored and the software on that system that provides the server functionality. In this case, the Web server I'm referring to is the software installed on a system, not an actual computer chip in a large beige case.

Server Technologies Supported by Dreamweaver

Dreamweaver supports these five server technologies (described in detail in the following sections):

- ✔ Active Server Pages (ASP)
- ✔ ASP.NET
- ✔ ColdFusion
- ✔ JavaServer Pages (JSP)
- ✔ PHP (which stands for PHP: Hypertext Preprocessor — a recursive acronym, for you wordsmiths)

The examples in this book use ASP in Microsoft Windows. In essence, all five work toward the same outcome: dynamic content on a Web page or Web site. They all provide the capability to generate HTML dynamically. Using server-side code, they can display information from a database and create HTML based on whether certain criteria are met or specified by a particular user. I selected ASP and Microsoft Windows for this book because ASP is one of the most common and relatively easy-to-use server software options.

To recommend one technology over the other really wouldn't be fair because they all offer similar functionality with slight variations in speed and efficiency. The most marketable language is ASP because of its widely used and mature features. If you dream of becoming a highly paid programmer, you can't go wrong with this one.

Check out these other titles, all published by Wiley Publishing, Inc.: *Active Server Pages For Dummies,* by Bill Hatfield; *ASP.NET For Dummies,* by Bill Hatfield; *JavaServer Pages For Dummies,* by MacCormac Rinehart; *ColdFusion MX For Dummies,* by John Paul Ashenfelter; and *PHP 5 For Dummies,* by Janet Valade.

The following sections provide more detail on each of these scripting languages.

ASP

ASP is a server technology that comes, at no additional cost, built into Windows 2003 Server, Windows 2000, Windows XP Professional, and it can be easily installed into Windows 98 and NT. Used in conjunction with Microsoft IIS or Personal Web Server, ASP isn't a stand-alone programming language because much of the code you write for ASP pages is in VB Script or JavaScript. You can check out www.4guysfromrolla.com to find out more about ASP in what more closely resembles plain English.

ASP.NET

ASP.NET is a relatively new server technology. It's not a revision of ASP 3.0; in fact, it's almost a complete overhaul of it. This latest installment of ASP isn't what 3.0 was to 2.0 — Microsoft has done more than add new tags. The language is more similar to traditional programming languages, such as C++, where code is compiled. This arrangement suggests that applications written in ASP.NET can run faster than anything now available because Web servers work more efficiently with less coding overhead. However, ASP.NET isn't as verbose as ASP 3.0, so it's much harder for novice programmers to read. ASP.NET is a Microsoft technology, and you can find more information at http://msdn.microsoft.com/asp.net/. You can also find more about ASP.NET from http://aspnet.4guysfromrolla.com/.

JavaServerPages (JSP)

JSP is from Sun Microsystems. Because its dynamic code is based on Java, you can run the pages from non-Microsoft Web servers. You can use JSP on Allaire JRun Server and IBM WebSphere. Using JSP, you can create and keep the dynamic code separated from the HTML pages (by using JavaBeans), or you can embed the JSP code into the page. Unless you're a hard-core programmer, however, this language isn't for you. JSP is horribly complex.

ColdFusion MX

ColdFusion MX, owned by Macromedia, uses its own server and scripting language. ColdFusion is probably the easiest language to figure out; and it offers built-in XML processing and custom tags that also allow you to separate dynamic code from HTML, which makes it similar to JSP. Like JSP, it's also ultimately based on Java.

PHP

PHP was originally native to Unix-based servers. However, you can now download Windows binaries from www.php.net to run Apache (a server software typically used with PHP) from any version of Windows as well as IIS on NT, 2000, XP Professional, and 2003 Server. You can even configure PHP to run on Personal Web Server (although it's rather tricky). The PHP scripting language is based on C, Perl, and Java. You can get more functionality with PHP right out of the box than you can with ASP. For example, virtually every ASP add-on that's on sale at www.serverobjects.com comes built-in standard or is available for free from PHP.net.

Making the Data Connection

To set up a *Web server*, you need server software. A Web server, sometimes called an HTTP server, responds to requests from a Web browser by serving up Web pages based on those requests.

You also need to set up an *application server*, which helps the Web server to process specially marked Web pages. When the browser requests one of these pages, the Web server hands the page off to the application server, which processes it before sending the page to the browser.

I use ASP specifically for the examples in this section because it's much easier to set up than any of the other technologies. Assuming that you're rather new at this task, I wouldn't want to throw you into the deep end (not yet, anyway).

In order to use ASP, the server choices are Microsoft IIS or Personal Web Server (PWS). Either one of these servers works as both a Web server and an application server. PWS runs with Windows 98 or Windows NT, and you can install it from your Windows CD. If you have Windows 2000 Server, Windows NT 4, or Windows XP Professional, IIS is part of the package. If you can't find your CD, you can always download IIS or PWS for free from the Microsoft Web site.

At this point, if you're running Windows 95, Windows 98 SE, or Windows NT, make sure that you have PWS installed. If you're running Windows 2000 or Windows XP Professional, IIS is already in your system, and all you have to do is make sure that it's started.

If you're running Windows 2000 or Windows XP Professional and IIS isn't enabled, you can install it by choosing Control Panel➪Add/Remove Programs➪ Add/Remove Windows Components. When the Windows Components screen appears, scroll down the list and make sure that a check mark appears next to the Internet Information Server option.

IIS doesn't work on Windows XP Home Edition. You must upgrade to Windows XP Professional to use it.

To download and install Microsoft Personal Web Server, go to `www.microsoft.com/downloads/` and search for **option pack**. Click the Windows NT 4.0 Option Pack option. If you're using Windows 98, choose Windows 95 from the list of operating systems — it's the same file — and follow the downloading instructions.

Setting up a DSN

A *Data Source Name,* or *DSN,* is basically a name associated with your database that helps you to keep your connection with the database intact even if the database changes to a new location.

Although you don't need a DSN to connect to a database using Dreamweaver, a DSN is the easiest way to get your dynamic Dreamweaver site to work.

To follow along with the steps in this section, you need an existing Microsoft Access database file, and you need to make sure that your Access Database Driver is installed. Follow these steps to ensure that it's already there and to create the DSN:

1. **In Windows XP Professional, choose Start⇨Programs⇨Administrative Tools⇨Data Sources (ODBC).**

   You see the ODBC Data Source Administrator dialog box (see Figure 13-2). On the first tab (User DSN), you see MS Access Database and Microsoft Access Driver (*mdb) on one line.

Figure 13-2: The ODBC Data Source Administrator dialog box.

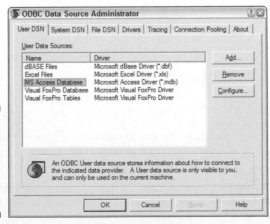

2. **Click the System DSN tab.**

   You see a list of database connections.

3. **Click Add.**

   A list of drivers appears (see Figure 13-3).

Figure 13-3:
The list of drivers from the Systems DSN tab.

4. **Select Microsoft Access Driver and then click Finish.**

   The ODBC Microsoft Access Setup dialog box appears (see Figure 13-4).

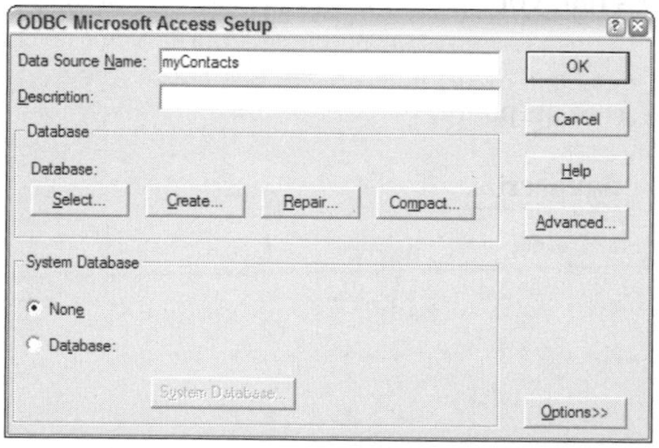

Figure 13-4:
The ODBC Microsoft Access Setup dialog box.

5. **Enter a name for your database in the Data Source Name text box. You don't** *have* **to type something in the Description box, but you can if you want.**

   Because the examples later in the chapter have to do with contacts, I assume that your database is called *contacts.mdb* and that you type **myContacts** as the Data Source Name. But you can call it whatever you want, as long as you remember what you called it.

6. **Click Select.**

   The Select Database dialog box appears.

7. **Find the database you want to use and click OK.**

   As you can see, the path to the database is now listed in the Database area in the ODBC Microsoft Access Setup dialog box.

8. **You can click the Advanced button to fill out authorization information if your database requires a username and password. Otherwise, don't worry about it.**

9. **Click OK in the ODBC Microsoft Access Setup dialog box to close it; then click OK to close the ODBC Data Source Administrator dialog box.**

Setting up Dreamweaver for Windows

Creating the data connection in Dreamweaver takes a few quick steps. You should start by setting up your site's local information and remote site information, which Chapter 2 explains in detail. Check out that chapter to get reacquainted if you're not already comfortable with this process.

In this example, I assume that you're running IIS (or PWS) on the same machine you run Dreamweaver on, so I show you how to set up a local connection.

If your IIS or PWS is enabled, when you go to your browser and type **http:// localhost** in the address bar, you see a page confirming that your Web server is up and running.

To get started, follow these steps:

1. **Create a new ASP Javascript page by choosing File⇨New.**

   The New Document dialog box opens (see Figure 13-5).

2. **Click Dynamic Page in the Category list.**

3. **Click ASP JavaScript and then click Create.**

   You have to have a document open to do anything with the Application panel.

4. **Click the Application panel to expand it and click the Databases tab (see Figure 13-6).**

   You can open the Databases tab by choosing Window⇨Databases from the Dreamweaver main menu.

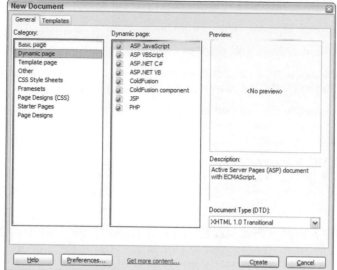

Figure 13-5:
New
Document
dialog box.

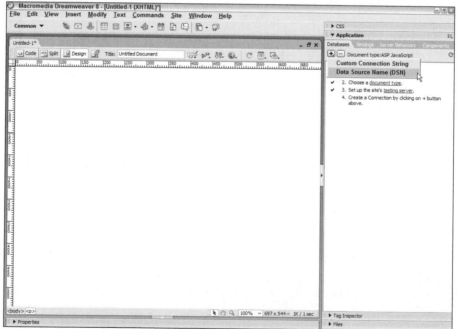

Figure 13-6:
The
Databases
tab.

5. **Click the plus sign (+) and select Data Source Name (DSN) from the list.**

You see the Data Source Name dialog box, as shown in Figure 13-7.

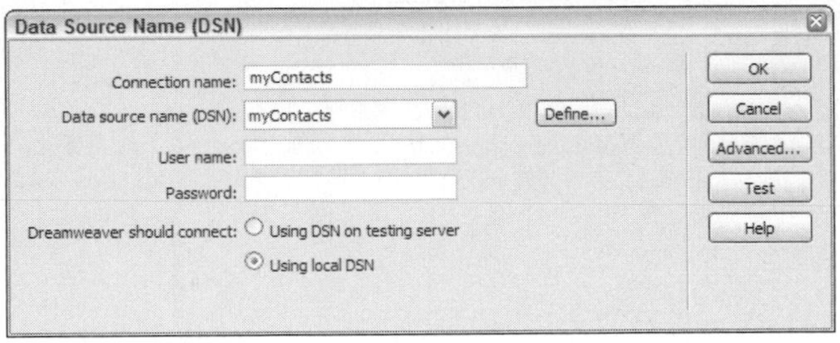

Figure 13-7:
The Data
Source
Name (DSN)
dialog box.

6. **Enter the name for the new connection.**

   For example, type **myContacts**.

7. **Select your database from the list of DSNs. Make sure you indicate that Dreamweaver should connect using local DSN.**

   If the name of your connection is myContacts, then you select the myContacts database.

   If you want to use a remote application server, make sure, of course, that you indicate that Dreamweaver should connect using DSN on the testing server.

8. **Click the Test button.**

   You see a pop-up message letting you know that the connection was made successfully, and you see your database listed on the Databases tab (see Figure 13-8).

   In the Files panel, you also see on your local drive a Connections folder, which contains an ASP file with the connection information for this database. Dreamweaver automatically references this file on any page you create that uses this database connection, saving you from having to insert it every time.

The ASP files in the Connections folder store necessary information that makes your page work correctly with the database. Upload this folder when you upload your site files to the application server.

If your connection fails, check your DSN again, and check the URL prefix for the application server. You can also check the Dreamweaver Help Index for other troubleshooting tips.

Now you're ready to build a dynamic Web site. In Chapters 14 and 15, I get into more details so that you can put these great Dreamweaver features to use on your site right away.

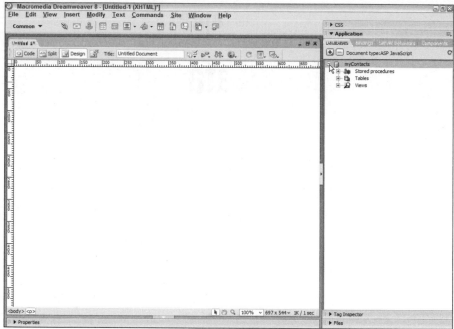

Figure 13-8:
The
Database
tab
displaying
the new
connection.

Setting up Dreamweaver for Mac users

Setting up a data connection on a Mac is a little more complicated because you can't run one of Dreamweaver's support Web servers or application servers locally, unless you're running OS X; you must connect to a remote server. Ideally, you can connect your Mac to an NT server with permission to browse the Mac, and after you're networked, make the data connection. Dreamweaver includes information in its help files that specifically covers this process for Mac users.

OS X users can alternatively download Apache's HTTP server from `http://httpd.apache.org/`. However, anyone using OS 9 and earlier is out of luck.

Chapter 14

Bringing Data into the Mix

*I*f you've never used the dynamic development capabilities of Dreamweaver, you'll want to get familiar with the windows and inspectors covered in the beginning of this chapter before you start creating your first project. In the rest of this chapter, you find out how these elements work together to create a Web site full of dynamic features.

For the purposes of illustration, all the figures and steps in this chapter are based on an example site with a contact management system that features information for various people — names, addresses, and pictures. If your site features another kind of data, such as product descriptions or articles, don't worry — these steps show you how to use Dreamweaver to create any kind of dynamic site. You can apply the info in this chapter to your own data to create any kind of dynamic Web site.

Make sure your application server is running and, because this chapter assumes that you're using Internet Information Server or Peer Web Services for Windows, make sure that you save all the pages as ASP pages (`filename.asp`) so that the server parses the code correctly. For a quick reminder on how to set up the application server, refer to Chapter 13.

Exploring the Panel

In Dreamweaver, the most fundamental elements of creating a dynamic Web site are in the Application panel, which includes the Databases, Bindings, Components, and Server Behaviors panels. In this section, I introduce you to these panels, which help you create your dynamic site.

The Databases panel

The Databases panel lets you look at the databases on your application server without creating a recordset. In the Databases panel, you can view your entire database structure within Dreamweaver — tables, fields, views, and stored procedures — without needing to use separate database software.

You can find the Databases panel by choosing Window➪Databases on the main menu.

You can create a Data Source Name (DSN) or a custom connection string by clicking the plus (+) sign in the Databases panel (shown in Figure 14-1). To see how you can create a Data Source Name using the Databases panel, refer to Chapter 13.

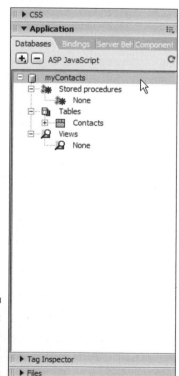

Figure 14-1:
The
Databases
panel.

The Bindings panel

The Bindings panel enables you to add and remove dynamic content data sources from your document. The number and kinds of available data sources can vary depending on whether you use ASP, JSP, or any other server technology (see Chapter 13 for a refresher on servers if you need to). A *data source* is where you get information to use on your dynamic Web page. An example of a data source is a recordset from a database, which you further explore in the next few sections of this chapter.

If you don't see the Bindings panel, you can open it by choosing Window⇨ Bindings on the main menu.

With the Bindings panel, you can access data sources in several ways. You can find out what data source objects you have available by clicking the plus (+) sign in the Bindings panel to get the Add Bindings pop-up menu (see Figure 14-2).

The Add Bindings pop-up menu includes

- ✓ **Recordset (Query):** A recordset stores data from your database for use on a page or set of pages. I explain recordsets in more detail in this chapter.

- ✓ **Command (Stored Procedure):** Commands, or *stored procedures,* are reusable database items that contain SQL code and are commonly used to modify a database (insert, update, or delete records).

- ✓ **Request Variable:** Commonly used wherever a search is involved, a Request Variable carries information from one page to another. When you use a form to submit data to another page, a request variable is created.

- ✓ **Session Variable:** *Session variables* store and display information for the duration of a user's session (or visit). A different session is created on the server for each user and is kept in use either for a set period of time or until a specific action on the site terminates the session (such as a logging out).

- ✓ **Application Variable:** *Application variables* store and display information that must be present for all users and is constant throughout the lifetime of an application. These types of variables are commonly used for page counters or date and time counters. Application variables are available only for ASP and ColdFusion pages, not for PHP and JSP.

- ✓ **Get More Data Sources:** Use this option to open Dreamweaver Exchange in your browser. You can use Exchange to download extensions for Dreamweaver. For more information about extensions, see Chapter 15.

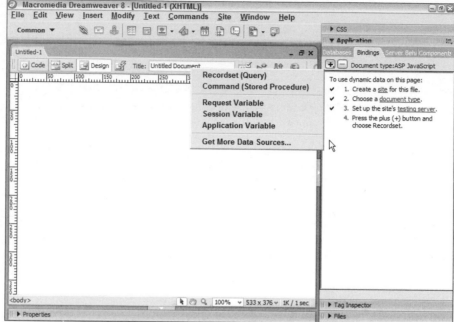

The Server Behaviors panel

Server behaviors are server-side scripts that perform some type of action. Through the Server Behaviors panel, you can add server-side scripts to your pages, such as user authentication and record navigation, which you can read more about in this chapter and Chapter 15. Server behaviors available to you vary depending on the server technology you use.

You can get to the Server Behaviors panel by choosing Window➪Server Behaviors on the Dreamweaver main menu.

You can view the available server behaviors by clicking the plus (+) sign in the Server Behaviors panel to get the Server Behaviors pop-up menu (see Figure 14-3).

The Server Behaviors pop-up menu includes

- **Recordset (Query):** A recordset stores data from your database for use on a page or set of pages. I explain recordsets in more detail in this chapter.
- **Command (Stored Procedure):** Stored procedures are reusable database items that contain SQL code and are commonly used to modify a database (insert, update, or delete records).

✔ **Repeat Region:** This server object displays multiple records on a page. Repeat Region is most commonly used on HTML tables or HTML table rows. You can see more about this behavior later in this chapter.

✔ **Recordset Paging:** If you have to display a large number of records, and want them to display a page at a time, this set of behaviors allows you to navigate from page to page or from record to record.

✔ **Show Region:** With this set of server behaviors, you can show or hide record navigation based on the records displayed. For instance, if you have Next and Previous links on the bottom of every page and your user is on the first page or first record of the recordset, you can set a behavior to display only the Next link. The same goes if the user is on the last page or record — you can set it to hide the Next link and display only the Previous link.

✔ **Dynamic Text:** The Dynamic Text option allows you to display information from your recordset anywhere on the page.

✔ **Go to Detail Page:** Using this behavior, you can link each record in your repeated region to a detail page for that particular record. The behavior also tells the detail page which record's information to display.

✔ **Go to Related Page:** You can use this behavior to link a particular dynamic page to another page that contains related information, passing the parameters of the first page to the related page.

✔ **Insert Record:** Use this behavior on a page to add new records to a database via a Web browser.

✔ **Update Record:** Use this behavior on a page to update existing records in a database via a Web browser.

✔ **Delete Record:** Use this behavior on a page to permanently delete a record from a database via a Web browser.

✔ **Dynamic Form Elements:** This set of server behaviors turns text fields, list/menu fields, radio buttons, or check boxes into dynamic form elements, which you can set to retrieve and display particular information from a recordset.

✔ **User Authentication:** The User Authentication set of behaviors allows you to log in a user, log out a user, check a username against the information in your database, and restrict access to a page.

✔ **XSL Transformation:** *EX*tensible *S*tylesheet *L*anguage *T*ransformations (XSLT) is a language that displays XML data on a Web page after transforming it into HTML.

✔ **Edit Server Behaviors:** Use this option to customize or remove existing server behaviors. Unless you are very comfortable with coding or SQL, I advise you not to mess with this option. (If you're curious about SQL, see *SQL For Dummies,* 5th Edition, by Allen G. Taylor, published by Wiley Publishing, Inc.)

✔ **New Server Behavior:** Use this option to create new server behaviors and add them to the list of existing behaviors. Again, this option is for the more advanced users who are comfortable with coding.

✔ **Get More Server Behaviors:** Use this option to open Dreamweaver Exchange in your browser. You can use Exchange to download extensions for Dreamweaver. For more information about extensions, see Chapter 15.

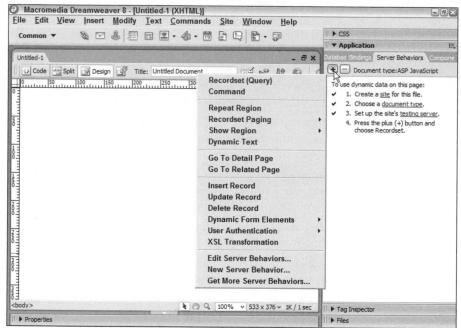

Figure 14-3:
The Server Behaviors panel and its pop-up menu.

The Components panel

Components are reusable bits of code that you can create and insert directly into your pages. With Dreamweaver, you can create components for JSP, Cold Fusion, and ASP.NET pages to consume Web services, display information, or any other use that you can imagine.

Creating a Recordset

The *recordset* holds data from your database for use on a page or set of pages by creating a query. A *query* gathers information from a database to be used on a page, selecting only the records matching the fields and conditions you select for the particular query. The queries for a recordset are built with SQL (Structured Query Language), but you don't need to know SQL in order to get the job done. Dreamweaver writes it all for you.

With your recordset in place, you can display information from your database in various ways.

Before you can create a recordset, you must first connect to a database. Chapter 13 goes over this in more detail.

To define a recordset in Dreamweaver:

1. **Open the ASP page that will use the recordset.**

2. **In the Bindings panel, click the plus sign and select Recordset (Query).**

   You see the Recordset dialog box, as shown in Figure 14-4.

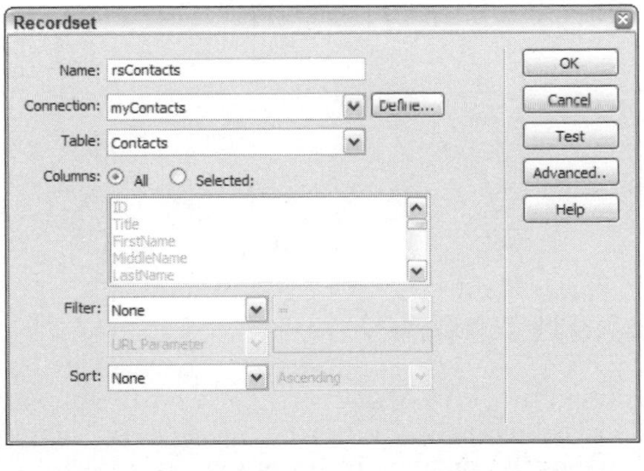

Figure 14-4:
The
Recordset
dialog box.

3. **Enter a name for your recordset in the Name box.**

   Usually, adding the letters *rs* to the beginning of the name is recommended to distinguish it as a recordset in your code, but it isn't necessary. I used *rsContacts* in Figure 14-4.

4. **Select your connection from the Connection drop-down list.**

   This list includes any data connections defined from the Databases panel. Chapter 13 explains how to create a connection.

5. **Choose a database table to collect the data for your recordset from the Table drop-down list.**

   You can select all the columns or only specific columns of data to be displayed.

6. **(Optional) If you want the available information to show only records that meet specific criteria, select a filter from the Filter area.**

7. **If you want the displayed records to sort in ascending or descending order, specify it in the Sort menu by selecting the field by which you want the records sorted (Name, Phone Number, and so on).**

   If you want to tweak the results further and you feel comfortable working with SQL, you can click the Advanced button to edit the SQL statement directly.

8. **To test the connection to the database, click the Test button.**

   You can find the Databases panel by choosing Window➪Databases on the main menu. To create more complicated recordsets, click the Advanced button and you can create SQL statements directly.

   If the test is successful, you see a window with the data in the recordset (similar to Figure 14-5).

Figure 14-5:
A success-
ful test
screen.

9. **Click OK to close the Test screen.**

10. **Click OK to complete the Recordset dialog box.**

    The Bindings panel shows the recordset (see Figure 14-6). You can expand it by clicking the plus sign next to the recordset.

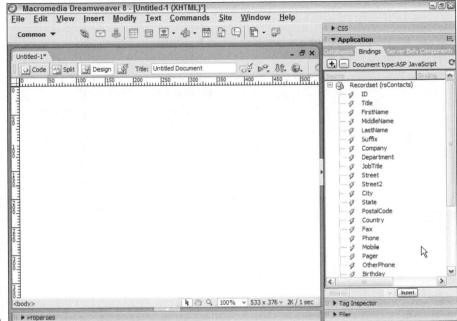

Figure 14-6:
Your recordset now displays in the Bindings panel.

Using a Recordset on Your Page

After you create a recordset, you can place the information on your page as you want. For this section, I made a basic list of all the contacts in the database, with a name, e-mail address, phone number, and Web site URL.

I already built a page with a table showing the appropriate number of cells for all the dynamic text that I'm inserting (see Figure 14-7).

After you set up the document the way you want it, you can drag and drop each data source to its appropriate spot on the page by following these steps:

1. **From the Bindings panel, select your first data source and drag it onto your page, dropping it where you want it to go.**

    The name of the dynamic text appears inside curly brackets. You can now format this piece of text any way you want, treating it like normal HTML text (see Figure 14-8).

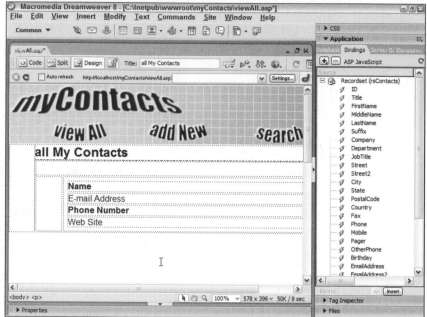

Figure 14-7:
I created
a page
showing
where each
piece of
information
goes.

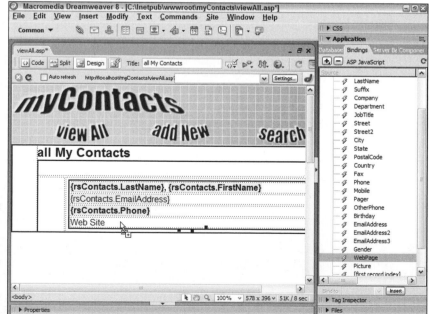

Figure 14-8:
The
dynamic
text is
inserted and
formatted.

2. **Test the result by clicking the LiveData button.**

   The first record of your database appears in place of the dynamic text code (see Figure 14-9). To show more than the first record, you need to define and repeat a region.

Repeating a Region

You probably want to show more than one record at a time on a page that's supposed to list all your contacts. You can do this by applying a server behavior to your region.

A *region* is any area of a page that displays information from a database on your page. After you define your region, you can apply a Repeat Region server behavior, which causes that area to be written to the page over and over, displaying every record, or as many as you tell it to, in the database defined by your recordset until all records display. Repeat Region is most commonly used on HTML tables or table rows.

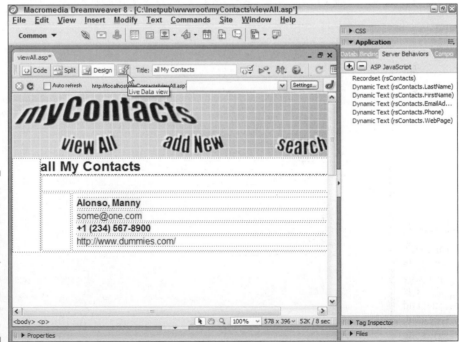

Figure 14-9:
The information from the first record in your database replaces the data source code.

To add a Repeat Region server behavior to your page:

1. **Select the area on your page that you want to define as a region.**

2. **Click the Server Behaviors panel, click the plus (+) sign, and select Repeat Region from the menu that appears.**

   The Repeat Region dialog box appears (see Figure 14-10).

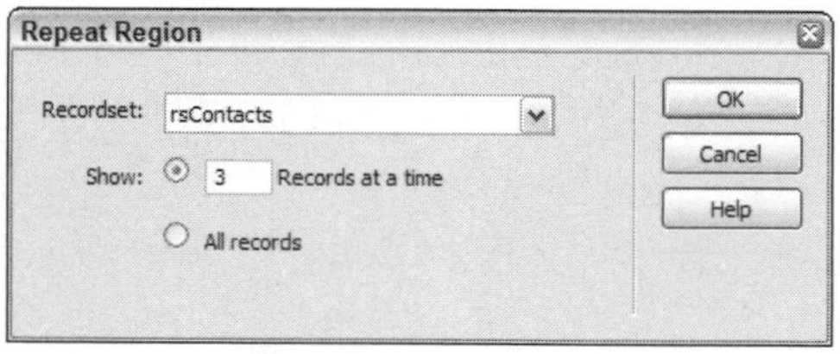

Figure 14-10: Define a region in the Repeat Region dialog box.

3. **Select the number of records that you want to show on the page and then click OK.**

4. **Click the LiveData button to see the results (see Figure 14-11).**

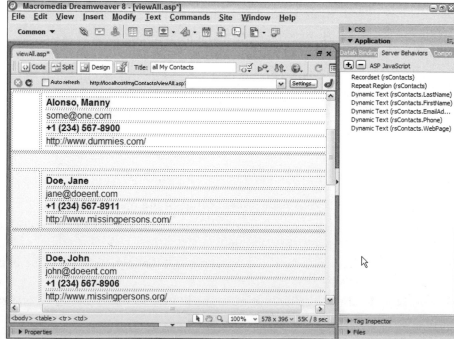

Figure 14-11: With Repeat Region, you can show more than one record at a time.

Adding a Dynamic Image

Whenever you have a dynamic Web site, images are usually involved, whether it is a catalog Web site or a news archive. You can bind an image to a recordset in various easy ways so that your images change depending on the other parts of the page that are bound to the same recordset. Before you bind the image, though, you need to take a few preliminary steps:

1. **Make sure that you have a field for each record in your database that lists the actual path of the image for that record.**

   For example, if your images reside in a folder called images, one level above your dynamic page, you enter the following in the image field in your database: **images/*imagename.gif*,** remembering to replace the *imagename.gif* part with the actual filename for each image.

2. **Upload your image folder to the server.**

   This step is necessary if you want to preview the page with images in LiveData view.

3. **Place a placeholder image in the spot where you want an image to appear for all the records.**

   You can use any of the images in your image folder as a placeholder, or choose Insert⇨Image Object⇨Image Placeholder to use the built-in image placeholder.

   You can find out more about inserting images in Chapter 2.

Binding the Image

After you insert the placeholder image, you can bind images two easy ways — with the Bindings panel or the Properties inspector.

Follow these steps to bind images using the Bindings panel:

1. **Select your placeholder image in the open document.**

2. **Click the plus (+) sign to expand your recordset. (If you're using a Mac, click the triangle.)**

3. **Select the field in your recordset that contains the name of the image file.**

4. **Click the Bind button at the bottom of the Bindings panel (see Figure 14-12).**

Figure 14-12:
The
Bindings
panel
makes an
image
dynamic.

Follow these steps to bind images using the Properties inspector:

1. **Click your placeholder image in the open document to select it.**

2. **Click the Browse button in the Properties inspector next to the Src box.**

   The Select Image Source dialog box appears (see Figure 14-13).

3. **In the Select File Name From section (at the top), select the Data Sources option.**

4. **Select the field that contains your image information.**

5. **Click OK.**

The image changes to a tree with a lightning bolt along its side.

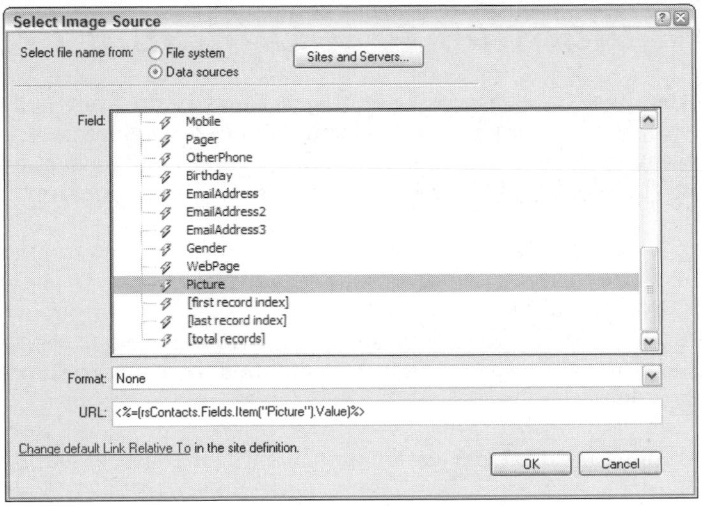

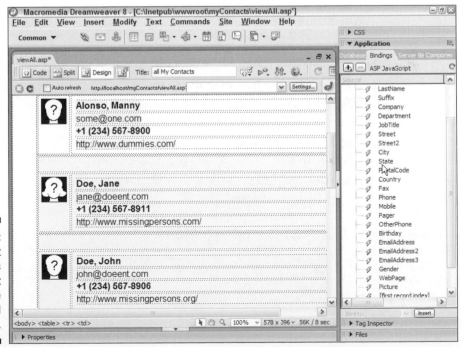

Figure 14-13:
The Select
Image
Source
dialog box.

After performing either of these two methods to bind your images to the
page, click the LiveData button (the button with a lightning bolt) to check out
the results (see Figure 14-14).

Figure 14-14:
You can test
your images
to find out
if they're
bound
correctly.

Adding Navigation to a Dynamic Page

If your database contains many records, you may opt to show only a small number of records per page, so that you don't overwhelm the user. The Dreamweaver Server Behaviors panel allows you to add navigation to your pages so that you can move forward or backward through records.

Define your Repeat Region, which I explain how to do earlier in this chapter, and make sure that you do not select a value large enough to show all records. You can add button images or text links at the bottom of the page to indicate some kind of navigation, such as Previous Page and Next Page links. With the buttons in place, you can activate them by using the Server Behaviors panel.

For example, to add the navigation movements for the Next and Previous buttons:

1. **Select the Previous Page button you added in the Document window.**

2. **Open the Server Behaviors panel.**

   You can open the Server Behaviors panel by choosing Window➪Server Behaviors on the main menu.

3. **Click the plus (+) sign and select Recordset Paging from the menu (see Figure 14-15).**

Figure 14-15: Select Recordset Paging and choose the appropriate navigation movement.

4. **From the submenu, choose the appropriate navigation movement (Move to Next Record or Move to Previous Record).**

   The Move to Record dialog box appears, and in most cases, you can just click OK because the defaults are right.

5. **Follow Steps 1 through 4 for the Next button.**

6. **Choose File➪Preview in Browser and select the browser you set up as your default preview browser.**

   You can now page through your records.

That's a pretty nifty trick. But did you notice that on the first page, the Previous Page button or link still appears, even though there is no previous page? Not to worry — a server behavior tells the navigation button when to show up.

1. **Click the Previous Page button in the Document window to select it.**

2. **Click the plus (+) sign in the Server Behaviors panel, and select Show Region from the menu (see Figure 14-16).**

3. **If you are working with the Previous Page button, select Show Region If Not First Record. If you are working with the Next Page button, select Show Region If Not Last Record.**

   The Show Region dialog box appears. Usually the selected recordset is correct, so just click OK.

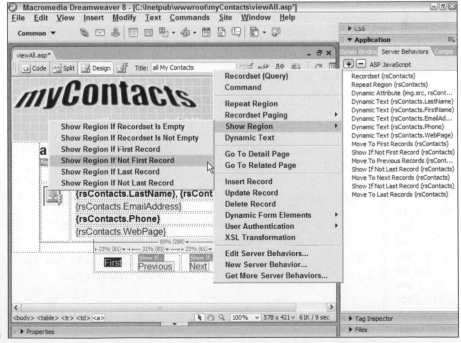

Figure 14-16:
Select
Show
Region and
make the
appropriate
selection
from the
submenu.

4. **Preview in your browser by clicking the Preview in Browser button on the Document toolbar.**

   Notice that now when you're on the first page of records, the Previous Page button does not show, and when you're on the last page, the Next Page button does not show.

Now that you know how to add navigation to your recordsets, you can get really fancy and add buttons to go to the first or last record. So if you have, say, 100 pages of records, you can jump from page 1 to page 100 without having to click Previous Page or Next Page through countless other pages of records. The server behaviors for those two are Move to Record⇨Move to First Record and Move to Record⇨Move to Last Record. It's pretty useful stuff to know.

Creating a Master-Detail Page Set

A very common way to display information on a Web site is to show a list of records, such as a list of contacts, with a link to each individual record for more detailed information.

A master page displays a list of records and a link for each record. When a user clicks a particular link, a detail page appears with more information about that record. There are two types of master pages. The first type is a list of records determined by you. Users can't alter the list of records on this page; they can only click to view more information about those records displayed. The second type is a dynamically created master page. A good example of this type of master page is a search results page that appears when a user performs a search for specific records.

A detail page is the page that displays when a user clicks a particular link from a master page. This page can either display more information about a record (such as an online catalog), or it can be set up for administrative purposes, such as updating or deleting a record.

Creating a Master-Detail page requires just a few clicks of the mouse. Using the functions described earlier in this chapter, create a page that lists all your contacts. This is your master page. Next, create the page you use as the detail page. Now you're ready to create the Master-Detail Page Set:

1. **Open the page you created to be the master page and choose Insert⇨Application Objects⇨Master Detail Page Set.**

   The Insert Master-Detail Page Set dialog box opens (see Figure 14-17). The top part of the dialog box is for defining the properties of the master page. The bottom part is for defining the detail page.

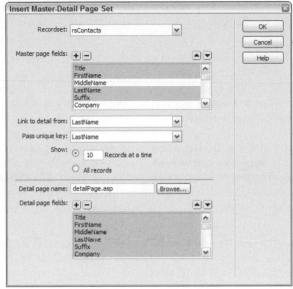

Figure 14-17:
The Insert
Master-
Detail
Page Set
dialog box.

2. **Select the recordset from the drop-down list that you use for your master page.**

3. **Next to Master Page Fields, use the plus (+) and minus (–) signs to add or remove fields that you want or don't want to display on the master page.**

4. **Select the field from which you want to provide a link to the detail page for each record.**

   For example, if you list a bunch of contacts, you can use the contact's name as the link to the detail.

5. **In the Pass Unique Key drop-down list, usually the default is correct; if it is not, select the unique identifier that you want to pass on to the detail page.**

6. **Select the number of records you want to show at one time on the master page.**

   Showing only a partial listing is okay because you can add navigation to view more records.

7. **Type the filename for the detail page in the Detail Page Name text box or click the Browse button to search for the file.**

8. **Just as with the Master Page section, use the plus and minus signs to add or remove fields that you want or don't want to show on the detail page.**

9. **Click OK.**

Dreamweaver automatically adds all the necessary recordset information and SQL code for you to begin using your Master-Detail Page Set. Everything from navigation to record status is in there.

After you create the master and detail pages, you may want to rearrange and format the fields in a way that is more aesthetic because Dreamweaver just plops the stuff onto the pages, which looks really generic. For example, you can change the column labels to read in a friendlier way. You can also format the font, color, and size, add padding to the table cells, and change the order of the columns.

Chapter 15

Using Forms to Manage Your Dynamic Web Site

*D*ynamic Web sites let you do a lot more than provide content and product listings to your Web site visitors. You can use Dreamweaver to create various types of forms that serve many useful purposes. Some examples include a login page so that users can register to use your Web site, a search page so that users can search your Web site for specific information, a shopping cart system for e-commerce, or a data entry form to safely allow non-technical data-entry personnel to easily edit the content of a Web site.

Establishing User Authentication

One of the good things about a dynamic Web site is that you can retain a lot more control over it, from who can view it and how much a user can view, to who can edit it and how much that person can edit. You can also assign different users different levels of access depending on criteria that you determine. For example, you may have an employee directory online that all employees can use to look up departmental information, titles, and phone extensions. However, if that directory also contains every employee's home phone number and home address, you wouldn't want the entire company to have access to everyone's personal information, right? The Dreamweaver User Authentication Server Behavior enables you to create different levels of access that restrict the kind of information a user can see; so you can make things such as personal information something only certain people may access.

Creating a login page

In the first exercise for this chapter, you create a user login form that checks information against a database. I use a sample database of employees that contains the following fields:

- ✔ Employee number
- ✔ Password
- ✔ Last name
- ✔ First name
- ✔ Department
- ✔ Title
- ✔ Access level

If you want to use a prebuilt database, I have provided a sample database called `employees.mdb` on my Web site at www.digitalfamily.com/dwd. I created it using Microsoft Access 2000.

After you have a database in place, create a page that contains a form with the following fields: a Username text box, a Password text box, and a Submit button. Refer to Chapter 12 for more details on how to create a form. Next, create a Data Source Name (DSN), database connection, and recordset that contains your employee number, last name, first name, password, department, title, and access level. Check out Chapters 13 and 14 if you need a quick review on this stuff.

Now that you have everything in place, you're ready to add user authentication to your form. These steps walk you through the setup for user authentication on a company's employee directory. I use the employee number as the username.

1. **Select the form and click the plus sign (+) in the Server Behaviors panel (see Figure 15-1).**

   Selecting a form in Dreamweaver can be a little bit tricky sometimes. A quick way to select the entire form is to click anywhere inside the form and then select the word *form* from the status bar at the bottom of the Dreamweaver window. This selects the entire form.

2. **From the menu, select User Authentication and select Log In User from the submenu that appears.**

   The Log In User dialog box appears (see Figure 15-2).

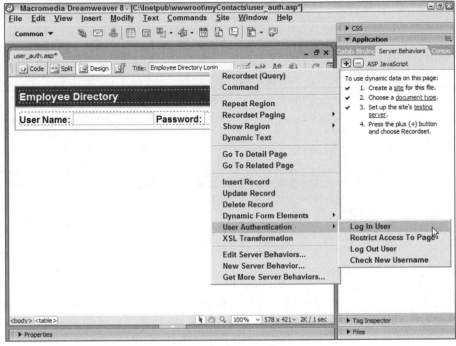

Figure 15-1:
The User
Authenti-
cation menu
in the
Server
Behaviors
panel.

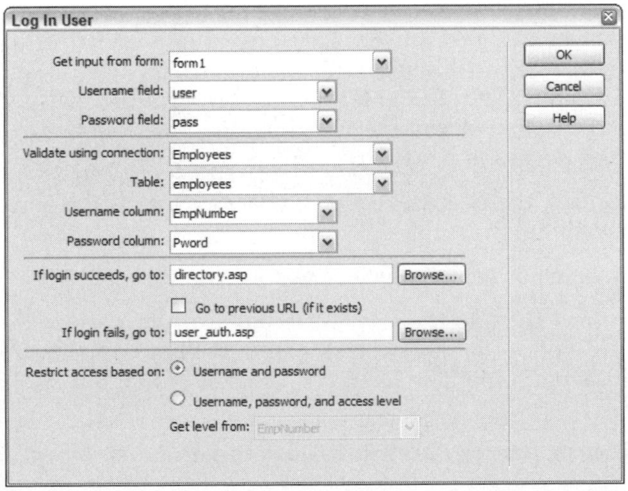

Figure 15-2:
The Log
In User
dialog box.

3. In the Get Input From Form field, enter the form name.

Naming forms is good practice, especially if you have a page with multiple forms. Naming your forms makes each one easier to identify within the code.

4. **Enter the name of the appropriate text box from your form in the Username Field and Password Field boxes.**

   In my example, the username field is called *user,* and the password field is called *pass*.

5. **From the Validate Using Connection and Table drop-down lists, make the appropriate selections.**

   Select the connection and table that corresponds to your user database. For example, if you're using the sample `employees.mdb` table, you'd use the Employees connection and the employees table.

6. **From the Username Column and Password Column drop-down lists, select the fields in your database that are used to verify the username and password provided by the user at login.**

   Because I use the employee number as the username, I selected that field as my Username Column, but if you have a specific username field in your database you select *that* one instead.

   At the time of this writing, Dreamweaver expects the username field to be a text field. If you decide to use a field such as an employee number, make sure that it is defined as a text field in the database or the page won't work.

7. **Enter the name of the page where users are redirected if the login succeeds.**

   If you want to use this as a generic page for logins, then check the Go to Previous URL box as well. That way, after a user tries to access a restricted page and is sent to this login page, the user is sent back to the restricted page after entering the correct username and password. Find out more about restricted pages in the following section, "Restricting access to pages."

   In my example, the page is `directory.asp`, which is the actual employee directory listing.

8. **Enter the name of the page where users are redirected if the login fails.**

   You can direct them to the same login page, or you can create a secondary login page that looks like the first one but contains an error message saying something like `That username and/or password is incorrect. Please try again`.

9. **Select Restrict Access Based on *Username and Password*.**

   If you want to further control access for users with a certain access level (say, Manager or Employee), you can define that in this area as well. The effect is that only the users in the database whose access level matches what you specify are taken to the login success page. The rest are redirected to the login failed page.

10. **Click OK.**

You can now preview this page in your browser and test the form by entering a username and password from your database.

Restricting access to pages

When you have a page you want to restrict (such as a user detail page) and a login page, you are ready to go. In the following steps, I assume that the name of the page that you want to restrict access to is `directory.asp`, that the name of your login page is `user_auth.asp`, and the Go To Previous URL option is defined for the login page (see the previous section, "Creating a login page," for more information).

To restrict access to a Web page, follow these steps:

1. **Open `employeeDirectory.asp` or whichever page you want to restrict.**

2. **In the Server Behaviors panel, click the plus sign and choose User Authentication⇨Restrict Access to Page from the menu.**

   The Restrict Access to Page dialog box opens (see Figure 15-3).

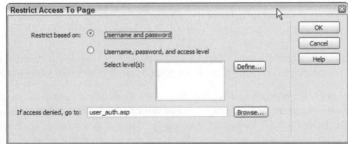

Figure 15-3:
The Restrict
Access
to Page
dialog box.

You can open the Server Behaviors panel by choosing Window⇨Server Behaviors from the main menu.

3. **Select Restrict Based on Username and Password.**

4. **Type the name of your login page in the If Access Denied, Go To box.**

   I used `user_auth.asp`. When users try to access this page directly, they're sent to `user_auth.asp` to log in before they can see this page.

5. **Click OK.**

6. **Press F12 to preview the page in your default browser.**

   Instead of the Employee Directory page, you see the user login page. Type a valid username and password to view the Employee Directory.

Securing Sensitive Information on Your Web Site

You can take security measures that help make your sensitive information more secure on the Web (some steps are for more advanced users):

- ✓ **Carefully choose the passwords you use.** Especially choose carefully for your FTP, database, and the admin login area of your Web site. Too often people use common words, names, and number combinations as passwords that are easy for hackers to figure out. An effective password consists of mixed letters and numbers — the more random the better — and is also a mix of upper- and lowercase letters whenever possible.

- ✓ **Protect your development machine.** Many Web site break-ins are inside jobs, where someone from within the company itself obtains the sensitive information because he or she has access to the Web site files. If your development machine is on a network and you must grant access to it, grant only restricted access.

- ✓ **On your Web server, turn Directory Browsing *off*.** Do this so folders without an index page don't display everything that's in them. If you're not the administrator for your Web server or don't know how to do this, ask a technical support representative at your hosting company to either walk you through it or do it for you. It's a fairly simple step.

- ✓ **Pages that require authentication, such as `directory.asp` from the previous example, should have code on that page that kicks out users who didn't log in to get to that page.** This way if someone happens to access the file without using the login page, they are sent elsewhere (see "Restricting access to pages," earlier in the chapter). One of the easiest ways to do this is with a cookie — of the ASP variety, not chocolate chip! In fact, this is how Dreamweaver's Server Behaviors does it behind the scenes. You can find out more about cookies and ASP in *Beginning Active Server Pages 3.0* by David Buser, et al. (published by Wrox Press).

- ✓ **Don't use an Access database for a serious Web site.** Not only is it slow, but stealing the info is simple because it's typically a single file. Even if a malicious person doesn't know SQL, he or she may be able to find the

Access file and read it off your Web server. If you are using an Access database, make sure it is stored in a folder outside the root folder of your Web site.

✔ **Keep your database on a dedicated machine, away from direct Internet access.** You can buff up database security by allowing only your Web server to access that machine through a local network infrastructure.

✔ **Use SSL technology to encrypt sensitive information sent back and forth from the server.** *Secure Sockets Layer* (SSL) is a form of encryption, developed originally by Netscape, used by Web servers and Web browsers to exchange sensitive information. You can find more about encryption and SSL at `http://computer.howstuffworks.com/encryption.htm`.

✔ **Don't copy and paste complex snippets of code that you found on the Web unless you absolutely trust the source and checked out all the stops.** Some hackers look for sites running this type of widely used code, and those who know its specific vulnerabilities can easily gain access to your machine.

Please keep in mind that the Dreamweaver Login Authentication can be a pretty basic method of restricting access to a page if you follow only the basic steps outlined in this book. An amateur hacker can quite possibly find your database, figure out passwords, or bypass the login page altogether to get to the information he or she wants. If you're building a site that contains sensitive information and you are not very familiar with Web site security, consider hiring a consultant to advise you. At the very least, read up on the subject so you can get a better understanding of the security risks you may encounter. *Web Security, Privacy and Commerce* by Simson Garfinkel (published by O'Reilly & Associates) provides a very thorough look into the subject.

Searching for Database Records

With Dreamweaver, you can create a form to search for records on your database using specific criteria. This is pretty useful if you have a large database. You don't want to make your users read through pages and pages of listings, whether they are employee records, or products, or anything else. Providing a search form allows your users to quickly find the information they want.

In this section, you discover a simple way to implement a database search on your dynamic Web site.

Setting up the search page

The search page is the simplest part to set up. All you need is a form with an action that goes to the results page, a form text field, and a Submit button:

1. **Create a new page that contains a form with the fields you want your users to search.**

   Check out Chapter 12 to go over forms in more detail.

   I use an employee directory database, so my text field is *Lname*, which allows my users to search by employee last names.

2. **In the Action field in the Properties inspector, enter the name of the results page.**

   See the next section to find out how to create this page.

   My result page is called *search_results.asp*.

3. **Save this page.**

Setting up the results page

The results page is a little bit more complex than the search page. The search actually takes place on this page, behind the scenes on the server, and what you see is only the result of that search. The text field that you determine in the search page is referred to as the *form variable* in the results page. The information you enter in this form is passed on to the results page in order for the search to take place.

1. **Create a new page that contains a table with a column for each field you want to show in the results.**

2. **Create a connection and a recordset for this page using the database or table from which you want to bring in the results.**

   See Chapters 13 and 14 if you need more detailed information on how to do this.

3. **In the Recordset dialog box (see Figure 15-4), select the appropriate connection and table.**

4. **Next to Filter drop-down list, select the column that corresponds with the field with which you want your users to search.**

5. **In the drop-down list directly below the Filter drop-down list, select Form Variable, and then enter the name of the text field element from your search form in the text box next to it.**

6. **In the Sort field, select the field by which you want to sort your results.**

7. **Click OK.**

Figure 15-4:
The
Recordset
dialog box
prepared for
search
results.

8. **Drag each field from your recordset in the Bindings panel to the appropriate column on the table in your results page. (See Figure 15-5.)**

   Chapter 13 shows you how to drag and drop fields.

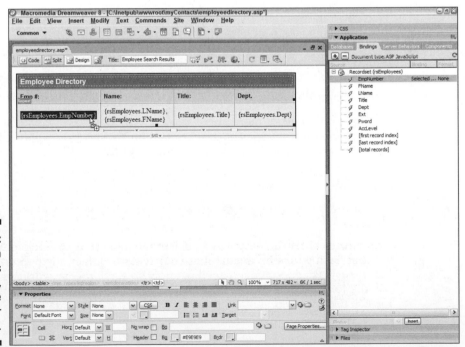

Figure 15-5:
The Search
Results
page,
dragging the
EmpNumber
field.

9. **Transfer your pages to the server and open your search page in a browser. Try searching for one of the entries in your database. The search finds the entry and lists it in your search results page, showing every field you requested on the results page.**

   I searched for *Hodges*, and Figure 15-6 shows my search results.

   If you want to return more than one matching row, you need to define a region and use the Repeat Region server behavior. You can find out more about this in Chapter 14.

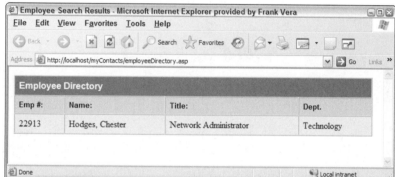

Figure 15-6:
The Search
Results
page,
working
properly.

That's it. Painless, right? This is a database search in its simplest form. The more advanced your understanding of Dreamweaver and the SQL language gets, the more complex you can make your search forms. Users with a basic understanding of SQL can enhance this page to search using multiple criteria, filter out search results, sort by various fields, and even display only certain results depending on the access level of the person performing the search.

If you want to find out more about working with databases and SQL, I recommend *Database Development For Dummies* and *SQL For Dummies,* both by Allen G. Taylor (published by Wiley Publishing, Inc.).

Editing a Database from a Browser

Using forms is also an easy way to perform data-entry tasks on a database without having to open the database application. In fact, the person performing those tasks doesn't even need to know how a database works in order to use the form. All the work is done right in the browser window. Through the form, a user can add, update, or delete a record from the database.

Say a manager wants to add a new employee and update some information in an employee directory for various employees who just received promotions. Using Dreamweaver, you can create a user-friendly interface where this manager can go to his browser, log in, and make those changes to the database. He can save his changes right there in his browser and view the updated information instantly, all without ever having to open a database application (such as Access).

You can secure content management pages (such as those discussed in this section) from the public by using the authentication features of Dreamweaver covered at the beginning of this chapter.

Adding a record to your database

A record in a database (a row) consists of a complete set of all the fields in the database.

In this section, you use a form to add a record to a database. Before starting, you must create a new dynamic page and connect it to the database you're editing. If you need to refresh your memory on how to do this, see Chapter 13.

After you create your page, you're ready to use the Dreamweaver Record Insertion Form Wizard Application Object. In one easy step, this Application Object Wizard creates a script that allows you to add a record to a database. It also creates the form with which you make the addition.

An *application object* lets you create a more complex function in one easy step.

Follow these steps to add a record using a form:

1. **Open your new page and place the cursor where you want the form to start.**

2. **Choose Insert⇨Application Objects⇨Insert Record⇨Record Insertion Form Wizard.**

   The Record Insertion Form dialog box opens (see Figure 15-7).

3. **Select the appropriate database connection, select the appropriate table from that database, and then enter the name of the page the user is redirected to after the new addition is made.**

4. **In the Form Fields section of the dialog box, verify that all the fields display.**

   In the Label column, you can change the actual name of the column by clicking a field from the list and editing the Label text. You can also determine what kind of form field (text, radio button, select menu) and what type of formatting (numeric, text, and so on) is used for each field. If any field has a default value, you can define that in this dialog box as well.

If your database table has an auto-number field (a field that the database automatically numbers sequentially for each record), you cannot submit data for that field; it needs to be removed from the Form Fields area.

5. Click OK.

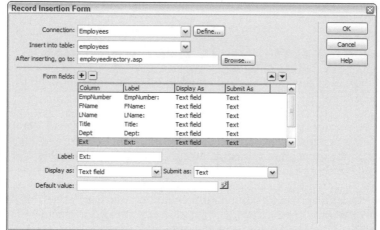

Figure 15-7:
The Record
Insertion
Form
dialog box.

You can now test your page (see Figure 15-8). Simply upload the page to your server, open it in your browser, and enter all the information for a new record. Click the Insert Record button. Your new record shows up in the database.

Upload the Connections folder when you upload your site files to the application server; otherwise, you get an ASP Include File Not Found error message.

When you create the database connection (refer to Chapter 13), a Connections folder is added to your site on the local drive. The ASP files in the Connections folder store necessary information that makes your page work correctly with the database. This type of file is typically called an *include file* because its content is referenced by the code in another page. Dreamweaver automatically *includes* the content of this file on any page you create that uses this database connection.

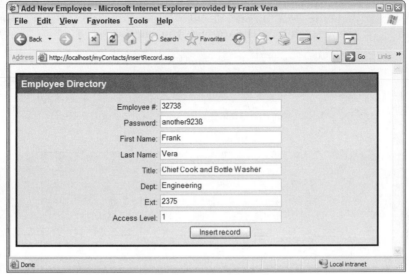

Figure 15-8:
The Record
Insertion
Form in
action.

Updating a record via a browser

To edit or *update* a record from a database, you first need to create a search form to search for the record you want to update, or a master page list where you can pick out the record. After you find the record, the Update Record form appears, which is where you perform the actual update.

Follow these steps to update an existing record:

1. **On a new page, create a simple search form with a text field element and a Submit button.**

   See the "Searching for Database Records" section, earlier in this chapter, if you need a refresher on creating search forms.

2. **Select the text field on your page, and in the Properties inspector, replace *textfield* with a more descriptive name. For example, *mysearch*.**

   This name helps differentiate one text field from another on a page that contains multiple fields.

3. **Create a recordset, and filter by the field that you use as your search criteria.**

   I used Employee Number (EmpNo) as my search criteria.

4. **From the drop-down list directly below the Filter list, select Form Variable. Next to Form Variable, type the name of the text field from your search form. In my case, I typed *mysearch*.**

5. **Click OK.**

6. **Choose Insert⇨Application Objects⇨Update Record⇨Record Update Form Wizard.**

   The Update Record dialog box opens (see Figure 15-9).

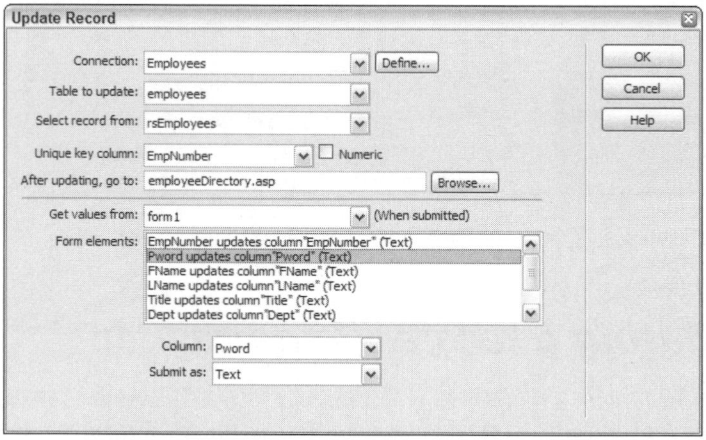

Figure 15-9:
The Update
Record
dialog box.

7. **Select the appropriate connection and table.**

8. **In the After Updating, Go To text box, enter the name of the page you want to show after the update is made.**

   I use `employeeDirectory.asp`, which is my default employee directory page.

9. **In the Form Elements box, make sure that the field labels are correct, or rename them to what you want to display on the update form. You can rename them later on your page by selecting and replacing the text for each field directly on your page.**

10. **Click OK.**

    A new form appears on your page. You can format the look of the form (font, color, and so on) to make it match the rest of your site.

11. **Select the Server Behaviors panel and click the plus sign (+). From the menu, choose Show Region⇨Show Region If Recordset Is Not Empty.**

    This last step ensures that you don't get an error if no recordset matches the criteria you enter into the search field.

Your Update form is now complete (see Figure 15-10).

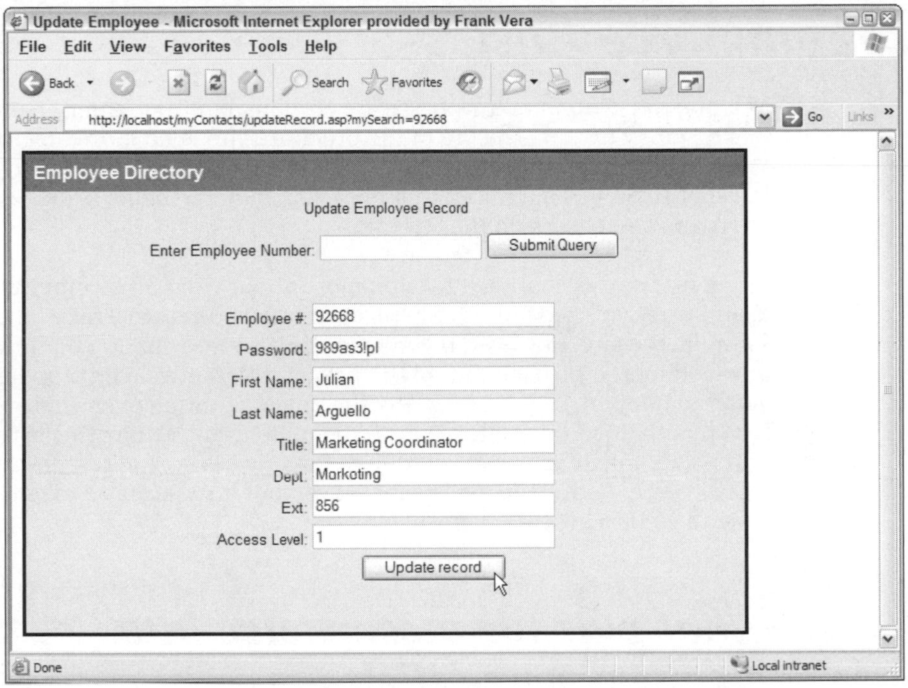

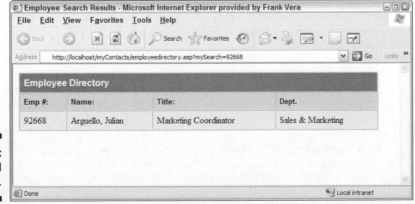

Figure 15-10:
The newly created Update form.

You can test the new page by previewing it in your browser. Enter a value that you know exists in that field in your database and click the Submit button. The Record Update form is now populated with the information for that record. You can now make any changes to that record and click the Update Record button to save the changes to the database. The next time you view that record online, the changes appear (see Figure 15-11).

Figure 15-11:
The updated record.

E-Commerce Basics

Most people who want a Web site are certain about one thing: They want to make money from it. The era of the brochure site is no more, my friends. People hawk everything from fine china to soil from the Holy Land on the Internet (I kid you not about that one). E-commerce helps bring together shoppers and sellers on the Internet.

In the rest of this chapter, I tell you more about what an e-commerce Web site is and what you need to have in place in order to create a fully functional e-commerce site. However, if you're looking for information on how to create an e-commerce site right out of the box with Dreamweaver, stop here. It's not going to happen. I don't know why the powers that be over at Macromedia haven't included this feature yet. To be quite frank, I think this is really one of the only major flaws I can find with Dreamweaver. You *can* create an e-commerce Web site using Dreamweaver, but it requires an extension, which I go into in just a moment.

What puts the e-commerce into an e-commerce Web site?

An e-commerce Web site, in a nutshell, is a Web site that accepts real-time payments for goods and services. For example, if you're looking for a weight loss supplement you can go to www.MetabolicNutrition.com, browse offerings in its weight loss product line, and have one shipped to you overnight.

Not all e-commerce Web sites are the same — many companies have built customized tools to aid users in the shopping process. For example, Metabolic Nutrition also allows you to store your shipping information so that you don't have to enter it every time you order. It also has a virtual personal assistant that recommends products based on your health, age, diet, and lifestyle.

The cost of an e-commerce Web site is significantly more than the cost of building a regular Web site because you have to figure in several third-party costs. Here's a quick run-down of the minimal (traditional) e-commerce requirements:

- **A shopping cart:** A shopping cart is a series of scripts and applications that displays items from your database, allows users to pick and choose which ones they want, and then collects payment and shipping information. Some Web-hosting accounts come with shopping carts included. A popular one is Miva Merchant (www.miva.com). Various Dreamweaver shopping cart extensions are also worth looking into. For example, PDG

Software (www.pdgsoft.com) offers a Dreamweaver extension that provides full integration with PDG's shopping cart with a price tag of about $400 for a lifetime license.

✔ **A merchant account:** This is literally an account with a bank or a financial institution that allows you to accept credit cards from your clients. Many merchant account providers also offer payment gateways and virtual terminals as a suite, which can save you money and time. Costs and transactions fees vary, as service providers set their own prices. Online Data Corp (www.onlinedatacorp.com) is a good one.

✔ **A payment gateway and virtual terminal:** A payment gateway is what ties your shopping cart to your merchant account. A virtual terminal is like an electronic bookkeeper and cash register in one — you can view your Web site transactions, issue refunds, and manage orders. The two most popular packages are the VeriSign PayFlow Pro and PayFlow Link (www.verisign.com).

✔ **A secure site certificate:** This encrypts information between your Web site and the client's computer to protect the information from being stolen as you make your purchase online. This is commonly referred to as Secure Sockets Layer (SSL) technology. Verisign and Thawte's 128-bit certificates are popular picks. If you're on a shared Web-hosting account, you may be able to share the server's certificate to save money; however, this is often regarded as unprofessional, because the security certificate doesn't display your company name on it — shoppers who check it see your Web-hosting company's name instead.

The definition of what a *traditional* e-commerce Web site is continues to change as new technologies and application service providers emerge. Services such as Yahoo! Stores allow you to create a site without purchasing any of the previously mentioned items. PayPal.com offers all-inclusive e-commerce services with free shopping cart tools.

Premade shopping carts and e-commerce systems save you time and money up front, and buying one is the fastest way to get a business online. The downside of using a premade shopping cart is that you often can't make it look like an integral part of your Web site, meaning that you usually have limited control over the graphical elements on shopping-cart–driven pages. Also, most shopping carts use their own databases and give you limited access to the code (because a lot of it may be compiled CGI, which Dreamweaver can't read), so you may run into brick walls when trying to build new features that you didn't buy out of the box.

Considering the investment and risk, many companies prefer to hire a professional programming team to create a system from scratch that looks and functions exactly how they want it to. Amazon.com, for example, has spent millions on its system to make it the incredibly smart and easy-to-use system it is today. But you don't have to break the bank — many very successful custom-built e-commerce Web sites are created for less than the cost of a used '94 Toyota Camry.

Extending Dreamweaver one feature at a time

At last count, a few minutes ago, Dreamweaver has 109 e-commerce-related extensions on the Macromedia Web site, from stand-alone shopping carts to a PayPal extension that allows shoppers to pay you via PayPal directly from your Web site.

However, e-commerce is just the proverbial ol' tip of the iceberg when extending Dreamweaver. At the Macromedia Exchange Web site, you can download an extension for just about any functionality your Web site can have.

You can add extensions to Dreamweaver two ways. The first is by going directly to the Web site at `www.macromedia.com/cfusion/exchange/index.cfm?view=sn120`.

The other way to access Macromedia Exchange is through Dreamweaver itself. You must be connected to the Internet in order for this to work. This can be done from various points within the application:

- **From the Insert menu:** Choose Insert⇨Get More Objects
- **From the Commands menu:** Choose Commands⇨Get More Commands
- **From the Help menu:** Choose Help⇨Dreamweaver Exchange
- **From the Server Behaviors panel:** Click the plus sign (+) and then select Get More Server Behaviors
- **From the Bindings panel:** Click the plus sign (+) and then select Get More Data Sources
- **From the Behaviors panel:** Click the plus sign (+) and then select Get More Behaviors
- **From the Insert Flash Button dialog box:** Click the Get More Styles button
- **From the New Document window:** Click the Get More Content button

When you are on Macromedia Exchange, if this is your first time there, you must register before downloading any extensions. Also, you need to make sure that your *Extension Manager* (which comes with Dreamweaver) is installed and running.

If you register and have the Extension Manager on your system, you can search for extensions and download them to your system. You can also choose to download the extensions (.mxp files) onto your computer and install them using the manager, or you can choose to install them on the spot, which downloads and installs the extension from the Web without saving the installation file on your hard drive.

You can run the Extension Manager for installing an extension in various ways. In Dreamweaver, you can choose Commands➪Manage Extensions. You must have a document open. In Windows, you can go to Start➪Programs➪ Macromedia➪Macromedia Extension Manager. You can also launch it by double-clicking an .mxp file in Explorer. On a Mac, you can run the Extension Manager by going to Help➪Manage Extensions.

When you open Extension Manager, you see all the extensions you installed on your system. To view the description for any of these extensions, simply click it once, and any pertinent information displays in the lower pane of the Extension Manager window.

Ready to add some extensions? Choose File➪Install Extension and follow the simple prompts to have your new extension up and running in no time. Uninstalling is just as simple: Choose File➪Remove Extension, and voilà!

Part VI
The Part of Tens

The 5th Wave   By Rich Tennant

WHERE'S THE DANG DOOR?!

In this part . . .

The Part of Tens features ten great Web sites designed in Dreamweaver to show you what's possible with this Web design program. You also find ten timesaving techniques to help you get the most out of Dreamweaver and ten great Web design ideas that you can use right away, including tips about how to score higher in search engines and how to add Google search features to your Web site for free.

Chapter 16

Ten Great Sites Designed with Dreamweaver

*D*reamweaver has become the clear choice of professional Web designers and is the program behind many of the best-designed sites on the Web.

Many of the sites featured in this chapter take advantage of the latest Web technologies, integrating Dynamic HTML, Flash, and more to create vivid animations and powerful interactivity.

The sites featured in this chapter provide an excellent overview of what you can do with Dreamweaver — and they're all great examples of what's possible on the Web today. Review the descriptions of these sites to discover what tools the designers used and how they made these great Web sites. Then spend some time online, visiting each site to appreciate the full impact of their design, navigation, and other features.

The Growing Digital Family

`www.digitalfamily.com`

With the help of my friends at `www.grupow.com`, I created the Digital Family Web site, shown in Figure 16-1, for my book, *Creating Family Web Sites For Dummies* (published by Wiley Publishing, Inc.). This site is designed for anyone who wants to create a Web site for a wedding, new baby, reunion, or any of the seemingly unlimited number of personal uses that have become popular on the Internet.

DigitalFamily.com is an example of how many authors, like myself, are creating Web sites to complement their books and provide updated information between revisions. It should be no surprise that I used Dreamweaver to create my newest Web site, relying heavily on the table layout features to create the page designs and the template features to make adding pages fast and easy, as well as to maintain a consistent design theme throughout the site.

You discover how to design templates in Chapter 4 and how to use the Layout features to create tables in Chapter 6.

Figure 16-1:
The Digital Family Web site was designed with Dream-weaver templates.

The Hum of World Journalism

www.worldhum.com

The World Hum Web site is an online travel magazine that focuses on destination journalism, offering tips on where to go, where to stay, and what to do. World Hum is run by editors Jim Benning and Michael Yessis. In 2005, World Hum began to work with Web design company Hop Studios to bring the site up to date, adding many of the bells and whistles of modern Web design: an RSS feed, a blog, a mailing list, search, CSS-powered design, comments, and contextual ads.

Behind a powerful content management system sits a set of templates and style sheets developed using Dreamweaver. In particular, the designers relied on Dreamweaver's style sheet capabilities to create a design that looks and feels the same from browser to browser, computer to computer.

The result is a Web site that is easily updated by its editors, who rely on the stability of the underlying code so that they can spend time thinking about where to take their readers next. (Chapter 4 covers Dreamweaver's template features.)

Listen to the Tracks at UnSound

www.unsoundtracks.com

Musician and composer Stefan Girardet's work has been featured in film and on television. When he decided to put up a Web site showcasing his work, Stefan turned to Web design company Hop Studios with a challenge: create a Web site design as organic and abstract as his music.

If the design wasn't a challenge, Stefan's ideas about handling the playback of his music were! The UnSound Tracks Web site, shown in Figure 16-2, includes a sample library (in MP3 format) of Stefan's musical compositions.

Stefan wanted visitors to the Web site to be able to sample his work without having to load hundreds of Web pages or get lost in a confusing navigational structure.

Hop Studios addressed the challenge by developing a way to integrate music directly into the page using layers and JavaScript programming. The site's complex code was made easier by using Dreamweaver's built-in tools for handling layers and behaviors that together give the user a seamless listening experience. (Find out how you can do similar tricks in Chapter 9.)

Figure 16-2:
UnSound
Tracks
relies on
Dream-
weaver's
layers and
behaviors
for smooth
functionality.

Friends of Washoe

```
www.friendsofwashoe.org
www.cwu.edu/~cwuchci
```

The Chimpanzee and Human Communication Institute runs a sanctuary for some very special chimpanzees in central Washington. Washoe and her family use American Sign Language to communicate with each other and with humans. Washoe is the first non-human animal to use sign language with humans.

The institute runs two Web sites, one at www.friendsofwashoe.org (shown in Figure 16-3) for the public and for students interested in learning about the chimps. The second, which focuses on its academic research and opportunities, is at www.cwu.edu/~cwuchci. Keeping the two sites updated is a challenge met with equanimity by Institute staff using Dreamweaver, along with a few graphics programs.

Dreamweaver's Check In/Check Out feature helps keep staff members from overwriting each other's work. Their Web design team appreciated Dreamweaver's site-management features when redesigning these sites in 2004, and they all use Library items to keep the navigation bars updated and in sync. (You find instructions for using Dreamweaver's site-management features, such as Check In/Check Out and Library items in Chapter 4.)

Figure 16-3:
The Friends
of Washoe
Web site
staff use
Dream-
weaver's
site-
management
features for
more
efficient
main-
tenance.

Alliance Environmental Group, Inc.

www.alliance-enviro.com

Alliance Environmental Group is an environmental contractor that specializes in commercial and residential air duct cleaning and demolition. Alliance also specializes in the safe removal of asbestos, lead paint, and other hazardous materials. Alliance is known for taking on big projects. When a home that was being fumigated exploded after a gas line was left open, Alliance staff responded quickly, repairing and cleaning up damage to 115 homes.

When Joe Mclean, president of Alliance Environmental Group, commissioned a redesign from Web design company Hop Studios, he wanted to get the twin messages of reliability and safety across to his customers by showcasing actual projects and customer testimonials.

Together with Alliance staff, Hop Studios reworked the site's user interface (shown in Figure 16-4) and organizational structure, looking for ways to implement consistent elements and timesaving features. Dreamweaver's Library items and templates were especially helpful, and a powerful and carefully crafted style sheet keeps design and formatting consistent.

Figure 16-4:
Alliance Environmental Group's Web designers use Dreamweaver to build new sections, while Alliance staff updates existing pages using Macromedia Contribute.

The Alliance staff updates the Web site using Macromedia Contribute, which works in concert with Dreamweaver to ensure smooth updates, revision saves, and consistent pages. (You find out how to create templates that work in Dreamweaver and Contribute in Chapter 4, and how to design style sheets in Chapter 8.)

Film Radar

```
www.filmradar.com/
```

Living in Hollywood is wonderful for a film fanatic, but the choice of movies in cinema's capital city can be overwhelming. Film Radar, shown in Figure 16-5, offers a guide to the best of the more interesting, obscure, specialty, and independent films screening in Los Angeles. Editor Karie Bible maintains the complex calendars and reviews as a one-woman-band using Dreamweaver.

She needed a site that was — above all — reliable, with code optimized to handle nearly constant updating. Web design company Hop Studios turned to Dreamweaver to build code that could meet those demands after it was integrated into a complex underlying publishing system.

Figure 16-5:
Film Radar's
constant
updates
mean that
the site's
code must
be flawless.

For example, the complex HTML tables that make up the navigation would have been almost impossible to create by hand — Dreamweaver made the layout a snap. For the dynamic pages of the calendar, mockups were created in Dreamweaver, and then given to the programmer to have appropriate programming code inserted. (Chapter 6 covers creating tables in Dreamweaver.)

Cartooning in Marin

`www.klemieux.com/`

Kathryn LeMieux is an award-winning cartoonist and fine art painter. Over the years her work for the *Point Reyes Light* newspaper in Western Marin County has won numerous California Newspaper Publisher Awards. Besides Feral West, she is one of the SIX CHIX, and contributes to that nationally syndicated comic strip. If you study the work on her Web site, you'll also discover that she is very fond of cows.

When Kathryn wanted to create a Web site for her comics and artwork, she turned to Sheila Castelli at DigitalCottage.com. Sheila used Photoshop CS and Dreamweaver to convert Kathryn's creative page designs into a user-friendly Web site shown in Figure 16-6. Because she's an artist and cartoonist, this site is filled with big, colorful images.

Figure 16-6:
Kathryn
LeMieux's
Web site
features
many
colorful,
carefully
optimized
images.

All the graphics at KLemieux.com were carefully converted for the Web and optimized to ensure they download quickly for Web site visitors. (You find tips about image formats, optimization, and more in Chapter 5.)

A Quiet Retreat

www.blackheroninn.com

The Black Heron Inn, shown in Figure 16-7, was created by professional Web designer Sheila Castelli (www.DigitalCottage.com). Sheila's goal was to create a clean, elegant design that prominently featured the views and architecture of this lovely bed and breakfast in Northern California. To capture the large windows that look out at the rolling hills of Point Reyes, Sheila optimized the photos on this site and set them off with a simple design, using tables to keep everything in place.

You can find more about image formats, optimization, and aligning text and images in Chapter 5. For tips and tricks that help you use tables to create page layouts like these, see Chapter 6.

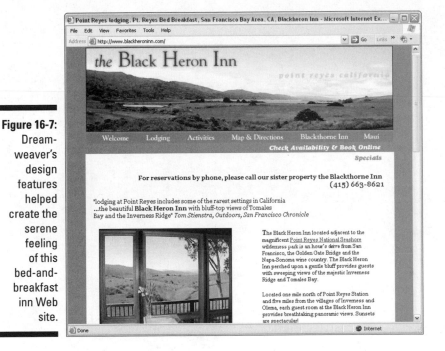

Figure 16-7:
Dream-
weaver's
design
features
helped
create the
serene
feeling
of this
bed-and-
breakfast
inn Web
site.

Dreamweaver, the Professional's Choice

`www.hopstudios.com/`

Dreamweaver is the clear choice of most professional Web designers these days, including those at Hop Studios, a Web design company in Vancouver owned and managed by one of the contributors to this book, Susannah Gardner.

Although Dreamweaver is great for the kinds of large, complex sites Susannah often creates for clients, you can also use it for sites with a bent for simplicity, such as her own company site shown in Figure 16-8.

Susannah chose Dreamweaver because she wanted the site to be quick loading, easy to navigate, and fun to use. Using Dreamweaver as the primary production tool has allowed the designers at Hop Studios to focus their energy on making a site that shows off their skills and talents, without taking too much time away from their clients. (You find design tips in Chapter 17 and timesaving tips for getting the most out of Dreamweaver in Chapter 18.)

Yours Truly

www.JCWarner.com/

I would love to take credit for the design of my own Web site (see Figure 16-9), but the truth is that my talented friend, Ivonne Berkowitz, came up with the design. I did build the site myself based on her design, and of course, I use Dreamweaver's great features to update and maintain it regularly. I've more than mastered the development of a Web site, but when it came time to make sure my site looked good, I turned to an expert, someone who was doing nothing but design work fulltime.

As the Web has gotten more complex, and the design standards higher, most good Web sites require a team of experts. Don't expect to be able to do everything yourself — seek out professional designers, programmers, writers, and editors when you need them to produce the best site possible. (And don't overlook your personal contacts. My mother, Malinda McCain, edits my site. She's a professional, too, with her own copy editing business, which you can find more about at www.sharewords.com/copyedit.)

I use Dreamweaver to make all the additions, updates, and changes to my site. (Just for the record, I really do think Dreamweaver is the best Web design program on the market, and I can't imagine using anything else on my own site.)

Figure 16-9:
My own
Web site
was, of
course, built
with Dream-
weaver.

Chapter 17

Ten Web Site Ideas You Can Use

Allgood Web sites grow and evolve. If you start with a strong design and pay close attention to some basic rules about interface, navigation, and style, you have a better foundation to build on. The following design ideas can help you create a compelling Web site that grows gracefully.

Design for Your Audience

No matter how technically sophisticated a Web site is or how great the writing, most people notice the design first. Make sure that you leave plenty of time and budget to develop an appropriate and attractive design for your Web site. The right design is one that best suits your audience — that may or may not mean lots of fancy graphics and animations.

Think about who you want to attract to your Web site before you develop the design. A gaming Web site geared toward teenagers should look very different from a Web site with gardening tips or an online banking site for adults. Review other sites designed for your target market. Consider your audience's time constraints and attention span, and, most important, consider your audience's goals. If you design your site to provide information to busy businesspeople, you want fast-loading pages with few graphics and little or no animation. If you design your site for entertainment, your audience may be willing to wait a little longer for animation and other interactive features.

Add Search Features with Google

If you're looking for an easy way to add a search engine to your Web site, consider using Google's AdSense service. This feature is tied into Google's advertising model and can even help you bring in more revenue if you have enough traffic on your site.

Google's search tools enable you to add a Web search section to your site, with a site search option that lets visitors choose to search the pages of your site. The program is free to use, but does require an application and approval. Google claim it's for businesses of all sizes, so even if you're relatively small, you may benefit from this service.

Visit `www.google.com/services/websearch.html` to find out more about paid search services, or visit `www.google.com/searchcode.html` for an easier option that doesn't give financial credit.

Use PDFs When They're Warranted

Adobe's Portable Document Format (PDF) has become increasingly popular on the Internet, and with good reason. Now that Acrobat Reader is widely distributed and even built into more recent browser versions, you can assume that most of your audience can read files in PDF.

Unfortunately, like many popular technologies, PDF has been overused and, dare I say, become a trick for people who don't want to take the time to design their pages in HTML. PDF is best used for files that you want to make easy to download in their entirety to be saved on someone's hard drive, as well as documents that you want to print exactly as they were designed.

However, PDF is not as fast as HTML, not as easy to browse and navigate, and the text is not searched by most search engines, making it harder for people to find your words. By all means, use PDF when it's warranted — it's a great option — but don't use it when HTML pages would be more accessible. Indeed, the best designers often provide both options to visitors, offering a text file in PDF that is easy to download or print and another version of the same content in HTML that is easy to browse or read online.

Let Visitors Enlarge Your Type

Although it is possible with CSS styles to disable a Web browser's capability to override your font size choices, please don't. Many of your visitors have adjusted their own systems to enlarge the text on Web sites because they can't read the small type that young Web designers prefer. Respect your elders (and anyone else who prefers larger type), and don't restrict their ability to resize the words on your pages — especially if you actually want them to read it.

If you really want to make it easy on your visitor's eyes, format your text with tags and options that use relative sizes, such as the Header tags (H1, H2, and so on) and use percents or the small, medium, and large font sizes instead of absolute pixels.

Accessible Designs

As you design your site, keep in mind that viewers come to your pages with a variety of computers, operating systems, and monitors. Ensure that your site is accessible to all your potential viewers by testing your pages on a variety of systems. If you want to attract a large audience to your site, you need to ensure that it looks good on a broad range of systems. A design that looks great in Firefox or Safari may be unreadable in Internet Explorer 3.0. And many people still use old browsers because they haven't bothered — or don't know how — to download new versions.

Accessible design on the Web also includes pages that can be read (actually, converted to synthesized speech) by special browsers used by the blind. Using the Alt attribute in your image tags is a simple way to ensure that all visitors can get the information they need. The Alt attribute specifies a text alternative that displays if the image doesn't appear. It's inserted into an image tag like this:

```
<IMG SRC="CAT.GIF" ALT="A picture of a black and white cat.">
```

Dreamweaver has many features designed to ensure you design your site with accessibility in mind. For example, in Preferences you can specify that you want accessibility alerts, which prompt you for <ALT> tags and other HTML design options that ensure your site displays well for all visitors.

Create a Consistent Design

Most Web sites work best and are easiest to navigate when they follow a consistent design. Case in point: Most readers take for granted that books don't change their design from page to page, and that newspapers don't change headline fonts and logos from day to day. Consistency is one of the primary tools used in books and newspapers to make it easy for readers to distinguish different elements and follow a story or theme.

As you lay out your Web page, keep related items close to one another and be consistent about how you design similar content elements. You want your viewers to instantly understand which pieces of information are related to each other. Distinguish different kinds of information by their

- Design
- Location
- Prominence

This type of organization makes following information visually much easier.

Make sure that similar elements follow the same design parameters, such as type style, banner size, and page background color. Give elements of similar importance the same weight on a page. If you use too many different elements on a page or on the same Web site, you can confuse your viewers.

To ensure a consistent style, define a set of colors, shapes, or other elements that you use throughout the site. Choose two or three fonts for your Web site and use those consistently as well. Using too many fonts makes your pages less appealing and harder to read.

Strive for consistency in your designs — except when you're trying to be unpredictable. A little surprise here and there can keep your Web site alive.

Follow the Three Clicks Rule

The Three Clicks Rule states that no important piece of information should ever be more than three clicks away from anywhere else on your Web site. The most important information should be even closer at hand. Some information, such as contact information, should never be more than one click away. You can make finding information easy for viewers by creating a site map (as I explain in the next section) and a *navigation bar* — a set of links to all the main sections on your site.

Map It Out

As your site gets larger, providing easy access to all the information on your Web site may get harder and harder. A great solution is to provide a *site map*, which is an outline or a diagram that illustrates the hierarchy and content of your site and includes links to the most important pages in the site.

The site map can get complicated and busy if you have a lot of pages and links, so it's usually best to create a site map in outline form. Don't put lots of graphics in your site map — it should be functional above all else. A site map doesn't have to look pretty; it has to allow your visitors to quickly get to any page on the site.

Be Prepared for Fast Updates

The Web provides a powerful vehicle for businesses and nonprofit organizations to present their side of any story and get the word out quickly when tragic events, bad press, and other crises arise.

But don't wait for an emergency to find out if you're prepared to add new information to your Web site quickly, and don't fool yourself into thinking that just because you don't manage a daily Internet newspaper you don't have to worry about speedy updates.

With a little planning and key systems set up in advance, you can be prepared for events that require timely information — whether an international crisis stops air travel, a flood closes your nonprofit, or an embarrassing event makes your CEO cringe and demand that the real story be told as soon as possible.

Most organizations develop Web sites that are updated on a weekly, monthly, or even annual basis. More sophisticated sites may link to databases that track inventory or update product listings in real time, but even high-end sites are often ill-prepared to update special information quickly.

Here are a few precautions you can take to be prepared for timely updates on your site:

✔ **Make sure you can send new information to your Web site quickly.**

Many Web sites are designed with testing systems that safeguard against careless mistakes, but these systems can add hours, or even days, to the time it takes to add new information to your Web site. Work with your technical staff or consultants to make sure you can update your site quickly if necessary. This may require creating a new section you can update independently from the rest of the site or override the regular update system.

✔ **Make updating important sections of your site easy.**

Consider building or buying a content management system that uses Web-based forms to post new information to your site. Such a system can be designed to change or add information to a Web page as easily as filling out an online order form. You need an experienced programmer to develop a form-based update system. Many Web consultants offer this kind of service for a reasonable fee. For example, this method works if you are a real estate agent and need to change listings or if you have a calendar of events. Include password protection so that you control access to the form. As an added advantage, a form enables you to make updates from any computer connected to the Internet. So you can update your Web site, even if you can't get back into your office.

✔ **Identify and train key staff to update the site.**

With the right systems in place, you do not need to have much technical experience to make simple updates to a site, but your staff needs some instruction and regular reminders. Make sure you also develop a schedule for retraining to ensure that no one forgets emergency procedures. Your most serious emergency could happen tomorrow or may not happen for years to come — you never know — but being prepared pays off in the end.

Back It Up

Make sure you have a system in place to back up your Web site. Always keep a copy of all the files that are on your server in a separate location and update it regularly to make sure you have the latest version of your site backed up at all times. Even the best Internet service providers sometimes have technical problems, so you should keep a backup of your site where you have easy access to it and can get it back online quickly if something does happen to delete any or all the files you have on the server.

Also keep a backup of your original source files, such as Photoshop images. For example, when you develop images for the Web, you usually start in a program such as Photoshop, creating a high-resolution image that may include layers and other elements. Before the image goes on your Web site, those layers get flattened and the image gets compressed or reduced and converted into a GIF or JPEG. If you ever want to go back and alter that image in the future, you'll want the original source file before it was compressed and the layers were flattened. Whether you create your own images or you hire a professional designer, make sure you develop a system for saving all these original elements when they are created.

Chapter 18

Ten Timesaving Dreamweaver Tips

*W*ith each new version, Dreamweaver gets even better, which makes creating Web sites faster and easier. As I put this book together, I collected tips and tricks and gathered them into this handy list. Take a moment to check out these tips, and you're sure to save time developing your Web site.

Splitting the View

If you like to switch back and forth between the HTML source code and Design view in Dreamweaver, you'll appreciate the option to split the window so that you can view both the source code and the page design at the same time. To split the window, choose View➪Code and Design or click the Show Code and Design Views button, located just under the Insert bar at the top of the Workspace.

With Dreamweaver 8, the source code has better color coding and tagging features, similar to those in the HTML editor HomeSite. Notice as you're working that if you select an image, text, or other element on a page in Design view, it is automatically highlighted in Code view, a great feature that makes it easier to find your place in the raw code. (You can find more on Dreamweaver's interface options in Chapter 1.)

Inserting Content with Formatting

Dreamweaver 8 gives you more options than ever for maintaining formatting when you copy and paste text from another program. You can change the default for how Dreamweaver handles formatting when you choose Edit➪ Paste and alter the Preferences in the Copy/Paste Category. And, you can choose Edit➪Paste Special to have all the options available each time you paste in new content. Here are your four options:

✔ **Text only:** Dreamweaver strips any formatting and inserts plain text.

✔ **Text with structure:** Dreamweaver includes paragraphs, lists, tables, and other structural formatting options.

✔ **Text with structure plus basic formatting:** Dreamweaver includes structural formatting as well as basic formatting, such as bold and italic.

✔ **Text with structure plus full formatting:** In addition to the previous options, Dreamweaver includes formatting created by style sheets in programs such as Microsoft Word.

Getting a Head Start on Your Designs

Dreamweaver 8 features many predesigned templates, as well as Starter Pages, which not only include topic-based designs, they actually include text. You may need to edit the text to meet your needs, but if you're creating a common site feature, such as a calendar or product listings, the general text already in place gives you a head start.

When you create a new file in Dreamweaver (such as by choosing File➪New), the New Document window offers you many ways to create a predesigned page, including the following:

✔ **Dynamic Template pages:** Choose the Template Page category to open a list of templates for dynamic Web site developing, including ASP Java-Script, VBScript, .Net C#, .Net VB, ColdFusion, HTML SSI, HTML, JSP, and PhP. Note that these formats require programming beyond the basic features of Dreamweaver and are designed for use with advanced, database-driven types of Web sites. You find more about these options in Chapters 13, 14, and 15.

✔ **Layout Designs for Frames:** Choose Framesets to open a collection of predesigned framesets. Because these templates can save you so much time, they're a "must use" feature if you're creating a site that uses frames.

✔ **CSS-Designed Pages:** Choose the Page Designs (CSS) category to open a list of page templates created using Cascading Style Sheets.

✔ **Predesigned Pages with Text:** Choose Starter Pages to open a list of common page designs that include content you can easily adapt for a wide variety of Web sites.

✔ **Regular Template Designs:** Choose Page Designs to open a list of basic HTML templates. Although they may seem simple by comparison, these are well-designed pages that can help you get a static Web site up and running with a lot less effort than creating it from scratch.

Tabling Your Designs

HTML tables still offer one of the most popular ways to create complex Web designs. Although getting tables just the way you want them can be challenging, Dreamweaver makes creating tables easier with its visual design features. In Layout mode, you can draw table cells on a page, drag them into place, and even group cells in nested tables — without ever worrying about how many rows and cells you need to create to make the table work.

Choose View➪Table Mode➪Layout Mode (or click the Layout button on the Layout Insert bar) to access Dreamweaver's special Layout environment. If you do want to do more standard table editing, such as merging or splitting cells, make sure to switch back to Standard mode. You can find cell and table options in the Properties dialog box when you select a table or cell in Standard mode, but not when you are in Layout mode. For more information about using Layout mode and working with HTML tables, check out Chapter 6.

Designing in a Flash

Flash rocks! The Macromedia vector-based design and animation program, Flash, is one of the coolest programs on the Web today because it makes creating fast-loading images and animations that dynamically adjust to fit any screen size possible. Now that the Flash plug-in is built into most current browsers, Flash has become a standard, and Dreamweaver has made adding a variety of common Flash features easier than ever — even if you don't own Flash.

In Dreamweaver 8, you can find premade Flash buttons, Flash text, Flash paper, and Flash movies available from the Common Insert bar by choosing one from the Media drop-down list. And then use Dreamweaver's integrated tools to customize the button, text, or other Flash element you've selected. You can even use Flash to create your own customized buttons, text, or other Flash files and add them to the list of available buttons for easy access within Dreamweaver.

You can add Flash text by choosing Insert➪Media➪Flash. For more on these integrated Flash features, turn to Chapter 11.

Making Fireworks Work with Your Images

The Dreamweaver integration with Fireworks, Macromedia's Web image program, makes editing images while you work in Dreamweaver easy. Need to change the text on a button or create a new banner? Just click the Edit button in the Properties inspector to launch Fireworks. Any changes you make to an image automatically appear in Dreamweaver. If you always use another image program, such as Photoshop, this level of integration should at least get you to consider using Fireworks. It can save you a ton of time in your design work, especially when your pesky colleagues and clients are always asking for last minute changes. For more on using Fireworks and Dreamweaver in tandem, check out Chapter 10.

Finding Functional Fonts

Designers get so excited when they find out that they can use any font on a Web page. But, in reality, your viewers must still have the font on their computers for it to display. The more common the font, the more likely it is to display the way you intend. If you want to use a more unusual font, go for it — just be sure that you also include alternatives. The Dreamweaver Font List already includes collections of common fonts, and you can always create your own Font List by choosing Text⇨Font⇨Edit Font List.

And here's another tip: Windows is by far the most common operating system that people use to browse the Net. To ensure the best — and fastest — results for the majority of your users, list a Windows font first.

In an effort to make text easier to read on the Web, Adobe and Microsoft have both created fonts especially suited to computer screens. To find out more, visit their Web sites at www.adobe.com and www.microsoft.com respectively and search for Web fonts.

Differentiating DHTML for All Browsers

If you like pushing the technical limits of what works on the Web, don't overlook Dreamweaver's Convert option. This feature automatically converts your complex page designs that work only in 4.0 and later browsers into alternative pages that display in 3.0 browsers. The feature converts the CSS and DHTML tags into regular HTML style tags by converting CSS formatting into HTML formatting tags and re-creating layers into HTML Tables.

To convert CSS and other features on a page, choose Modify⇨Convert⇨ Layers to Tables. Beware that HTML is not capable of the complex designs you can create using DHTML, so your converted pages may not look as much like the original as you would like. For example, the conversion can't do justice to a layer that moves across the screen in a static table cell. Chapter 9 walks you through the process in detail. The conversion isn't a perfect science, but it is a relatively easy way to ensure your pages are at least presentable in older browsers.

I've heard too many good designers say that users should upgrade their browsers and that they don't care about users who are so lame they're still using an old version of AOL. Here's a word of caution: It only takes one really important viewer to get you in trouble for not doing multibrowser designs. Beware that one of the most likely people to be using an older browser is the president of the company who is traveling with his laptop that has a browser he's never upgraded because he only uses it from hotel rooms on the road. Don't take the risk that your paying clients, your boss, or worse yet, your investors, are the ones with the old browsers. Make sure your designs work well for everyone — it's the sign of a truly high-end Web designer. For more on Dreamweaver's Convert feature, read Chapter 9.

Directing Your Viewers

Creating multiple pages is the most fail-safe solution for making sure that all your viewers are happy when you use cutting-edge page designs filled with DHTML and CSS. That means you create two or more sets of pages: one that uses the latest features and one that uses older, more universally supported HTML tags. But how do you ensure that viewers get to the right pages? Use the Check Browser behavior.

The Check Browser behavior is written in JavaScript and determines the browser type that each viewer who lands on your site uses. The behavior then directs users to the page design best suited to their browser versions. To use this feature, choose Window⇨Behaviors to open the Behaviors panel. You can also find this panel by opening the Tag panel and choosing the Behaviors tab.

Select the plus sign (+) to open the drop-down list of options on the Behaviors tab and choose the Check Browser option. In the Check Browser dialog box, specify what browser versions should be directed to what pages on your site. When users arrive at your site, they're automatically directed to the pages of your choice, based on the browser types and versions that you specify. For more on this and other behaviors, read Chapter 9.

Keeping Frequently Used Items Handy

Ever wished you could keep all your favorite Dreamweaver features in one convenient place? Now you can with the Favorites tab.

When you launch Dreamweaver, the Common tab is visible at the top of the Workspace. Click the arrow to the right of it, and you find a drop-down list with several options, including Layout, Forms, and HTML. At the bottom of that list is the newest addition of Macromedia, the Favorites bar.

Select the Favorites bar and you can customize it with all your favorite objects; just right-click (or Control+click) choose Customize Favorites. Use this bar as a convenient way to keep all your favorite features handy. You can even change it for special projects that require a series of steps or elements.

Index

Notes

Notes

Notes

Notes

Notes

Notes

Notes

BUSINESS, CAREERS & PERSONAL FINANCE

0-7645-9847-3   0-7645-2431-3

Also available:
- Business Plans Kit For Dummies
  0-7645-9794-9
- Economics For Dummies
  0-7645-5726-2
- Grant Writing For Dummies
  0-7645-8416-2
- Home Buying For Dummies
  0-7645-5331-3
- Managing For Dummies
  0-7645-1771-6
- Marketing For Dummies
  0-7645-5600-2

- Personal Finance For Dummies
  0-7645-2590-5*
- Resumes For Dummies
  0-7645-5471-9
- Selling For Dummies
  0-7645-5363-1
- Six Sigma For Dummies
  0-7645-6798-5
- Small Business Kit For Dummies
  0-7645-5984-2
- Starting an eBay Business For Dummies
  0-7645-6924-4
- Your Dream Career For Dummies
  0-7645-9795-7

HOME & BUSINESS COMPUTER BASICS

0-470-05432-8   0-471-75421-8

Also available:
- Cleaning Windows Vista For Dummies
  0-471-78293-9
- Excel 2007 For Dummies
  0-470-03737-7
- Mac OS X Tiger For Dummies
  0-7645-7675-5
- MacBook For Dummies
  0-470-04859-X
- Macs For Dummies
  0-470-04849-2
- Office 2007 For Dummies
  0-470-00923-3

- Outlook 2007 For Dummies
  0-470-03830-6
- PCs For Dummies
  0-7645-8958-X
- Salesforce.com For Dummies
  0-470-04893-X
- Upgrading & Fixing Laptops For Dummies
  0-7645-8959-8
- Word 2007 For Dummies
  0-470-03658-3
- Quicken 2007 For Dummies
  0-470-04600-7

FOOD, HOME, GARDEN, HOBBIES, MUSIC & PETS

0-7645-8404-9   0-7645-9904-6

Also available:
- Candy Making For Dummies
  0-7645-9734-5
- Card Games For Dummies
  0-7645-9910-0
- Crocheting For Dummies
  0-7645-4151-X
- Dog Training For Dummies
  0-7645-8418-9
- Healthy Carb Cookbook For Dummies
  0-7645-8476-6
- Home Maintenance For Dummies
  0-7645-5215-5

- Horses For Dummies
  0-7645-9797-3
- Jewelry Making & Beading For Dummies
  0-7645-2571-9
- Orchids For Dummies
  0-7645-6759-4
- Puppies For Dummies
  0-7645-5255-4
- Rock Guitar For Dummies
  0-7645-5356-9
- Sewing For Dummies
  0-7645-6847-7
- Singing For Dummies
  0-7645-2475-5

INTERNET & DIGITAL MEDIA

0-470-04529-9   0-470-04894-8

Also available:
- Blogging For Dummies
  0-471-77084-1
- Digital Photography For Dummies
  0-7645-9802-3
- Digital Photography All-in-One Desk Reference For Dummies
  0-470-03743-1
- Digital SLR Cameras and Photography For Dummies
  0-7645-9803-1
- eBay Business All-in-One Desk Reference For Dummies
  0-7645-8438-3
- HDTV For Dummies
  0-470-09673-X

- Home Entertainment PCs For Dummies
  0-470-05523-5
- MySpace For Dummies
  0-470-09529-6
- Search Engine Optimization For Dummies
  0-471-97998-8
- Skype For Dummies
  0-470-04891-3
- The Internet For Dummies
  0-7645-8996-2
- Wiring Your Digital Home For Dummies
  0-471-91830-X

* Separate Canadian edition also available
† Separate U.K. edition also available

Available wherever books are sold. For more information or to order direct: U.S. customers visit www.dummies.com or call 1-877-762-2974.
U.K. customers visit www.wileyeurope.com or call 0800 243407. Canadian customers visit www.wiley.ca or call 1-800-567-4797.

SPORTS, FITNESS, PARENTING, RELIGION & SPIRITUALITY

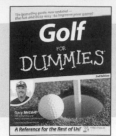

0-471-76871-5

0-7645-7841-3

Also available:

- Catholicism For Dummies
  0-7645-5391-7
- Exercise Balls For Dummies
  0-7645-5623-1
- Fitness For Dummies
  0-7645-7851-0
- Football For Dummies
  0-7645-3936-1
- Judaism For Dummies
  0-7645-5299-6
- Potty Training For Dummies
  0-7645-5417-4
- Buddhism For Dummies
  0-7645-5359-3

- Pregnancy For Dummies
  0-7645-4483-7 †
- Ten Minute Tone-Ups For Dummies
  0-7645-7207-5
- NASCAR For Dummies
  0-7645-7681-X
- Religion For Dummies
  0-7645-5264-3
- Soccer For Dummies
  0 7645 5229 5
- Women in the Bible For Dummies
  0-7645-8475-8

TRAVEL

0-7645-7749-2

0-7645-6945-7

Also available:

- Alaska For Dummies
  0-7645-7746-8
- Cruise Vacations For Dummies
  0-7645-6941-4
- England For Dummies
  0-7645-4276-1
- Europe For Dummies
  0-7645-7529-5
- Germany For Dummies
  0-7645-7823-5
- Hawaii For Dummies
  0-7645-7402-7

- Italy For Dummies
  0-7645-7386-1
- Las Vegas For Dummies
  0-7645-7382-9
- London For Dummies
  0-7645-4277-X
- Paris For Dummies
  0-7645-7630-5
- RV Vacations For Dummies
  0-7645-4442-X
- Walt Disney World & Orlando
  For Dummies
  0-7645-9660-8

GRAPHICS, DESIGN & WEB DEVELOPMENT

0-7645-8815-X

0-7645-9571-7

Also available:

- 3D Game Animation For Dummies
  0-7645-8789-7
- AutoCAD 2006 For Dummies
  0-7645-8925-3
- Building a Web Site For Dummies
  0-7645-7144-3
- Creating Web Pages For Dummies
  0-470-08030-2
- Creating Web Pages All-in-One Desk
  Reference For Dummies
  0-7645-4345-8
- Dreamweaver 8 For Dummies
  0-7645-9649-7

- InDesign CS2 For Dummies
  0-7645-9572-5
- Macromedia Flash 8 For Dummies
  0-7645-9691-8
- Photoshop CS2 and Digital
  Photography For Dummies
  0-7645-9580-6
- Photoshop Elements 4 For Dummies
  0-471-77483-9
- Syndicating Web Sites with RSS Feeds
  For Dummies
  0-7645-8848-6
- Yahoo! SiteBuilder For Dummies
  0-7645-9800-7

NETWORKING, SECURITY, PROGRAMMING & DATABASES

0-7645-7728-X

0-471-74940-0

Also available:

- Access 2007 For Dummies
  0-470-04612-0
- ASP.NET 2 For Dummies
  0-7645-7907-X
- C# 2005 For Dummies
  0-7645-9704-3
- Hacking For Dummies
  0-470-05235-X
- Hacking Wireless Networks
  For Dummies
  0-7645-9730-2
- Java For Dummies
  0-470-08716-1

- Microsoft SQL Server 2005 For Dummies
  0-7645-7755-7
- Networking All-in-One Desk Reference
  For Dummies
  0-7645-9939-9
- Preventing Identity Theft For Dummies
  0-7645-7336-5
- Telecom For Dummies
  0-471-77085-X
- Visual Studio 2005 All-in-One Desk
  Reference For Dummies
  0-7645-9775-2
- XML For Dummies
  0-7645-8845-1

HEALTH & SELF-HELP

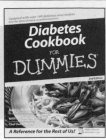

0-7645-8450-2

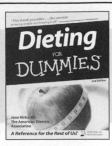

0-7645-4149-8

Also available:

- Bipolar Disorder For Dummies
  0-7645-8451-0
- Chemotherapy and Radiation
  For Dummies
  0-7645-7832-4
- Controlling Cholesterol For Dummies
  0-7645-5440-9
- Diabetes For Dummies
  0-7645-6820-5* †
- Divorce For Dummies
  0-7645-8417-0 †

- Fibromyalgia For Dummies
  0-7645-5441-7
- Low-Calorie Dieting For Dummies
  0-7645-9905-4
- Meditation For Dummies
  0-471-77774-9
- Osteoporosis For Dummies
  0-7645-7621-6
- Overcoming Anxiety For Dummies
  0-7645-5447-6
- Reiki For Dummies
  0-7645-9907-0
- Stress Management For Dummies
  0-7645-5144-2

EDUCATION, HISTORY, REFERENCE & TEST PREPARATION

0-7645-8381-6

0-7645-9554-7

Also available:

- The ACT For Dummies
  0-7645-9652-7
- Algebra For Dummies
  0-7645-5325-9
- Algebra Workbook For Dummies
  0-7645-8467-7
- Astronomy For Dummies
  0-7645-8465-0
- Calculus For Dummies
  0-7645-2498-4
- Chemistry For Dummies
  0-7645-5430-1
- Forensics For Dummies
  0-7645-5580-4

- Freemasons For Dummies
  0-7645-9796-5
- French For Dummies
  0-7645-5193-0
- Geometry For Dummies
  0-7645-5324-0
- Organic Chemistry I For Dummies
  0-7645-6902-3
- The SAT I For Dummies
  0-7645-7193-1
- Spanish For Dummies
  0-7645-5194-9
- Statistics For Dummies
  0-7645-5423-9

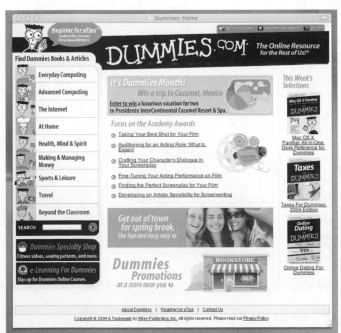

Get smart @ dummies.com®

- **Find a full list of Dummies titles**
- **Look into loads of FREE on-site articles**
- **Sign up for FREE eTips e-mailed to you weekly**
- **See what other products carry the Dummies name**
- **Shop directly from the Dummies bookstore**
- **Enter to win new prizes every month!**

* Separate Canadian edition also available
† Separate U.K. edition also available

Available wherever books are sold. For more information or to order direct: U.S. customers visit www.dummies.com or call 1-877-762-2974.
U.K. customers visit www.wileyeurope.com or call 0800 243407. Canadian customers visit www.wiley.ca or call 1-800-567-4797.